Contributions to Decision Making - I

Contributions to
Decision Making - I

Edited by

Jean-Paul Caverni
Université de Provence
Aix-en-Provence, France

Maya Bar-Hillel
The Hebrew University
Jerusalem, Israel

F. Hutton Barron
University of Alabama
Tuscaloosa, AL, U.S.A.

Helmut Jungermann
Technische Universität Berlin
Berlin, Germany

1995

ELSEVIER

Amsterdam – Lausanne – New York – Oxford – Shannon – Tokyo

ELSEVIER SCIENCE B.V.
Sara Burgerhartstraat 25
P.O. Box 211, 1000 AE Amsterdam, The Netherlands

Library of Congress Cataloging-in-Publication Data

Research Conference on Subjective Probability, Utility, and Decision
  Making (14th : 1993)
    Contributions to decision making / edited by Jean-Paul Caverni ...
  [et al].
      p.   cm.
    "SPUDM 1993"--CIP t.p.
    Includes bibliographical references.
    ISBN 0-444-82181-3 (alk. paper)
    1. Decision-making--Congresses. 2. Choice (Psychology)-
  -Congresses.   I. Caverni, Jean-Paul. II. Title.
  BF448.R473 1993
    153.8'3--dc20   95-2215
                                                             CIP

ISBN: 0 444 82181 3

This book is printed on acid-free paper.

Printed in The Netherlands.

PREFACE

This volume presents a selection of the papers presented at the 14th Research Conference on Subjective Probability, Utility, and Decision Making (SPUDM-14). The general theme is decision research and its application, primarily from a psychological perspective, but representing a broad spectrum including economics, computer science, operations research and social science as well.

The conference attracted over 150 participants from Europe, North America, Asia, and Australia. Over 90 papers were presented, of which 19 have been selected for this volume. Selection was based on a review process of two referees together with subsequent editorial judgment. Thus, these papers have been judged by peers to be of outstanding quality.

Publication of selected papers is an important SPUDM tradition. With the exception of the 3rd Conference (1971), twelve previous volumes of selected papers have been published (References are provided below). These volumes reflect a distinct shift over time from the classical maximization of subjective expected utility (SEU) paradigm to a wide array of theoretical and empirical aspects of descriptive psychological decision research. The newer approaches include prospect theory and its implications for personal spending and saving decisions (mental accounting), axiomatic generalizations such as rank dependent expected utility theories and an extension of decision field theory to multiattribute problems.

Two other theories were discussed in plenary sessions - SP/A theory and Image theory. In SP/A theory security (S) - avoiding risk - and potential (P) - some exceptional outcome are combined in various rank dependent ways. Aspiration level (A), allows the decision to be made by trying to maximize the probability that an acceptable level (A) is achieved. Image theory looks at everyday decisions - not as gambles - but as involving compatibility of options, goals and strategies with stored knowledge and beliefs.

Two of the major papers presented comprehensive reviews. Marcus Spies discussed the problem of cognitive presentation of relevant knowledge for expert systems involving uncertainty. He showed that biases in probability judgments can be explained using belief functions. Incomplete expert knowledge can be modeled using conditional events. Borcherding, Schmeer and Weber reviewed comprehensively research on weighting attributes in multiattribute decision making, including biases and sensitivity to choice of methods.

The 1993 Conference extended the geographical scope of SPUDM, and fortunately, will change its name as well. This was the first time the conference was held in France. The next conference will be held in Jerusalem, hosted by Maya Bar-Hillel. Finally, SPUDM has become a formal society - the European Association for Decision Making. The association's purpose is

> the advancement and diffusion of knowledge about judgment and decision making and the interchange of information relating to this subject between the members and other associations throughout the world as well as between members and other interested institutions and/or individuals.

For the about 25 years SPUDM has survived as an informal, collegial, self perpetuating biennial conference open to all interested in decision research. Much of the work has been done by Organizing Committees, and by participants serving as referees. With the formation of the association, the nature of future organizing committes will change, but the enthusiasm, collegiality and quality of our conferences will continue.

Thus it is our pleasure to thank the other members of the organizing committee, Oswald Huber (Switzerland), Joop van der Pligt (Netherlands) and Helen Moshkovich (Russia). We also thank those organized the symposium and workshops: Lee Beach (USA), Jean-Marc Fabre (France) and Allen Parducci (USA), Vittorio Girotto and Paolo Legrenzi (Italy), Nick Pidgeon (UK) and Michael Smithson

(Australia), and Peter Politser (USA), Danielle Timmermans (Netherlands) and Peter Wakker (Netherlands).

Finally we gratefully acknowledge the assistance of those who served as referees: P. Ayton (UK), L. Babcock (USA), C. Ball (Australia), J.-P. Barthélémy (France), L. Beach (USA), J. Beattie (UK), R. Beyth-Marom (Israel), A. Blaye (France), K. Borcherding (Germany), A. Bostrom (USA), B. Brehmer (Sweden), D. Budescu (USA), T. Connolly (USA), A. Cooke (USA), D. Erev (Israel), J.-M. Fabre (France), K. Fischer (Germany), J. Fox (UK), B. Gibbs (USA), V. Girotto (Italy), N. Harvey (UK), L. Hendricks (Netherlands), O. Huber (Switzerland), J. Klayman (USA), P. Koele (Netherlands), M. Lewicka (Poland), R. Lipshitz (Israel), L. Lopes (USA), L. Mann (Australia). B. Mellers (USA), D. Messick (USA), J.L. Mumpower (USA), M. Omodei (Australia), W. Otten (Netherlands), D. Over (UK), A. Parducci (USA), A. Pearman (UK), H.-R. Pfister (Germany), N. Pidgeon (UK), R.F. Pohl (Germany), P. Politser (USA), R. Ranyard (UK), I. Ritov (Israel), E. Shafir (USA), J. Shanteau (USA), Z. Shapira (USA), M. Spies (Germany), K. Teigen (Norway), R. Thaler (USA), D. Timmermans (Netherlands), J. van der Pligt (Netherlands), Ch. Vlek (Netherlands), P. Wakker (Netherlands), S. Watson (UK), A. Wearing (Australia), M. Weber (Germany), G. Wright (UK).

REFERENCES

[SPUDM-1, Hamburg] Wendt, D. (Ed.) (1969). *Proceedings of a research conference on subjective probability and related fields.* Report of the Psychological Institute, University of Hamburg.

[SPUDM-2, Amsterdam] Zeeuw, G. de, Vlek, Ch. & Wagenaar, W.A. (Eds.) (1970). Subjective probability: theory, experiments, applications. *Acta Psychologica, 34,* (n° 2/3).

[SPUDM-4, Rome] Wendt, D. & Vlek, Ch. (Eds.) (1975). *Utility, probability and human decision making.* Dordrecht/Boston: Reidel.

[SPUDM-5, Darmstadt] Jungermann, H. & Zeeuw, G. de (Eds.) (1977). *Decision making and change in human affairs.* Dordrecht/Boston: Reidel.

[SPUDM-6, Warsaw] Sjoberg, L., Tyszka, T. & Wise, J.A. (Eds.) (1983). *Human decision making.* Lund: Doxa.

[SPUDM-7, Goteborg] Beach, L.R., Humphreys, P.C., Svenson, O. & Wagenaar, W.A. (Eds.) (1980). *Exploring human decision making.* Amsterdam: North-Holland. *Acta Psychologica, 45.*

[SPUDM-8, Budapest] Humphreys, P.C., Svenson, O. & Vari, A. (Eds.) (1983). *Analysing and aiding decision processes.* Amsterdam: North-Holland and Budapest: Akademiai Kiado.

[SPUDM-9, Groningen] Borcherding, K., Brehmer, B., Vlek, Ch. & Wagenaar, W.A. (Eds.) (1984). *Research perspectives on decision making under uncertainty.* Amsterdam: North-Holland. *Acta Psychologica, 56.*

[SPUDM-10, Helsinki] Brehmer, B., Jungermann, H., Lourens, P. & Sevon, G. (Eds) (1986). *New directions in research on decision making.* Amsterdam: North-Holland.

[SPUDM-11, Cambridge] Rohrmann, B., Beach, L.R., Vlek, Ch. & Watson, S.R. (Eds.) (1989). *Advances in decision research.* Amsterdam: Noth-Holland. *Acta Psychologica, 68,* (1988).

[SPUDM-12, Moscow] Borcherding, K., Larichev, O.I. & Messick, D.M. (Eds.) (1990). *Contemporary Issues in Decision Making.* Amsterdam: North-Holland.

[SPUDM-13, Fribourg] Huber, O., Mumpower, J., van der Pligt, J. & Koele, P. (Eds.) (1993). *Current Themes in Psychological Decision Research.* Amsterdam: North-Holland. *Acta Psychologica, 80,* (1992).

TABLE OF CONTENTS

SECTION 1

Conceptual and review papers

Contributions to Decision Making - I
J.-P. Caverni, M. Bar-Hillel, F.H. Barron and H. Jungermann (Editors)
1995 Elsevier Science B.V.

3

BIASES IN MULTIATTRIBUTE WEIGHT ELICITATION

Katrin Borcherding[1], Stefanie Schmeer[1] and Martin Weber[2]

[1] Institut für Psychologie; Technische Hochschule Darmstadt,
Steubenplatz 12, D-64293 Darmstadt, Germany
[2] Fakultät für Betriebswirtschaftslehre; Universität Mannheim,
D-68131 Mannheim, Germany

Abstract. In multiattribute decision models the quality of the model output strongly depends on the validity of the attribute weights. Therefore the determination of attribute weights is a central step in eliciting the decision maker's preferences. The set of weights and weight judgments as well as actual preferences depend on a variety of factors such as aspects of the value tree, weight elicitation procedures, selection of attributes and attribute ranges, response mode, and framing. Here we review descriptive studies which have investigated behavioral influences on weights. These studies are important for improving the application of prescriptive decision analysis as a decision aid.

1. INTRODUCTION

Both in our private and professional life we constantly make decisions without giving much attention to it. Only when the decisions are important and difficult do we carefully consider the alternatives and balance the various advantages and disadvantages. Decisions become problematical when we have simultaneously to consider several relevant and often conflicting criteria and where no alternative is clearly superior to the others. A decision maker (DM) can be confused by the amount of information that has to be correctly searched, evaluated, weighted and aggregated. These processes have all been shown to be susceptible to biases due to cognitive overload and mental shortcomings (Kahneman, Slovic & Tversky, 1982; Nisbett & Ross, 1980) as well as personal needs (Festinger, 1964; Svenson, 1992).

Multiattribute utility theory deals with how to evaluate rationally and choose accordingly among alternatives in a multicriteria decision problem (Keeney & Raiffa, 1976; von Winterfeldt & Edwards, 1986). As a social scientific tool it can be applied to support the DM and improve decision making. Usually this is done in four successive steps which involve structuring objectives, eliciting preferences, scoring alternatives and finally aggregating preferences and scores. Firstly, the DM has to specify and structure objectives in terms of a value tree with broad objectives at the top and specific subobjectives at the bottom level. The objectives (or goals or criteria or values) at the bottom have to be operationalized in terms of measurable attributes. As a next step, the DM's preferences have to be elicited. Here, the DM has to specify the relationship between the outcomes of an attribute and the degree to which the corresponding subobjective is satisfied (unidimensional value or utility function) as well as the relevance of each subobjective with respect to the top level or overall objective in terms of attribute weight. The third step is to collect information about the alternatives, i.e. to score all alternatives with regard to their consequences on all attributes. Finally, the DM's preferences and the scores of alternatives are aggregated to derive overall evaluations of alternatives. The alternative with the highest evaluation should be chosen. Sensitivity analyses may be performed to build up the DM's confidence in the prescribed choice. This involves changing attribute weights slightly and observing its effect on resulting decisions. Then the focus can switch to the implementation of action.

Let $A = (x_1, x_2, \dots x_j, \dots x_n)$ be an alternative described by an n-tuple of specific outcomes (x_j) on a set of relevant attributes $(X_j, j=1\dots n)$ or a probability distribution over this n-tuple. The evaluation of such decision alternatives requires the DM to specify n-dimensional preference functions. Multiattribute value or utility theory specifies the conditions under which these can be broken down into and aggregated from lower dimensional, preferably n one-dimensional functions. The simplest aggregation rule is the additive value model with no uncertainty involved (Desirable properties for a set of attributes defined by Keeney & Raiffa, 1976, appear in italics in the following text.) In addition to some very basic consistency axioms one assumes that for evaluation the alternatives are described *completely* by the (*measurable*) attributes and that "additive" preferential independence (*de- and recomposition*) holds, i.e. the additive difference independence condition is satisfied (Dyer & Sarin, 1979). The overall evaluation of an alternative is given by

$$V(A) = \sum_j w_j \cdot v_j(x_j)$$

where v_j is the unidimensional value function for the j-th attribute. Value functions are defined as interval scales, and as long as unidimensional value functions are anchored at 0 for the realistic worst and at 1 for the realistic best outcome and weights are normalized, i.e. sum to one, the resulting evaluation of alternatives, V(A), is on an interval scale, also with a range from 0 to 1.

The weights are scaling constants and provided that the attributes do *not overlap* they express the relative contribution of one attribute to the overall evaluation of alternatives, i.e., they adjust the units (standard intervals) of qualitatively different attributes with respect to their value. Necessarily, these scaling constants or weights are positive and have to be expressed on ratio scales. Where uncertainty is involved, value functions have to be replaced by utility functions for which similar aggregation rules exist if (additive) utility independence holds.

It has often been shown that for a reasonably structured value tree simple additive multiattribute value models are sufficient to describe the DM's preferences. This is partly a consequence of linear models not being sensitive to modest model violations (Einhorn & Hogarth, 1975; Dawes, 1982). If multiattribute value analysis is applied, the determination of weights becomes central, since they reflect the DM's basic concerns. Unfortunately, however, DMs are not familiar with expressing these in terms of "hard" numbers.

If at least some attributes are positively correlated across alternatives, decisions are quite robust to changes in corresponding weights. Consider the evaluation of students. A student with a good grade in one subject area is more likely to have a good grade in others as well, making adequate weighting less important. These situations probably occur more often than we are aware of, just because they are less problematic. If, however, as in most complex decision problems, either outcomes generally are negatively correlated or the outcomes of the efficient set of alternatives are negatively correlated, small changes in weights can result in different alternatives becoming the best ones (Kleinmuntz, 1983: Johnson, Meyer & Ghose, 1989). Consider the case of employing a student. The problem becomes difficult when promising students differ considerably in their particular strengths. In such cases small changes in the weights given to different attributes will result in different students being employed. From a descriptive viewpoint this problem is not new. In dissonance theory (Festinger, 1964) the difficulty of a decision is high when alternatives appear similar in overall attractiveness but are different on single attribute outcomes, i.e., have a 'small cognitive overlap'. According to the theory, making a difficult decision leads to cognitive dissonance, a tension arising from anticipating the negative consequences of the decision: specifically, losing the advantages of the non-chosen and having to accept the disadvantages of the chosen alternative. Strategies that reduce this tension or dissonance must raise the attractiveness of the chosen and/or decrease the attractiveness of the non-chosen alternative. A strategy that is very suitable for dissonance reduction is biasing attribute weights, i.e., raising the weights for the attributes where the outcomes of the chosen alternative are good while reducing the weights where these outcomes are bad. Since weights are crucial model inputs provided by the DM, it is wise to investigate behavioral influences on weight judgments in order to be able to compensate for biased weight judgments and thus improve decision making.

2. ATTRIBUTE WEIGHTING METHODS

2.1. Weight elicitation procedures

Numerous procedures exist for deriving attribute weights and weighting procedures can be classified with respect to several criteria. In measurement theory direct and indirect procedures are distinguished. In direct measurement, numerical judgments are elicited on response scales for which scale properties are assumed to apply. Indirect measurement involves eliciting multiple simple ordinal judgments and then deriving scaling as well as scale properties that can be tested (Krantz, Luce, Suppes & Tversky, 1971; von Winterfeldt & Edwards, 1986). Also, the weighting can be achieved through either decomposed or holistic approaches. In the former case attributes are weighted through direct attribute comparisons whereas in the latter case alternatives are presented and weights are inferred from judgments of these alternatives. A third distinction can be made with regard to whether the measurement approach is algebraic or statistical, i.e. whether weights are calculated from just a few (at least n-1) judgments or whether weights are derived statistically from a redundant set of judgments, using, for example, averaging or least square or maximum likelihood solutions.

Depending on the purpose, different procedures have their advantages and disadvantages and none seems to be generally superior. When, however, decisions are made in complex decision situations, particularly those encountered by institutions, then weighting procedures that are direct, decomposed and algebraic predominate. They are more efficient and almost as good as indirect procedures, do not overtax the DM by presenting complex alternatives for comparison but instead focus on only a few, relevant attributes. Cross-checks may be made to test the stability of the elicited weight judgments. Any discrepancies between the weight judgments may be fed back to the DM to reconcile or they may be removed through averaging, or they may be understood to result from uncertainties associated with weight judgments whose effects on resulting decisions can be tested by sensitivity analysis. In line with these arguments the direct weighting procedures that will be described here are decomposed and algebraic. A special emphasis will be given to hierarchical and non-hierarchical approaches. A discussion of these and other weighting methods can be found in von Winterfeldt and Edwards (1986).

2.2. Direct weight elicitation methods

The **ratio method** (Edwards, 1977) typically requires the DM first to rank the attributes according to their relative importance taking attribute ranges into account. The least important attribute is arbitrarily assigned a raw weight of 10 and all other attributes are judged to be multiples thereof. The final weights are arrived at by normalizing the raw weights to sum to one. Although cross-checks for weight ratios between several pairs of attributes are recommended, the weights strongly depend on the comparisons with the least important attribute. It would therefore seem necessary first to check that the least important attribute happens not to be one of too little importance which would result in ratio judgments that are high, difficult to make, and possibly low in reliability and validity. The ratio method can be varied by using an anchor different from 10 or by using other attribute comparisons than comparison with the least important attribute. Other methods such as point allocation or Saaty's (1986) intensity scale can be seen as predecessors or crude versions of the ratio method as long as the task is understood as one of magnitude and not of category scaling.

The **swing method** (von Winterfeldt & Edwards, 1986) uses the concept of "swings" instead of weights. It focuses on how much a DM values an attribute swing from the "worst" to the "best" outcome. An alternative with worst outcomes on all attributes is presented and the DM is allowed to change one attribute from the worst to the best outcome. The DM is then asked which attribute swing would result in the largest, second largest, etc..., improvement of the alternative, thus specifying a rank order from the most to the least important attribute. The swing of the most important attribute is set to 100 and the magnitude of all other swings have to be specified as percentages thereof. These percentages are normalized to yield final weights. The swing method, like the ratio method, is easy to understand. With the focus on swings instead of weights, it has the advantage of being more vivid and of explicitly taking attribute ranges into account.

The **trade-off method** (Keeney & Raiffa, 1976) is more sound than the previous ones; attribute importance is derived by considering ranges but in addition relying more explicitly on the properties of the compensatory model. The basic idea of the procedure is to compare two alternatives that differ with respect to their descriptions on only two attributes. One alternative has the best outcome on one attribute and the worst on the other attribute. For the other alternative it is vice versa. The DM chooses the preferred alternative and thereby indicates the attribute that is more important to him or her. It is the attribute on which the chosen alternative has the best outcome. The outcomes are then adjusted to yield indifference between the alternatives. To maintain the original attribute ranges, either the good outcome of the chosen alternative is made worse or the bad outcome of the non-chosen alternative is made better. The adjustments can only be made on continuous attributes or at least on attributes with a sufficient number of possible intermediate outcomes. Also, these comparisons are more natural for some pairs of attributes than for others. If indifferences are elicited for at least n-1 meaningfully selected pairs of alternatives, attribute weights can be calculated.

The **pricing-out method** can be seen as a special case of the trade-off method. Here, for all attributes the DM has to specify the highest amount of money he or she would be willing to pay in order to have the best instead of the worst outcome. The trade-off is done by comparing all attribute outcomes to the cost attribute and the indifference is established by adjusting costs. Merkhofer and Keeney (1987) applied a variant of the trade-off and pricing-out method in a nuclear waste disposal siting problem. They did not use the whole attribute range but instead took small meaningful units. For example, they asked the DM to trade off the life of one resident with the lives of a number of workers, and only then did they make a link to a money attribute by having the DM specify the money equivalent of the life of a resident. Provided that value functions are linear, attribute weights can easily be arrived at from these trade-offs. Sometimes trade-offs involving money are extremely difficult to make, particularly when values like lives are involved (Lichtenstein et al., 1990), although the DM can sometimes base his or her judgments on already existing, socially agreed costs, such as compensations agreed by courts.

The swing and the trade-off methods are similar in that in both cases attribute ranges are compared. The difference between them lies in the fact that in the swing method the attribute ranges remain unchanged and the relevance of one attribute range is expressed in comparison to another, whereas in the trade-off method attribute ranges are adjusted in such a way that the adjusted ranges have the same relevance.

The **utility weighting method** differs from the previous ones in that uncertainty is taken into account. The method relies on the BRLT-method (Basic Reference Lottery Ticket; Keeney & Raiffa, 1976), where a DM has to specify the probability h_j for which s/he is indifferent to whether he or she obtains a safe option, an alternative with the best outcome on attribute j and the worst outcomes on all other attributes, or a probabilistic option where an alternative with best outcomes on all attributes is obtained with probability h_j and an alternative with only worst outcomes is obtained with the complimentary probability. Although this method is intriguing, to our knowledge it is hardly used in applied settings any more, only for eliciting unidimensional value functions. This is due to the difficulty of the method. Specifically it is difficult to elicit weights for attributes like costs, where less is preferred to more. Another reason why the method is not often applied, is the close relationship found between risky and riskless utility functions (Barron, von Winterfeldt & Fischer, 1984, although not supported by Keller, 1987). If, for whatever reason, utility weights seem to be more appropriate than value weights, value weights can be transformed into utility weights by using only one basic reference lottery in the elicitation procedure (Dyer & Sarin, 1979).

2.3. Hierarchical versus non-hierarchical approaches

The previously described weight elicitation methods can be applied in both a hierarchical and a non-hierarchical fashion. In the non-hierarchical mode, weights for attributes are elicited only on the bottom level of the value tree. The hierarchical mode uses the hierarchical objectives of the tree and elicits and normalizes weights separately for attributes belonging to the same branch or sub-branch. Starting at the bottom of the tree relative weights are elicited only for attributes belonging to the same sub-branch. On higher levels, the same procedure is repeated for sub-branches belonging to the same branch or for branches belonging to the same basic objectives. When this has been done for all levels, final attribute weights are arrived at by 'multiplying through the tree' in such a way that the final weight of an attribute is the product of all normalized weights on the path from bottom to top.

In the hierarchical mode, only those few attributes or objectives have to be compared that are connected with each other by belonging to the same branch. This is an advantage because it is both less demanding and more meaningful. The disadvantage lies in the fact that in the hierarchical mode objectives have to be compared that lack usually on all but the bottom level simple attribute operationalization. These objectives are complex and have attribute ranges which are difficult to imagine. The ratio method is usually applied in the hierarchical mode, the others in the non-hierarchical one.

In the following sections, biases in weights judgments will be reported with an emphasis on those that result from multiattribute structure.

3. BIASES IN WEIGHT ASSESSMENTS

3.1. Possible biases

In the last section we presented several methods for weight elicitation in multiattribute utility or value measurement. The literature of preference elicitation contains various biases in preference assessment for single attribute utility measurement (Hershey, Kunreuther & Schoemaker, 1982). It follows that we would also expect similar biases when weights are assessed. Asking a DM for weight judgments in one specific way usually results in a different set of weights than the sets derived via different elicitation procedures (Borcherding, Eppel & von Winterfeldt, 1991; Eppel, 1990; Jaccard, Brinberg & Ackerman, 1986; John, Edwards & Collins, 1980; Pfister, Jungermann & Kauffmann, 1991; Schoemaker & Waid, 1982; Steward & Ely, 1984). In addition to this general problem, however, there are specific biases which arise due to the multiattribute structure of the problem. These biases are discussed in this section.

From a prescriptive point of view weights should only depend on the DM's preference system and comply with certain prescriptive requirements. There are, however, a range of biases which can arise which violate these requirements:

(a) Sometimes it is necessary to use 'proxy' attributes instead of real ones. A proxy attribute is one that indirectly measures the achievement on a stated objective ('means' versus 'ends', Keeney & Raiffa, 1976). As the relationship between a proxy attribute and a stated objective is usually imperfect, the proxy attribute should receive less weight than the stated 'end-objective'. If the reduction is insufficient, a proxy overweighting bias is said to exist (see 3.2.).

(b) In assessing attribute importance, attribute ranges are crucial. Through weighting, the importance of one attribute range or part of it is related to the importance of another attribute range. Hence, changing ranges should influence weight judgments to a high degree. If a DM does not adjust weights sufficiently, a range insensitivity bias is said to arise (see 3.3.).

(c) Attributes are evaluated in a multiattribute context. Since different value trees can be formulated for any decision problem, the number of attributes and the structure of the tree can differ. The

particular structure can exert an effect on evaluations that will be
referred to as a structuring bias. There are two variants: the splitting
bias and the hierarchy bias. Eliciting a weight directly for a main
attribute or arriving at it by adding the weights of its subattributes
should give the same result. If the splitting of an attribute affects the
final weights, a splitting bias is said to exist. Also, an attribute
weight should not depend on how and where this attribute is linked
to the tree. If it does, this will be called a hierarchy bias (see 3.4.).

3.2. Proxy overweighting bias

Proxy attributes are common in multiattribute decision
making. Although in most cases the DM knows which fundamental
objective s/he cares about, it is difficult for him or her to acquire
relevant information about the alternatives, i.e., to score the
alternatives with respect to their specific outcomes on fundamental
objectives. For example, assume you have a siting and construction
problem for a chemical plant. One of your major objectives is to
minimize adverse 'health effects' because of air pollution due to the
plant. It is easier to predict or measure real consequences for the
'air pollution level' than for health effects. However, the air pollution
level may only be a proxy attribute for the 'health effect' attribute the
DM is actually concerned about.

When a proxy attribute has to be evaluated, a DM has to
perform a difficult task: s/he has to consider the relation between
the proxy attribute and the fundamental attribute in order to weight
the proxy attribute. Since this relation is usually a probabilistic one,
the weight for the proxy attribute should be lower than when a
perfect relation exists. This effect is also known as the 'regression
effect' in other areas. In adjusting weights some systematic errors,
namely biases, might be expected.

Fischer, Damodaran, Laskey and Lincoln (1987) conducted an
empirical study investigating an air pollution problem. Using 'level of
dust emission' as a proxy attribute for 'person days per year of
asthma' they found that the DM tended systematically to overweight
the proxy attribute. The DM did not adjust for the probabilistic link
between the proxy and the fundamental attribute.

3.3 Range insensitivity bias

Suppose you want to purchase a consumer hardware item, for example a mixer. As long as it has the features you require, you are concerned about price and design. Imagine both seem to be equally important when you assume a price range of $20. This would result in weights of .5 for design and .5 for price. Once in the shop, you learn that the price range is only $5, i.e., the range you originally expected is cut to one fourth. This information should immediately switch your attention to the design attribute. Design should seem more important now than price. Provided that value functions are linear, weight ratios should now be 1:0.25, i.e., design should be four times as important as price. The resulting weight for design should be 1/1.25=.8 and the weight for price .25/1.25=.2. As required by MAUT, the weight for design is now 4 times as high as the weight for price. The example shows that weight judgments depend (and should depend) on the range of outcomes. Increasing/decreasing the range of attribute outcomes should produce corresponding changes in attribute weights.

Whether subjects adequately consider attribute ranges when assessing attribute weights can best be tested by changing the range of attribute outcomes and observing the corresponding changes in weight judgments. Gabrielli and von Winterfeldt (1978) elicited weights using the direct ratio method: moderate changes in attribute ranges did not lead to systematic changes in attribute weights. Using a between-subject design, Fischer (1991) also found that weights elicited by the direct ratio method were insensitive to changes in range. He found, however, significant range sensitivity in swing weights and trade-off weights. Nevertheless, as in the study by von Nitzsch and Weber (1993) which used a within-subject design, the empirically-observed adjustment to manipulations of the range was significantly smaller than prescriptively predicted.

While the above studies were conducted in the framework of MAUT, Beattie and Baron (1991) reported similar results when calculating weights from intuitive holistic evaluations, using a multiple regression approach. In regression analysis, (beta) weights are given for standardized input (predictor) variables. The evaluation of a set of alternatives (job applicants) that shows a small variance on one of the variables (attributes) should only slightly depend on the outcomes on this variable. Consequently the variable, being a poor predictor, receives a small beta weight. If, in the same context and for another set of alternatives, the variability is high, outcomes with regard to this variable should have a high impact on overall evaluation and the resulting beta weight should also be high. Interpreting Beattie and Baron's result in the light of MAUT, they found some adjustment. Again, however, it was not as large as predicted.

In a recent study by Mellers and Cooke (1992) apartments described in terms of rent and distance from campus were evaluated. Either the rent range was narrow and the distance range was large, or vice versa. The evaluations of particular apartments of which one was closer and the other cheaper were compared. In many cases either the cheaper or the closer appartement was preferred, no matter what the attribute ranges were like. Preference reversals, however, were observed as well. They always occurred in such a way that the closer appartement tended to be preferred when the distance range was narrow whereas the cheaper tended to be preferred when the rent range was narrow. The authors concluded that preferences are range-dependent. This effect can be explained by a range insensitivity bias in weighting. In a decomposed approach, range insensitivity is present when weights are too large for narrow ranges compared to wide ranges. As a result of this, model-derived overall evaluations of alternatives will too much depend on those attributes with a narrow range. This corresponds to Mellers and Cooke's findings analysing holistic overall evaluations: With a narrow rent range, rent might have become overly important in comparison to distance, whereas, with a narrow distance range, distance might have become overly important, leading to the preference reversals mentioned above.

3.4. Structuring bias

Consider a job choice problem. A DM has to choose between a number of different jobs and s/he decides on the following list of attributes: salary, job security, and career opportunity. We can derive a value tree out of this non-hierarchical list of attributes by splitting up at least one attribute, e.g., job security, into two subattributes, e.g., personal job security and security of the firm. Multiattribute utility and value theories predict that for subattributes which are complete and not overlapping, the sum of weights should be equal to the weights of the main attribute.

Contrary to this prediction, Weber, Eisenführ and von Winterfeldt (1988) showed that for ratio and swing procedures as well as for a decomposed statistical procedure, the sum of weights for the subattributes is significantly greater than the weight for the main attribute when the latter is directly elicited. This splitting bias also appeared in other studies (Borcherding & von Winterfeldt 1988, Eppel 1990, and Weber 1989). It seems to hold across most weighting methods and situational contexts, but only if the weighting methods are applied in a non-hierarchical fashion (Borcherding & von Winterfeldt, 1988; Eppel, 1990). If weighting methods are applied in a hierarchical way, the hierarchical structure of the value tree exerts a strong influence on weights. Including one of the objectives at a different level of the value tree should not affect the weight of an attribute. This is not the case, however. Borcherding and von Winterfeldt (1988) showed that the superstructure of a value tree greatly influenced ratio weights that were elicited in a hierarchical fashion. Greater weights resulted when objectives were added at a higher level of the tree. No effect was observed with three other non-hierarchical methods. It seems that one general principle underlies both effects. If weights for objectives are compared on a specific level of a value tree, variations in the structure above this level (i.e., different hierarchies) affect weights if the elicitation is carried out in a hierarchical way. Variations in the structure below this level (i.e., splitting of attributes) affect weight judgments, if they are elicited in a non-hierarchical way.

The effect of hierarchy was explicitly analyzed by Stillwell, von Winterfeldt and John (1987) who found that the two ways of eliciting preferences resulted in different weights. Assessing weights hierarchically, i.e. on each level separately, resulted in steeper weights than assessing the weights non-hierarchically, i.e., only on the lowest level. The result probably depends on specific aspects of the DM's preferences. In the hierarchical mode, attribute weights depend on the number of intermediate levels between the top and bottom of the tree. The higher this number is for any of the attributes, the smaller are the weights in comparison to when they are elicited by the non-hierarchical mode. Also, the higher the level where attributes are added to the tree, the higher are the resulting weights, again in comparison to when weights are elicited by the non-hierarchical approach. Both effects stem from the fact that using a hierarchical approach, weights are derived by multiplying through the tree. The more probabilities that have to be multiplied in order to derive an attribute weight, the smaller the weight. If in applied settings important objectives are subdivided, there is a risk that these objectives will be underweighted using a hierarchical approach and overweighted using a non-hierarchical one.

3.5. A unifying interpretation

Structuring bias, range insensitivity bias and proxy overweighting bias would all seem to stem from the inability of subjects to adjust their weight judgments in accordance with changes in attributes or in the value tree structure. Consider, for example, the attribute of monthly salary with a range from 3.000 Deutsche Mark to 6.000 Deutsche Mark . This attribute could be split into two subranges, basic salary, ranging from 3.000 Deutsche Mark to 4.000 Deutsche Mark, and success-dependent salary, ranging from nothing up to 2.000 Deutsche Mark. If a splitting bias exists, the sum of weights for the two subattributes should be higher than the weight for the main attribute. Such an effect could also be explained by a range insensitivity bias. When a range insensitivity bias exists, subjects insufficiently take into account the decrease in range with the result that weights are too high. A similar relation can exist between the range insensitivity bias and the proxy bias. The probabilistic link between fundamental and proxy attributes leads to a loss in true variance, i.e., a smaller range for the proxy attribute. Not adjusting weights in accordance with a decrease in range of the proxy attribute will result in overweighting the proxy attribute in comparison with the fundamental one.

Some of the mentioned biases in weight judgments have counterparts in the area of probability judgments. Fischhoff, Slovic and Lichtenstein (1978), for example, demonstrated a bias in a fault tree analysis which is similar to the splitting bias and to which the same theoretical explanations may apply. Support theory developed by Tversky and Koehler (1993) is a major step towards formally modeling the behavior demonstrated in Fischhoff, Slovic and Lichtenstein (1978) as well as the biases described here. The theory assumes that subjects derive probabilities according to the number of specific hypotheses they can generate. Applying this idea to the area of preference elicitation, weight judgments might depend on the specific consequences a subject can think of. Those consequences depend on the number of specific attributes and not on attribute ranges.

4. BIASES IN DECISION MAKING

Systematic distortions occur not only when eliciting weight judgments but also when asking for holistic evaluations of alternatives. The reason for this can be found in people using a variety of heuristics rather than normative rules when making a decision. These heuristics can be described as cognitive 'shortcuts', i.e., simplifying strategies which reduce the cognitive overload that typically occurs in multi-attribute decision situations, but still approximate the accuracy of normative procedures. Decision-makers appear to be highly adaptive in their strategy selection (Payne, 1982; Payne, Bettman & Johnson, 1988, 1990) which depends on many task and context variables such as response mode, the framing of the decision problem, time pressure, and incomplete information about the alternatives. Here the influence of these strategies on resulting decisions and, specifically, their influence on the weights and weight judgments that may be inferred from the decisions, will be reported.

4.1. Response mode effects

In making a decision, different response modes can be applied. Amongst others, the best alternative may be directly selected, dominated or inferior alternatives may be successively rejected, or the choice may be inferred, e.g., from evaluations of all alternatives (judgments) or from constructed indifferences between alternatives (matching). All response modes yield preference orders of alternatives. According to the prescriptive principle of procedure invariance, these should be the same for all response modes. As has been shown many times, however, this is not the case. The discrepancies can be as large that even reversals of preference occur, i.e., different alternatives emerge as the best ones when different response modes are applied. The preference reversal phenomenon occurs in risky as well as non-risky contexts (Slovic, 1975; Tversky, Sattath & Slovic, 1988; Slovic, Griffin & Tversky, 1990) and has proven to be exceptionally robust (Grether & Plott,

1979), thus underlining the importance of response mode effects in decision making.

Lichtenstein and Slovic (1971) proposed a process of anchoring and adjustment, based on compatibility between an attribute and the required response, as an explanation for these findings. Supporting evidence for this was provided by Schkade and Johnson (1989). Subjects apparently use the score on the compatible attribute (e.g. payoff when asked to set prices) as an anchor for their response and then make upward or downward adjustments to accommodate the score on the noncompatible attribute. Since these adjustments are typically insufficient, the compatible attribute is overweighted. Accordingly, Schkade and Johnson were able to show that manipulating the starting point on the response scale significantly reduced the rate of preference reversals. However, other processes might be involved as well (Slovic, Griffin & Tversky, 1990).

Tversky, Sattath and Slovic (1988) analyzed preferences from matching and choice and found that attribute weights derived from choices were steeper than those derived from matching. They interpreted their findings as supporting the prominence hypothesis which states that the more prominent attribute weighs more heavily in choice than in matching. One rationale for the prominence hypothesis is that justification processes play an important role in choice, but less so in matching. Accordingly, Slovic, Fischhoff and Lichtenstein (1988) stated that "much of the deliberation prior to choice consists of finding a concise, coherent set of reasons that justify the selection of one option over the others" (p.159) whereas for matching this is not the case.

Although compatibility and prominence effects have been established independently, they may jointly contribute to preference reversals and thus help to explain the size and robustness of this phenomenon (Slovic, Griffin & Tversky, 1990). There have been attempts to integrate both explanations. Tversky et al. (1988) suggested that a qualitative strategy, such as selecting the option that is superior on the more important dimension, is more likely to be used in the qualitative method of choice, whereas a quantitative strategy, such as making trade-offs between dimensions is more likely to be employed in the quantitative method of matching. This suggests the prominence effect can be attributed to a more general compatibility between the nature of the task and the nature of the strategy it invokes. Alternatively, one could argue that attributes become prominent either because they are more important or because they are compatible with the required response mode. In this case, the prominence hypothesis is regarded as the more extensive principle that can also explain compatibility effects.

Since weight elicitation in MAUT is done for previously selected attributes which might vary in their degree of compatibility with the required response mode of elicitation, it is quite likely that response mode effects also occur for different methods of eliciting weights. Also, if response modes have a stable impact on final evaluations of alternatives, the problem arises as to which final evaluations to model.

4.2. Framing effects

In decision making under risk, framing effects have been known for some time. Contrary to the prescriptive assumption of descriptive invariance, alternative descriptions of a decision problem often result in different preferences of the DM (Kahneman & Tversky, 1979, 1984; Tversky & Kahneman, 1981; 1986). According to Kahneman and Tversky's prospect theory, different formulations of the same decision problem induce decision makers to adopt different decision frames, i.e., different internal representations of the "acts, outcomes and contingencies associated with a particular choice" (Tversky & Kahneman, 1981, p. 453). Outcomes are evaluated in terms of changes from a current reference point (gains or losses) rather than in terms of final wealth. In the domain of losses, DMs tend to be risk-seeking, whereas they tend to be risk-averse in the domain of gains. In addition, loss aversion can be observed; losses are assigned a greater value than corresponding gains.

Recently, the idea that reference points play an important role has been extended to riskless decision making. Tversky and Kahneman (1991) demonstrated that weights depend on the status quo of the decision maker. Subjects weighted the attribute where they lost something relative to their status quo more heavily than the attribute where they gained something, which can be explained by loss aversion. This implies that when eliciting indifference points, it matters on which attribute the match has to be made.

Having to give something up on an attribute will make the respective attribute more important and can result in indifference curves crossing each other (Delquié, 1993). Slovic, Griffin and Tversky (1990), however, were able to demonstrate that their similar finding can again also be explained by compatibility effects. Shapira (1981) asked senior executives of a company to make trade-offs of job attributes in relation to their current job, varying the direction of the trade-off. In one condition, for example, subjects had to indicate the maximum amount of decrease in interest and challenge they were willing to accept for a certain increase in their salary. In the other condition they had to indicate the minimum increase in interest and challenge needed to offset an equivalent decrease in salary. In accordance with prospect theory, the relative weights of the attributes were higher when a decrease (loss) was expected than when an increase (gain) was expected. This effect might also occur with other methods of weight elicitation where an anchor or reference point is set, i.e., with more or less all direct elicitation methods for weights.

Obviously, there are different ways of setting reference points. Another possibility might be to present people with 'phantom' alternatives, i.e., alternatives that are not available (Farquhar & Pratkanis, 1993). If a subject is indifferent to which of two alternatives X and Y they obtain, the presentation of a phantom alternative that dominates Y makes the decision maker (to a small degree) prefer X to Y. When alternative X is chosen, the loss of the outcome on the attribute on which Y is superior to X has a smaller impact when a phantom alternative is introduced. The question of how additional alternatives affect the trade-off between a given pair of alternatives, however, is far from being resolved.

A more general perspective of framing is taken by Keeney (1992). Decisions are often framed as problems, not as the opportunities which they often are or can be. Framing decision situations as opportunities might lead to different decisions and might let them appear to be less stressful and even enjoyable. In a broader sense, impacts of personal variables such as induced moods, needs or expectations and environmental variables like having to justify something in public on decision making could all be regarded as framing effects.

As pointed out above, research on response mode and framing effects has identified two important strategies employed by DMs in multiattribute decision situations: first, the tendency to further increase the weight of already important attributes and decrease the weight of less important ones, thereby reducing the dimensions of the evaluation task, and secondly, the tendency to place a higher weight on negative outcomes than on corresponding positive ones. These strategies can be observed in a variety of other contexts as well, e.g., in decision making under time pressure (Wright, 1974; Wright & Weitz, 1977; Ben Zur & Breznitz, 1981; Payne, Bettman & Johnson, 1988; Svenson & Edland, 1989). Weighting negative information more heavily than positive information is also a common finding in the area of impression formation. Anderson (1965), for example, found that when subjects were asked to evaluate a hypothetical person described by adjectives varying on the positive-negative dimension, highly negative adjectives lowered the overall evaluation more than would be predicted by either an adding model or an averaging model of information integration. No parallel effect was found for highly positive adjectives. Furthermore, differential weighting occurs when alternatives are described incompletely. Slovic and MacPhillamy (1974) studied choices between alternatives for which information was provided on one common and one unique attribute. They found that subjects weighted attributes more heavily when they were common than when they were unique. This can again be explained by prominence as well as compatibility effects. Only the common attribute allows to compare scores for both alternatives directly. This might have made the common attribute more prominent and at the same time served as an anchor for the response. Differential weighting even occured when subjects had been warned not to yield to such a tendency. This highlights again how powerful such effects can be.

5. CONCLUDING REMARKS

It is often argued that multiattribute utility procedures are particularly suited to being applied to decision situations that are important, complex and difficult. In MAUT the evaluations that have to be made are less complex and are aggregated in a consistent manner in arriving at an overall evaluation. This is assumed to improve decision making. Many applications of MAUT have demonstrated that this is true. Nevertheless, the quality of the output of a multiattribute model is limited by the quality of the input: namely, the quality of the weight judgments. This paper has focused on the quality of weight judgments and their proneness to behavioral biases.

It has been shown that several weight judgment biases exist. Inconsistencies in weight judgments can emerge even when only one weighting method is applied but can be even greater when different weighting methods are applied (Weber & Borcherding, 1993). That these inconsistencies are very stable was impressively demonstrated by Eppel (1990). When subjects were asked to reconcile inconsistencies between weights elicited with different methods, final weights again depended on the method applied for reconciliation.

In this paper we have reported weighting biases which arise from the multiattribute structure of decision problems and which violate MAUT's prescriptive invariance requirements. Subjects show a range insensitivity bias and a proxy overweighting bias as well as biases due to the structure of the value tree such as a splitting bias and a hierarchy bias. Because a particular value tree with its attributes and attribute ranges has a high impact on resulting weights and because there are no 'correct' value trees, the value tree has to be chosen with great care. Keeney and Raiffa's (1976) criteria for objectives and attributes and the checklist of von Winterfeldt and Edward's (1986) should be completed in order to allow for subjects strengths and weaknesses. In most of the experiments reported here the DM gave weight judgments for a value tree that was presented to him or her. In real decision situations, however, the value tree is elicited from the DM. Adelman, Sticha and Donnell (1986) found that different approaches of eliciting value trees resulted in equally good but systematically different trees. The top-down and bottom-up approaches they used yielded the same number of lowest level objectives, but compared to the bottom-up approach the top-down approach produced more intermediate levels between top and bottom levels and a higher variance in the number of intermediate levels. This shows that the method used for eliciting a value tree affects the 'steepness' of the tree and can thus exert a strong influence on weights if they are elicited hierarchically.

In the light of the biases which can afflict weight judgments, the question arises whether decomposed methods such as MAUT are really superior to holistic evaluations of decision alternatives. It has been shown, however, that not only weight judgments but also holistic evaluations of alternatives can be biased. For example, a response mode bias can arise such that for the same set of identically described alternatives different overall evaluations emerge as a function of the particular response mode applied. Also, a framing bias can exist such that when response mode is held constant, evaluations differ as a function of how alternatives are described, i.e., how alternatives are framed. Since both biases have found to be very robust, the problem arises as to which overall evaluation to model when applying multiattribute utility measurement. Differing overall evaluations can be explained by different attribute weights. When attribute weights are elicited directly, the problem of 'true' overall evaluations becomes one of 'true' weights.

The decomposed and the holistic approach are alike in being prone to substantial biases. Currently it is difficult to compare them with respect to the magnitude of the biases. If one approach has to be selected for application to a complex decision situation, however, the decomposed approach is still the preferable one. The correlation between holistic and model-derived evaluations of alternatives is high when only a few attributes have to be considered. The fact that the correlation decreases when the number of attributes increases can only be attributed to changes in the quality of holistic evaluations. Increasing the number of attributes leaves evaluations in a decomposed approach unchanged but makes holistic evaluations more complex because more information has to be simultaneously taken into account. Human beings are, however, not good at processing complex information, so that the quality of holistic evaluations deteriorates with increasing numbers of attributes.

Clearly, in order to improve complex decision making the emphasis must be to resolve the weaknesses of the decomposed approach. One important route to tackling these weaknesses is to understand the biases which affect weight judgments. The studies reported here mostly used student subjects. Often, however, in real world applications the DM is highly trained or expert. Experts might be expected to be less susceptible to biases in weight judgments because of their greater knowledge of the subject area and their greater familiarity with the decision problem and its different frames. Still, the same sorts of biases are likely to occur. Generally, ratio weights seem to be more biased than weights elicited with other weighting methods because attribute ranges are not explicitly included in their elicitation and because the ratio method is usually applied hierarchically. Other weighting methods are typically applied in a non-hierarchical way where the influence of hierarchical aspects of value tree structures on weights is less strong.

There remain, however, the splitting bias and the range insensitivity bias. In the process of deriving a value tree objectives are split into attributes. The problem arises as to how much objectives should be split. Objectives are split in order to find a set of less complex attributes with the primary desirable properties of being complete, operational, decomposable and non-redundant (Keeney & Raiffa, 1976). Subject to these criteria the set should be as small as possible. Splitting should therefore only be performed if it helps to reduce the complexity of the problem but at the same time keeps the focus on few relevant aspects of the situation as opposed to many minor aspects. This implies that a further subdivision is only recommended for very important aspects. These considerations suggest that one should aim for a set of attributes with similar importances. If such a set can be found, weight judgments may become more valid.

The degree to which attribute outcomes determine overall evaluations is a function of the actual range of outcomes as well as the importance of the attribute. Von Winterfeldt and Edwards (1986, p. 230 ff) discussed several ways of setting ranges. Although the range of attribute outcomes is of major importance, it might not be wise to use the actual range of outcomes for the weight elicitation, particularly not if it is new to the DM. It might be more desirable to elicit meaningful anchors from the DM, e.g., likely good and bad outcomes of potential alternatives, and then to elicit weights for these ranges. The reason for insufficient adjustment of weight judgments to changes in range is presumably that for the DM importance exists even in the absence of explicitly given attribute ranges. This importance has been learned from past experience. Taking this past experience into account when specifying attribute ranges could also make weight judgments more valid.

Finally, it should be emphasized how helpful a tool sensitivity analysis is for showing the DM the implications of his or her weight judgments for the overall evaluations of alternatives. It can indicate sensitive attributes and demonstrate where their sensitivity stems from. Also, sensitivity analysis provides model-derived evaluations for alternatives at all levels of the value tree including the intermediate levels. This allows the DM to compare model-derived evaluations with his or her intuitively-derived ones not only on the top and bottom levels but also on intermediate levels. Also it switches the DM's focus to different branches of the tree. Thereby sensitivity analysis provides the opportunity for considerable cross-checking. It is assumed that cross-checking substantially reduces biases.

6. REFERENCES

Adelman, L., Sticha, P.L. & Donnell, M.L. (1986). An experimental investigation of the relative effectiveness of two techniques for structuring multiattribute hierarchies. *Organizational Behavior and Human Decision Processes, 37,* 188-196.

Anderson, N.H. (1965). Averaging versus adding as a stimulus-combination rule in impression formation. *Journal of Personality and Social Psychology, 11,* 214- 219.

Barron, H.F., von Winterfeldt, D. & Fischer, G.W. (1984). Theoretical and empirical relationships between risky and riskless utility functions. *Acta Psychologica, 56,* 233-244.

Beattie, J. & Baron, J. (1991). Investigating the effect of stimulus range on attribute weight. *Journal of Experimental Psychology: Human Perception and Performance , 17,* 571-585.

Ben Zur, H. & Breznitz, S.J. (1981). The effects of time pressure on risky choice behavior. *Acta Psychologica, 47,* 89-104.

Borcherding, K., Eppel, T. & von Winterfeldt, D. (1991). Comparison of weighting judgments in multiattribute utility measurement. *Management Science, 37,* 1603-1619.

Borcherding, K. & von Winterfeldt, D. (1988). The effect of varying value trees on multiattribute evaluations. *Acta Psychologica, 68,* 153-170.

Dawes, R.M. (1982). The robust beauty of improper linear models in decision making. In D. Kahneman, P. Slovic & A. Tversky, (Eds.), *Judgment under uncertainty - Heuristics and biases.* Cambridge: University Press, 391-407.

Delquié, P. (1993). Inconsistent trade-offs between attributes: New evidence in preference assessment biases. *Management Science, 39,* 1322-1395.

Dyer, J.S. & Sarin, R.A. (1979). Measurable multiattribute value functions. *Operations Research,,27,* 810-822.

Edwards, W. (1977). How to use multiattribute utility measurement for social decision making. *IEEE Transaction on Systems, Man, and Cybernetics, 7,* 326-340.

Einhorn, H.J. & Hogarth, R.M. (1975). Unit weighting schemes for decision making. *Organizational Behavior and Human Performance, 13*, 171-192.

Eppel, T. (1990). Eliciting and reconciling multiattribute utility weights. Los Angeles: University of Southern California.

Farquhar, P.H. & Pratkanis, A. (1993). Decision structuring with phantom alternatives. *Management Science, 39*, 1214-1226.

Festinger, L. (1964). *Conflict, decision, and dissonance.* Stanford: Stanford University Press.

Fischer, G.W. (1991). Range sensitivity of attribute weights in multiattribute utility assessment. Technical Report, Center for Decision Studies, Fuqua School of Business, Duke University, Durham, NC.

Fischer, G.W., Damodaran, N., Laskey, K.B. & Lincoln, D. (1987). Preferences for proxy attributes. *Management Science, 33*, 198-214.

Fischhoff, B., Slovic, P. & Lichtenstein, S. (1978). Fault trees: Sensitivity of estimated failure probabilities to problem representation. *Journal of Experimental Psychology: Human Perception and Performance, 4*, 330-334.

Gabrielli, W. & von Winterfeldt, D. (1978). Are importance weights sensitive to the range of alternatives in multiattribute utility measurement? *SSRI Report* No.78-6, Los Angeles: University of Southern California.

Grether, D.M. & Plott, C.R. (1979). Economic theory of choice and the preference reversal phenomenon. *The American Economic Review, 69*, 623-638.

Hershey, J.C., Kunreuther, H.C. & Schoemaker, P.J.H. (1982). Sources of bias in assessment procedures for utility functions. *Management Science, 28*, 936-954.

Jaccard J., Brinberg, D. & Ackerman, L.J. (1986). Assessing attribute importance: A comparison of six methods. *Journal of Consumer Research, 12*, 463-468.

John, R.S., Edwards, W. & Collins, L. (1980). A comparison of importance weights for MAU analysis derived from holistic, indifference, direct subjective, and rank order judgments. *SSRI Technical Report* No.80-4. Los Angeles: University of Southern California.

Johnson, E.J., Meyer, R.J. & Ghose, S. (1989). When choice models fail: Compensatory models in negatively correlated environments. *Journal of Marketing Research, 26*, 255-270.

Kahneman, D., Slovic, P. & Tversky, A. (Eds.) (1982). *Judgment under uncertainty - Heuristics and biases.* Cambridge: University Press.

Kahneman, D. & Tversky, A. (1979). Prospect theory - An analysis of decision under risk. *Econometrica, 47*, 263-292.

Kahneman, D. & Tversky, A. (1984). Choices, values, and frames. *American Psychologist, 34*, 341-350.

Keeney, R.L. (1992). *Value focused thinking: A path to creative decision making.* Cambridge: Harvard University Press.

Keeney, R.L. & Raiffa, H. (1976). *Decisions with multiple objectives.* New York: Wiley.

Keller, L.R. (1987). Decision problem structuring: Generating options. Unpublished paper, Fuqua School of Business, Duke University.

Kleinmuntz, D.N. (1983). The sensitivity of linear multiattribute utility models to attribute formulation. Working paper No. 82/83-4-27. Austin: Department of Management, Graduate School of Business, University of Texas.

Krantz, D.H., Luce, R.D., Suppes, P. & Tversky, A. (1971). *Foundations of measurement, Vol 1;* New York: Academic Press.

Lichtenstein, S., Gregory, R., Slovic, P. & Wagenaar, W. A. (1990). When lives are in your hands: Dilemmas of the societal decision maker. In R.M. Hogarth (Ed.): *Insights in decision making,* Chicago: University of Chicago Press, 91-106.

Lichtenstein, S. & Slovic, P. (1971). Reversals of preference between bids and choices in gambling decisions. *Journal of Experimental Psychology, 89,* 46-55.

Merkhofer, M.W. & Keeney, R.L. (1987). A multiattribute utility analysis of alternative sites for the disposal of nuclear waste. *Risk Analysis, 7,* 173-194.

Mellers, B.A. & Cooke, A.D.J. (1992). When tradeoffs depend on attribute range. Working Paper, UC Berkeley, Berkeley,CA.

Nisbett, R.E. & Ross, L. (1980). *Human inference: Strategies and shortcomings of social judgement.* Englewood Cliffs, NJ: Prentice Hall.

Payne, J.W. (1982). Contingent decision behavior. *Psychological Bulletin, 92,* 382-402.

Payne, J.W., Bettman, J.R. & Johnson, E.J. (1988). Adaptive strategy selection in decision making. *Journal of Experimental Psychology: Learning, Memory, and Cognition, 14,* 534-552.

Payne, J.W., Bettman, J.R. & Johnson, E.J. (1990). The adaptive decision maker: Effort and accuracy in choice. In R.M. Hogarth (Ed.): *Insights in decision making,* Chicago: University of Chicago Press, 129-153.

Pfister, H.-R., Jungermann, H. & Kauffmann, R.(1991). Assessing importance weights in decision analysis: Simple methods and complex structures. Working Paper.

Saaty, T.L. (1986). Axiomatic foundation of the analytic hierarchy process. *Management Science, 32,* 841-855.

Schkade, D.A. & Johnson, E.J. (1989). Cognitive processes in preference reversals. *Organizational Behavior and Human Decision Processes, 44,* 203-231.

Schoemaker, P.J.H. & Waid, C.D. (1982). An experimental comparison of different approaches to determining weights in additive utility models. *Management Science, 28,* 182-196.

Shapira, Z. (1981). Making trade-offs beween job attributes. *Organizational Behavior and Human Performance, 28,* 331-335.

Slovic, P. (1975). Choice between equally valued alternatives. *Journal of Experimental Psychology: Human Perception and Performance, 1,* 280-287.

Slovic, P., Fischhoff, B. & Lichtenstein, S. (1988). Response mode, framing, and information-processing effects in risk assessment. In D.E. Bell, H. Raiffa & A. Tversky (Eds.), *Decision making: Descriptive, normative and prescriptive interactions.* Cambridge: CPU, 152-166.

Slovic, P., Griffin, D. & Tversky, A. (1990). Compatibility effects in judgment and choice. In R.M. Hogarth (Ed.), *Insights in decision making.* Chicago: University of Chicago Press, 5-27.

Slovic, P. & MacPhillamy, D. (1974). Dimensional commensurability and cue utilization in comparative judgment. *Organizational Behavior and Human Performance, 11,* 172-194.

Steward, T.R. & Ely, D.W. (1984). Range sensitivity: A necessary condition and a test for the validity of weights. Report No.270. Boulder, Colorado: Center for

Research on Judgment and Policy, Institute of Cognitive Science, University of Colorado.

Stillwell, W.G., von Winterfeldt, D. & John, R.S. (1987). Comparing hierarchical and nonhierarchical weighting methods for eliciting multiattribute value models, *Management Science, 33*, 442-450

Svenson, O. (1992). Differentiation and consolidation theory of human decision making: A frame of reference for the study of pre- and post-decision processes. *Acta Psychologica, 80*, 143-168.

Svenson, O. & Edland, A. (1989). Change of preference under time pressure: Choices and judgments. In H. Montgomery & O. Svenson (Eds.): *Process and structure in human decision making*, New York: Wiley, 225-236.

Tversky, A. & Kahneman, D. (1981). The framing of decisions and the psychology of choice. *Science, 211*, 453-458.

Tversky, A. & Kahneman, D. (1986). Rational choice and the framing of decisions. *Journal of Business, 59*, 251-278.

Tversky, A. & Kahneman, D. (1991). Loss aversion in riskless choice: A reference-dependent model. *The Quarterly Journal of Economics*, 1039-1061.

Tversky, A. & Koehler, D. (1993). Support theory: A nonextensional representation of subjective probability. In preparation, Stanford University, Stanford.

Tversky, A., Sattath, S. & Slovic, P. (1988). Contingent weighting in judgment and choice. *Psychological Review, 95*, 371-384.

von Nitzsch, R. & Weber, M. (1993). The effect of attribute ranges on weights in multiattribute utility measurements. *Management Science, 39*, 937-943.

von Winterfeldt, D. & Edwards, W. (1986). *Decision analysis and behavioral research*. Cambridge: University Press.

Weber, M. (1989). Availability as an explanation of the splitting bias. Working Paper, Universität Mannheim.

Weber, M. & Borcherding, K. (1993). Behavioral influences on weight judgments in multiattribute decision making. *European Journal of Operations Research, 67*, 1-12.

Weber, M., Eisenführ, F. & von Winterfeldt, D. (1988). The effects of splitting attributes on weights in multiattribute utility measurement. *Management Science, 34*, 431-445.

Westenberg, M.R.M. & Koele, P. (1990). Response modes and decision strategies. In K. Borcherding, O.I. Larichev & D.M. Messick (Eds.), *Contemporary issues in decision making*. Amsterdam: North-Holland, 159-170.

Wright, P. (1974). The harassed decision maker: Time pressures, distractions, and the use of evidence. *Journal of Applied Psychology, 59*, 555-561.

Wright, P. & Weitz, B. (1977). Time horizon effects on product evaluation strategies. *Journal of Marketing Research*, 429-443.

Acknowledgements. We would like to thank Hutton Barron and two anonymous reviewers for their helpful comments. Also, we gratefully acknowledge the improvement of this paper due to the changes suggested by Karina Linnell. They were intended to be language corrections, but actually made us think more about what we wanted to say.

Contributions to Decision Making - I
J.-P. Caverni, M. Bar-Hillel, F.H. Barron and H. Jungermann (Editors)
© 1995 Elsevier Science B.V. All rights reserved.

ON MODELING RISKY CHOICE: WHY REASONS MATTER

Lola L. Lopes

College of Business, University of Iowa
Iowa City, IA 52242, USA

Abstract : Three classic phenomena of risky choice (risk aversion, risk seeking, and the Allais paradox) are examined from the point of view of the goals that people express by their choices. It is argued that models of the risky choice process that do not provide a theoretical role for these goals are descriptively inaccurate and prescriptively inappropriate. SP/A theory (Lopes 1987, 1990) is proposed as one means by which people's expressed goals can be incorporated into the modeling of risky choice and related to subsidiary forms of data such as choice protocols.

Research on decision making comes in three flavors: descriptive, predictive, and prescriptive. If we consider also that decision research is often predicated on normative economic models, there is plenty of room for confusion about what it is that we are actually doing. The thesis to be defended in this paper is that accurate description is prerequisite to prediction and to prescription. We will focus at present on decision making under risk, but the argument extends easily to alternative areas such as research on linear models and on probability judgment.

In making description prerequisite to prediction and to prescription, I am explicitly rejecting positivist conventions for talking about the relation between theory and the world, conventions that were popularized in economics by Milton Friedman (1953) in his famous paper on positive economics. Friedman's main points have become part of conventional wisdom. Most famous is the dictum that one tests the adequacy of a theory by the accuracy of its predictions and not by the realism of its assumptions. Secondary points include the ideas that simplicity and fruitfulness should figure in breaking ties between theories that predict equally well, and that the relation between theory and reality boils down to "as if" rather than to "is." On Friedman's view, theories are no more than heuristic frameworks for organizing empirical data and for specifying the language in which phenomena are discussed. They are not intrinsically right or wrong but are only more or less accurate in predicting.

Michael Polanyi (1962) has argued a quite different case. For Polanyi, the most basic criterion for theory is truthfulness, which in turn resides in the contact of theory with reality. On his argument, wrong theories, no matter how elegant, are fruitful only in producing error. Polanyi's science does not reside in the cool application of scientific method but rather in the passionate pursuit of an unobstructed glimpse of the world. In Polanyi's words, "Scientists—that is, creative scientists—spend their lives in trying to guess right. They are sustained and guided therein by their heuristic passion" (p. 143).

Friedman and Polanyi differ sharply in the degree to which pure description is seen as contributing to right prediction. Friedman cares about right prediction because only right prediction can provide the foundation for economic policy. Provided that a theory predicts rightly, its descriptive accuracy is irrelevant. This is exactly the functional link that underlies behaviorism's focus on prediction and control. Polanyi's position is more in line with cognitivism in asking theories to do more than generate right predictions. In his view, science should seek truthful theories that illuminate our understanding. Truthful theories generate right predictions because they embody right reasons.

In what follows, I will suggest how theories of human risk taking might have evolved differently if more attention had been given to accurate description at different points in history. In particular, I focus on the three basic phenomena that theories of risk taking aim to explain. The first is risk aversion which we can consider in its most behavioral formulation as a tendency for gambles to be less preferred than their expected values. The second is risk seeking which is the tendency for gambles to be preferred to equivalent sure things. The third is the Allais paradox which we can think of as a violation of the linearity assumptions of expected utility theory (EU). In each case, my intent will be to show how people's choices relate to their immediate goals (i.e., the proximate and consciously-accessible reasons for their preferences) and to argue that tying theory more closely to people's goals enhances theoretical validity both descriptively and predictively.

UTILITY AND RISK ATTITUDE

Bernoullian Origins

As early as the mid- 17th century, mathematicians converged on the idea that what we nowadays term "expected value" (EV) is a proper measure of a gamble's worth. In the 18th century, however, the idea was challenged by a hypothetical gamble known as the St. Petersburg paradox[1] , a gamble that has infinite EV but that most people judge to be worth only a few dollars (see Lopes, 1981, for more on the St. Petersburg paradox). Many solutions were proposed for the paradox, one of which permanently set the mold for explaining why people undervalue gambles. This was the invention of Daniel Bernoulli (1738/1967) that we now call expected utility (EU) theory. Bernoulli pointed out that in computing expected value, the subjective value of money (utility) is implicitly assumed to be equal to its objective value. If we focus on subjective value, however, the St. Petersburg game looks much less attractive.

The explanatory device that Bernoulli used is known today under the name "diminishing marginal utility". Mathematically, we assume that utility (subjective value) is a concave (negatively accelerated) function of objective value. If we then replace objective dollars with utilities and compute the expectation of the utilities, it becomes apparent that the gamble is not worth much. The reason is that the concave utility function effectively compresses higher values, shifting the mean downward, and thereby reducing the game's average (i.e., probability weighted) value.

Bernoulli's utility construct provided *an* explanation for risk aversion, but he provided no supporting arguments to suggest that it was *the* explanation. In order to nail down the descriptive validity of his construct, he would have needed to move beyond the single datum that he was concerned with (i.e., the small value given to the St. Petersburg game) and figure out what sorts of subsidiary evidence might lend support to the role of diminishing marginal utility in producing risk aversion. In some sense, he would have needed to invent not only

---

[1] A fair coin is tossed repeatly until it comes up tails, at which point the player is paid a sum equal to 2^n, where n is the toss on which tails appears. For $n = 1$, the prize is $2; for $n = 2$, $4; for $n = 3$, $8, and so forth. How much should a person pay for a single play of the game? According to the EV criterion, one should pay all one has because the EV of the game is infinite.

psychophysics (of which the utility construct is a precursor) but also cognitive psychology.

It is interesting to speculate how the history of research in risky choice might have evolved if Bernoulli and his contemporaries had been more concerned with descriptive accuracy. Several different questions might have been addressed. One clear tack would have been to verify that diminishing marginal utility has measurable impacts over the outcome ranges that occur in the St. Petersburg game and other large-prize lotteries. Examples of this tack can be found in direct measurements of utility reported by Allais (1986a). More telling, however, would have been attempts to link process measures such as protocols to pricing judgments. The latter tack would have required Bernoulli to confront the issue of how diminishing marginal utility affects judgments.

Taken as mathematics, diminishing marginal utility reduces differences among large outcomes. The theoretical action, so to speak, is on the high end of the outcome continuum. This would lead one to predict that protocols concerning the St. Petersburg game would focus on comparisons among large outcomes. But when students in classroom settings are asked to decide (hypothetically, of course) how much they would pay to play the game just once and then to explain their choices, explanations almost invariably focus on small outcomes. One sort of explanation says, more or less, "I choose [a small number] because most of the possible outcomes are small." Another says, "I wouldn't pay more than [a small number] because I am unlikely to win more than that back." The explanations differ in whether or not they invoke a specific target or aspiration level but neither sort involves comparisons among large outcomes[2].

---

[2] It is worth noting that, in other contexts, people are quite willing to use small subjective differences among large outcomes as explanations for risk aversion. For example, in the constant difference form of the Allais paradox, most people prefer $1 million for sure to .10 to win $5 million, .89 to win $1 million, and .01 to win zero. In defending their preference for the certain outcome, such people frequently point out that subjectively there is a much bigger difference between zero and $1 million than between $1 million and $5 million. This explanation would be consistent with Bernoulli's utility construct.

INFLECTED UTILITY AND LINEARITY

Research on risk taking took a sharp turn against description following the publication of von Neumann and Morgenstern's (1944/1947) axiomatic restatement of the EU model. There is no need to get into specific axioms. The important point is that von Neumann and Morgenstern shifted the focus of theory away from description of underlying process and toward measurement and representation of preferences that were themselves taken to be primitive. Although von Neumann and Morgenstern defended their axioms as being psychologically plausible, their utility construct was to be seen as a device for summarizing preferences rather than for causing them. Similarly, the decision maker was considered to choose as if to maximize expected utility, though neither the mechanistic nor teleological aspects of maximization were taken to apply psychologically.

The von Neumann and Morgenstern theory not only eschewed description of process, it made it scientifically suspect. At the same time that the theory broadened the behavioral domain to include risk-seeking preferences as well as risk aversion, it trivialized description to mere insertion of kinks in a utility function, a move that now abjured psychological content (including psychophysics) as "nonsensical" (Savage 1954/1972, p. 96) and "meaningless" (Arrow 1951, p. 425). Although at one time there had been lively interest in the role of regret and ambiguity in risky choice (reviewed in Lee, 1971), these ideas did not make sense within an expected utility context. Consequently, they were banished from theoretical description for almost thirty years and have only recently been reclaimed descriptively as EU theory has begun to lose its luster. Similarly, the prominence of EU theory blurred and eventually erased the theoretical distinction between unique and repeated decisions even though it continued (and continues) to be central in actuarial contexts.

At the same time that EU theory was expunging the psychological content in the utility function and in the idea of EU maximization, its axiomatic focus opened the door to better understanding of the structural relations among preferences entailed by the EU principle. In this regard, Allais (1953/1979) contributed mightily by recasting EU theory into the proposition that preferences among lotteries should be linear in probability. His two paradoxical problems showed clearly that, contrary to linearity requirements, preferences were not constant over either additive (constant difference) or multiplicative (constant ratio) transformations of probabilities. Moreover, his focus on people's desire for certainty and on their need to trade off EU maximization with the prevention of ruin reasserted the primacy of psychological description in theory development.

Allais' critique had practical as well as theoretical significance since the failures of linearity that he exposed vitiated prescriptive applications of EU theory that used arbitrary reference gambles to measure utility (see Hershey, Kunreuther, & Schoemaker, 1982; McCord & De Neufville, 1985). But despite the theoretical relevance and intuitive cogency of Allais' counterarguments (even Savage succumbed to the paradoxes), his critique was virtually ignored for thirty years by most economists and most psychologists. (See Lopes 1988 for an analysis of how this occurred.) By the late 1970s, however, economists and psychologists geared up to cope with Allais, a process that effectively redirected the energies of both groups to description.

RISK THEORY IN THE WAKE OF ALLAIS

Weighted Utility and Rank Dependency

Theory development after Allais can be divided into two phases. In the first phase, researchers tried to remedy the problems with EU theory by substituting subjective weights for probabilities much as Bernoulli had substituted utilities for objective values. Prospect theory (Kahneman & Tversky, 1979) was the most important development in this line, but it was soon recognized that the weighting tack Kahneman and Tversky had taken led to some undesirable mathematical consequences such as the possibility of preference for stochastically dominated alternatives. Much more important from a descriptive point of view was their suggestion that the utility function is S-shaped about the status quo with risk aversion predicted for gains and risk seeking predicted for losses. Unlike the versions of inflected utility that had been proposed in the von Neumann and Morgenstern mold, Kahneman and Tversky's proposal reasserted the role of psychophysics in mediating risk attitude. Their version differed from that of Bernoulli, however, in that the mechanism operated on absolute magnitudes (producing mirror-image effects for gains and losses) and not on overall asset levels.

More recently, both psychologists (e.g., Birnbaum et al, 1992; Lopes 1984, 1990; Tversky & Kahneman, 1992) and economists (e.g., Allais, 1986b; Quiggen, 1982; Yaari, 1987) have moved toward a more radical reformulation of EU theory, one that gives up linearity while still retaining important mathematical properties of generalized averaging notions. The term that has evolved for referring to these theories is "rank dependent." While the term is not perfect (since rank per se is not really at issue) I will follow current convention and use it here as well.

The basic idea in rank dependent utility is quite simple. For simplicity, let us first examine a simple computational illustration. Consider a gamble of the form {.05,$1;.15,$25;.6,$50;.15,$75;.05,$99}. We would ordinarily compute the expected value as follows: (.05)($1) + (.15)($25) + (.60)($50) + (.15)($75) (.05)($99) = $50. It is in this form that one can immediately see the possibility for replacing dollar values by their utilities and for replacing probabilities by decision weights.

However, there is an alternative way to compute EV in which one writes the equation in decumulative form[3] : (1.00)($1) + (.95)($24) + (.80)($25) + (.20)($25) + (.05)($24) = $50. This can be interpreted as indicating that one gets at least $1 for sure, with probability .95 gets yet another $24, with probability .80 gets yet another $25, with probability .20 gets yet another $25, and with probability .05 gets yet another $24. The final EV, $50, is unchanged by the decumulative computation but the apparent possibilities for psychological transformation shift. One can still replace differences in values by differences in utility, but transformation on probability would now involve decumulative probabilities rather than raw probabilities. For example, the original lottery has two outcomes each of which occur with probability .05. If raw probabilities were transformed (as in prospect theory), the same transformation would apply to both. In rank dependent theories, however, quite different things could happen to the .05 probability attached to the worst outcome and the .05 probability attached to the best outcome.

Three important possibilities for the decumulative transformation operation can be seen in Figure 1. On the abscissa of each graph are objective decumulative probabilities, D. A probability of 1.00 (to the

---

[3] (1.00)($1) + (1.00 − .05)($25 − $1) + (1.00 − .05 − .15)($50 − $25) + (1.00 − .05 − .15 − .60)($75 − $50) + (1.00 − .05 − .15 − .60 − .15)($99 − $75) = $50.

right of the graph) is the decumulative probability attached to the worst outcome (i.e., you get at least the worst outcome for sure). To the left are decumulative probabilities for successively better and better outcomes, limiting at zero which is the probability of exceeding the best outcome. The ordinate shows psychologically transformed values, h(D), under three weighting scenarios.

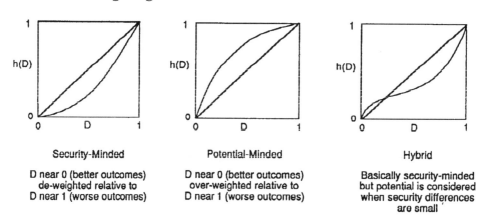

Security-Minded

D near 0 (better outcomes) de-weighted relative to D near 1 (worse outcomes)

Potential-Minded

D near 0 (better outcomes) over-weighted relative to D near 1 (worse outcomes)

Hybrid

Basically security-minded but potential is considered when security differences are small

Figure 1.

The left panel displays what I call security-mindedness. The decumulative probability attached to the worst outcome (1.00) receives full weight. Successively better outcomes receive proportionally less and less of their objective weight (i.e., the weight they would receive in an EV computation). In terms of observable preferences, a person displaying this pattern of weighting would appear to be risk averse in the classic sense: sure things would be preferred to actuarially equivalent gambles. Mild risk aversion would be entailed by a curve bowing only a little from the diagonal. Extreme and even pathological forms of risk aversion (i.e., strict maximining) would be entailed by a curve running tight against the graph's vertical and horizontal axes.

The middle panel is the rank dependent analog to risk seeking in EU theory. The decumulative probability attached to the worst outcome receives a weight of 1.00, but weights attached to successively better and better outcomes receive proportionally more and more weight. I call this pattern potential-mindedness. It corresponds behaviorally to a preference for lotteries over actuarially equivalent sure things.

The right panel, labeled hybrid, has been proposed by Allais (1986) and by me (1990) to represent the weighting pattern for the typical decision maker. The weighting curve is basically security-minded for low outcomes (i.e., proportionally more attention is devoted to worse outcomes than to moderate outcomes) but there is some additional attention (over-weighting) for the very best outcomes in a distribution.

Protocols and Psychological Description

I have been arguing for some time based on protocols that psychological processes of this sort underlie the expression of risk attitude in choices among gambles (Lopes, 1987). Let me reiterate very briefly some of those arguments. For illustration, consider the two lotteries displayed in Figure 2. The 100 tally marks in each represent lottery tickets and the values to the left of each row represent possible outcomes. Each of the two lotteries has an expected value of $100. The labels printed below each lottery are for expository convenience only. Subjects saw unlabeled lotteries and referred to them by their position in the display (e.g., left lottery or right lottery).

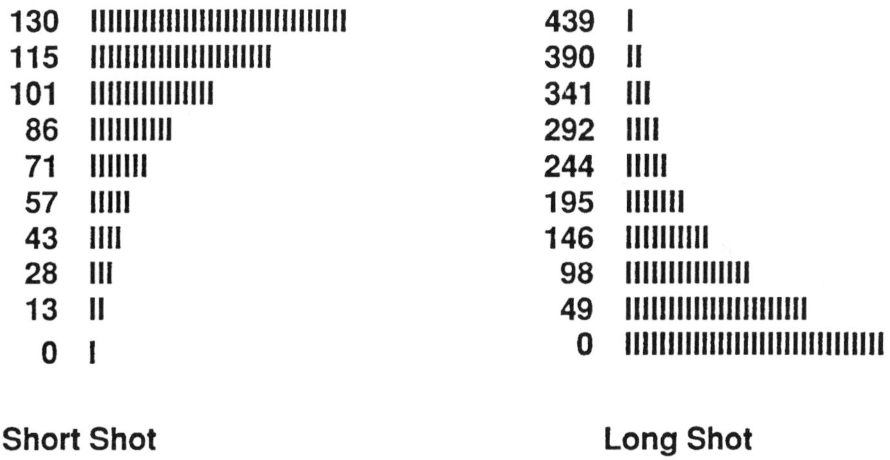

130																													439		
115																							390			
101																	341				
86												292					
71									244						
57							195								
43						146										
28					98													
13				49																				
0			0																															

Short Shot   **Long Shot**

Figure 2.

When people with preferences that we would tend to label "risk averse" choose between these lotteries, they tend to prefer the short shot. A representative explanation runs as follows: "I choose the [short shot] because there is only one chance of me losing and the best odds indicate a good chance of winning $71 or more. The [long shot] has too many opportunities to lose—it is too risky." People with preferences that we would label risk seeking have quite a different slant on things. They tend to prefer the long shot, explaining themselves as follows: "The chance for winning nothing is small with the [short shot] but since the dollar amount in the [long shot] is attractive I run the risk of losing and go for the [long shot]." Protocols such as these were my first clue that people were processing lotteries in decumulative form (i.e., as nested inequalities) and that their risk attitudes were reflections of the relative attention that they paid to bad and good outcomes.

A recent doctoral thesis by Lindemann (1993) has substantiated the importance of security and potential in real-world decisions involving substantial risk. Lindemann studied the decisions of farm couples (husband and wife teams) to sell or hold grain. This is a continuing and complex decision for small farmers who must decide among forward pricing their grain (selling before the crop is harvested), selling at harvest to producers or in local spot markets, storing grain in hopes that prices will rise, or using options or futures markets to hedge against risk.

Lindemann found that most farmers could easily be classified as either security-minded or potential-minded. Security-minded farmers speak in terms of "protection," of "locking in prices," of "being sure of something," and of "avoiding loss." For example, as one woman commented on the decision of a farm couple who chose to postpone selling in hopes of higher prices: "They're gambling. Hopefully they don't gamble if they need the money or have to borrow for operating expenses. They could lose big." Farmers such as these tend to sell early, when the price covers costs plus a small profit.

Potential-minded farmers, on the other hand, typically wait to sell and often miss opportunities to sell at reasonable profit. These farmers frequently speak of "hope," of "opportunities," and of "rising prices." They "shoot for prices" but do not necessarily see this as gambling. In one farmer's words: "Most farmers like to take even that remote chance to hit the highs." Another said "Farmers just naturally wait for a higher price even if there's a good price."

Lindemann also found that the women tended to be more security-minded than the men. She attributed the latter finding to the fact that women in farm couples tend to keep the books and so are more likely to be concerned with meeting costs plus a small profit. The men, on the other hand, regularly participate in "coffee shop" conversations with other farmers where social interaction and competition keeps everyone's focus on catching the season's high price.

Rank Dependence and Psychological Process

Although one tends to think of rank dependent models in algebraic terms and hence in terms of weighted averaging, the process can also be related to choice mechanisms. Strict security-mindedness corresponds as process to maximining in which the chooser compares risky options according to their worst outcomes. If they differ, the option with the better worst outcome is chosen. If they are the same, the attention switches to the second worst option and the comparison is repeated. In the same way, strict potential-mindedness corresponds to maximaxing in which choice is determined by a comparison of the best outcomes.

Strict security-mindedness and strict potential-mindedness are equivalent to strict maximining and strict maximaxing, respectively, and can lead to very foolish choices when security or potential differences are small (e.g., a few pennies difference among worst outcomes for security-mindedness or among best outcomes for potential-mindedness). Milder versions of the two, however, are not excessively affected by small differences in the critical regions of lotteries (i.e., at low or high ends of the distributions). But both processes are relentlessly single-minded in the sense that the weighting operation focuses on either worst outcomes or best outcomes, but not both.

The hybrid function that Allais and I prefer (see again Figure 1) allows both worst outcomes and best outcomes to be considered. In terms of process, it has some relation to processing by what has been called a lexicographic semiorder (Tversky 1969). If two distributions are very different in their lower regions, the choice between them will probably reflect security-mindedness. On the other hand, if the two lotteries are similar in their lower regions, attention will shift to the best outcomes and the tie will be broken in favor of potential-mindedness. This kind of reasoning process applies both to the purchase of lottery tickets (in which the expenditure of $1 has little impact on one's overall fortunes, but the possibility of winning millions has major attractions) and for explaining both constant difference and constant ratio versions of the Allais paradox (see Lopes 1990 for a detailed explanation).

The idea of rank dependent weighting holds promise for linking traditional laboratory studies of risky choice involving experimental lotteries with studies of risk perception involving natural and technological hazards. One of the well-replicated findings of Slovic (1987) is that lay people's judgments of risks fall into a two dimensional space. One of the dimensions seems to correspond to "dread" or catastrophic potential and the other seems to correspond to lack of firm scientific knowledge (i.e., uncertainty) in the risk estimates.

These two dimensions have natural interpretations in a rank dependent model. In rank dependent terms, risk distributions that have potentially catastrophic outcomes (e.g., nuclear energy production) differ fundamentally at the low end from distributions with worse average outcomes but no catastrophic potential (e.g., production of energy from coal). Decision makers who combine outcomes and probabilities with the sort of security-minded weighting function shown in the left panel of Figure 1 would tend to prefer risks without catastrophic potential even if the probability of the catastrophic outcome were small and even if the average outcome of the more secure risk were worse.

Uncertainty or ambiguity in risk estimates also decreases the acceptability of risks in a rank dependent model. To see this, consider a technology that experts estimate will cause no annual fatalities with probability .99 and one or more fatalities with probability .01. To the extent that these estimates are firm (i.e., based on solid actuarial data), the numerical values will enter the weighting process as given. But if there is uncertainty in the estimates (as there often is with new and untried technologies) either the probabilities will be adjusted to allow for increased probabilities of bad outcomes (e.g., Einhorn & Hogarth, 1985) or the outcome levels will be adjusted to allow for worse outcome levels (i.e., more fatalities) or both. In either case, the option will become less acceptable in a rank dependent weighting scheme even if the adjustments to probability and value are symmetric about the estimated values.

Beyond Rank Dependence

Rank dependent models of risky choice appear to do a good job of describing human judgments. While providing a natural place for capturing how people directly weight bad and good outcomes, they also allow for influences on judgment from psychophysical or utility effects of outcome magnitudes. However, rank dependence may not be sufficient to describe all risky choices even in fairly simple situations. I will briefly describe two such cases for illustration.

Risk Seeking for Losses

It has long been noted that people frequently take risks when they are confronted with possible losses (Bowman, 1982; Kunreuther & Wright, 1979; Williams, 1966). Prospect theory (Kahneman & Tversky, 1979) provided a formal explanation for this phenomenon by proposing that the utility function is S-shaped, being concave (risk averse) for gains and convex (risk seeking) for losses. This idea has been retained in the new, rank dependent version of prospect theory (Tversky & Kahneman, 1992). However, close examination of the data from studies comparing choices for gains with choices for losses reveals frequent failures of reflection and framing predictions based on the S-shaped function (e.g., Cohen et al 1987; Fagley & Miller 1987; Fischhoff 1983; Hershey & Schoemaker 1990; Miller & Fagley 1991; Schneider 1992; Schneider & Lopes 1986). Although choices for gains are often risk averse, choices for losses are variable both between and within subjects. In addition, subjects express conflict much more frequently when choosing among losses than when choosing among gains (Lopes, 1987).

If people's greater willingness to take risks for losses were being caused by an S-shaped utility function, one would expect reasonable degrees of symmetry to hold for gains and losses. Although there might be small differences for particular comparisons reflecting the interaction of the weighting function with the utility function, by and large there should be similar patterns for gains and for losses, both in terms of preference and in terms of conflict. Absence of such symmetry suggests that some other mechanism may be causing the observed increased willingness of people to take risks for losses[4].

---

[4] Although most studies of prospect therory (Kahneman & Tversky, 1979) focus on the reflection hypothesis, few deal with the difficulty of pin-pointing the cases in which reflection will not occur. An early and notable exception is Hershey and Schoemaker (1980). The problem of prediction is even more pronounced in the rank dependent version of prospect theory (Tversky & Kahneman, 1992) since that theory features two multiply-inflected functions (one for values, another for weights) that oppose one another in their effects. In the latter case, simulation based on estimated functions might provide a general picture of when reflection is predicted, but predictions for specific cases would remain difficult.

The variability in choices among losses and the experience of increased conflict may signal the operation of more than one psychological process in risky choice. This idea has been formalized as a two-factor model called SP/A theory (Lopes 1987, 1990). SP refers to security-potential. This component uses rank dependent weighting to capture the way that a lottery's probabilities and outcomes are combined into an overall index of attractiveness. The three weighting forms shown previously in Figure 1 are from SP/A theory.

SP/A theory also proposes that people's choices are often aimed at maximizing the probability that they will achieve some aspiration level (the A in SP/A). For example, recall that in the St. Petersburg game many subjects would refuse to pay more than a small amount for the gamble because they believe that they would have too little chance of (at least) breaking even if they paid more. This would be an example of aspiration level thinking. Such processes are probability driven and are related conceptually to the sorts of "bold play" mechanisms that were initially described by Dubins and Savage (1965/1976) and now are considered part of the study of stochastic control[5] .

Subjects who face choices among losses often describe their dilemmas in terms that suggest a conflict between their aspiration to lose little or nothing and their overall assessment that a lottery is potentially dangerous. To illustrate, Figure 3 compares the short shot lottery with a rectangular lottery having the same expected value. Most risk averse subjects prefer the short shot for gains, expressing little or no conflict about the choice. For losses, however, preferences are more variable and conflict between aspiration and security is more prominent. For example, one subject who chose the (riskier) rectangular lottery said "Another difficult one. I chose the [rectangular] lottery because the odds are equal on each dollar amount, whereas the [short shot] shows the odds in favor of a loss of $70 or more, and very good odds of losing $130. The [rectangular] seems to be a safer risk despite the potential for a higher loss, i.e., $200 max."

---

[5] "Bold play" refer to the strategy of placing all of one's stake (or as much as is necessary) on whichever option provides the best probability of achieving one's goal.

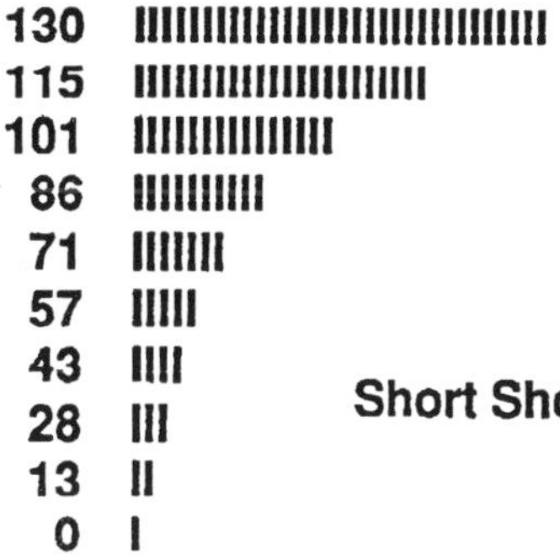

200	IIIII
189	IIIII
178	IIIII
168	IIIII
158	IIIII
147	IIIII
136	IIIII
126	IIIII
116	IIIII
105	IIIII
94	IIIII
84	IIIII
74	IIIII
63	IIIII
52	IIIII
42	IIIII
32	IIIII
21	IIIII
10	IIIII
0	IIIII

130	IIIIIIIIIIIIIIIIIIIIIIIIIIIIIII
115	IIIIIIIIIIIIIIIIIIIIIII
101	IIIIIIIIIIIIIII
86	IIIIIIIIII
71	IIIIIII
57	IIIII
43	IIII
28	III
13	II
0	I

Short Shot

Risk Averse Pattern

	SECURITY	ASPIRATION
GAINS	Short Shot	Short Shot
LOSSES	Short Shot	Rectangular

Rectangular

Figure 3.

The 2x2 table in Figure 3 schematizes the hypothesized difference between gain and loss choices. According to SP/A theory, risk averse subjects tend to be security-minded in rank dependent terms and tend to have modest aspiration levels for gains. If we suppose, for example, that some particular subject would be content to win $50 in a choice between the short shot and the rectangular lotteries, it follows that both the security-weighting mechanism and aspiration level considerations would favor the short shot. On the other hand, if we assume that the same subject facing a loss aspires to lose no more than $50, we see that the security mechanism and the aspiration mechanism now push in opposite directions. Security-mindedness prefers the short shot since it has a considerably lower maximum loss ($130 versus $200) but aspiration level prefers the rectangular since it gives the greater chance of losing less than $50 (25% versus 10%). The conflict between the two factors produces individual uncertainty and greater choice variability both between and within subjects[6].

Regret and Aspiration

At one time, before modern (axiomatic) EU theory had achieved theoretical hegemony in the area of risky choice, there was considerable interest in the idea that people's choices might be aimed at reducing or minimizing the possibility of regret once the outcome of a decision was known (see Lee, 1971, for a review). There were even attempts to incorporate regret into normative theory (Luce & Raiffa 1957), though these eventually were abandoned because they led to unacceptable consequences such as intransitivity and influence from irrelevant alternatives. Descriptive interest in regret has been rekindled recently, however, by theorists who have used the idea to explain and justify behavior that violates EU (Bell, 1982; Loomes & Sugden, 1982, 1987) and by laboratory research that confirms that regret plays an important role in choice and in our experience of outcomes (e.g., Johnson, 1986; Landman, 1988).

Even more telling, however, is the evidence of regret and other emotion-based thinking in the protocols of Lindemann's (1993) farm couples. In one task, for example, respondents were asked to comment on the experience of a farm couple (the Grays) who had passed up an opportunity to sell in April at a small profit and then at harvest were fortunate to sell at an even higher profit. Although one might suppose that the Greys were elated, one security-minded respondent saw the Greys as foolhardy. As he said, "They had to be anxious....They should feel lucky they were rescued by a price increase." For security-minded respondents, avoiding regret appears to be the norm and early sales (forward pricing) are described as "peace of mind during the growing season when the price is locked in."

For potential-minded respondents, regret works the other way. When another couple (the Browns) were described as selling in April at a small profit only to find prices at harvest even higher, potential-

---

[6] The present chapter focuses on risk averters because they are more common than risk seekers. It is worth noting, however, that SP/A theory predicts an opposite pattern for risk-seekers in which potential-weighting and aspiration level considerations coincide for losses but conflict for gains. Confirmation of the predicted reversed pattern for a pre-selected group of risk-seekers can be found in Schneider and Lopes (1986).

minded respondents expected them to be "disappointed that they did not sell when the price was at its highest." Respondents such as these think that "forward pricing is taking too big a gamble" and readily see the possibility for painful regret ("It hurt too much to harvest beans that they could have received 40 cents per bushel more for..."). As Lindemann (herself the co-owner of a family farm) remarked of this all-too-real situation, "What student of regret theory understands what it is like to measure regret by the bushel as it pours into a combine grain tank?" (p. 93).

Lindemann's protocols are filled with emotional language. They are also keenly attuned to aspirations set on the basis of a myriad of goals and needs (e.g., meeting costs, loans coming due, memories of past highs and lows, coffee-shop braggadocio, competition among neighbors and family members). Although some of these factors may be interpreted as affecting weights in a rank dependent scheme, conflicts among incompatible goals will require additional theoretical mechanisms (as in SP/A theory) as will both pre-decisional and post-outcome comparisons involving outcomes and aspirations (as in regret theory). Real-life risk taking is richly textured and many dimensioned, well beyond the limits of what most theoretical models can describe. Still, if we wish to predict human behavior in such settings and especially if we wish to help people make better decisions, we must grapple with the process as it exists, complexity and all.

Predicting and Prescribing for Real

As I noted in the introduction, there are three distinct lines of research in risky choice: descriptive, predictive, and prescriptive. These lines originate at a common point—the invention of modern EU theory—and they intertwine so tightly and so incessantly thereafter that even well-versed readers of the literature on risk taking may be hard pressed to know at any given point whether an author is describing what actually is, what is likely, or what ought to be.

Like the Hydra, which grew two new heads for each one lopped off, early laboratory results suggesting the descriptive inaccuracy of EU were met by more and more hardened resistance to the idea that decision making might or should deviate from EU axioms. Evidence of this resistance is made apparent by holes in the literature signaling the suppression of entire topics of study during the first three decades after von Neumann and Morgenstern. I have already mentioned the moratorium on regret research. But this is just one of many suppressed topics. Allais' (1953/1979) penetrating critique of EU's linearity assumptions were met by a combination of smug superiority (i.e., if you really understood the axioms you would accept them) and stony silence. Ellsberg's (1961) commentary on ambiguity came to a similar fate. The familiar and previously undisputed distinction between unique and repeated gambles faded into obscurity. Only in the last 15 years have these topics resurfaced in descriptive research. Still, the belief lingers, especially among psychologists, that deviations from EU theory represent misunderstandings and human limitations in information processing rather than alternative conceptions of rationality.

In recent years, economists and decision analysts have reluctantly come to accept the existence of preference reversals and other sorts of judgmental context effects and well-understand the serious impediments such phenomena place in the way of psychological measurement. Serious as these may be, however, the technical problems may be surmountable if attention is given to finding the "best" response mode for measuring or predicting values in particular contexts. In contrast, most of the failures of EU theory that have been discussed in this paper cannot be "fixed" even in principle because they represent fundamental differences between what people seem to care about and what adherence to EU provides.

Classical Dutch book and money pump defenses of EU axioms are on par with parental threats of the bogeyman. Sadly, perhaps, for children and for adults, what is out there in the world is much more immediate and threatening than what might be under the bed. The idea of counseling decision makers to eschew considering potential regret because it might hypothetically lead to intransitivity is silly and useless. If there is virtue in trying to help people avoid the potentially negative impacts of emotions and reasoning errors on decision making, such help will only be acceptable if it also aids the decision makers in achieving their own goals, including such positive emotional states as security, predictability, and even fun.

For illustration, let me return one last time to Lindemann's (1993) study of farm couples. It is an inescapable truth known to farmers and to bureaucrats alike that farming is a financially dangerous occupation. Nor is good advice scarce. Farm agencies of all sorts routinely council farmers on such sound principles as setting price targets in advance and abiding by them even when it seems that prices might go higher, considering the hidden shrinkage and storage costs of choosing to hold grain, and turning a deaf ear to coffee-shop advice from friends and neighbors. Unfortunately, few farmers follow the advice even though they know from hard experience that they should.

One particularly interesting example of a failed federal attempt to help farmers manage the risks of farming better was a program introduced by the U.S. Department of Agriculture in 1985 to encourage grain producers to use commodity futures and options markets to hedge against risk. The program was introduced with great fanfare and with the expectation that eventually it would involve thousands of producers. Three years later, however, the program quietly expired with only five grain producers having participated. This failure would have been entirely predictable had agency experts bothered to ask farmers about their perceptions of the relative risks and benefits of alternative risk reduction schemes. Had they done so, they would have found (as Lindemann did) that farmers and agency experts differ radically in terms of the perceived riskiness of holding grain versus using the futures market as a hedge. For the experts, hedging is judged to be the least risky of all alternatives and holding to be second most risky. For farmers, however, holding grain is second in safety only to selling while hedging ranks somewhere in the middle of the list.

Lindemann argues that prescriptions for curing the ills that plague small farmers ought to be based on realistic description of the producers' financial and social world. For example, she suggests that the cost-based caution that the women tend to show should be exploited when selling decisions are made. At present, even though women are more likely than men to have a proper idea of what costs are and what a profitable price would be, women participate very little in the final stage of making selling decisions. The reasons for this separation between costing and selling is mostly coincidental, reflecting the fact that cost computations are done at home by the women whereas selling decisions are made away from home by the men. Finding a way to involve the women at the point of sale is just one way to increase the influence of costs on decisions and decrease unwanted social influences.

Lindemann also suggests that decisions oriented solely to achieving security are unlikely to appeal to potential-minded farmers. She suggests that a strategy that acknowledges both kinds of goal and allows for their expression might work better than strategies aimed at stamping out all speculative and competitive urges. Her prescription is to separate these motives by dividing the available crop into two bundles: the security bundle and the opportunity bundle. The quantity allotted to the security bundle should be as large as necessary to cover the basic needs of the operation. Spouses would agree to sell this bundle when a certain price is reached or by a certain date. The opportunity bundle would be available for speculation by the potential-minded member of the team, with suitable conditions imposed to make sure that such speculation in no way endangers the income in the security bundle.

For most of the last fifty years, researchers in risk theory have supposed that accurate description is nice but unnecessary to prediction and prescription. This position is baffling given the important role that advances in description have played in improving prediction and prescription in the physical and biological sciences. In retrospect, there is a chicken-and-egg quality to the question of whether it was the normative allure of EU that hampered good descriptive studies of risk taking or the absence of good descriptive data that bolstered the empirically unsupported claims of the normative theory. Whichever it was, however, the chickens have flown the coop, one hopes never to return.

Much of the original normative appeal of EU theory lay in its potential usefulness for psychological measurement. But measurement doesn't require normative theory: descriptive theory will do just fine so long as it is accurate enough to allow researchers to devise measurement tools that reach beyond superficial responses to deeper values. Although it is humanly understandable that applied researchers will mourn the demise of techniques based on the assumption that EU describes both human behaviors and human intentions, let us hope that the time spent grieving will be brief. Time is precious and there is critical work to be done in rebuilding predictive and prescriptive tools for risk taking from today's new and more accurate descriptive base.

REFERENCES

Allais, M. (1953/1979). The foundations of a positive theory of choice involving risk and a criticism of the postulates and axioms of the American school. In M Allais, O Hagen, (Eds.), *Expected Utility Hypotheses and the Allais Paradox*, Boston: Reidel, 27-145.

Allais, M. (1986a). Determination of cardinal utility according to an intrinsic invariant model. In L Daboni, A Montesano, M Lines (Eds.) *Recent Developments in the Foundations of Utility and Risk Theory*, Boston: Reidel, 83-120.

Allais, M. (1986b). The general theory of random choices in relation to the invariant cardinal utility function and the specific probability function. Working Paper C4475, Centre d'Analyse Economique, École des Mines, Paris, France

Arrow, K.J. (1951). Alternative approaches to the theory of choice in risk-taking situations. *Econometrica. 19*, 404-37.

Bell, D.E. (1982). Regret in decision making under uncertainty. *Oper. Res. 3,0* 961-81

Bernoulli, D. (1738, 1967). *Exposition of a New Theory on the Measurement of Risk*. Farnborough Hants, England: Gregg. L. Sommer, trans.

Birnbaum, M.H., Coffey, G., Mellers, B.A, & Weiss, R. (1992). Utility measurement: Configural-weight theory and the judge's point of view. *J. Exp. Psychol: Hum. Percept. Perform. 18*, 331-346

Bowman, E.H. (1982). Risk seeking by troubled firms. *Sloan Mgt. Rev. 23*, 33-42

Cohen, M., Jaffray, J-Y. & Said, T. (1987). Experimental comparison of individual behavior under risk and under uncertainty for gains and for losses. *Organ. Behav. Hum. Decis. Process. 39*, 1-22

Dubins, L.E. & Savage, L.J. (1965/1976). *Inequalities for Stochastic Processes: How to Gamble If You Must*. New York: Dover.

Einhorn, H.J. & Hogarth R.M. (1985). Ambiguity and uncertainty in probabilistic inference. *Psychol. Rev. 92*, 433-61

Ellsberg, D. (1961). Risk, ambiguity, and the Savage axioms. *Q. J. Econ. 75*, 643-69

Fagley, N.S. & Miller, P.M. (1987). The effects of decision framing on choice of risky vs certain options. *Organ. Behav. Hum. Decis. Process. 39*, 264-77

Fischhoff , B. (1983). Predicting frames. *J. Exp. Psychol.: Learn. Mem. Cognit. 9*: 03-16

Friedman, M.. (1953). *Essays in Positive Economics*. Chicago: Univ. Chicago Press.

Hershey, J.C., Kunreuther, H.C. & Schoemaker, P.J.H. (1982). Sources of bias in assessment procedures for utility functions. *Manage. Sci., 28*, 936-54

Hershey, J.C. & Schoemaker, P.J.H. (1980). Prospect theory's reflection hypothesis: A critical examination. *Organ. Behav. Hum. Perform. 25*, 395-418

Johnson, J.T. (1986). The knowledge of what might have been: Affective and attributional consequences of near outcomes. *Pers. Soc. Psychol. Bull. 12*, 51-62

Kahneman D, Tversky A. 1979. Prospect theory: An analysis of decision under risk. *Econometrica. 47*:263-91

Kunreuther, H. & Wright, G. (1979). Safety-first, gambling, and the subsistence farmer. In J.A .Roumasset, J. Boussard, I. Singh (Eds.) *Risk, Uncertainty, and Agricultural Development*, New York: Agricultural Development Council 213-230.

Landman, J. (1988). Regret and elation following action and inaction: Affective responses to positive versus negative outcomes. *Pers. Soc. Psychol. Bull. 13*, 524-36

Lee, W. (1971). *Decision Theory and Human Behavior*. New York: Wiley

Lindemann, B.L. (1993). The effects of social context on grain producers' decisions to sell or hold grain. PhD thesis. Univ. Iowa.

Loomes, G. & Sugden, R. (1982). Regret theory: An alternative theory of rational choice under uncertainty. *Econ. J. 92*, 805-24.

Loomes, G. & Sugden, R. (1987). Some implications of a more general form of regret theory. *J. Econ. Theory. 41*, 270-87

Lopes, L.L. (1981). Decision making in the short run. *J. Exp. Psychol.: Hum. Learn. Mem. 7*, 377-85

Lopes, L.L. (1984). Risk and distributional inequality. *J. Exp. Psychol.: Hum. Percept. Perform. 10*, 465-85

Lopes, L.L. (1987). Between hope and fear: The psychology of risk. *Adv. Exper. Soc. Psychol. 20*, 255-295

Lopes, L.L. (1988). Economics as psychology: A cognitive assay of the French and American Schools of risk theory. In B.R. Munier (Ed.) *Risk, Decision, and Rationality*, Boston: Reidel, 405-16.

Lopes, L.L. (1990). Re-modeling risk aversion: A comparison of Bernoullian and rank dependent value approaches. In G.M. von Furstenberg (Ed.), *Acting Under Uncertainty*, Boston: Kluwer, 267-99.

Luce, R.D. & Raiffa, H. (1957). *Games and Decisions: Introduction and Critical Survey.* New York: Wiley

McCord, M.R. & De Neufville, R. (1985). Assessment response surface: Investigating utility dependence on probability. *Theory Decis. 18*, 263-85

Miller, P.M. & Fagley, N.S. (1991). The effects of framing, problem variations, and providing rationale on choice. *Pers. Soc. Psychol. Bull. 17*, 517-22

Polanyi, M. (1962). *Personal Knowledge: Towards a Post-Critical Philosophy.* Chicago: Univ. Chicago Press

Quiggen, J. (1982). A theory of anticipated utility. *J. Econ. Behav. Organ. 3*, 323-43

Savage, L.J. (1954/1972). *The Foundations of Statistics.* New York: Dover.

Schneider, S.L. (1992). Framing and conflict: Aspiration level contingency, the status quo, and current theories of risky choice. *J. Exp. Psychol.: Learn. Mem. Cognit. 18*, 1040-57

Schneider, S.L. & Lopes, L.L. (1986). Reflection in preferences under risk: who and when may suggest why. *J. Exp. Psychol.: Hum. Percept. Perform. 12*, 535-48

Slovic, P. (1987). Perception of risk. *Science. 236*, 280-85

Tversky, A. (1969). Intransitivity of preferences. *Psychol. Rev. 76*, 31-48,

Tversky, A. & Kahneman, D. (1992). Advances in prospect theory: Cumulative representation of uncertainty. *J. Risk Uncertain. 5*, 297-323

von Neumann, J. & Morgenstern, O. (1944/1947). *Theory of Games and Economic Behavior.* Princeton: Princeton Univ. Press

Williams, A.C. (1966). Attitudes toward speculative risks as an indicator of attitudes toward pure risks. *J. Risk Ins. 33*, 577-86

Yaari, M.E. (1987). The dual theory of choice under risk. *Econometrica. 55*, 95-115

Contributions to Decision Making - I
J.-P. Caverni, M. Bar-Hillel, F.H. Barron and H. Jungermann (Editors)
1995 Elsevier Science B.V.

UNCERTAINTY AND DECISION MAKING - EXPERT TREATMENT OF HUMAN EXPERTISE

Marcus Spies

Institute for Knowledge-based Systems, IBM Germany—Scientific Center,
Vangerowstr. 18, D - 69115 Heidelberg
e-mail: spies @ vnet.ibm.com

Abstract. Probabilistic expert systems today use Bayesian networks to process complex multivariate models in application domains. The successful application of Bayesian networks presupposes valuation of conditional knowledge. It is argued that human expertise, for empirical as well as logical reasons, is largely constrained to incomplete conditional knowledge. Incomplete conditional knowledge cannot be treated within a traditional probabilistic framework. A qualitative theory of such knowledge is formulated using conditional events. Probabilities on conditional events naturally come as random sets. In a digression, the relevance of random sets and evidential reasoning to recent developments in nonexpected utility theory is demonstrated. It is shown that the theory of valuated conditional events allows probabilistic reasoning on the basis of incomplete conditional knowledge.

1. INTRODUCTION: EXPERTISE AND EXPERT SYSTEMS

Human decision making and inference are commonly based on knowledge. Thus, if decision making under risk or uncertainty is being scientifically investigated, evaluation of knowledge has to be taken into account. The present paper deals with structures of knowledge that establish a framework for decision making. Speaking of knowledge structures it is natural to start with a look at the state of the art in artificial intelligence.

Historically, one of the truisms in expert systems research was that human experts were able to evaluate knowledge and to make decisions in a more intelligent way than conventional computer software could. This truism merely reflected implementation issues, not modeling issues. A conventional computer program crunches numbers or even symbols and evaluates conditions in a fixed sequence. It was assumed that human intelligent systems would process data in a more flexible way, testing only relevant conditions, economizing on the numbers of rules that had to be used, and so on. However, what this truism overlooked is our ability to build formal models that are much better than individual intuition, better even than that of the most advanced experts. This is true for many domains, from optimizing resource mixtures in operations research to evaluating diagnostic probabilities in clinical decision making. Our collective reason can go beyond the capabilities of individual reasoning. This is what makes the truism concerning the fantastic abilities of human experts sound a bit odd today.

As a consequence, expert systems have not been able to fulfill exaggerated expectations of either the scientific or the computer users' community. To a great extent, they even fell short of adequately modeling expert knowledge where this knowledge was undoubtedly individual and could not be formulated more precisely by using a formal model. Therefore, today, expert systems come along with much more moderate promises than they used to. They are increasingly designed such as to help carrying out administrative tasks that require browsing large amounts of facts and rules, like customs regulations. The replacement of men or women by intelligent machines seems as remote a vision as it did 40 years ago; today, the use of "intelligent" computing technology is based on a more restricted and, perhaps, more realistic perspective.

All this leaves the opaqueness of human knowledge structures quite unresolved. The hope that computer expert systems would help us to ever better understand human experts or human cognitive systems has only been fulfilled in limited domains, such as semantic memory and procedural knowledge.

It seems to me that the issue of human vs. computer reasoning is ill-posed. Either the purpose of doing AI programming is to simulate human cognitive processes or it is to solve problems in computing technology. Both purposes should not be mixed up. A much more promising view for cognitive science is that of the computer as an external reasoning device (like we use notes on a piece of paper as external memory devices when calculating a 6-digit division) that allows to precisiate reasoning patterns (see Schönpflug, 1986). In this perspective, the question is not whether humans reason like a computer calculates (they better should not), or whether computers calculate like a human being reasons (again, they better should not), but, rather, what is the best way to bring human reasoning and computer calculation to synergy. It seems that precisely in the realm of reasoning with probabilities and decision-making under risk such a synergy is possible. The present paper intends to establish some basic ideas that seem necessary for such a kind of synergy.

2. PROBABILITIES IN EXPERT SYSTEMS: THE SYNERGY OF KNOWLEDGE AND DATA ANALYSIS

For the past eight years, the issue of uncertainty in expert knowledge has attracted an ever greater number of computer scientists all over the world (perhaps the most encompassing monograph on the state of the art as of that time is Goodman & Nguyen, 1985). Both a yearly American and a biennial European series of conferences is devoted to this theme. Expert systems using probabilistic calculus have become wide-spread since Pearl's book (1988) and a seminal paper by Lauritzen & Spiegelhalter (1988). Basically, probabilistic expert systems are built on conditional dependence and independence assumptions that are the probabilistic counterparts of rules in rule-based systems. Such assumptions over multivariate domains make up a formal structure known as *Bayesian network*.

An important property of modeling highly multivariate domains (i.e., domains with some 10,000 or more variables) with Bayesian networks is the strict local nature of independence assumptions being maintained throughout the whole knowledge base. Only very few variables will be (marginally) independent, most independencies will be conditional. Conditional independence is much easier to verify, because it states independence only if *all other things are equal*. A simple interpretation of conditional independence, given by Pearl (1988), is that specifying a conditioning variable makes conditionally independent variables uninformative to each other. (There is a close relationship between these models and independence models in the analysis of contingeny tables, see Bishop, Fienberg, & Holland, 1975. There is also a relationship to discrete independence models used in database design theory, see Fagin, 1977; Beeri, Fagin, Howard, 1977; Ozsoyoglu & Yuan, 1987; Spies, 1991a).

In setting up a Bayesian network, experts are asked to provide structural rather than numerical information. As in traditional rule-based systems, experts are asked to state possible dependencies between variables describing phenomena in the to-be-modeled domain. Such dependencies can then be used to derive an economic representation of the joint probability distribution of very high dimensional domains, like medical diagnosis or fault analysis. These distributions are written as products of likelihoods on small subsets of variables. These subsets, in turn, are found out via a graph-theoretic analysis of the structure of the dependence relationships provided by experts. Given a particular graph representation, the tasks of propagating evidence, updating marginal probabilities of variables, and even of learning conditional probabilities can be tackled using efficient algorithms. For details, the reader is invited to consult Lauritzen & Spiegelhalter (1988), Pearl (1988), Spies (1993).

It would require immense computing resources to find out arbitrary dependencies in highly multivariate domains with discrete variables empirically; therefore, in these approaches, human expertise goes into a synergy with statistical analysis. Thus, it is *the expert treatment of human expertise* that makes it a valuable source of knowledge.

The approach of Bayesian networks has, to some extent, alleviated the burden of giving probability judgments for experts. Their heuristics and biases in judgmental tasks *seem* to be of less relevance to judgments of influence of variables on other variables than to judgments that somehow imply valuations of whatever kind of degree of uncertainty - despite the fact that this is not proven at all by empirical psychological research (see the papers on covariance and control in Kahneman, Slovic, and Tversky, 1982).

The meaning of independence assumptions for decision research is quite similar to that for probabilistic expert systems. In decision research, different kinds of independence are distinguished that help making value functions and utility functions easier to assess and to express. A link between probabilistic independence and additive independence in multiattribute utility functions has been established by Keeney & Raiffa (1976, p. 242). They prove that, under two equivalent conditions, certainty equivalents for probability mixtures of values of different single attributes under fixed values of independent attributes can be combined into a joint certainty equivalent for a risky commodity bundle composed of realizations of all attributes in question. The first condition requires marginal independence of attribute probabilities and a multilinear utility function. The second condition is additive independence of the attributes. This result generalizes easily to conditional independence in both utility functions and probabilities. This is a remarkable relationship; it shows that structures which help simplify decision making also help simplify the architecture of expert systems. To my knowledge, this relationship has not been exploited yet in practice.

2.1 A challenge to probabilistic knowledge representation

It would be an unrealistic approach to designing expert systems, if one assumed that all domains could be modeled by statistical data alone once an expert (team) has identified the necessary independence and dependence relationships among variables. Expert judgment of probabilities, as odd a phenomenon as it may seem, is still often a valuable and the only accessible source of valuation. Moreover, the psychological question of how humans derive their judgments of perceived uncertainty or risk is not answered by the development of techniques making them largely superfluous. In this paper I want to discuss one particular aspect of the knowledge structures that seems to be used by humans in forming their judgments of conditional probability or risk. This aspect may be stated briefly as follows:

Human evaluation of uncertainty is based on incomplete conditional knowledge.

By *conditional knowledge* I understand a rule-like structure of knowledge. Empirically, it seems that human experts are rather able to state conditional uncertainties than unconditional ones. For instance, if a surgeon assesses the odds of a disease given a symptom, no knowledge of the base rate of this disease is needed. Formally, conditioning assures an indispensable restriction of variable interactions. Without this restriction, models of high-dimensional domains become unmanageable.

By *incomplete conditional knowledge* I mean that often human knowledge relates only to some of the possible antecedents of a rule. For instance, the combination of two swollen cheeks indicates mumps, but is it hard to say whether one swollen cheek of a child on one day indicates mumps or not. Generally, not all combinations of antecedents are considered in human knowledge. Some may even be unreasonable. As a consequence, human conditional knowledge often cannot fulfil the requirements of a Bayesian model of uncertainty (this will be explained in more detail below). A second consequence is that if evidence concerning antecedents of rules comes in, often only partial matches exist that fail to lead to a clear conclusion about the uncertainty valuation of any rule consequent.

The principle of incomplete conditional knowledge is meant normatively in this paper; I am not saying that a language that is based on incomplete conditional knowledge could describe any human judgment pattern without having to refer to the heuristics and biases investigated principally by Kahneman, Slovic, and Tversky (1982). However, it can be shown that incomplete conditional knowledge can explain at least some of the observed biases in human judgments. For the conservatism bias, I have shown this in a previous paper (Spies, 1991b; see also Edwards, 1982). I will not reiterate this argument here. I rather wish to concentrate on how incomplete conditional knowledge can be described and used to predict human reasoning.

Incomplete conditional knowledge is one possible language for expressing uncertainty among others (see Shafer & Tversky, 1985; Dubois &

Prade, 1988, 1989). It is particularly suited to what we experience in practice when working with domain experts: the necessity to base judgments on some specific antecedents and the impossibility of assessing uncertainty judgments under all combinations of relevant antecedents.

3. INCOMPLETE CONDITIONAL KNOWLEDGE

3.1 Conditioning and rules

There are three levels of modeling knowledge on which incomplete conditional knowledge can appear.

First, it is a common problem in knowledge assessment that experts know the result of some process if some antecedent data are given, but that they cannot tell anything about the outcomes of the process if the antecedent conditions are not met. This happens very frequently in the process of setting up expert systems.

Second, and more theoretically, it is essential to the logic of scientific explanation that we only can tell about the occurrence of the *explanandum* if the antecedent conditions are fulfilled (according to the Hempel-Oppenheim scheme of scientific explanation). Due to possible other causation mechanisms, the absence of antecedent conditions does not warrant any inference concerning the explanandum.

Finally, in elementary propositional calculus we have the (formal) implication, which evaluates to true if the antecedent is false. Intuitively, this means that a state of nature that is irrelevant to an *explanandum* cannot falsify an implication.

In contrast to this, in probabilistic reasoning systems like Bayesian networks it is necessary to assess the probability of any *explanandum* on the condition that the antecedents do *not* occur. Thus, by defintion, these systems cannot handle incomplete conditional knowledge.

In order to show this, let me recall that conditional probabilities are defined on a subspace of a probability space with universe Ω, σ—algebra A and probability measure P. The meaning of conditioning is that some subset $A \in$ A has been found to contain the true realization of the random outcome $\omega \in \Omega$. Thus, the probability textbook definition of conditional probability given some event A with $0 < P(A)$ reads, in the discrete case,

$$P(B|A) = \frac{P(A \cap B)}{P(A)} \qquad (1)$$

Sometimes I will call A the antecedent and B the consequent of the conditional $B|A$, thus establishing a terminological link to rule-based modeling.

The probabilistic uncertainty attached to rules in expert knowledge is usually modeled by conditional probabilities. The principle underlying the use of such probabilities as quantifications of uncertainty w.r.t. facts and rules is Jeffrey's rule, the *law of total probability.* This law tells us how to compute the updated probability of an event given some antecedent variable with several states. This computation is analogous to deduction in a conventional rule-based system. In order to apply Jeffrey's rule, we must know the marginal probabilities of each of the states of the antecedent variable and the conditional probabilities of the event given *each* state. Let D_1 to D_n denote a set of mutually exclusive and exhaustive states of antecedent variable $D,$ and let S be the *explanandum,* that is, some event in a probability space $(\Omega, A\ P)$. Then Jeffrey's rule reads

$$P(S) = \sum_{i=1}^{n} P(S|D_i)P(D_i) \qquad (2)$$

In case the antecedent variable is a proposition that can be true or false the application of Jeffrey's rule necessitates the evaluation of the conditional probability of the *explanandum* given the proposition is false. This may be, in many applications, a quantity that is either difficult to assess or even meaningless (consider epidemiological studies involved in estimating diagnostic probabilities in medicine: if a disease is absent, it is difficult to assess the probability of a symptom).

It is this necessity to evaluate conditional statements which do sometimes not correspond to anything meaningful at all that makes probabilities hard to apply to expert knowledge in real world settings. I contend that it is possible to overcome this necessity if one uses the formalism of conditional events and belief functions which I will now introduce.

3.2 Conditioning and probability

The notion of conditional events refers to the structure which is introduced on the universe (Ω) of a probability space by conditional probabilities.

It has been observed (Goodman & Nguyen, 1988) that there is no element X of any σ-algebra A such that X is obtained by usual set-theoretic operations on A, B, ... and that in probability space (Ω, A P) $P(B|A) = P(X)$ for any A, B $\in$ A. Thus, *conditional probabilities are not probabilities of events in* A. Rather, they are probabilities of events in A $\cap$ A, the so-called trace of A in A. However, *the event whose conditional probability we are assessing does not need to be itself a subset of A.* Therefore it is natural to search for events in our original $\sigma-$ algebra that qualify as conditional.

The easiest way to determine such events is to take all sets whose conditional probability, given A, is the same. Which events could this be? Let us answer this question intuitively. If we know the true outcome to lie in a subset $A \in$ A then we know that $\overline{A}$ and all of its subsets have conditional probabilities of zero (mathematicians say $\overline{A}$ is a P_A-null set.). Similarly, if we take any event $B \in$ A that has non-empty intersection with $\overline{A}$, its conditional probability will remain unchanged if we add or take away any of the null-sets in A. Thus, denoting symmetric difference by Δ, we have

$$P(B\Delta C|A) = P(B|A) \text{ if } C \subseteq \overline{A} \qquad (3)$$

(It is recalled that, for any sets U, V, the symmetric difference is defined as $(U \cap \overline{V}) \cup (\overline{U} \cap V)$. In terms of bit strings, symmetric difference can be easily implemented by the XOR-function). A little technical detail is neccessary: It can happen that there are atoms $\omega \in A$ with $P(\omega) = 0$. In this case, the P_A null sets contain even a part of A itself. Let the set of all such ω be $C \subset A$. For the following development it is assumed that, in such a situation, we condition on $A \setminus C$ instead of A.

Thus, we can see that the event a conditional probability refers to actually is a set of events, namely, the set of symmetric differences of the event whose conditional probability is being stated with all subsets of the complement of the antecedent of the conditional. Now let us define this set of events as a *conditional event* (see Goodman & Nguyen, 1998; Goodman, Nguyen, & Walker, 1991; Dubois & Prade, 1991; Spies, l991a, 1994), denoted by [B|A]. We have:

$$[B|A] = \left\{ X | X = B\Delta C, C \subseteq \overline{A} \right\} \qquad (4)$$

Thus, a conditional event is precisely the set of events obtained by taking away or adding any subset of the null sets under conditioning with antecedent *A* to a given event *B*. Conditional events have been defined for the first time by Goodman & Nguyen (1988). Since then, there has been a considerable amount of work on this mathematical topic (see Goodman et al., 1991).

3.3 Rules, conditioning and probability

What does the definition of conditional events imply for our understanding of conditioning? First, this definition tells us that conditioning is actually a simplification. It establishes equivalence classes in our event algebra and chunks single events into them. This is analogous to what stating a rule in expert knowledge does. Second, it allows us to examine closely which events a rule (whatever its probability may be) refers to. Let us see this in more detail.

If we take $C = \overline{A} \cap B$ we have $X = B \triangle C = B \cap A$, the intersection of events corresponding to antecedent and consequent. This intersection contains all elements ω of the universe that lie both in the antecedent and in the consequent event, or all ω that can serve as *verifying instances* of the rule "if ω is in *A*, then it is in *B*."

On the other hand, if we take $C' = \overline{A} \cap \overline{B}$ we obtain $X' = B \triangle C' = \overline{A} \cup B$ the formal implication of the consequent, given the antecedent. This event contains all elements ω of the universe that *cannot* serve as counter-examples or *falsifying instances* of the rule "if ω is in *A*, then it is in *B*".

Now, it can be shown that each element of the set $[B|A]$ lies in between *C* and *C'* (see, for instance, Nguyen & Rogers, 1991). The converse is true, as well. Thus, a conditional event corresponding to antecedent *A* and consequent *B* extends from the event of all elements verifying the formal implication of antecedent and consequent up to the event consisting of all elements that do not definitely falsify this implication. Therefore, a conditional event is an interval of events that *describe different variants of matching the rule "if ω is in A, then it is in B",* ranging from purely verifying instances to all instances that are not in conflict with this rule. We can write this in a formula:

$$[B|A] = \left\{ X | B \cap A \subseteq X \subseteq \overline{A} \cup B \right\} \tag{5}$$

To sum it up, conditional events offer a language that seems eminently suited to describing partial matching and incomplete knowledge of rules.

4. VALUATIONS OF INCOMPLETE KNOWLEDGE

Having established a qualitative model of incomplete conditional knowledge, the next step is to ask what happens if there are (probabilistic) valuations on the elements of the model, namely conditional events. Obviously, there is a little problem, since conditional events are sets of events and conditional events of different antecedents may be very differently looking sets. It would be helpful to have some mapping that transports a probability on a universe to the set of conditional events given one antecedent. Such a mapping would then generalize conditional probabilities to incomplete conditional knowledge structures. Fortunately, such mappings exist; they are the principal ingredient of the theory of *random sets* to which I will therefore turn now.

A random set is defined as a set-valued mapping from a probability space into some outcome space. Intuitively, expert knowledge very often takes the form of such an imprecise, set-valued prediction. As an example, take the list of candidate substances that may appear in a sample of soil where some known poisonous substances have leaked. Each of these substances will react with other substances present in the soil. This will produce a set of different substances via so-called metabolism. If you know a probability distribution of the leaking substances, your knowledge about metabolism etc. will take the probability distribution of initial substances to a random set of different substances produced by metabolism etc.

The notion of an imprecisely known probability distribution seems to be applicable to many aspects of human expertise. In expert systems research, such generalizations of probabilistic models have therefore become a cornerstone of discussion. They were considered initially because classical probabilities are too rigid for many applications. Random sets, viewed as a description of knowledge structures, give rise to evidential reasoning (Shafer, 1976; Ruspini, 1987). Let us next review some of the essential aspects of evidential reasoning.

4.1 Evidence theory: A short introduction

Evidence theory (see Dempster, 1967; Shafer, 1976, 1982; Shafer et al., 1987; Kohlas, 1990; Spies 1991b, 1993) rests on the assumption that expert valuations of knowledge (in the normative as well as the descriptive sense) are often less precise than a probability distribution. This is what decision analysts have expressed when they differentiated between decision making under risk (where a probability distribution is known) and decision making under uncertainty (where the distribution is unknown, or known only up to some set of parameters).

The essential ingredients of evidence theory are a (usually discrete) probability space (Ω, A, P) and a set-valued mapping $T: \Omega \to P(\Theta)$ such that $T^{-1}(X) \in A$ for all X in some σ-algebra on $P(\Theta)$. Θ is usually called the *frame of discernment*. The set-valuedness of T expresses the uncertainty that goes beyond classical probability. Note that this uncertainty is qualitative rather than quantitative: T induces some imprecision into the events realized by choosing a given element of Ω, not the quantitative expression of uncertainty itself (like the probabilities of probabilities sometimes encountered in statistical inference, or like a fuzzy set of probabilities). A set-valued random variable (or, briefly, a random set) thus describes incomplete knowledge "on top of" random fluctuations (see also Spies, 1993).

A classical random variable is described by taking the sets of outcomes that are realized with some probability. Since a random set is more imprecise, we have only "traces" it leaves on Θ, the outcome space. One trace is given by the probability that $T(\omega)$ falls entirely into a given set $X \in \Theta$; this is termed lower probability or *degree of belief* (in the evidential terminology).

$$Bel(X) = P(T(A) \subseteq X)$$

The other trace is given by the "hitting" probability that $T(\omega)$ just intersects a given set X. This is termed the degree of plausibility or upper probability of the set in question.

$$Pl(X) = P(T(A) \cap X \neq \emptyset)$$

Evidently, these two "traces" are related. If the image of a given ω lies entirely outside a set X, it must lie entirely inside $\overline{X}$. This is expressed in the fundamental identity of evidence theory.

$$Bel(X) = 1 - Pl(\overline{X}) \qquad (6)$$

It can be shown that a belief function is characterized by a generalized form of additivity. Recall that a probability measure is additive over disjoint events. Now, a belief function is always superadditive over disjoint events (this property is called supermodularity in Kampke, 1992).

Finally, evidence theory tells us how to combine different sources of evidence, if they are independent. The easiest way to combine random sets is to take the so-called Möbius-inverse of a belief function, which is sometimes termed basic probability assignment:

$$m(X) = \sum_{Y \subseteq X} (-1)^{|X-Y|} Bel(Y) \qquad (7)$$

This horrendous equation has a simple meaning. It says that you compute m-numbers just by looking at the smallest sets possessing degrees of belief greater than zero. These smallest sets may overlap, in contrast to a classical probability distribution. Adding up degrees of belief of all subsets of X, you keep removing beliefs attributed to subsets already included. —Adding up the m-numbers of subsets of $X \subseteq \Theta$ you get back the original belief function.

$$Bel(X) = \sum_{Y \subseteq X} m(Y) \qquad (8)$$

Sets X with $m(X) > 0$ are called *focal elements*.

Assuming m-numbers are available, independent random sets are combined like independent random variables, but with the additional proviso that an empty intersection of focal elements is not allowed. Probability mass attached to the empty set is proportionally redistributed among all non-empty intersections of focal elements of the two belief functions. This operation is usually called orthogonal sum or Dempster's rule of combination. Given two sets of m-numbers, we obtain

$$m_1 \oplus m_2 (X) = k \cdot \sum_{B_1 \cap B_2 = X} m_1(B_1) \cdot m_2(B_2)$$

where
$$k = \frac{1}{1 - \sum_{B_1 \cap B_2 = \phi} m_1(B_1) \cdot m_2(B_2)}$$

This notation is particularly suited for computational purposes. If the m-numbers stem from two random sets T_1 and T_2 we can write the operation in a more abstract and logically clearer way:

$$Bel_1 \oplus Bel_2 (X) = P(T_1 \cap T_2 \subseteq X | T_1 \cap T_2 \neq \phi) \qquad (9)$$

It has been shown by Dempster (1967) that a random set describes a convex set of probability distributions, while the converse does not hold (see also Kyburg, 1987). Thus, belief functions are not entirely the same thing as convex sets of probability distributions. Using belief functions we restrict nature more severely than by mere probability intervals.

The development of independence structures in probabilistic expert systems has been extended to belief functions as well (see Kong, 1986; Shafer et al., 1987). However, the difficulty of empirically defining degrees of belief has prevented evidence theory from becoming a widely accepted tool. Fishburn (1985, 1986) has established a strong connection between probability intervals (which correspond to a superset of belief functions) and interval orders. He also gives a purely judgment-based assessment procedure for belief functions. To my knowledge, this method has not been used in applications.

Dempster's rule has been criticized because of its behaviour under conditioning (see Jaffray, 1990). Conditioning is not well described by a model of independent random sets. Therefore, several researchers have begun to tackle the problem of conditioning in belief structures more fundamentally (again, see Jaffray, 1990; see Nguyen, Hestir, and Rogers, 1991; Spies, l991a, 1994). Below, I will show that the introduction of conditional events solves at least a good part of the problem, and that this solution sheds light on cognitive processes that we assume in experts' incomplete conditional knowledge.

At this point I wish to digress to some decision-making applications of evidential reasoning.

4.2 A case in point: Random sets and decision making

The classical definition of decision making under risk presumes knowledge of the probability distribution of the states of nature on the part of the decision maker. Keeney & Raiffa (1976) show how lottery preferences translate into a scaling of probabilities that obeys expected utility theory. However, in the view of many violations of EU-theory that may not legitimately be viewed as being biased, generalizations of the notion of risk have been introduced in order to formulate more flexible normative models. Such models have become known as anticipated utility (AU) or rank-dependent utility models (see Schmeidler, 1989; Wakker, 1898, 1990; Jaffray & Wakker, 1993).

In this section I wish to make the point that belief functions form at least a useful subset of those probability distortions that are employed to formulate rank dependent utility.

To start, let me show that a well known violation of expected utility theory by decision makers can be taken into account if we allow for partially known probabilities given by belief functions. Thus, if we allow uncertainty beyond the classical paradigm of decision making under risk, we get a normative model that is in better accord with decision makers' behaviour.

The Allais paradox is one of the most famous examples of a human preference pattern that violates the axioms of expected utility theory (see Chankong & Haimes, 1983, p. 181). The paradox is constructed by contrasting two pairs of gambles. In the first pair, the two gambles are

Gamble 1.1   •Win 1 million $ with certainty.

Gamble 1.2   • Win 2 million $ with $p = 0.09$,

                  • win 1 million $ with $p = 0.9$,

                  • nothing with $p = 0.01$.

The two gambles in the second pair are

Gamble 2.1   • Win 2 million $ with $p = 0.09$,

                  • nothing with $p = 0.91$.

Gamble 2.2   • Win 1 million $ with $p = 0.1$,

                  • nothing with $p = 0.9$.

It is supposed to be reasonable (while not rational) to prefer gamble 1.1 over 1.2 and to prefer gamble 2.1 over 2.2. The reasoning behind this pattern of preferences, in the first pair, is that a certain prospect is better than a slightly uncertain one with higher expected value, and that, in the second pair, the higher probability of winning is traded off against the smaller gain being obtained. An expected utility model for this pattern of preferences would require that

$$0.1u(\$10^6) > 0.09u(\$2 \cdot 10^6) + 0.01u(\$0) \tag{10}$$

and

$$0.09u(\$2 \cdot 10^6) + 0.01u(\$0) > 0.1u(\$10^6) \tag{11}$$

The first inequality follows from the first pair of gambles by subtracting $0.9u(\$10^6)$ from both sides of the relation between the corresponding expected utilities. The second inequality follows from subtracting $0.9u(\$0)$ from both sides of the corresponding relation between expected utilities. Obviously, there is a contradiction between the two inequalities describing the preferences in terms of expected utilities.

It has been noticed (Kämpke, 1992) that this contradiction can disappear if we allow the numerical probabilities to be distorted. In the continuous case, such a distortion ϕ is assumed to be a monotone function from the unit interval (the range of probabilities) onto the unit interval (the range of distorted probabilities) which is continuous from the right. Moreover, we assume that $\phi(0) = 0$ and $\phi(1) = 1$. From the decision-theoretic viewpoint, such a distortion corresponds to a subjective rescaling of, so to speak, the objective subjective probabilities.

A probability that is distorted in such a manner is called a *capacity* (see Kämpke, 1992, following Kohlas, 1990, and the basic work of Choquet, 1954). Formally, we can write $\phi \circ P$, where the operator $\circ$ denotes composition of functions. It has been shown in several papers (Schmeidler, 1989; Wakker, 1989, 1990) that the expectation operation w.r.t. a capacity should be the so-called Choquet-integral. Intuitively, this integration requires that you should *not* just multiply utilities with corresponding capacities and add up these products. Rather (in the discrete case), you take successive differences of decreasing utilities and multiply by the capacity of the event corresponding to these differences. (This is exemplified graphically in Wakker, 1989).

Let me rephrase the pattern of preferences in the Allais paradox using a capacity in the following inequalities. (For simplicity, I assume the gains to be rescaled.) For gamble 1.1, we simply have $AU = u(1)$. For gamble 1.2, we find

$$AU = \phi(0.09)(u(2) - u(1))$$
$$+ \phi(0.99)(u(1) - u(0))$$
$$+ \phi(1)u(0) \tag{12}$$

The difference $u(2) - u(1)$ corresponds to the event that the gamble ends up with a gain higher than 1. The probability of this is 0.09. The difference $u(1) - u(0)$ corresponds to the event that the gamble yields more than 0. The probability of this is 0.99. Finally, the event that the gamble yields at least 0, has the probability 1. Note that if you take the identity for ϕ you get standard expected utility. In the same manner we find for gamble 2.1

$$AU = \phi(0.09)(u(2) - u(0)) + \phi(1)u(0) \tag{13}$$

and for gamble 2.2

$$AU = \phi(0.1)(u(1) - u(0)) + \phi(1)u(0) \tag{14}$$

Taking the observed preference pattern over the two pairs of gambles, we obtain two inequalities. For the sake of brevity, it is assumed, without loss of generality, that $u(0) = 0$, $u(1) \neq 0$, and $u(2) = 1$, since u is defined only up to a positive linear transformation. For the gambles in the first pair, it results that

$$\phi(0.09)(1 - u(1)) + \phi(0.99)u(1) < u(1) \tag{15}$$

for those in second pair

$$\phi(0.09) > \phi(0.1)u(1) \tag{16}$$

Adding the two inequalities, simplifying and rearranging finally yields

$$\phi(0.99) + \phi(0.1) - \phi(0.09) < 1 \tag{17}$$

Note that this cannot be fulfilled by taking ϕ to be the identity, i.e., by a usual probability distribution. I will now show that there is a straightforward construction of a random set that allows this inequality to be fulfilled.

Since ϕ is defined on probabilities P, let us take the following sets whose probabilities are being used: Let $B \subset \overline{A}$ and $P(\overline{A}) = 0.1$. Then take $P(B) = 0.09$ and, consequently, $P(A \cup B) = 0.99$.

Assuming there exists a belief function *Bel* fulfilling the inequality (17) describing the Allais paradox, this belief function should then obey the following relation:

$$Bel(A \cup B) + Bel(\overline{A}) - Bel(B) < 1 \tag{18}$$

or, equivalently

$$Bel(A \cup B) - Bel(B) < 1 - Bel(\overline{A}) = Pl(A) \tag{19}$$

There are actually many belief functions fulfilling this inequality. To simplify even further, assume there is no focal element of the random set that is spread among A and B, i.e., assume *Bel(A ∪ B) = Bel(A) + Bel(B)*. Then all that is required to resolve the Allais paradox is

$$Bel(A) < Pl(A) \tag{20}$$

which only means that there should be at least one focal element different from A and its subsets that intersects A (without intersecting B). That is, the random set should not be trivial w.r.t. A. This seems to be a very mild requirement.

There have been predecessors of anticipated utility models; they used a probability distortion without Choquet integration. As Wakker (1989) argued, this can lead to violations of stochastic dominance. In these predecessing models, one substituted the classical expected utility theory with a *bilinear model,* a model that is linear both in the utility function and in the capacity (or the subjective (subjective) probability function). Models of this kind have been successfully used for explaining major human biases in decision making by Kahneman & Tversky in their *prospect theory* (Kahneman & Tversky, 1979) and by Coombs & Lehner (1984) in an analysis of compensatory changes on (subjective subjective) probabilities and gains / losses in decision making under risk. Recently, prospect theory has been further developed to include Choquet integration (*cumulative prospect theory,* Kahneman & Tversky, 1992).

Let me sum up. Rank dependent or anticipated utility theory uses probability distortions, which take the form of capacities (named after Choquet and integrated as he proposed). From the probabilistic point of view it seems desirable to restrict the class of capacities to some meaningful subset. I contend that such a subset is formed by *random sets* (see Kendall, 1974; Shafer, 1976). Random sets require a form of additivity that gives the capacity constructed this way a special meaning that can be traced in the belief and plausibility functions. Moreover, the language of random sets is sufficiently rich to emulate those decision problems anticipated utility is designed to describe: It is possible to construct random sets that allow to resolve the Allais paradox (for the Ellsberg paradox, a construction has been proposed in Jaffray, 1989). As a consequence, random sets are proposed as a sufficiently rich and yet clearly restricted form of probability distortion that is useful in utility modeling.

4.3 Coping with incompleteness: Conditional random sets

Coming back to incomplete conditional knowledge structures, I will now illustrate the meaning and use of conditional events in analyzing such structures. The structures I will refer to have been used by Jungermann and Thüring (1993) to develop the notions of ambiguity and validity in judgment under uncertainty. I think it is useful to take knowledge structures in order to show that it is the incompleteness of evidence rather than some dogma that compels to advocate the use of belief functions (or conditional belief functions, as it will turn out) instead of classical probabilities for the valuation of uncertainty.

The first structure, used by Jungermann and Thüring (1993), demands no more than a standard classical probability model. It is characterized by two rules, given here under two conditional probabilities of a symptom (the fictitious Nagami fever), given a diagnosis (a virus):

1. $p(F|V) = \alpha$

2. $p(\overline{F}|\overline{V}) = \beta$

In this case, α is simply the sensitivity of the symptom w.r.t. the diagnosis, while β is the specificity. These two numbers are frequently used in medical testing and they have a clear interpretation without any need to go into something beyond classical probability (see Spies, 1993). Using sensitivity and specificity, we can compute the marginal probability of the fever F if the probability of the virus is given.

The scenario changes somewhat if we consider a second knowledge structure. Here, a new variable enters the picture: it is the organism's inability to produce antibodies (*D*).

1. $p(F|V, D) = \alpha$

2. $p(\overline{F}|\overline{V}) = \beta$

3. $p(\overline{F}|\overline{D}) = \gamma$

Here, the rule valuation is such that a simple interpretation of the numbers in terms of medical testing is impossible. Since not all combinations of antecedents occur in the rules, we are not ready to apply Bayes' theorem or Jeffrey's rule, even if marginal probabilities of *D* and *V* are given. For instance, assume we are told the marginal probabilities of the states *D* and $\overline{D}$ we then know the specificity of the diagnosis "inability to produce antibodies" w.r.t. the diagnosis of the Nagami fever; but we lack the sensitivity information that is needed to compute a marginal probability of the symptomatic Nagami fever. This also makes it impossible, given the probability of the symptom, to use Bayes' theorem to compute the posterior probability of the diagnosis. Thus, we encounter the problem that no updating of probabilities can take place even if evidence about marginal probabilities comes in.

One solution is to let the probabilities in the above knowledge structure refer to the conditional events belonging to the conditional statements above. However, if we do so, these probabilities will refer to sets of events in our original space. Thus, we have to shift to the aforementioned belief functions in order to state probabilities properly. Table 1 shows the situation.

Table 1. An unspecific interpretation of incomplete conditional knowledge

rules:	1	2	3
a	$m([F \mid D, V]) = \alpha$	$m([F \mid \overline{V}]) = \beta$	$m([F \mid \overline{D}]) = \gamma$
b	$m([\Theta \mid D, V]) = 1 - \alpha$	$m([\Theta \mid \overline{V}]) = 1 - \beta$	$m([\Theta \mid \overline{D}]) = 1 - \gamma$

We can put up several models of uncertain rules with conditional events. The first model assumes that some probability is attached to the rule, and with the remaining probability nothing is known about the behaviour of the system being described by the rule (Kohlas, 1990). This is known as the leaky capacitor model of uncertainty, I will call it here the unspecific model. The second model is the usual probabilistic model, where a certain probability is attached to a rule and the remaining probability is attached to the contrary rule, namely the rule that predicts the negation of the consequent, given the antecedent. I call this model the specific model. An interpretation of our Nagami-fever rules in terms of this model is given in table 2.

Table 2. A specific interpretation of incomplete conditional knowledge

rules:	1	2	3
a	$m([F \mid D, V]) = \alpha$	$m([F \mid \overline{V}]) = \beta$	$m([F \mid \overline{D}]) = \gamma$
b	$m([\overline{F} \mid D, V]) = 1 - \alpha$	$m([\overline{F} \mid \overline{V}]) = 1 - \beta$	$m([\overline{F} \mid \overline{D}]) = 1 - \gamma$

Finally, the third model combines the two previous ones. Here, some probability *p* is attached to the rule, some probability $q \leq 1 - p$ is attached to the contrary rule, and the remaining probability $(1 - (p + q))$ is attached to the whole universe or frame of discernment. I call this model the dichotomous belief model; it is treated in some detail (without reference to conditional events, however) in Baldwin (1986) and Spies (1989). I will not consider it here any further, because it can be viewed as a combination of the specific and the unspecific model.—It is by no means clear which of these models apply empirically when we either wish to model a particular domain or a particular human expert. Human knowledge structures show delicate nuances as to conditioning (see Wason & Johnson-Laird, 1972).

In a conventional model, the probabilities of each model would be attached to conditional expressions; as shown before, in many cases these quantifications cannot be used to derive anything about marginal probabilities. This changes if we attach the probabilities to the conditional events corresponding to the rules. We can then use the formalisms of combining belief functions such as to give *a priori* bounds on at least some marginal probabilities. We also can infer to which kind of evidence the model being examined is most sensitive.

To continue with the example let us combine the belief functions on conditional events in the unspecific and the specific model. Table 3 gives the result according to Dempster's rule for the unspecific model.

Table 3. Result of combining *a priori* incomplete conditional knowledge in the unspecific model

Event Rows	Intersection	Probability
aaa	F	$\alpha\beta\gamma$
aab	$\overline{D} \cup F$	$\alpha\beta(1-\gamma)$
aba	$\overline{V} \cup F$	$\alpha(1-\beta)\gamma$
abb	$\overline{V} \cup \overline{D} \cup F$	$\alpha(1-\beta)(1-\gamma)$
baa	$(D \cap V) \cup F$	$(1-\alpha)\beta\gamma$
bab	$\overline{D} \cup (V \cup F)$	$(1-\alpha)\beta(1-\gamma)$
bba	$\overline{V} \cup (D \cup F)$	$(1-\alpha)(1-\beta)\gamma$
bbb	Θ	$(1-\alpha)(1-\beta)(1-\gamma)$

The computations involved in this combination can be accomplished using an intersection theorem on conditional events (Goodman et al., 1991; Spies, 1994).

Let us examine the results for the *unspecific* model. We get one clear support of event *F*, and one clear support for the whole frame of discernment. The remaining probabilities are committed to events that, mostly, correspond to formal implications. For instance *abb* corresponds to $(D \cap V) \supset F$ which is just the formal implication corresponding to the first rule. Note that, by the assumption underlying the unspecific model, all these events contain $\omega \in \Omega$ that *do not falsify* the rules in question.

The results of combining *a priori* evidence in the *specific* model are markedly different. Table 4 gives the results according to Dempster's rule.

Table 4. Result of combining *a priori* incomplete conditional knowledge in the specific model

Event Rows	Intersection	Probability
aaa	F	$\alpha\beta\gamma$
aab	$(F\cap D\cap V)\cup(\bar{V}\cap F)\cup(\bar{D}\cap\bar{F})$	$\alpha\beta(1-\gamma)$
aba	$(F\cap D\cap V)\cup(\bar{V}\cap\bar{F})\cup(\bar{D}\cap F)$	$\alpha(1-\beta)\gamma$
abb	$(\bar{F}\cap(\bar{D}\cup\bar{V}))\cup(D\cap V\cap F)$	$\alpha(1-\beta)(1-\gamma)$
baa	$(F\cap(\bar{D}\cup\bar{V}))\cup(D\cap V\cap F)$	$(1-\alpha)\beta\gamma$
bab	$(\bar{F}\cap D\cap V)\cup(\bar{V}\cap F)\cup(\bar{D}\cap\bar{F})$	$(1-\alpha)\beta(1-\gamma)$
bba	$(\bar{F}\cap D\cap V)\cup(\bar{V}\cap\bar{F})\cup(\bar{D}\cap F)$	$(1-\alpha)(1-\beta)\gamma$
bbb	$\bar{F}$	$(1-\alpha)(1-\beta)(1-\gamma)$

In the specific model, we find clear support both in favor and against event F (cases *aaa* and *bbb*); all remaining probabilities are committed to mixtures of verifying and falsifying instances confirming and disconfirming some of the rules. As an example, take case *baa*. The event $\bar{F}\cap D\cap V$ falsifies rule 1, which predicts fever, given the virus infection and the weakness of the infected body's immune system (conditional event $[F|D\cap V]$). The event $F\cap(\bar{D}\cup\bar{V})$ contains verifying instances of at least one of the rules relating to the prediction of fever given no virus infection, or to the prediction of fever given in intact immune system of the patient. These rules were expressed by stating probabilities on conditional events $[F|\bar{D}]$ and $[F|\bar{V}]$ respectively. As a consequence, the posterior plausibility of violating a rule is usually higher in the specific than in the unspecific model.

In the specific model, there is a simple Bayesian interpretation of the resulting probability interval on event F, the occurrence of the Nagarni fever. The support in favor of the fever is $\alpha\beta\gamma$. This is simply the probability that all three rules are true. On the other hand, the support of its non-occurrence is *p*

= $(1-\alpha)(1-\beta)(1-\gamma)$. Therefore, the plausibility of the fever occuring is $1-p$ which is nothing but the probability that any of the three rules fires. Thus, the degrees of belief and plausibility reflect the probabilities of an AND- vs. an OR-connection of the rules, or, as Shafer (1986) has put it, of the concurrent vs. successive testimony implied by the rules.

In the unspecific model, if either rule can be fulfilled, the support goes to the entire frame of discernment (Θ).

We have thus derived, for both models, intervals of probability of the predicted event and of verifying or falsifying the implications given by the rules and other implications that are not explicitly stated in the knowledge structure. This would have been impossible without conditional events. The result is simple and plausible. Moreover, we are now in a position to predict the effect of incoming evidence on either model. These predictions can be used in practice to decide which model to choose or to describe a human expert.

Let me briefly comment on the normative content of the combination of incomplete conditional knowledge I have demonstrated here. In an accompanying paper (Spies, 1994) it is shown that this combination reduces to Jeffey's and Bayes' rule in case of complete conditional knowledge and given marginal probabilities of the antecedents.

5. THE EFFECT OF EVIDENCE ON INCOMPLETE CONDITIONAL KNOWLEDGE STRUCTURES

To summarize the resulting situation after evaluating the *a priori* information in both models, let me introduce the notion of consistency of a belief function, as introduced by Dubois & Prade (1987). Intuitively, a belief function is consistent, if its focal elements largely overlap, else it becomes more and more inconsistent. (A numerical definition of dissonance is used in Dubois' and Prade's paper to quantify this intuitive notion).

Now, let us imagine what happens in these two models if evidence comes in. By evidence, I mean some new probability statement or belief function that can be combined with the *a priori* beliefs or our models to give new, *a posteriori* beliefs. I will discuss the impact of evidence separately for evidence providing non-falsifying information w.r.t. the rules being used in the conditional events and for evidence providing falsifying information. Either evidence can be understood in terms of a hypothesis-testing paradigm of subjective knowledge processing (see Klayman & Ha, 1987).

In the unspecific model, the effect of verifying (or, more generally, non-falsifying) instances is to make the model more specific, i.e., to break down the support for the frame of discernment into support for smaller events that correspond to rule-verifying instances. The consistency of the model, however, will remain large. In the specific model, on the other hand, the effect of verifying instances is to make the model ever less consistent, because these instances will produce empty intersections with the events found by combining the *a priori* conditional knowledge. Now, according to Dempster's rule, probability mass attached to the empty set is summed up and proportionally distributed among all non-empty intersections of events. As a consequence, more and more probability mass will flow "downward", to the atomic events. As a further consequence, the model will become more specific, since ever sharper contradicting events will be emphasized. Thus, both models are made more specific by non-falsifying evidence; the specific model is made less consistent.

If evidence in the form of falsifying instances comes in, the effect on the two models will be different. In the unspecific model, we now generate empty intersections between the events after combining *a priori* information and the evidence. Therefore, this model will lose consistency: belief will spread over non-intersecting events increasingly. In the specific model, the effect of falsifying instances will not be harmful to overall consistency, since the events in this model mainly consist of disjunctions of falsifying elements. Again, both models will become more specific.

Thus, we can make the following predictions for experts using either model. If we assume that consistency makes the processing of a model easier, we can predict that non-falsifying information will be easier to integrate in the unspecific model and that falsifying information will be easier to integrate for people relying on the specific model. Since the specific model contains focal elements that correspond to violations of rules, some general processing difficulty could be assumed for this model w.r.t. human cognition. This would confirm earlier findings (Spies, 1989).

These considerations show that conditional event evaluations of probabilities in incomplete conditional knowledge reveal a deeper structure in the rules. It becomes clear what kind of evidence will have what kind of impact on the model. It seems interesting to test these impacts empirically for human subjects and to implement them in evidence combining devices like sensor fusion software. Moreover, they allow one to generate *a priori* probability intervals, which would have been impossible with classical conditional probabilities.

6. CONCLUSION

It is assumed throughout this paper that human expertise is characterized by incomplete conditional knowledge. This is a challenge to old and recent techniques of uncertainty management based on conditional probabilities. A deeper look into the nature of conditioning reveals that a new structure is established on the universe of discourse once conditioning takes place. This structure is composed of conditional events. In terms of probabilities, conditional events are sets of equally valued events under conditioning. In terms of logic, conditional events comprise all sets for which a given implication from antecedent to consequent is true. They comprise all variants of matching a rule relating antecedent and consequent. Valuating conditional events presupposes a theory of random sets; this theory is mostly treated under the heading of evidential reasoning. Applying methods of evidential reasoning to conditional events yields a solution to the problem of managing uncertainty under the incomplete conditional knowledge.

The usefulness of random set theory to recent theories of nonexpected utility is demonstrated. In these theories, distorted probabilities are used in order to overcome some classical paradoxes in decision making. It is shown that random sets, and, with them, the theory of belief and plausibility functions, provide a useful subset to which to restrict the distortions of probability. This subset is rich enough to allow for resolving well known paradoxes by Allais and Ellsberg. Constructing a random set, however, seems easier than constructing an otherwise unrestricted probability distortion.

REFERENCES

Baldwin, J. F. (1986). Support logic programming. In: A. Jones, A. Kaufmann, H.-J. Zimmermann (Eds.) *Fuzzy Sets Theory and Applications*, NATO ASI Series, Reidel, Dordrecht - Boston, 133-170.

Beeri, C., Fagin, R., & Howard, J. (1977). A complete Axiomatization for function and Multivalued Dependencies in Database Relations. *Int. Conf. Mgmt. of Data*, ACM, NY, 47-61.

Bishop, Y., Fienberg, & S., Holland, P. (1975). *Discrete Multivariate Analysis: Theory and Practice*. MIT Press, Cambridge, MA.

Chankong, V., & Haimes, Y. (1983). *Multiobjective Decision Making*. Armsterdam, North Hol land.

Choquet, G. (1954). Theory of Capacities. *Annales de l'Institut Fourier 5*,131- 291.

Coombs, C., & Lehner, P. (1984). Conjoint Design and Analysis of the Bilinear Model. *J. Math. Psych., 28*, 1- 42.

Dubois, D., & Prade, H. (1987). Properties of measures of information in evidence and possibility theories. *Fuzzy Sets and Systems, 24 (2)*,161-182.

Dubois, D., & Prade, H. (1988). Conditioning in Possibility and Evidence Theories - A logical Viewpoint. In: B. Bouchon, L. Saitta, R. Yager (Eds.). *Uncertainty and Intelligent Systems* (Proc. Second IPMU, Urbino 1988), 401-408.

Dubois, D., & Prade, H. (1989). Measure-free Conditioning, Probability, and Non-monotonic Reasoning. *Proc. 11th IJCAI*, Detroit, 1110-1114.

Edwards, W. (1982). Conservatism in human information processing. In: Kahneman, Slovic, Tversky (Eds). *Judgment under uncertainty*, New york, Cambridge University Press, 359-369.

Erné, M. (1987). *Ordnungs- und Verbandstheorie*, University of Hagen Press.

Fagin, R. (1977). Multivalued Dependencies and a new Normal Form for relational Databases. *ACM Transactions on Database System, 2*, 262-278.

Fishburn, P. (1985). *Interval orders ant Interval Graphs*. New York, Wiley.

Fishburn, P. (1986). Interval Models for Comparative Probability on Finite Sets. *J. Math. Psych., 30*, 221-242.

Goodman, I., & Nguyen, H. (1985). *Uncertainty Models for Knowledge-based Systems*. North Holland, Amsterdam.

Goodman, I., & Nguyen, H. (1988). Conditional Objects and the Modelling of Uncertainties. In M. Gupta, T. Yamakawa (Eds.). *Fuzzy Computing*, Elsevier Science, New York, 119 - 138.

Goodman, I., Nguyen, H., & Walker, E. (1991). *Conditional inference ant logic for intelligent systems*. Amsterdam: Elsevier.

Goodman, I., Gupta, M., Nguyen, N., & Rogers S., (Eds.) (1991). Conditional Logic in Expert Systems, Amsterdam: North Holland.

Heckerman, D. (1986). Probabilistic interpretations for MYCIN's Certainty Factors. In: L.N. Kanal, J.F. Lemmer (Eds.). *Uncertainty in Artificial Intelligence (1)*, North Holland, 167 196.

Jaffray, J.-Y. (1989). Linear Utility Theory for Belief Functions. *Operations Research Letters, 8,*107- 112.

Jaffray, J.-Y. (1990). Bayesian Conditioning ant Belief Functions. *Working Paper. Université Paris VI, Laboratoire d'Informatique de la décision.*

Jaffray J.-Y., & Wakker, P. (1993). Decision making with belief functions: Compatibility and Incompatibility with the sure-thing principle. *Working Paper. Université Paris VI, Laboratoire d' Informatique de la décision, and University of Leiden, Dept. Medical Decision Making.*

Johnson-Laird, P.N. (1983). *Mental Models,* Cambridge University Press, Cambridge.

Jungermann, H., & Thüring, M. (1993). Causal Knowledge and the expression of uncertainty. In: G. Strube, K. Wender (Eds.). *The cognitive psychology of knowledge.* Elsevier, Amsterdam, 53-73.

Kahneman, D., Slovic, P., & Tversky, A. (Eds.) (1982). *Judgment under Uncertainty: Heuristics and Biases.* New York, Cambridge University Press.

Kahneman, D., & Tversky, A. (1979). Prospect Theory: An Analysis of Decision under Risk. *Econometrica, 47,* 263-291.

Kämpke, T. (1992). Diskrete und stochastische Strukturen zur Verarbeitung unsicherer Information. *Habilitation Thesis, Universität Ulm.*

Keeney, R., & Raiffa, H. (1976). *Decisions with Multiple Objectives.* New York, Wiley.

Kendall, D. (1974). Foundations of a Theory of Random Sets. In: E. Harding, D. Kendall (Eds.). *Stochastic Geometry.* New York, Wiley, pp. 322- 376.

Klayman, J., & Ha, Y.-W. (1987). Confirmation, Disconfirmation, and Information in Hypothesis Testing. *Psychologial Review, 94 (2),* 211- 228.

Kohlas, J. (1990). Evidenztheorie: Ein Kalkuel mit Hinweisen. *FAW, University of Ulm, Research Report* FAW-TR-90002.

Kohlas, J., & Monney, P.A. (1990). Modeling and Reasoning with Hints. *University of Fribourg, Inst. for Automation and OR, Working Paper* 174.

Kong, A. (1986). Multivariate Belief Functions and Graphical Models, Diss., Dept. of Statistics, Harward University.

Kyburg, H. (1987). Bayesian and Non-Bayesian Evidential Updating. *Artificial Intelligence, 31,* 271 - 293.

Lauritzen, S., & Spiegelhalter, D. (1988). Local Computations with Probabilities on Graphical Structures ant their Application to Expert System. *J. R. Statistical Society, 50 (2),* 157 - 224.

Lichtenstein, S., Fischoff, B., & Phillips, L. D. (1982). Calibration of probabilities: The tate of the art to 1980 in: D. Kahneman, P. Slovic, A. Tversky (Eds). *Judgement under uncertainty,* Cambridge, Cambridge University Press, 306-335.

Ozsoyoglu, Z. M., & Yuan, L.Y. (1987). A new Normal Form for Nested Relations. *ACM transactions on Database Systems, 12 (1)*,111-136.

Pearl, J. (1988). *Probabilistic Reasoning in intelligent Systems: Networks of Plausible Inference*. Morgan Kaufman, San Mateo, CA.

Ruspini, E. (1987). The Logical Foundations of Evidential Reasoning. *Technical Note 408*. SRI International, Menlo Park, CA.

Schmeidler, D. (1989). Subjective Probability and expectet utility without additivity. *Econometrica, 57 (3)*, 571- 587.

Shafer, G. (1976). *A mathematical Theory of Evidence*. Princeton, Princeton University Press.

Shafer, G. (1982). Belief Functions and Parametric Models. *J. R. Stat. Society, B, 44 (3)*, 322 - 352.

Shafer, G. (1986). The Combination of Evidence. *Int. J. Intell. Systems*, 155-179.

Shafer, G., Tversky, A. (1985). Languages and Designs for Probability Judgment, *Cognitive Science, 9*, 309- 339.

Shafer, G., Shenoy, P., & Mellouli, K. (1987). Propagating Belief Functions in Qualitative Markov Trees. *Int. J. Approx. Reasoning, 1(4)*, 349-400.

Scholz, R. (1987). Cognitive Strategies in Stochastic Thinking. Reidel, Dordrecht - Boston.

Schönpflug, W. (1986). The trade-off between internal and external information storage. *J. of Memory ant Language, 25*, 657-675.

Spies, M. (1988). A Model for the Management of imprecise Queries in relational Database . in: B. Bouchon, L. Saitta, R. Yager (Eds). *Uncertainty and Intelligent Systems*. Springer Lecture Notes on Computer Science, vol. 313, Heidelberg, 146-153.

Spies, M. (1989). *Syllogistic inference under uncertainty - An empirical contribution to uncertainty modelling in knowledge-based systems with fuzzy quantifiers ant support logic*. Munich, Psychologie Verlags Union.

Spies, M. (1990a). Impresision in Human Combination of Evidence. In: W. Janko, M. Roubens, H.-J. Zimmermann (Eds.). *Advances in Fuzzy Systems*. Kluwer, Boston, 161-175.

Spies, M. (1991a). Applications Aspects of Qualitative Conditional Independence. Proc. 3rd IPMU Conference, Springer Lect. *Notes Comp. Sc., 521*, 31-39.

Spies, M. (1991b). Combination of Evidence with Conditional Objects and its Application to Cognitive Modelling. In: I. Goodman, M. Gupta, N. Nguyen, S. Rogers (Eds.). *Conditional Logic in Expert Systems*, Amsterdam: North Holland, 181-210.

Spies, M. (1993). *Unsicheres Wissen..* (Monograph). Spektrum Akademischer Verlag - Scientific American, Heidelberg.

Spies, M. (1994). Evidential Reasoning with Conditional Events. In: M. Fedrizzi, J. Kacprzyk, R. Yager (Eds.). *Advances in the Dempster-Shafer theory of Evidence*. New York, Wiley, 493-511.

Wakker, P. (1989). Tranforming Probabilities without violating stochastic dominance. In: E. Roskam (Ed.). *Mathematical Psychology in Progress*. Berlin, Springer, 29-47.

Wakker, P. (1990). A behavioural foundation for fuzzy Measures. *Fuzzy Sets and Systems, 37,* 327-350.

Wason, J., & Johnson-Laird, P.N. (1972). *Psychology of Reasoning: Structure and Content,* Batsford, London.

Zadeh, L.A. (1985). Syllogistic reasoning in fuzzy logic and its application to usuality and reasoning with disposisions, University of California at Berkeley. *Institiute of Cognitive Studies, Report 34.*

ACKNOWLEDGEMENT. I wish to thank Helmut Jungermann for his comments on an earlier version of this paper; his curiosity in relationships between the knowledge structures in Jungermann & Thuring (1993) and conditional events inspired several topics of this paper. I am grateful to Peter Wakker who made his work on rank dependent utility available to me soon after the SPUDM 14 conference. Moreover, I am indebted to all those who encouraged my work on conditional events, particularly to Didier Dubois, Irwin Goodman, Jean-Yves Jaffray, Janus Kacprzyk, Juerg Kohlas, Hung Nguyen, and Franz-Josef Radermacher. Finally, I received lots of helpful comments during the SPUDM 14 conference in Aix-en-Provence.

SECTION 2

Symposium and workshop papers

Contributions to Decision Making - I
J.-P. Caverni, M. Bar-Hillel, F.H. Barron and H. Jungermann (Editors)
1995 Elsevier Science B.V.

THE THEORY OF IMAGE THEORY:

AN EXAMINATION OF THE CENTRAL CONCEPTUAL STRUCTURE

Terry Connolly and Lee Roy Beach

Dept. of Management and Policy College of Business and Public
Administration, University of Arizona Tucson, AZ 85721 U.S.A.
email: connolly@ccit.arizona.edu

INTRODUCTION

For some time decision researchers have known that the subjective expected utility (SEU) model, and its near relatives offer only an imperfect description of how most humans make decisions. Despite vigorous attempts to improve descriptive accuracy, many researchers suspect that the remedies offered (e.g., inflected utility functions, non-probabilistic weighting schemes, non-maximizing combination rules) are largely cosmetic, preserving the basic logic of the model only by the use of ad hoc expedients. Only recently has it become clear that this collective body of work, which we will call Traditional Decision Theory (TDT), is being seriously challenged by alternative theories which offer a different view of decision making than that provided by TDT.

TDT is the result of some three hundred years of work by many scholars, and is, by any standard, a major intellectual achievement. Because it is the dominant paradigm for thinking about decision making, challengers are required to offer a great deal before their claims and alternative views are taken seriously. As a result, such alternatives, inevitably embrionic, are liable to be rejected in their entirety at the first empirical set-back, even if complete rejection is not warranted. The purpose of this article to outline the challenge to TDT, and to argue for giving alternatives to TDT the leeway to develop to their potential in spite of inevitable initial empirical failures.

Space limitations prevent any complete survey of all of the alternatives to TDT that have been proposed. We will concentrate our attention on one example, image theory (Beach, 1990, 1993; Beach & Mitchell, 1987; 1990). We will take the position that image theory (IT), in its current (1993) version, is exemplary of a class of theories each of which, though differing in specifics, shares a group of assumptions and orientations different from those of TDT. By clarifying which elements are specific to the current version of IT and which are generic to the class of theories. we hope to promote the survival of the class even if the current version of IT does not itself survive.

In what follows, we first give a brief description of the frontrunners among the challengers to TDT, and a somewhat fuller summary of the main points of IT. Next we explore the points of contrast between IT and TDT, emphasizing the types of phenomena each addresses, the assumptions each makes, and the contrasts of theory and prediction between the two. From this contrast we develop the foundations of a research agenda which will serve the survival and development of both IT and the other challenging theories.

Some Non-Traditional Decision Theories

There have recently appeared a number of descriptive models of decision making that depart markedly from the normative, economic logic of TDT. We are limited here to a brief description of the central idea of each of these theories; the interested reader is referred to Klein, Orasanu, Calderwood and Zsambok (1993) for more complete discussions.

Recognition-Primed decision making (Klein, 1989) states that the majority of 'decisions' actually involve recognition of the situation as one for which the decision maker has a prepared course of action or a course of action that can be modified to suit the situation. Noble's (1989) *cognitive situation assessment* theory is similar in that the focus of the theory is on how the decision maker identifies the requirements of the situation and uses past experience as a source for ways of satisfying those requirements. In a similar vein, Lipshitz's (1989) theory of *argument-driven decision making* views decision making as relying on causal logic to derive reasonable ways of dealing with environmental demands. Pennington and Hastie's (1988) theory of *explanation-based decision making* fits well with the other theories except that it assumes that situation assessment involves elaboration of a story that incorporates the decision maker's knowledge about what led up to the present situation and the implications of that knowledge and that story for what will happen in the future. These four theories focus on the role of situation assessment, past experience, and causal thinking in decision making. None of these is an explicit part of TDT.

In a slightly different vein, Connolly's (Connolly & Wagner, 1988) theory of *decision cycles* sees decision making as an incremental process in which the decision maker's view of the situation is refined as behavior is implemented, and behavior is modified thereby to better suit the demands of the situation; thus what may have been a 'bad' decision to begin with is molded into a 'good' decision in light of feedback. Montgomery's (1983) *search for dominance structure* model is a theory of post-decisional behavior in which the favored decision alternative is bolstered to become the clearly dominant alternative. Finally, Hammond's (1988) *cognitive continuum theory* considers the nature of, and implications of, intuitive and analytical processes in decision making. These last three theories emphasize the roles of cognitive processes in guiding and justifying decisions, and do so in a much richer way than is afforded by TDT.

Image Theory

Image theory contains many of the elements of the theories briefly described above. It acknowledges that situation assessment is a prior condition for decision making; that past experience is fundamental, often making reflective decision making unnecessary; that causal reasoning often is central when decisions must be made; that intuition is a familiar component of decision making; and that feedback obtained in the course of implementation not only guides behavior but also leads to further decisions in support of goal attainment.

Image theory views the decision maker as a manager of knowledge and information who attempts to keep a reasonable degree of consistency among his or her images of what is right, what he or she is attempting to achieve, and what he or she is doing to promote those achievements. Together, these images encompass the decision maker's store of knowledge.

The labels for the images are: the value image (beliefs and values that define what is right), the trajectory image (the goal agenda describing what he or she is attempting to achieve), and the strategic image (the plans aimed at achievement of the goals on the trajectory image - plans are the blueprints that guide tactical behavior and that can be used to forecast the future that they will promote).

Not all of the decision maker's knowledge is relevant in every situation. Framing is the process by which a partition of the entire knowledge store is defined such that it contains those aspects of the three images that are relevant to the situation at hand. These relevant aspects of the images constitute standards against which the suitability of decision options are evaluated. The theory (Beach, 1990) describes how framing takes place.

There are two kinds of decisions, adoption decisions and progress decisions. These are made using either or both of two kinds of decision tests, the compatibility test or the profitability test. Adoption decisions can be further divided into screening decisions and choice decisions. Adoption decisions are about adoption or rejection of candidate goals or plans as constituents of the trajectory or strategic images. Screening consists of eliminating unacceptable candidates. Choice consists of selecting the most promising candidate from among the survivors of screening.

Progress decisions consist of assaying the compatibility ('fit') between the forecasted future if a given plan is implemented (or continues to be implemented) and the ideal future as defined by the trajectory image. Incompatibility triggers rejection of the plan and adoption of a substitute. Failure to find a feasible substitute prompts reconsideration of the plan's goal.

The compatibility test assays the fit between a candidate goal or plan and the decision standards defined by those aspects of the three images that constitute the frame. It is a single mechanism, in contrast to the profitability test which is the decision maker's unique repertory of choice strategies for selecting the best option from among the survivors of screening by the compatibility test.

Image theory sees decision making proceeding in the following way: the decision maker frames the situation in terms of knowledge about how it arose and its place in the large perspective of events. If the situation requires decision making and the decision is one that has been made before, the decision maker probes memory to find a strategy for dealing with it, called a policy. If the decision is unique or if the former policy failed, the decision maker must consider the options (which are goals or plans), screen them using the compatibility test, and adopt the best survivor using the profitability test. If only one option is considered, and if it survives the compatibility test, it is the choice without having to evoke the profitability test. Similarly, if more than one option is considered and only one survives, it is the choice. If more than one option is considered and more than one survives, the profitability test is used to break the tie by selecting the best choice, where best is defined by the particular choice strategy that is used.

Progress decisions proceed in a different manner. Here the question is whether a given plan is forecasted to achieve its goal if implementation is continued. The key is the compatibility between those aspects of the trajectory image included in the frame and the forecast generated by running the plan fast-forward. Sufficient compatibility implies retention of the plan and its continued implementation. Insufficient compatibility implies cessation of implementation and replacement of the plan with one that is more promising - often only a slight modification of the original plan in light of the discrepancy between the trajectory image and the forecast. This process is engaged in periodically during implementation in order to monitor progress toward goal achievement.

Image theory research has focused strongly on adoption decisions-screening and choice (summarized in Beach, 1990, 1993). Dunegan (1993) has initiated research on progress decisions that shows promise and that is supportive of the image theory position. There has been limited research on the nature of images (Brown, Mitchell & Beach, 1987; Beach, Smith, Lundell & Mitchell, 1988; Bissell & Beach, 1993). The theory has generated two books and 25 papers, of which 9 papers are empirical studies and the rest are elaborations of the theory and attempts to apply it to such areas as auditing, job search, management, consumer behavior, family planning, political decisions, and so on. In short, image theory is in its infancy and empirical testing has just begun.

Contrasting Theoretical Concerns

To better understand the difference between the theoretical concerns of Image Theory (IT) and those of traditional decision theory (TDT), let us apply both to a concrete practical example. Suppose that you find yourself with an unexpected free afternoon in a city you know and like, with several hours to fill before your flight home. How will you spend your time? A walk seems appealing, and you are faced with a decision as to which favorite old haunts you will visit. How do TDT and IT approach the problem?

Note first that the problem, though not in the least exotic, is quite complex. It assumes that one wishes to act purposively - some possible afternoons would certainly be better than others - though no clear single purpose is specified. There are a variety of ways to have fun: the art gallery. the museum, a stroll through old town, a teashop, a view. Not all of these will be reachable in the time available, some will complement one another (the stroll followed by a rest at tea), others will compete (having tea at one place perhaps precludes coffee immediately afterwards somewhere else). Extensive knowledge is assumed of both the environment (the city and its delights) and oneself (one's tastes and their likely shifts as the afternoon unfolds energy lags. hunger increases). More may be learned about both as the afternoon proceeds: previously unvisited parts of the city may offer new surprises; a new taste may be discovered at a market stand. There are uncertainties and contingencies: Will it rain, will I get lost? And there are important contingencies: one road leads on to another, closing off the road not taken; one lunch precludes a second, while invigorating the traveller for a stroll rather than a book shop.

These complexities are noted primarily because they must all be ignored in a TDT formulation of the problem. If, following Korzybski, we recall that the map is not the territory, we should recall also that the decision tree is not the map. TDT abstracts the traveller's problem as a current choice between alternative paths which are attractive only because of the destinations to which they (may) later lead. Note how the complex intertwinings of streets. satisfactions, contingencies and opportunities are simplified and packaged in the abstraction. Time is bifurcated into "Now", the time at which choice is made, and "Later", the time at which outcomes are experienced and evaluated. A road chosen now is treated only as a value-neutral path to a unitary 'destination" or "outcome" - perhaps formulated as "Spend afternoon in Area A", "Spend afternoon in Area B", and so on. Any number of issues are treated as exogenous, or not treated at all: why are these and only these options considered ? (Is the possibility of an earlier flight home considered? Why? Or why not?) Is a destination equally liked or disliked regardless of the path by which it is approached? How long is the time-frame within which the afternoon's activities will be evaluated? How does one evaluate a "destination" when the activities it includes are themselves branched, capricious, opportunistic? unexpected? And so on.

None of this is intended as either comprehensive or novel as a critique of TDT. It is simply to try to recapture, for those of us long steeped in TDT, what a very strange abstraction is at its core. We assume that the root interest of decision theory, orthodox or heterodox is with how people do, or better could, get around on the ground. The concern is with real roads, really taken or not, that lead to real destinations. satisfactory or not. TDT operates at two removes of abstraction from that real world: first the abstraction from territory to map. then the abstraction from map to decision tree. The brilliant achievements of TDT have been won at the level of the tree. It should not surprise us that the two-way path from world to tree and back is sometimes fraught with difficulties. To refer to these simply as issues of "framing" (Tversky & Kahneman, 1981) or "implementation" (Harrison, 1975) seems to diminish the conceptual distance that needs to be covered in moving from world to model and back.

It is at this basic, architectural level of theory that we see IT as most sharply confronting the orthodoxy of TDT. The core of IT is a richly interconnected network, embedding acts, actions, plans, projections of future outcome streams and other organized sequences of actions with purposes, objectives, principles and values. IT is thus highly contextualized - it addresses first the decision maker's understanding of the world, the actions he or she might take, their relationships to one another and to later consequences, and the linkages between these consequences and his or her value structure. For expository and pedagogical reasons this network has generally been presented in terms of the three somewhat distinct "images", noted earlier: the Value Image, clustered around principles and purposes; the Strategic Image, clustered around actions and their organization; and the Trajectory Image. clustered around the intersection of action and purpose. But the central thrust of IT is to confront head-on the fact that actions, purposes and goals are often richly interconnected. It is, perhaps, the empirical exception rather than the rule that the three elements are linked in the minimal sense captured in traditional decision trees. More commonly IT turns our attention to a network of connections, built up over time in the mind of the decision maker. Action selection is only marginally the result of conscious deliberation at the moment of decision. It is closer to an output of a production system in which complex responses are generated by discrete triggering conditions. The spirit is that of Simon's (1947) description of "programmed decisions" or Miller, Galanter and Pribram's (1960) discussion of plans and actions.

The core contrast between TDT and IT, then, turns on two conceptual partitions. One partition divides what is thought to be "inside", what "outside" the decision maker. The second partition is between those matters that are specific to the focal decision, and those that are stored or relatively stable over time. To overdraw the contrast only slightly:

TDT treats the decision maker as somehow "owning" an abstract decision mechanism, something like an unlabelled decision tree, and the computational skills to analyse it. In making a specific decision, this general-purpose machine is first loaded with content relevant to the decision (option names, values, a selection rule, etc.) and the computations are done to select an action. The output of this process is then back-translated or "implemented" as a real action in the real world.

IT treats the decision maker as "owning" a context-specific network, slowly assembled over time, connecting values, preferences, goals, actions, plans and strategies. In making a specific decision, this network is activated by either external stimuli (e.g. loss of status quo, presentation of a new possibility) or internal stimuli (e.g. discrepancy between actual and anticipated outcomes). This activation leads to search for the closest feasible path through the net. and new action choice.

Even this rather oversimplified contrast leads to a number of potentially testable empirical propositions. For example:

1. Typical number of options considered by a competent decision maker

TDT would predict many. IT few. (Note that the proposition concerns *competent* decision makers. A narrow search for options could be read as evidence either of an IT process or of an incompetent TDT process. Narrow search with good long-run effectiveness would thus be the crucial evidence.)

2. Extent of deliberation, speed of decision

TDT would imply relatively extensive deliberation, since large amounts of information need to be processed. IT predicts much less processing at the moment of choice, since most of the relevant considerations in matching action to purpose have been previously embedded in the network connections.

3. Cross-context transferability of decision skills

TDT predicts that individuals capable of skilled decision making in one context are likely to excell similarly in different contexts: they own and operate excellent decision engines. IT predicts much less transfer, since the network is specific to a particular context - a given disease group for a physician, a given investment category for a stockbroker.

4. Reliance on potentially flawed cognitive processes

Given the enormous recent interest in cognitive biases, illusions. fallacies and the like, it is worth noting that TDT appears heavily reliant on such inference-like processes, while IT is not. The latter may thus offer a more plausible account of good performance in real contexts than does TDT.

5. Implementation concerns

TDT yields action choice only at the highly abstract, model level, and thus faces potential difficulties translating this abstract recommendation into action on the ground. IT. in contrast, is concerned throughout with recognizable, concrete actions and consequences, so problems of back-translation arise much less.

6. Locus of subject-matter expertise

In TDT, subject-matter expertise is essentially "off-line", and distinct from decision making expertise. Indeed, the two types of expertise may well reside in different heads, with the decision maker acquiring subject-matter information from advisers or local experts as need arises. In IT, subject-matter expertise is central to the decision apparatus itself. It is difficult to imagine an IT decision maker delegating action selection to another, even a high-priced decision analyst!

7. Linkage to central values and principles

In TDT, action is linked to the decision maker's central values only indirectly, by means of an exogenous process by which values are made manifest as preferences over outcomes. In principle, as long as the decision maker can express preferences at the level of specific outcomes, issues of central, higher-level values need not arise. In contrast, IT explicitly links these higher-level values into the lower-level objectives, goals. and preferences, opening the possibility for a treatment of values endogenous to the decision process itself.

8. Articulability of decision process and results

Interestingly, either a TDT or an IT mode of arriving at a choice can be articulated or defended, though the terms of doing so differ from one to the other. A TDT explanation stresses the comprehensiveness of the analysis, the conformity with canons of rationality, the extent of computations and sensitivity analyses, the care with which optimal action was selected. An IT explanation would stress more the linkages: between the action chosen and other actions contemplated or already in process; and between the action chosen and important goals, values and objectives .

9. Selection of research subjects and tasks

TDT, with its implicit assumption of the generic central process, is free to use essentially any convenient subjects and tasks. College students playing low-stakes gambles are a perfectly reasonable and cost-effective choice. IT, in contrast, requires tasks and subjects for whom there has been reasonable opportunity to develop the postulated issue-specific network interconnections. This does not exclude student subjects, of course - students do in fact choose apartments, friends, sexual practices, work habits and areas of study, and may well have developed something more than rudimentary connections among the elements involved. They probably do not, however, routinely gamble with million-dollar stakes at known odds. Their performance in such tasks will thus tell us little of interest to IT.

As these examples suggest, there is substantial empirical content to the contrast we are drawing between TDT and IT conceptualizations. (We would claim, indeed, that substantial empirical support favors the IT over the TDT predictions in many of these issues, but our purpose here is theoretical rather than empirical comparison between the two). In retrospect, it is perhaps unfortunate that the majority of IT research to date has concerned a relatively peripheral cluster of concerns, those associated with the screening of options into a short list of serious candidates. Such screening processes are, certainly, of real interest, but they do not bear on the central theoretical contrasts between IT and TDT. The latter is simply silent on the matter: Options are generally treated as "given" or, in some models, as the results of (costly) search. IT does. of course, make specific predictions as to how screening will proceed - that it will be done by EBA or negative lexicographic filters, ignoring differences on any above-threshold dimension; and that information used in screening is not reused in later choice. Much evidence consistent with such mechanisms has been generated (see Beach 1993 for review). However, IT's predictions in this area are not central to the network vs. tree issues sketched above. and the mechanisms, if established, could as easily be appropriated by TDT as an exogenous, predecision process as taken as evidence hostile to it.

It is time now to take up the more central IT issues: just how interconnected and organized is the hypothesized network of values, strategies and goals in the mind of the competent decision maker? How is this net built up over time? Can alternative network structures yield equivalent performance in terms of successful choices? How broad are subject-matter domains? What elements do they include? Is the three-way division proposed in current versions of IT empirically supported, or is it merely an expository convenience? This line of inquiry is not much illuminated by research that takes, say, a value image and reduces it to a simple list. The guiding metaphor, after all. is that of the image. The items comprising it are not simply an ear, a nose, a mouth, an eye: they are a face, the elements organized, orderly, interconnected. These organizational issues have been central to psychology at least since the work of Bartlett (1932) on the importance of "active organization" in schemas. They have surfaced more recently in the decision making context in such work as that of Margolis (1987) on the role of patterns in cognition and thinking; in Pennington and Hastie's (1988) work on how stories are used to organize complex bodies of information, as in jury decisions; and in Jungermann's (1985) work on scenarios (stories about the future) in decision making. Future research on IT will need to address these issues of network scope, content and organization more seriously if it is to live up to its central metaphor: the image.

CONCLUSION

This essay has explored some of the central theoretical contrasts between Image Theory (IT) and Traditional Decision Theory (TDT). We have identified several such contrasts, and drawn from them a number of implications, some with real empirical content: number of options considered, generalizability of decision making skills, the importance of subject-matter expertise, and others. In each of these, the current version of IT, sketched earlier makes specific predictions, and will live or die on the empirical evidence.

We have not sought here to survey the empirical evidence to date (though we do believe it to be generally supportive of most predictions of current IT). Our purpose has been to anticipate the inevitable empirical setbacks, and to set out what is central to theories of the IT sort, what peripheral. We have identified several points of fundamental contrast between IT and TDT: the sorts of research that will illuminate each, the types of subjects and research tasks required. These are the seeds of an extensive research agenda.

We do not expect the current version of IT to survive unscathed. As particular predictions are sharpened and tested, we fully expect that IT will require major modification, even rethinking - as. indeed. TDT has been modified and refined in the empirical fires. What we have argued for here is precisely for the scope that allows such refinement. IT represents not a single theory but a class of theories: less generic, more contextual, more networked, less deliberative, than TDT. Our hope is that the work of constructing an empirically justified theory of this sort will not be abandoned at the first empirical set-back. What we now treat as TDT represents the flowering of several centuries of revision and refinement. We hope some of the same tolerance will be extended to the new theretical efforts currently represented by IT.

REFERENCES

Bartlett, F.C. (1932). *Remembering: a study in experimental and social psycholooy.* Cambridge, U.K.: Cambridge University Press.

Beach, L.R. (1990). *Image theory: Decision making in personal and organizational contexts.* Chichester, UK: Wiley

Beach, L.R. (1993). Image theory: Personal and organizational decisions. In G.A. Klein, J. Orasanu, R. Calderwood & C.E. Zsambok (Eds.). (1993), *Decision Making in Action: Models and Methods.* Norwood, N.J.: Ablex Publishing Co.

Beach, L.R. & Mitchell, T.R. (1987). Image theory: Principles, goals and plans in decision making. *Acta Psychologica, 66,* 201-220.

Beach, L.R. & Mitchell. T.R. (1990). Image theory: A behavioral theory of decisions in organizations. In B.M. Staw & L.L. Cummings (Eds.), *Research in organizational behavior, 12,* Greenwich, CT: JAI Press.

Beach, L.R., Smith, B., Lundell, J. & Mitchell. T.R. (1988), Image theory: Descriptive sufficiency of a simple rule for the compatibility test. *Journal of Behavioral Decision Making, 1,* 17-28.

Bissell, B.L. & Beach, L.R. (1993). *Image theory: The role of the compatibility test in situational diagnosis.* Technical report 93-12, University of Arizona. Department of Management and Policy.

Brown, F., Mitchell, T.R. & Beach,L.R. (1987). *Images and decision making: The dynamics of personal choice.* Technical report # 87-1. Seattle, WA, University of Washington, Department of Psychology.

Connolly, T. (1988). Hedge-clipping, tree-felling, and the management of ambiguity. In M.B. McCaskey, L.R. Pondy & H. Thomas (Eds.). *Managing; the challenge of ambiguity and change.* New York: Wiley.

Connolly, T. & Wagner, W.G. (1988). Decision cycles. In R.L. Cardy, S.M. Puffer & M.M. Newman (Eds.), *Advances in information processing in organizations (Vol.3.)* 183-205. Greenwich, CT: JAI Press.

Dunegan, K.J. (1993), Framing, cognitive modes and image theory: Toward an understanding of a glass half-full. *Journal of applied Psvchology, 78,* 491-503.

Hammond, K.R. (1988). Judgment and decision making in dynamic tasks. *Information and Decision Technologies, 14,* 3-14.

Harrison, E.F. (1975). *The Managerial Decision-Making Process.* Boston: Houghton Mifflin .

Jungermann. H. (1985), Inferential processes in the construction of scenarios. *Journal of Forecasting, 4,* 321-327.

Klein. G.A. (1989) "Recognition-primed decisions". In W.B. Rouse (Ed.), *Advances in man-machine system research,* 5, 47-92. Greenwich, CT: JAI Press.

Klein, G.A., Orasanu, J., Calderwood, R. & Zsambok, C.E. (Eds.) (1993), *Decision Making in Action: Models and Methods.* Norwood, N.J.: Ablex Publishing Co.

Lipschitz, R. (1989). *Decision making as argument driven action.* Boston: Boston University Center for Applied Social Science.

Margolis, H. (1987). *Patterns. thinking and cognition: A theory of judgment.* Chicago: University of Chicago Press.

Miller, G.A., Galanter, E. & Pribram, K.H. (1960). *Plans and the structure of behavior.* New York: Holt, Rinehart & Winston.

Montgomery, H. (1983). Decision rules and the search for dominance structure: Towards a process model of decision making. In P. Humphreys, O. Svenson & A. Vari (Eds.), *Advances in Psychology.* Amsterdam: North-Holland.

Noble, D. (1989). *Application of a theory of cognition to situation assessment.* Vienna. VA: Engineering Research Associates.

Pennington, N. & Hastie, R. (1988). Explanation-based decision making: Effects of memory structure on judgment. *Journal of Experimental Psychology: Learning. Memory and Cognition, 14 (3).* 521-533.

Simon, H.A. (1947), *Administrative behavior.* New York: Macmillan. 1947.

Tversky. A. & Kahneman. D. (1981). The framing of decisions and the psychology of choice. *Science, 211,* 453-458.

Contributions to Decision Making - I
J.-P. Caverni, M. Bar-Hillel, F.H. Barron and H. Jungermann (Editors)
© 1995 Elsevier Science B.V. All rights reserved.

CONTEXTUAL EFFECTS IN JUDGMENT AND CHOICE

Allen Parducci[1] and Jean-Marc Fabre[2]

1 University of California UCLA, Dept. of Psychology
CA 90024-1563 Los Angeles, USA
2 Université de Provence, 29, av. Robert Schuman,
13621 Aix-en-Provence Cedex 1, France

Abstract. The range and relative frequencies of contextual stimuli are shown to affect judgments and also choices. Consistency of response is a central theme of alternative models of frequency effects: Haubensak emphasized memory for previous responses to the same stimuli, Boillaud and Fabre the reduction of response ambiguity to maximize transmission of information. An experiment by Fabre and Molina demonstrated neutral-point anchoring of judgments of examination scores. Another, by Fabre and Besson, demonstrated that differing effects of sexual identification on judgments of income depend upon contextual differences induced by between-subject vs. within-subject designs. Mellers described how reversals of choice depend upon the range values of stimulus components just as judgments depend upon the contextual range. Parducci distinguished between utility and pleasure in a theory of happiness based on his range-frequency theory of judgment.

Contextual effects loom large in research on decision making and also in research on evaluative judgment. However, demonstrations that choices depend upon how the alternatives are "framed" have seemed a world apart from demonstrations that category ratings depend upon the frequency distribution of contextual stimuli. Where the research on decision making has focused more on marketplace types of choices, research on judgment has remained closer to the traditional psychophysical concern with the measurement of subjective experience and value.

Although our two workshops on contextual effects included efforts to bridge these differences, their main thrust was upon contextual effects as traditionally conceived in the study of evaluative judgments. The judgment of any stimulus reflects the relationship of that stimulus to the other stimuli with which it is presented. This is most clear in the case of simple psychophysical judgments: experimental manipulations of the range, relative frequencies, or spacings of contextual stimuli produce highly predictable shifts in the category ratings of any particular stimulus. Controversy tends to center on the theoretical interpretation of these well-established empirical phenomena.

RANGE-FREQUENCY THEORY

The range-frequency theory of judgment (e.g., Parducci, 1983) provided a starting point for theoretical discussion in this workshop. Range-frequency theory assumes that stimuli, whether presented simultaneously or successively, are represented in a context for the judgment of any particular stimulus. This context is conceived as a frequency distribution of values on an underlying stimulus dimension. The internal judgment of any particular stimulus is assumed to be a weighted average of its place in the range of contextual representations (its range value) and its percentile rank in the same context (its frequency value). The overt category rating is then a linear transformation of this internal judgment. In addition to psychophysical stimuli, like sizes of squares or pleasantness of tastes, range-frequency theory has had predictive success for judgments of cognitive materials, like imaginary scores on tests or verbal descriptions of different life situations.

Two, somewhat surprising phenomena have encouraged alternative interpretations of how the frequency distribution of contextual stimuli determines the judgments. When the stimuli are presented with unequal frequencies in distributions that are skewed, the effects of this skewing vary inversely with the number of rating categories but directly with the number of stimuli (Parducci and Wedell, 1986). Wedell's (1984) consistency model was developed to explain these phenomena without having to assume changes in the range-frequency weighting but instead by reducing the number of alternative categories that would have to be assigned to the same stimulus. The model assumes a very small context in which representations of any particular stimulus are limited to the size of the context divided by the number of rating categories (e.g., when the context has just 12 representations and ratings are in terms of just 4 categories, this limit would be 3). Two of the contributions to the workshop presented theoretical alternatives to this model.

HAUBENSAK'S CONSISTENCY THEORY

The first was the consistency theory developed by Gert Haubensak (Haubensak, 1992) in what may seem, at least initially, a radical departure from range-frequency theory. According to Haubensak, category ratings reflect attempts by the subject to provide a consistent set of responses to whatever stimuli are presented. Unless the range has changed, the subject gives the same response previously given to the same stimulus--insofar as it is remembered. Short- and long-term memory are described by two empirical parameters. When a presentation is either of a new stimulus or of an old stimulus that has been forgotten, it is assigned a category reflecting the direction of its difference from the closest of the remembered stimuli (or an intermediate category if it falls between two remembered stimuli).

Besides providing an alternative explanation of how the effects of skewing are affected by the number of categories and stimuli, Haubensak's consistency model gives a trial-by-trial account of the development of the rating scale at the level of individual subjects. It is at this level that the model has run into special difficulties, predicting a variability of response not found in empirical data (Parducci, 1992b). In the discussion, Haubensak suggested how these difficulties might be overcome, perhaps by incorporating the stimulus background as a determinant of one endpoint of the rating scale.

Haubensak also emphasized the usefulness of his consistency theory for explaining the transfer effects obtained when the frequency distribution of presented stimuli is shifted abruptly to another distribution. This elicited considerable discussion. Different experimenters have found wide differences in the tendency of subjects to hold on to their pre-shift scales, and even in whether initial presentations have any long-term effects (Parducci, 1992b).

Haubensak also presented the results of a new transfer experiment in which one stimulus near the middle of the set was anchored by instructions first to one category, then to a different category. Paradoxically, subjects shifted their scales so quickly and so completely that the data could be combined across the two orders of anchoring. By assuming a high rate of "forgetting" (in this case, a willingness to conform to the anchoring instructions), the data were shown to be highly consistent with the consistency model. However,

Haubensak also showed that a simple adaptation of the range-frequency model did almost as well.

Discussion brought agreement that, in spite of the apparent difference between Haubensak's approach and that of range-frequency theory, it has proven difficult to devise crucial tests. Haubensak argued for the theoretical simplicity of his own theory, emphasizing the explicit openness of its operations. However, he agreed that predictions from his theory were anything but intuitively simple, requiring averaging across many computer simulations for any particular experimental condition. There was little agreement on whether this version of consistency theory provides a better explanation of the quick development of the rating scale or whether it could account for category ratings of stimuli presented simultaneously.

MAXIMIZING INFORMATION TRANSMISSION

The second alternative to the Wedell model for explaining the effects of number of categories and number of stimuli was a process model developed by Eric Boillaud and Jean-Marc Fabre. Their approach is rooted in the idea that each evaluative judgment transmits information about which among a set of stimuli is being identified. This was the original interpretation of the frequency principle in range-frequency theory (Parducci, 1968), and it was this idea that was implemented by Wedell through his consistency model.

Following Fabre (1987, 1993), the discriminational-informational model presented by Boillaud and Fabre is based on an approach in which frequency and consistency principles are brought together under a single framework of information transmission: when a set of response categories has to be assigned to a set of stimuli, information theory shows that the maximum transmission of information is achieved by maximizing the amount of information in the responses. The latter measure depends both on the frequency principle (equalization of response frequencies) and the consistency principle (only one of the alternative categories of response assigned to each stimulus). The discriminability of the stimuli and the size of the past sequence used for computations are determined, respectively, by the model's two parameters: 1) a discriminational parameter determining the size of the intervals within which different stimulus values are not discriminated and are thus assigned the same response category, and 2) a parameter for the size of the working memory determining the number of past trials used to compute the response category to be assigned the currently presented stimulus, i.e., its momentary context for judgment.

Boillaud presented the results of computer simulations showing how this model captures major features of the empirical data on skewing, number of categories, and number of stimuli, including the effects of presenting one stimulus much more often than the others. The discussion concentrated on the difference between this model and Haubensak's with respect to its conception of consistency. According to Boillaud and Fabre, although consistency does allow for the assignment of a single category to different stimuli, it precludes assignment of different categories to successive presentations of the same stimulus that occur within the same limited span of working memory. Haubensak's algorithm for generating consistency can assign different categories to successive presentations of the same stimulus whenever the previous stimulus-response association has been forgotten. As in the model proposed by Wedell (1984), the present model also allows for a modification of the category scale within an experiment. Hence the Boillaud and Fabre model explicitly predicts an adaptation to contextual changes, contrary to Haubensak's conception of consistency. Discussion emphasized that the model's discriminational parameter is not simply a measure of discriminability but that it reflects the size of the attentional steps a subject uses for creating stimulus intervals. Within a given interval, different stimulus values may be perceived as identical or as similar enough to be treated as identical. Again, there is the problem of finding crucial experiments to discriminate between the alternative models of how the skewing of the context determines the judgments.

NEUTRAL-POINT ANCHORING

Jean-Marc Fabre described two new experiments, both studying shifts in category ratings that implied shifts in their contexts as these interacted with concrete representations of stimuli. The first of these, the work of Fabre and Guylaine Molina, bore on the social anchoring of the rating scale at a natural neutral-point of the stimuli, in partial replication of an experiment by Marsh and Parducci (1978). Although the same numerals were again employed as stimuli, these were now identified as scores achieved by different students on an examination rather than as monetary gains or losses. The between-subjects, factorial design manipulated the contexts (either wide range, narrow range, negatively skewed, or positively skewed) and the centering of scores (either all positive and centered at 100 or both negative and positive, centered at 0). The narrow range ran between either 70 and 130 or between -30 and +30, the wide range between either 50 and 150 or -50 and +50. Skewing was produced by varying the spacing of scores within each range; the positively-skewed context varied between either 70 and 150 or between -30 and +50; the negatively-skewed context between 50 and 130 or between -50 and +30. A third factor was whether the middle category of the rating scale was labeled neutral or "moyen" (average). The experimental instructions required subjects to rate the performance represented by each score, using one of five categories.

Although the results replicated Marsh and Parducci's demonstration of neutral-point anchoring at the zero point, the major new finding was that the ratings were also anchored at 100 for the sets of scores that were all positive. Thus, the occurrence of neutral-point anchoring seems more ubiquitous than suggested by Marsh and Parducci who speculated that it would be found only when there was a natural neutral point, such as the break-even point in gambling or the threshold between good and bad moral behaviors. However, the neutral-point anchoring found in the experiment by Fabre and Molina, whether at 0 or at 100, did not produce the symmetrical extensions of the contextual range that had been posited to explain the results of the earlier study: for example, -30 received the lowest possible rating, 1, whether it was presented in the positively-skewed or in the narrow-range context; similarly, +30 received the highest possible rating, 5, whether in the negatively-skewed or in the narrow-range context.

A possible explanation for these differences lies in the French custom of using the term "moyen" (average) to describe scores that have been graded as at least satisfactory or passing. This was the reason for the third factor in the experimental design, viz., whether the middle category of the rating scale was labelled "neutral" or "moyen." Although this difference in labeling did not have marked effects on the ratings, it suggests that for the French students who served as experimental subjects in this research, the score of 100 was interpreted as a just- passing grade. This would mean that the scores were themselves interpreted as grades that had already been assigned by the professor rather than as absolute levels of performance, such as number of items answered correctly on an exam. This would mean that the score of 100 was also interpreted as a natural neutral-point, like the break-even point in gambling or the threshold between good and bad moral acts. Even accepting this interpretation, there still remains the question of why the symmetry of inferred contextual ranges does not apply to professors' grades. One possibility that Molina is pursuing experimentally is that the subjects made global assessments of the skewed sets of scores. Since most of the scores in the positively-skewed set were below "moyen" or the passing level, the class as a whole was judged as failing. Given this judgment, the worst of these scores must be rated low indeed.

PERCEIVED SEXUAL DISCRIMINATION IN SALARIES

Between-subjects vs. Within Subjects Designs

The second of these empirical studies, this one by Fabre and Catherine Besson, takes a contextual approach to the ratings of the income of an imaginary employee who is described as either male or female. Because of the much publicized claims of sexual discrimination in this area, it seemed that the sex of employees might be an important factor determining the perceived adequacy of their incomes. The particular methodological goal of the study was to pursue a contextual distinction made by Birnbaum (1982) with respect to judgments of the responsibility of women who had been raped. Birnbaum replicated a study by Jones and Aronson (1973) who had concluded that the judged reponsibility depended on the social status of the victim: both married women and virgins were judged more responsible than women who had been divorced. Birnbaum demonstrated that although the counter-intuitive direction of these results is obtained using a between-subjects design in which the each subject judges the responsibility of only one classification of woman, the reverse is found using a within-subjects design in which each subject judges the responsibility of women in all three classifications. Birnbaum ascribed this difference to the establishment of separate contexts for each classification in the between-subject design but an overall context including all three classifications in the within-subject design.

Fabre and Besson hypothesized that identification of the sex of employees would affect the context for rating how high or low their incomes seem, with different contexts being established depending upon experimental design: in a within-subject design, the context represents the incomes of both sexes; but in a between-subject design, the context depends on the sex of the employee whose income is being rated.

For each of the subjects, all of whom were female students at the University of Provence, the stimuli were descriptions of two imaginary employees. The two could differ with respect to sex and also with respect to length of service and type of diploma (with the descriptions for each sex balanced for these last two factors and also for the order of presentation). In the between-subject design, the two descriptions presented each subject were either both male or both female. In the within-subject design, one was male and the other female. Subjects' task was to rate how high or low they judged the supposed income to be for both of the persons described, using seven categories from "very low" to "very high."

The results seem to confirm Birnbaum's analysis: in the between-subject design, the supposed income receives higher ratings when the imaginary employee is identified as female; and the reverse is true for the within-subjects design. Thus, in a context that includes the incomes of men, the supposed income is rated lower when it is earned by a woman.

Besson is currently conducting pilot studies in which the subjects are not students but rather are themselves employees. Surprisingly, the initial data suggest that the difference in results obtained in between- and within-subject designs disappears for these subjects. In both designs, the supposed income is rated higher when earned by a male than by a female, but overall these employees rate both men's and women's incomes lower than they were rated by students. It is still not clear whether this is because as employees they already have a single context of incomes for both sexes or whether it is because this sample of subjects includes both men and women.

TOWARDS A CONTEXTUAL THEORY OF CHOICE

In a contribution that addressed itself directly to contemporary concerns with effects of context upon choices, Barbara Mellers presented a theoretical analysis and also powerful empirical evidence for choice reversals produced by the range effects that have been a central concern in studying evaluative judgments. In her experiments, co-authored with Alan Cooke, student subjects were offered choices between apartments that varied both in price of rent and in distance from the university. The contextual ranges of both the rents and distances were varied independently in a factorial design, with comparisons focused on choices common to all conditions. When the range of rents was narrow, cheaper apartments were preferred to closer ones. When the range of rents was wide, closer apartments were preferred to cheaper ones.

Mellers and Cooke were also able to demonstrate these systematic reversals of preference in an experiment with only three trials, two of which extended the common range of either rents or distances. This answers the objection that such results depend on artificial conditions with hundreds of trials exposing the different levels of a factorial design.

Similar results were demonstrated when, instead of making choices, subjects judged the attractiveness of the same combinations of rent and distance. Subjects assign a higher rating to the cheaper apartment than to the closer apartment when the contextual range of rents is narrow, but the closer apartment gets the higher rating when this range is wide. Indeed, the effects of range were even more pronounced with attractiveness ratings than with choices.

These preference reversals, whether illustrated by choices or by differences in ratings of attractiveness, were well-predicted by a very simple theory. Mellers and Cooke assumed that subjects average the information about rent and distance to arrive at an overall evaluation of the apartment. Just as each average determines an apartment's rating of attractiveness, the direction of the difference between any two averages determines the choice. In computing each average, the scale values of the rent and the distance were assumed to reflect their places in the ranges of their respective contexts. These range values change to reflect the ranges in the different experimental conditions. In accordance with range-frequency theory, the difference in inferred range values for any two rents is greater when the range of rents in narrower. So too with distances.

Mellers concluded with a recommendation that we draw upon our understanding of the contexts for evaluative judgments in order to achieve a better understanding of the contexts for choices. Her research with Cooke supports this integration across what are typically treated as separate domains of research. She described the challenge of trying to relate particular types of framing effects upon choice behavior to contextual effects in judgment, emphasizing the absence of a more general theory of framing.

Much of the discussion focused upon Mellers' distinction between global effects of context upon choice (due to background stimulus distribution or reference level) and local effects (due to the particular choice set under consideration). She reviewed various examples of choice reversals contingent upon the framing of the choice or upon the particular reference level that had been established, both classified as global effects. Her present study clearly falls among the global. Discussants speculated about the generality of this distinction between global and local effects.

PLEASURES AND UTILITIES

A Contextual Theory of Happiness

Going back to the original, 18th-century conception of utility as the subjective experience of pleasure, Parducci (1968, 1984) adopts Bentham's utilitarian definition of happiness as a theoretical sum or mean across all hedonic experiences. This can be very different from contemporary conceptions of utility as inferred from preference or choice (cf., Kahneman and Varey, 1991). The distinction is exhibited by experimental subjects who respond differently to questions about pleasure and choice (e.g., Tversky and Griffin, 1992).

Parducci identifies pleasures and pains as internal judgments made on the dimension of utility or preference. Like any other evaluative judgment, the pleasantness of an experience is determined by its place in a context representing, in this case, other hedonic experiences. These contextual representations are conceived as a frequency distribution of values on the underlying dimension of utility. The scaling of this dimension is inferred from category ratings of pleasantness, using a range-frequency model of contextual effects in judgment.

The assumption that hedonic judgments follow range-frequency principles implies that the mean of all such judgments is proportional to the skewing of the contextual representations--insofar as these are representative of the actual hedonic experiences. Even when contexts are not truly representative, it is the piling up of these experiences near the upper endpoints of their contextual ranges that is crucial for the happiness defined by classical utilitarianism. One outcome might be preferred to another; but the less preferred is more pleasant when it is higher in its context than the more preferred is in its context. Only when different experiences share the same context can their pleasures be assumed to be a monotonic function of their utilities. However, in the spirit of Savage (1950), it would be consistent with utility theory to take future contexts and a theory of contextual effects into account when trying to decide between alternative choices.

Applications of this contextual theory of happiness run into the problem of inferring particular contexts for hedonic experiences. Although in part representative of recent experiences in the same domain, contexts can be biased by systematic drifts along the preference scale or by differential retention of pleasant or unpleasant experiences. Retention here is usually unconscious, implicit memories that affect the judgments without themselves being remembered in the sense of recall or recognition (Tulving and Schacter, 1990). Counter-intuitively, happiness would be greater when the contextual drift was downward or when the more painful experiences remained longer in the context.

Biological domains, such as eating or sex, may be the happiest, perhaps because they include natural optimums. However, most hedonic experiences seem to occur in the imagination, as with the pleasures of anticipating, remembering, and fantasizing. These are often stimulated by real-world activities, such as reading or conversation. Careful choices among these sources of stimulation help us control our daydreams and fantasies. Although setting high goals can diminish our pleasures from actual achievements, the joys of imagined success can more than counterbalance the negative effects of such high contextual endpoints. At least this is what is suggested by computer simulations that explored the range-frequency implications of establishing different kinds of context (Parducci, 1992a).

Discussion of the theory centered on its counter-intuitive implication that ecstasy is more frequent in negatively-skewed distributions. Although the frequency principle reduces the average judgment of experiences close to the upper endpoint, the greater frequency of such experiences insures more of the highest judgments. Whatever its position on the scale of preference, the worst of any hedonic context will be experienced as painful. The apparent inefficacy of Pollyanna-like social comparisons with the less fortunate was attributed by Parducci to their not being experienced as painful and thus not being represented in hedonic contexts.

AFTERTHOUGHTS

The various contributions to our workshops illustrate an extraordinarily diverse set of approaches to the study of contextual effects, from experimental studies of choice and judgment, through theories developed to explain psychophysical data and specific models of judgment that differ more in their algebraic details than in the general thrust of their ideas, and even a theory of happiness that is perhaps untestable in a truly scientific sense. The common thread is the predominant role that all of the contributions assign to contextual effects. The effects themselves are either directly observable, as in the experimental research, or at least imaginable as in the discussion of happiness. However, it is the nature of the context that must be inferred in all of these approaches. In the various models of judgment, the context may be identified with a set of stimuli actually presented for judgment or it may be inferred from shifts in the ratings obtained in actual experiments. Such inferences become much more conjectural for social judgments and the hedonic judgments of everyday life. However, one advantage of applying conceptions of context developed to explain judgments in situations where the contextual stimuli are so directly observable to situations in which they are not so directly observable is that the ambiguities of everyday discourse are constrained by the more precise conceptions.

REFERENCES

Birnbaum, M.H. (1982). Controversies in psychological measurement. In B. Wegener (Ed.), *Social attitudes and psychological measurement* (pp.401-485). Hillsdale, NJ: Erlbaum.

Fabre, J.-M. (1987). *La relativisation des jugements.* Thèse d'Etat, Université de Provence.

Fabre, J.-M. (1993). *Contexte et jugement.* Lille: Presses Universitaires de Lille.

Haubensak, G. (1992). The consistency model: A process model for absolute judgments. *Journal of Experimental Psychology: Human Perception and Performance, 18,* 303-309.

Jones, C., & Aronson, E. (1973). Attribution of fault to a rape victim as a function of the respectability of the victim. *Journal of Personality and Social Psychology, 26,* 415-419.

Kahneman, D., & Varey, C. (1991). Notes on the psychology of Utility. In J. Roemer and J. Elster (Eds.), *Interpersonal comparisons of well-being.* Cambridge: Cambridge University Press.

Marsh, H.W., & Parducci, A. (1978). Natural anchoring at the neutral point of category rating scales, *Journal of Experimental Social Psychology, 14,* 193-204.

Parducci, A. (1968). The relativism of absolute judgment. *Scientific American, 219,* 84-90.

Parducci, A. (1983). Category ratings and the relational character of judgment. In H.-G. Geissler, P. Petzold, H.F.J.M. Buffart, E.L.J. Leevwenerg, & V. Sarris (Eds.), *Modern issues in perception.* Berlin: VEB Deutscher Verlag der Wissenschaften.

Parducci, A. (1984). Value judgments: Toward a relational theory of happiness. In R. Eiser (Ed.), *Attitudinal judgment.* New York: Springer.

Parducci, A. (1992a). Elaborations upon psychophysical contexts for judgment: Implications of cognitive models. In H.-G. Geissler, S.W. Link, & J.T. Townsend (Eds), *Cognition, information processing, and psychophysics: Basic issues.* Hillsdale, NJ: Erlbaum.

Parducci, A. (1992b). Comment on Haubensak's Theory of judgment. *Journal of Experimental Psychology: Human Perception and Performance, 18,* 310-313.

Parducci, A., & Wedell, D.H. (1986). The category effect with rating scales: Number of categories, number of stimuli, and method of presentation. *Journal of Experimental Psychology: Human Perception and Performance, 12,* 496-516.

Savage, L.J. (1950). *The foundations of statistics.* New York: Wiley.

Tulving, E., & Schacter, E.L. (1990). Priming and human memory systems. *Science, 247,* 301-306.

Tversky, A., & Griffin, D. (1992). Endowment and contrast in judgments of well-being. In F. Strack, M. Argyle, & N. Schwartz (Eds.), *Subjective well being: An interdiciplinary perspective.* Oxford: Pergamon Press.

Wedell, D.H. (1984). A process model for psychophysical judgment. *Dissertation Abstracts International, 45,* 3102-B (University Microfilms International 8428589).

Contributions to Decision Making - I
J.-P. Caverni, M. Bar-Hillel, F.H. Barron and H. Jungermann (Editors)
111

AGGREGATION, RATIONALITY, AND RISK COMMUNICATION :THREE CURRENT DEBATES IN MEDICAL DECISION MAKING

D.R.M. Timmermans[1] P. Politser[2] and P.P. Wakker[1]

1 University of Leiden, Medical Decision Making Unit, PO Box 9600,
Bldg.43, 2300 RC Leiden, The Netherlands
2 M.I.T., 50 Memorial Drive 52-533
MA 02139 Cambridge, U.S.A.

Decision analysis prescribes a systematic way of decision making under uncertainty based on probability theory and utility theory. It is often used to solve complex medical decision problems, such as the following. "A 70 years old male who is a heavy smoker, has for over 10 years complained of chest pain indicative for angina pectoris. The nitroglycerine his physician prescribed relieved the pain immediately, but the pain returned occasionally over the past few weeks. His physician thinks the diagnosis of a progressive angina pectoris is very likely. This is the reason why this patient is eligible for a coronary bypass operation. There is a reasonably large chance that this operation will lead to a relief of the pain. A very small percentage of the patients dies during the operation. However, this patient has an increased mortality risk, because he suffers from hemophilia A. An angiogram shows that the angina pectoris is rather serious. There is a low chance that the result is a false positive."

The workshop addressed the following treee dilemnas in medical and other applications of decision analysis : individual versus aggregate analysis, deviations from EU theory, and the communication and the perception of risks.

DILEMMA 1: The individual versus the aggregate level

Aggregated empirical data play an important role in medical decision analysis. These data lead to probability and utility estimates for specific groups, and help to provide guidelines for now to deal with groups of patients. The use of such estimates has raised many questions. For instance, should we consider patients comparable and divisible into subgroups, and therefore most efficiently managed with aggregate guidelines, or are patients unique? Who, for instance, should have the greatest role in deciding whether the patient should undergo a coronary artery bypass operation: the patient, who takes a concrete individual view, or the doctor, who takes a more abstract aggregate view for similar patients, or third parties like hospitals or insurers, who balance aggregate costs and benefits in allocating resources?

In the first presentation Peter Politser (MIT) presented some data showing that lay people rely on different factors when making decisions than doctors. The former focus more on welfare conditions, while the latter focus more on the uncertainties in the decision. In the discussion Jim Shanteau (Kansas State University) emphasized that lay people and experts take different factors into account when making decisions which might cause miscommunications between patients and physicians.

The second issue was equity in health care. How do we adequately consider the equity of resource allocation in health care? Which methods do we need to assess preferences for the distribution of resources? Is it fair that the patient from the opening example with his age and history of smoking is eligible for a coronary bypass operation, while there is a long waiting list with patients who are younger and did not smoke? In the second presentation Rakesh Sarin (UCLA) discussed the issue of equity from individual, group and social viewpoints. Generally, people believe that good but also bad things should more or less be equally divided among people. In relation to health care, it is assumed undesirable that some privileged groups benefit more from health care than others. When formalizing equity issues, different divisions of people into specific groups may lead to differences in the equity of health benefits. When dividing people, for instance, into men and women health policies might seem fair, while a division into blacks and whites of the same group of people seems unfair. Equity in health care is thus related to how one defines groups. Martin Weber (University of Mannheim) emphasized this in his discussion of the paper. He also drew the attention to different kinds of risks. Things are different for voluntary and involuntary risks. Surely, people are free to endure the risks they want (such as mountain climbing), but should they have the same rights to health care as people who do not take these risks? What is the criterion of fairness in relation to health risks such as infant mortality: should one measure it against infant mortality in earlier days or against the risk of the group with the lowest infant mortality? What is the reference point? Most physicians, however, refuse to make decisions on other than medical grounds. Equity is not an useful criterion for them, because what is equitable is difficult to determine. It is simply not possible to find out who is most "guilty" of his/her disease. In their view, the patient with angina pectoris can only be refused treatment, if his chances to survive the operation are much lower than those of a non-smoker.

The general discussion continued by emphasizing the complexity of the equity issue which can be viewed from different perspectives. This leaves also ample room for manipulation by policy makers. A conclusion was that more research is needed about the different roles of patients and physicians in medical decisions, and that the issue of equity in relation to health care is becoming more important.

DILEMMA 2: Deviations from EU theory

People do not always make decisions according to EU theory. They may overweigh small probabilities and do not always revise probabilities adequately after receiving new information. In treatment problems, they may judge unfavorable outcomes attributed to doctors' actions as more serious than those caused by inaction. In diagnostic problems they may do the opposite. How should we deal with decision makers' deviations from the EU model? Is it sensible that the physician, when deciding what to do, takes into account the regret she might feel when the patient from the opening example, who is in a bad shape, dies during the operation and the angina turns out not to have been very serious? Should we include factors such as responsibility and anticipated regret in a normative model?

Jane Beattie (University of Sussex) discussed the notion of decision aversion, which might be caused by the anticipated regret involved in making a decision. There is a trend in medicine to increase patients' involvement in treatment decisions. Although this involvement yields many benefits, there are also some costs. If a pregnant woman, for instance, has a choice whether or not to do prenatal screening, this may lead to stress. Because these tests induce a risk for the unborn baby, the woman has to trade-off the risk of having a handicapped baby (when no screening is done) against having a spontaneous abortion due to the tests. Data show that some women are very averse to making this kind of decisions.

George Wu (Harvard University), in his discussion of the paper, mentioned that regret can be reduced by a proper framing of decisions, and discussed whether regret should be modelled as an attribute of utility. Important in this context is how much one might want to pay (in terms of a reduction in expected utility) for taking into account the anticipated regret. Furthermore, participants of the workshop felt that the regret patients would feel, should play a role in decisions. Physicians, however, should not let their personal emotions influence the optimal decision for the patient.

Another issue which was discussed, is how physicians assess probabilities, e.g. the probability that the angina pectoris is progressive after learning about the result of the angiogram, and how physicians process probabilities in general. John Fox (Imperial Cancer Research Fund) argued that decision analysis is inadequate for medical practice, because it leaves out the important step of recognizing that there is a problem and how to structure that decision problem. Instead of a Bayesian reasoning model to establish the most probable disease on the basis of symptoms and test results, he proposed a model that makes use of argumentations. Argumentations for or against a certain disease increase or decrease the probability of disease. Embedded in a formal mathematical framework, a set of argumentations leads to a decision network or argumentation structure suggesting the most plausible outcome. This approach is assumed to be more natural for physicians to use than Bayesian reasoning, and is part of a general decision technology that has been developed by Fox and his colleagues to achieve maximal flexibility.

Patrick Bossuyt (University of Amsterdam), in his discussion of the paper, pointed out that decision technologies should not only be flexible, but should also satisfy optimality criteria. The advantage of using decision analysis in medicine compared with AI applications, is that decision analysis provides objective criteria to compare clinical strategies, and can thus justify clinical practice. He also called attention to the growing role of decision analysis in medical practice. He argued that, contrary to some years ago, decision analysis is widely accepted as an approach to solve medical problems, even to the extent that people accept decision analytic solutions without critically examining the model or the data used in the model. In the general discussion, some participants argued that a decision analytic framework may very well be used in medical practice and that an argumentation based decision model should be considered as an additional tool for, e.g., the generation of alternatives.

DILEMMA 3: Communication and perception of risks

Legal doctrine often allows medical interventions once the patient is informed of the risks, and approves. Often risks are communicated in verbal terms. The question is how the physician should communicate the risks of surgery versus continuation of medication to the patient. Is the description in the opening example sufficient or should the physician provide numerical information? Would percentages enable the patient to make a rational trade-off of the different risks? Many researchers have tried to explain why people use verbal terms to communicate risks. Ido Erev (Technion Haifa) disagreed with the view that verbal terms are used because people can communicate risks more efficiently in verbal terms than in percentages. He argued that we should adapt a game theoretical approach. Communication could be seen as a game, in which people have different goals they want to achieve. A hypothetical example is the following. Although physicians want to choose the best treatment for the specific patient, they might also want to introduce some vagueness in the communication of the different risks. This vagueness of risks involved induces a variability in the treatment preferred by different patients. Not all patients prefer the same treatment. This in turn might provide physicians with a wider experience in treatments. Processes like this may play a role in patient-physician communications and could be studied from a game theoretical perspective. More attention should be given to the functions, other that conveying the truth, that verbal probability terms play in communication.

Karl Teigen (Tromsφ University), in his discussion of the paper, elaborated on this. To create behavioral variability is just one of the possible functions. Whether a person prefers to use verbal or numerical probabilities may depend on the different aims in a communicative setting. Does a person want to be maximally informative or simply to sound convincing? Is the aim to create agreement or to be encouraging? Or is the primary aim not to be blamed if proven wrong? Or does a person have several (maybe contradictory) goals, he/she wants to achieve? Different needs may lead to different preferences for the sender and receiver of the communication. In the general discussion it was argued that in a medical setting the vagueness of verbal terms make risks more acceptable to patients.

People's interpretation of these verbal terms may differ and may also depend on context. It is possible that patients and physicians differ in the appraisal of the several risks involved, i.e., the risk of surgery and a possible increased risk of an heart attack when continuing the medication. What are the factors that influence the acceptability of medical risks? How do people handle these risks? How much impact on risk perception do the following factors have: whether the risk is controllable, ambiguous, and whether it is caused by action or inaction? Willem Albert Wagenaar (University of Leiden) presented some data about framing experiments (cf. Asian disease problem) in which subjects were asked to give verbal terms to percentages. Results show that subjects, by means of giving labels, construct a dominance structure of the decision problem which is no longer a dilemma, because one alternative is clearly dominant. However, subjects turned out to give different interpretations to percentages depending on the outcomes, e.g. if there are human lives at stake or "only" butterflies etc.

Ilana Ritov (Ben Gurion University), in her discussion of the paper, called attention to other factors which might affect patients' perception of risks, such as whether the risk is caused by action or inaction, and the ambiguity of risks which might change people's perception of the risk. The general discussion further dealt with what should be the best way to communicate risks to patients. Verbal terms have the advantage of vagueness, but percentages are more exact. However, if patients do not interpret percentages in an exact way, but attach verbal labels to them, are percentages still preferable? The general discussion led to the conclusion that more research is needed on the communication of risks, especially between patients and physicians in relation to how patients handle these risks.

In conclusion: the papers and the discussions in this workshop all referred to three dilemmas related to the prescriptive role of EU theory, which are:

(1) *Equity: the individual versus the group.* How should we give health care to people in a fair way when budgets are shrinking? Who should decide whether or not a certain treatment for a specific patient is appropriate?

(2) *Rationality: normative versus descriptive models.* How should we model violations of EU theory such as regret? What should we do with deviations from Bayesian reasoning?

(3) *Ambiguity: verbal versus numerical risks.* Is ambiguity in the communication between physicians and patients by using verbal risk terms good or bad? How do patients perceive risks?

The workshop and several other presentations at the conference, showed an increasing interest in the study of medical decisions from a psychological point of view. It also showed that the themes discussed in the workshop are of interest to (psychological) researchers as well as practitioners in the field of medical decision making.

SECTION 3

Experimental and modeling papers

Contributions to Decision Making - I
J.-P. Caverni, M. Bar-Hillel, F.H. Barron and H. Jungermann (Editors)
121

RATIONALITY OF EXPECTATIONS IN

JUDGMENTAL EXTRAPOLATION OF TIME SERIES

Fergus Bolger and Nigel Harvey

University College, Gower Street
WC1E 6BT London, UK

Abstract. A major assumption upon which current macroeconomic theory is based is that expectations are "rational", that is, judgmental forecasts make use of all relevant available information. An alternative view, taken from forecasting practice, is that forecasts are made so that a trend apparent in historic data is extrapolated into the future. Within psychology the rationality of judgment and decision making has been assessed relative to normative models and generally has been found to be wanting. The widely accepted explanation for these findings is that, because of capacity limitations, people reason using heuristics which usually work but sometimes lead to biases. One type of heuristic, the anchor-and-adjust heuristic, can be used to form expectations in a manner consistent with the extrapolative hypothesis. We report an experiment designed to test whether judgmental forecasts are made according to the rational expectations hypothesis or by using heuristics. Subjects viewed graphs of simulated sales over a 45-day period and forecast sales for the next day. The graphs were varied according to the trend and serial dependence that they contained in order to simulate forecasting conditions in the real world. Our results revealed that forecasts were suboptimal and biased. This leads us to reject the rational expectations hypothesis and conclude that people make judgmental forecasts through the use of heuristics.

Are the expectations that people form "rational" and, if not, upon what basis is the future anticipated? The answers to these questions have practical implications for econometric and forecasting practice in particular, and decision support in general. They also have theoretical implications for our conception of human rationality and what this implies for cognitive models of judgment and decision making.

Expectations play a key role in macroeconomics, where the value of expected variables such as future income or interest rates directly influences important economic relationships such as consumption and money-demand functions. These relationships are then combined into full macroeconomic models with significant policy implications (see Attfield, Demery & Duck, 1991). Within economics several different expectation-formation hypotheses have been proposed; of these, the one currently dominant is known as the *rational expectations hypothesis* (Pennant-Rea & Crook, 1986; Attfield et al., 1991). According to this hypothesis, people take all relevant sources of information into account when forming their expectations and do so in an optimal manner (Muth, 1961; Minford, 1992). The predictions from this hypothesis are that the mean of forecast errors will be zero, that these errors will exhibit no pattern, and that the variance of errors will be equal to or lower than the variance of errors produced by any other forecasting technique (see Attfield et al., 1991). Expectations also play an important role in microeconomic models. Models in which people solve dynamic optimization problems also invoke the assumption of rational expectations (see Hanson and Sargent, 1980).

The rational expectations hypothesis is at odds with evidence from psychological research into judgment and decision making. A considerable body of work suggests that people neither take into account all relevant sources of information when making a decision nor make use of this information in an optimal manner (see Kahneman, Slovic and Tversky, 1982; Payne, Bettman, & Johnson, 1992). Rather, the generally accepted view is that — because of cognitive capacity limitations — people use *heuristics* which by their nature are fallible. Heuristic use consequently results in *biases* in judgment from time to time (e.g. Simon, 1956; Tversky & Kahneman, 1974). People are therefore seen as being irrational relative to optimal normative procedures, and this is used as justification for aiding judgment or replacing it with statistical methods. Expectation formation is not excepted from this conclusion regarding the limits of human reasoning. Several studies of forecasting have found suboptimalities in estimation relative to statistical forecasting techniques (e.g. Lawrence & Makridakis, 1989; Sanders & Ritzman, 1992; Timmers & Wagenaar, 1977; Wagenaar & Sagaria, 1975; Wagenaar & Timmers, 1978, 1979). Further, specific heuristics which forecasters employ have been identified (Bolger & Harvey, 1993; Harvey, Bolger & McClelland, 1994; Lawrence & O'Connor, 1992).

Given these psychological findings, where does the rational expectations hypothesis stand? To date few attempts have been made to test the rational expectations hypothesis directly but those tests which have been conducted provide little support for the hypothesis (see Hudson, 1982; Pesaran, 1987; Sheffrin, 1983). However, economists seem content to accept that expectations are rational on pragmatic grounds alone, namely, that assuming rationality permits the construction of consistent and stable econometric models. These models seem to account for the observed data as well as, if not better than, models based on different assumptions of expectation formation. Since economists do not appear to have looked to psychologists for guidance about the actual processes of expectation formation, nor have psychologists spent much time on this issue, there is a lack of a realistic alternative to the assumption of rationality. In view of this lack of competition it is not surprising that econometric models incorporating the rational expectations hypothesis can be upheld on pragmatic grounds.

Against this background, the current study was designed to investigate the rational expectations hypothesis and to identify the true mechanisms of expectation formation if and when judgmental forecasting departs from optimal. From a practical perspective, such a strategy should at worst provide empirical support for the most prevalent approach to econometric modelling, and at best permit improved modelling. Hence we shall examine whether forecasting error is larger than that to be expected on the basis of rational expectations and provide some estimate of the size of any such mismatch. From a theoretical standpoint, research into the cognitive processes involved in expectation formation will shed light on the status of human rationality in general and, more particularly, increase our understanding of what is an important everyday psychological function — anticipation of the future.

METHOD

Subjects

Forty-three subjects participated in the experiment. These subjects were all prospective undergraduate psychologists who were visiting the University College London Psychology Department on open-days or for interviews. Ages ranged from 16 to 30 years, with the majority being under 20 years old. Approximately two-thirds were female. The subjects were not paid for their participation but prizes were awarded for the best forecasters.

Materials

The stimuli consisted of one hundred and five 45-point time-series plots. The graphs were generated by computer before the start of the experiment. Series varied in terms of trend (none, up or down), which was achieved by incrementing or decrementing the mean by a small constant at each time interval. Series also varied in the degree of correlation between each point and its immediate predecessor (first-order autocorrelation), and between each point and the point two behind (second order autocorrelation). The first-order autocorrelation ranged from −.87 to +.77 and the second-order autocorrelation ranged from −.69 to +.49. All series were generated using a model which contained parameters for both first- and second-order autocorrelation — these parameters were varied in order to produce individual series. Gaussian noise was added to each series by randomly sampling from a normal distribution with a mean of zero and a standard deviation of 2. The series were labelled *sales* on the ordinate and *days* on the abscissa. The scale was such that sales were always substantially above zero and the level of sales to be forecast was around 91 (range 74 to 109) in all series. Examples of stimulus series are given in Figure 1.

Design and Procedure

Each subject participated in one of five experimental sessions. All the subjects within an experimental session saw the same 21 stimulus series selected from the total of 105 so as to be approximately balanced in terms of trend and spread of autocorrelation. Within each session, which lasted about 20 minutes, the subjects were first briefed orally as a group. They were told that they would be taking part in a computer-controlled experiment concerned with forecasting. Specifically, they were asked to regard themselves as factory managers who were required to predict sales for the next day on the basis of sales for the previous 45 days. They were told that forecasts were to be made for each of 21 products made in the factory. A couple of example trials were then demonstrated on a large monitor.

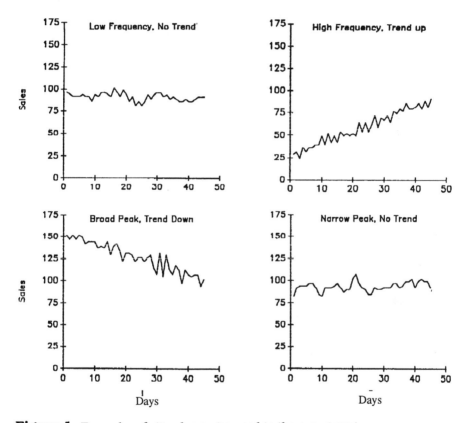

Figure 1. Examples of stimulus series used in the experiment.

Next the subjects were shown into individual cubicles containing a microcomputer with a colour monitor and two joystick controls, one with red buttons and the other with yellow ones. Once the subjects had read the further written instructions provided, they could initiate the experimental session by pressing any red button on the left-hand joystick. When such a button was pressed, the first graph was presented on the screen. By moving the right-hand joystick a small dot could be made to move up and down the screen in the position of the 46th day. The forecast was made by positioning this dot then pressing one of the yellow buttons on this joystick. Pressing a red joystick button allowed the subject to move on to the sales graph for the next product. The "true" value of sales was indicated on the graph before the next trial began.

The experiment was self-paced. After all 21 trials were completed the subjects were presented with a message on the screen telling them that the experiment had finished and thanking them for participating. Each subject's 21 forecasts were then saved to disk.

RESULTS

Tests of the Rational Expectations Hypothesis

An assumption underlying the rational expectations hypothesis is that expectations should be formed on the basis of all information available at the time a forecast is made. This being the case, errors in forecasts can only be due to that aspect of the series which cannot be predicted from observation of the past: the random noise in the series. Put another way, the difference between the forecast for a given time and the true value of the series at that time should be equal to random error with a mean of zero and a constant variance. This assumption can therefore be tested by regressing the forecast for a given period on to the true value of the series at that period. For the assumption to be true the intercept should be zero, the slope should be unity, and the residuals shoud be random noise (see Attfield et al., 1991). The regression performed was therefore

$$F_t = \alpha + \beta X_t + e_t$$

where X_t and F_t are the true value and the forecast of time t respectively. If the rational expectations hypothesis is correct then α should be zero and β equal to one.

The mean forecast for each of the 105 different series was calculated. This involved averaging over the forecasts of all the subjects who saw a particular series (n = 8, 9, 11, 10 and 5 for each of the five blocks of stimulus items respectively). Averaging over different numbers of subjects can lead to heteroscedasticity;

however, no evidence for this was found in the plot of the residuals. The 46th point of each series had been generated along with the preceding points before the experiment but was withheld from subjects until after their forecast for that period. This true value of the 46th point in each of the 105 series was regressed on to the mean forecasts. The resulting value for the intercept was 35.7, not zero, as predicted by the rational expectations hypothesis, and the slope was 0.607 not unity. This underestimation in slope is consistent with what would be expected if judgments were subject to a range-contraction effect (see Poulton, 1989). The regression accounted for 44.8% of the variance (adjusted R^2). The correlation of the residuals against the fitted true values of the series did, however, indicate that the error term was noise since $r = 0.001$.

A second test of the rational expectations hypothesis is considered to be a stronger test than the first. It relies on the assumption that, to be rational, expectations must be formed in accordance with the process by which the true values of the series are produced (see Attfield et al., 1991). Thus if the to-be-forecast values of the series are regressed upon every preceding data point in the series, beta weights so obtained should equal the beta weights obtained by regressing the judgmental forecasts on to the same predictors. The residuals should again be uncorrelated with the fitted values of Y. The following two regressions were therefore performed:

$$X_{46} = \beta_1 X_1 + \beta_2 X_2 + ...\beta_{45} X_{45} + e$$

$$F_{46} = \tau_1 X_1 + \tau_2 X_2 + ...\tau_{45} X_{45} + e$$

where X_t is the true value and F_t the forecast at time t. For the rational expectations hypothesis to be correct β_t should equal τ_t.

These regressions were performed with 105 values of each variable. When predicting the true value of the series for the 46th time point, the previous values of the series accounted for 69.9% of the variance whereas in the prediction of the forecast 86.2% of the variance was accounted for (both figures are adjusted R^2 values). A repeated-measures t-test on the two sets of beta weights provided no evidence that the difference between these weights is equal to zero ($t(44) = 0.00$, $p = 1.00$); thus the rational expectations hypothesis can again be rejected. Inspection of the beta weights revealed that the main difference between the two sets is that the weighting at each time period is approximately equal for the regression of the true value of the series on to its predecessors whereas for the judgmental forecasts the last observed data point in the series is very heavily weighted relative to the other points in the series. Analysis of the residuals showed no systematic departure from the assumption of random error.

One problem with this test of the rational expectations hypothesis is that, for our data, four different autoregressive types are mixed together. This means that the relationship between the true value (X_{46}) and the previous values of the series is different from one type of series to another. In order to address this problem we separated out the four different autoregressive types and conducted a test for each type. Unfortunately the number of data points was reduced to as little as 20 for one type of series which forced us to limit the regressions to the 19 points immediately preceding the forecast (X_{27} to X_{45}). This analysis did not provide any support for the rational expectations hypothesis either (note that the degree of freedom for t-tests, which is given in parentheses, was reduced in two instances due to collinearity): narrow peak, $t(13) = .33$, $p = .75$; high frequency, $t(18) = -.42$, $p = .68$; low frequency, $t(18) = -.03$, $p = .98$; broad peak, $t(15) = -.09$, $p = .93$.

Analysis of Forecast Errors

Given that the judgmental forecasts of our subjects do not appear to have been formed in accordance with the rational expectations hypothesis it can be assumed that forecasts are suboptimal. In this section we examine both the degree of forecast error relative to the best forecast that could be made and the factors to which this suboptimality might be attributed.

Optimal forecasts were produced for each series by determining the first- and second-order autocorrelation in the series and using these parameters to extrapolate the next point, adding trend as appropriate. These optimal forecasts are similar to the actual one-step-ahead values of the series without the noise component. However, the values of the autoregressive parameters are empirically derived for the production of the optimal forecasts, but pre-determined for the generation of the original series. The difference between these two sets of values is attributable to sampling error.

Forecast error was summarized as mean absolute percent error (MAPE) of the judgmental forecasts from the optimal forecasts. Overall forecast error thus calculated was 5.96% or approximately 5.5 sales units on our graphs. If forecasts had been made optimally the error would of course have been 0%. It was expected on the basis of previous research that both trend and type of autoregressive pattern in the series would contribute to the size of forecast error (e.g. Bolger & Harvey, 1993; Lawrence & Makridakis, 1989). A 2-way repeated measures ANOVA was therefore performed on the MAPE scores. There were three levels of trend (flat, up, down) and four levels of autoregressive type which distinguished their spectral properties (a broad peak at mid-range frequencies, a narrow peak at mid-range frequencies, a peak at low frequencies only, a peak at high frequencies only). The four autoregressive types were determined a posteriori from their autoregressive parameters as described by Gottman (1981, chap. 12). There were approximately equal numbers of each type of stimulus. The MAPE scores from different stimulus series of the same type were averaged to produce 12 MAPE scores per subject (three kinds of trend times four autoregressive types) and the ANOVA was performed on these composite scores.

The ANOVA revealed significant main effects of both trend and autoregressive type: $F(2, 84) = 20.83$, $p < .001$ and $F(3, 126) = 18.83$, $p < .001$ respectively. There was also a significant two-way interaction of Trend x Autoregressive Type: $F(6, 252) = 8.27$, $p < .01$. The means and standard errors broken down by trend and autoregressive type are shown in Figure 2.

From an examination of Figure 2 it can be seen that errors for trended series are generally larger than those for untrended series, with the largest error being for upward trended series. Those autoregressive types which are characterized by a broad, mid-range frequency peak appear overall to have the highest errors but the series with by far the largest errors are those with both broad peaks and upward trends. Post hoc tests showed that the only significant effects were for the broad peaked series, where size of error is different for all levels of trend.

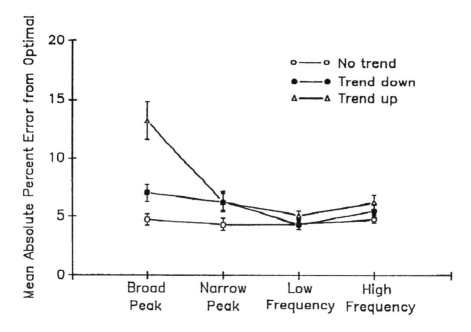

Figure 2. Mean absolute percent error from optimal for judgmental forecasts shown as a function of type of trend and autocorrelation. Standard errors shown by vertical lines.

Simulating Forecasting Strategy

Since our subjects' forecasts were imperfect they must have been using some strategy other than that described by the rational expectations hypothesis. It thus appears that our subjects were using a suboptimal forecasting strategy, or heuristic. This resulted in fairly large errors which were not attributable to the unpredictable noise in the series. From the regression of forecasts on to previous values of the series it appears that this heuristic places heavy weight on the last observed data point. Such a heuristic might be the commonly used forecasting strategy known as *Naive Forecast 1* (NF1), which requires no knowledge of the generating process in order to be applied and thus constitutes a benchmark against which supposedly more sophisticated strategies should show an improvement (see e.g. Makridakis, Wheelwright & McGee, 1983). NF1 makes no adjustment for trend or autocorrelation. Such lack of compensation for features of the series may have contributed to the higher forecasting errors for trended series than untrended, and for broad-peaked autoregressive types relative to the other types. To test this hypothesis we simulated the forecast errors which would have occurred if subjects made their forecasts by simply repeating the last data point. The pattern of errors relative to optimal produced by forecasting using this NF1 heuristic are shown in Figure 3.

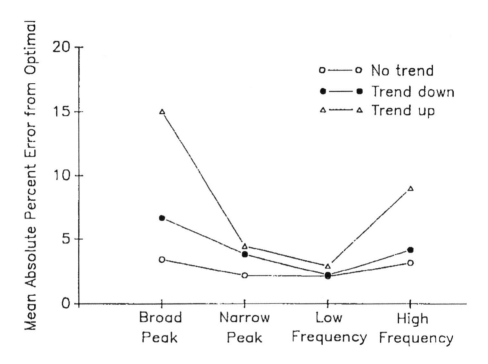

Figure 3. Mean absolute percent error from optimal for NF1 forecasts shown as a function of type of trend and autocorrelation.

Comparison of Figure 3 with Figure 2 reveals that the NF1 heuristic results in a pattern of errors which closely mirrors that found for the judgmental forecasts. The highest NF1 errors are for series with a broad-peaked frequency characteristic. Such series consist of a mixture of several mid-range frequencies and as such may be difficult to predict. Also broad-peaked series have negative first- and second-order autocorrelation, which would make a forecasting strategy based on repetition of the last or second-to-last points very prone to error. The next highest errors are for series with high frequency characteristics, which also have negative first-order correlation (although positive second order). Since the NF1 strategy makes no adjustment for trend, errors for trended series should be greater than errors for untrended series. However, why this should be largely restricted to upward trends is unclear. The fact that this effect of trend is replicated in the simulation suggests that it is not due to a feature of judgment such as compensation for differential proximity of the axes from the ends of upward- and downward-trended series. We therefore assume that the observed trend effect must reflect particular characteristics of the random sample of upward-trended series generated for the experiment. It is interesting to note that even using this rather crude heuristic the overall level of forecast error was lower than that of our subjects (4.83% compared with 5.96%).

DISCUSSION

Using stimulus series with characteristics which are common in real-world series, namely, trend and autocorrelation, we found no support for the rational expectations hypothesis either in terms of direct tests or in terms of the size of forecast errors relative to optimal "rational" forecasts. Rather than making their forecasts optimally on the basis of all the information in the series our subjects appeared to form their expectations on the basis of the last observed data point in the series only. No indication of any significant attempt to correct for autocorrelation in the series was found. The large errors for series which had negative first-order autocorrelation can be attributed to use of the NF1 heuristic, which performs poorly for these types of series. No compensation seems to have been made for trend either. The errors for trended series were therefore greater than for untrended series. Series with autocorrelation and/or trend are frequently encountered in real-world forecasting (see Box & Jenkins, 1976; McCleary & Hay, 1980; Pandit and Wu, 1983) thus the irrationality demonstrated by our subjects could equally well be manifest in practical settings.

Finally, a question arises for future research. Although the pattern of errors seems to be well characterized by the use of the NF1 heuristic for forecasting, this may not be an accurate reflection of what people are actually doing. Previous research (Bolger & Harvey, 1993) suggests that heuristic use is context-sensitive. In other words, different information is used as the basis of expectation formation depending on the type of series to be forecast. The global view of NF1 heuristic use may conceal more sophisticated heuristic selection at a finer level of analysis. In order to investigate this possibility it would be necessary to require that subjects make a larger number of forecasts for any given type of series than was the case in the current study. Such a procedure should also permit us to see whether the worryingly large errors for broad-peaked series with upward trends are a genuine effect or an artefact of the particular stimulus series that we used.

REFERENCES

Attfield, C.L.F., Demery, D. & Duck, N.W. (1991). *Rational expectations in macroeconomcs: An introduction to theory and evidence* (2nd ed.). Oxford: Blackwell.

Bolger, F. & Harvey, N. (1993). Context-sensitive heuristics in statistical reasoning. *Quarterly Journal of Experimental Psychology, 46A,* 779-811.

Box, G.E.P. & Jenkins, G.M. (1976). *Time series analysis: Forecasting and control, revised edition.* San Francisco: Holden-Day.

Gottman, J.M. (1981). *Time-series analysis: A comprehensive introduction* for *social scientists.* Cambridge: Cambridge University Press.

Hansen, L.P. & Sargent, T.J. (1980). Formulating and estimating dynamic linear rational expectations models. *Journal of Economic Dynamics and Control, 2,* 7-6.

Harvey, N., Bolger, F. & McClelland, A. (1994). On the nature of expectations. *British Journal of Psychology,* 85, 203-229.

Hudson, J. (1982). *Inflation: A theoretical survey and synthesis.* London: George Allen and Unwin.

Kahneman, D., Slovic, P. & Tversky, A. (Eds.). (1982). *Judgment under uncertainty: Heuristics and biases.* Cambridge: Cambridge University Press.

Lawrence, M. & Makridakis, S. (1989). Factors affecting judgmental forecasts and confidence intervals. *Organizational Behavior and Human Decision Processes, 42,* 172-187.

Lawrence, M. & O'Connor, M. (1992). Exploring judgmental forecasting. *International Journal of Forecasting, 8,* 15-26.

Makridakis, S., Wheelwright, S.G. & McGee, V.E. (1983). *Forecasting methods and applications.* New York: Wiley.

McCleary, R. & Hay, R.A. (1980). *Applied time series analysis for the social sciences.* Beverly Hills: Sage.

Minford, P. (1992). *Rational expectations macroeconomics: An introductory handbook.* Oxford: Blackwell.

Muth, J.F. (1961). Rational expectations and the theory of price movements. *Econometrica, 29,* 315-335.

Pandit, S.M. & Wu, S.M. (1983). *Time series and system analysis with applications.* New York: Wiley.

Payne, J.W., Bettman, J.R. & Johnson, E.J. (1992). Behavioral decision research: A constructive processing perspective. *Annual Review of Psychology, 43.*

Pennant-Rea, R. & Crook, C. (1986). *The Economist economics.* London: Penguin.

Pesaran, M.H. (1987). *The limits to rational expectations.* Oxford: Basil Blackwell.

Poulton, E.C. (1989). *Bias in quantifying judgment.* New Jersey: Erlbaum.

Sanders, N.R. & Ritzman, L.P. (1992). The need for contextual and technical knowledge in judgmental forecasting. *Journal of Behavioral Decision Making, 5,* 39-52.

Simon, H.A. (1956). Rational choice and the structure of the environment. *Psychological Review, 63,* 129-138.

Sheffrin, S.M. (1983). *Rational expectations.* Cambridge: Cambridge University Press.

Timmers, H. & Wagenaar, W.A. (1977). Inverse statistics and misperception of exponential growth. *Perception and Psychophysics, 21,* 558-562.

Tversky, A. & Kahneman, D. (1974). Judgment under uncertainty: Heuristics and biases. *Science, 185,* 1124-1131.

Wagenaar, W.A. & Sagaria, S.D. (1975). Misperception of exponential growth. *Perception and Psychophysics, 18,* 416-422.

Wagenaar, W.A. & Timmers, H. (1978). Extrapolation of exponential time series is not enhanced by having more data points. *Perception and Psychophysics, 24,* 182-184.

Wagenaar, W.A. & Timmers, H. (1979). The pond and duckweed problem: Three experiments on the misperception of exponential growth. *Acta Psychologica, 43,* 239-251.

ACKNOWLEDGEMENT. Preparation of this article was supported by the Economic and Social Research Council grant R000232646.

Contributions to Decision Making - I
J.-P. Caverni, M. Bar-Hillel, F.H. Barron and H. Jungermann (Editors)
© 1995 Elsevier Science B.V. All rights reserved.

THE PERSISTENCE DILEMMA: THE CAUSE OF THE LOSS AND THE "TRANSACTION" AND "SCRIPT" HYPOTHESES

Nicolao Bonini[1], Rino Rumiati[2] and Paolo Legrenzi[3]

1 CREPCO, Université de Provence, 29 Av. Robert Schuman,
F-13621 Aix-en-Provence Cedex 1, France
2 Dipartimento di Psicologia, Università di Padova, Italy
3 Istituto di Psicologia, Università di Milano, Italy

Abstract. Tversky and Kahneman (1981) found that people are less committed to a previous decision such as going to the theatre when they lose a "ticket" than when they lose a "note" of the same monetary value. Singer, Singer and Ritchie (1986) found that people are more reluctant to persist with the previous decision when they lose a note which was especially put aside to buy a ticket ("ticket directed note") than when they lose a "note" of the same monetary value. The "transaction" hypothesis has been proposed as an explanation of these findings (hereafter, the "target effect"). According to it, the presence (or the absence) of a transaction -be it real or fictitious- would induce people to take (or not to take) into account the suffered loss while deciding whether to persist or not with the previous decision. This should induce people to make different choices. An interpretation of the target effect in terms of "categorization and script" processes has also been proposed (cf. Henderson and Peterson, 1992). The present study investigates whether the target effect is affected by the presentation of information that specifies the cause of the loss. Furthemore, manipulating the cause of losing (or getting) a note, or a ticket, controls the predictive validity of the "transaction" and "script" hypotheses. Experiments 1 and 2 demonstrate that the target effect reduces and disappears when subjects are presented with causal information specifying "other people's fault" and "own fault" for the suffered loss, respectively. In Experiment 3, subjects were presented with a partial transaction such as to book a ticket. Results show that the target effect disappears. In Experiment 4, both the ticket and the note were presented as a gift. Results show that an effect similar to that reported by Tversky and Kahneman is found. We argue that the "transaction" hypothesis and the "script" one do not adequately account for the observed results.

INTRODUCTION

Let us consider the following situation (cf. Thaler, 1993). You have bought a ticket for your team's football game, a week in advance. The day of the match the weather is very bad: it is raining and very cold. Further, your ticket does not allow access to a covered stand. Will you still see the football match or not? This is a typical example of a persistence dilemma: you have to decide whether or not to maintain the previous course of action in the face of a negative event.

A decision procedure that might be used to resolve this dilemma is the consideration of the marginal costs and benefits of the two options "persist" vs. "change". By following this procedure, the subjects consider only future consequences, both positive or negative, associated with the two options, give them an utility value and, finally, choose the option with the greater utility. However, findings show that when people are facing a persistence dilemma, they tend to ignore this procedure. Their decision seems to be mainly affected by past choices (see the "sunk cost" effect discussed in Arkes and Blumer, 1985; Garland and Newport, 1991). For example, in the case of the football match problem, people tend to persist with the initial decision to go to see the match because they already bought the ticket. Furthermore, their degree of persistence should be affected mainly by the amount of money spent for buying the ticket, relative to their personal budget. Said differently, the extent to which people persist with a previous decision is a function of the presence/absence and relative amount of past commitment to that decision such as money, time spent, etc.

Tversky and Kahneman (1981) and Singer, Singer and Ritchie (1986) studied the effect of *qualitative manipulations* of the persistence dilemma on subjects's persistence decision. For example, keeping constant the monetary value, they manipulated the "type of loss" faced by subjects. Let us recall Singer and colleagues' experiment on the theater problem.

In that experiment, subjects were asked to imagine that they had decided to go to the theater. In one condition, subjects imagined that they lost a banknote which had been saved in order to purchase the ticket ("goal-directed note"). In another condition, subjects imagined that they lost a note of the same amount ("generic note"). Subjects were asked whether they would maintain their original decision to go to the theater or not.

The results of that experiment (replicated by Rumiati, Bonini, and Legrenzi, 1993) show that the affirmative answers are more frequent in the "generic note" loss condition than in the "goal-directed note" loss condition. This outcome is explained neither by the notion of "sunk cost" nor by the notion of "marginal cost".

Singer and colleagues (1986) interpret these results in the light of the mental accounting theory (cf. Thaler, 1993). Specifically, they argue for a so called "economic transaction" hypothesis. According to it, subjects in the "goal-directed note" condition *would take into account* the loss of the note while deciding whether to persist or not with the previous decision. This in turn would cause a decrease in their tendency to persist. On the contrary, subjects in the "generic note" condition *would not take into account* the loss of the note while deciding whether to persist or not . The consideration of the loss of money in the "goal-directed note" condition would be due to the presence of an economic transaction, although an imagined one: "I will give you some money, you will give me a ticket". Tversky and Kahneman (1981) used the "economic transaction" hypothesis for explaining a similar finding. They found that subjects were more reluctant to persist with the previous decision to go to the theater when they lose a "ticket" than when they lose a "note" of the same monetary value. Again, differences in the persistence decision across the two loss conditions were attributed to a different account of the suffered loss. In the "ticket" condition, subjects would take into account the suffered loss whereas subjects, in the "note" condition, would not do it.

Findings reported by Singer and colleagues and Tversky and Kahneman (hereafter, the "target effect") can also be interpreted in the light of the "cognitive script" hypothesis (cf. Henderson and Peterson, 1992). According to it, while the loss of a ticket (or a goal-directed note) is a "natural component" of the going to the theater script, the loss of the generic note is not. Said differently, "if it can be assumed that the going to the theater category includes the notion of buying a ticket, it is far less probable that it includes the notion of money loss" (p. 98). The different status of the two types of loss related to the "going to the theater" script would therefore be the cause of their different account. This in turn, would cause a different tendency to persist across the two loss conditions[1].

It should be noted that in the experiments reported by Tversky and Kahneman (1981) and Singer, Singer and Ritchie (1986), subjects were not presented with any causal information specifying *how the loss occurred*. Should the specification of the cause of the loss affect the persistence decision? Should it affect the target effect? To what extent the economic transaction and the script hypothesis may predict the effects of the specification of the cause of a loss on the persistence decision?

The aim of this study is twofold. First of all, it controls the effect of the *specification of the cause* of losing (or gaining) goods on the persistence decision. Said differently, keeping constant the "type of loss" and its "monetary value", this study investigates whether the different cause of losing (or getting) an object induces subjects to differently persist with a previous decision. For example, in the theater ticket problem, it will be assessed whether the specification (or not) of the cause of gaining (or losing) possession of a ticket, a note or a goal-directed note affects the persistence decision. Although the study is mainly an exploratory one, it can be argued that the encoding of an information related to a "loss" (or a "gain") of goods is affected by the way goods are lost (or gained). This, in turn, should affect subject's choices. For example, the encoding of the acquisition of a $100 note found by chance on the street may not be the same encoding of the acquisition of a $100 note received for one's own birthday. If encoding processes affect decisions, as argued by mental accounting theory, then the manipulation of the "modality" of getting (or losing) goods should also affect the persistence decision.

The second aim of the study is to assess *the predictive validity* of the economic transaction and the script hypotheses. This will be

---

[1] It should be noted that Henderson e Petersen (1992) do not consider the cognitive script hypothesis alternative to the economic transaction one. In fact, they suggest that the processes described in categorization, schema, and script theories are the same processes underlying mental accounting. Furthemore, they often underline that same predictions can be made from the mental accounting and the cognitive script theories.

accomplished by controlling to what extent the two hypotheses predict the effects on the persistence decision of the specification of the cause of losing (or getting) possession of goods in the theater ticket problem.

EXPERIMENT 1

Method

Subjects. The subjects taking part in this experiment were 479 students attending a psychology degree course at the Universities of Padova and Trieste.

Experimental design. Two factors make up the experimental design: the "cause" of loss ('control', 'other people's fault' and 'own fault' situations) and the "type of loss" ('ticket' and 'note' conditions). In the control situation, no information is given to subject about the cause of the loss (cf. Tversky and Kahneman, 1981). In the other two situations, subjects were provided with causal information specifying how the loss occurred. In the 'other people's fault' situation, subjects were presented with information suggesting that the loss occurred because of some one else fault. In the 'own fault' situation, subjects were presented with information suggesting that the loss occurred because of own fault. Students were randomly assigned to the six conditions. Subjects were given the following instructions: (in parentheses the instructions refer to the "note" condition):

Control

"You have decided to go to a show (the ticket costs 50,000 Lire) and have already bought the ticket which costs 50,000 Lire. You are just going into the theater when you realize you have lost the ticket (a 50,000 Lire note).The seats are not numbered and it is impossible to prove that you have actually bought the ticket.

Would you (still) spend (50,000 Lire to buy the ticket for the show) 50,000 Lire for another ticket?"

Tab.1c: Percentages of affirmative/negative answers in the "own fault" situation across the two types of losses.

Own fault

	Ticket	Note
Yes	38 (48%)	46 (58%)
No	41 (52%)	34 (42%)
	79	80

$\chi^2(1) = 1.42$, n.s.

The disappearance of the target effect in the "own fault" situation is not predicted neither by the economic transaction nor by the script hypothesis.

According to the economic transaction hypothesis, regardless of the way in which the loss occurred, persistence should be higher in the "note" condition than in the "ticket" one. This is determined by the presence of an economic transaction in the "ticket" condition that should induce subjects to take into account the suffered loss.

The script hypothesis also predicts a difference in the level of persistence between the two types of loss. Regardless of how the ticket or the note was lost, it is likely that the "going to the theater" script includes the notion of ticket-buying, whereas it is less likely that it includes the notion of money loss.

Thus, according to both hypotheses subjects should take into account the loss of the ticket whereas they should not take into account the loss of the money, regardless of the cause of the loss. This in turn, should induce subjects to persist more in the "note" condition than in the "ticket" one.

The decrease and the disappearance of the target effect are due to a different effect of the presence/absence of "causal information" on the persistence decision across the two "type of loss" conditions. Said differently, whereas the presence/absence of causal information did not affect choices in the "ticket" condition, the presence/absence of causal information affected choices in the "note" condition. Affirmative answers do not differ in the three situations related to the loss of the "ticket" $[X^2 (2) = . 78$, n.s.] while they differ when a "note" is lost $[X^2 (2) = 14.38$, p < .001].

The aim of the next experiment is to check whether the disappearance of the target effect in a situation of "own fault" can be extended to the situation studied by Singer, Singer, and Ritchie (1986). In other words, Experiment 2 controls whether the presentation of causal information specifying "personal responsibility" for the suffered loss eliminates the difference in the tendency to persist between the condition of loss of a "generic note" vs. the condition of loss of a "goal-directed note". Furthemore, Experiment 2 tests whether the disappearance of the target effect reported in the previous experiment can be replicated with a different scenario of "own fault".

EXPERIMENT 2

Method

Subjects. The subjects taking part in this experiment were 112 students attending a psychology degree course at the University of Trieste.

Experimental design. Two factors make up the design: the "cause" of the loss ("control" and "own fault" situations) and the "type of loss" ("ticket", "note", and "goal-directed note" conditions).

In the control situation no information is given about the cause of the loss. Six different experimental situations are possible. The "ticket-control" and the "note-control" situations were investigated in the previous experiment. The subjects of Experiment 2 were randomly assigned to the remaining four conditions. Instructions used in the "goal-directed note-control" situation are similar to those used in the experiment of Singer, Singer, and Ritchie (1986). A new scenario referring to an "own fault" situation is used in this experiment. Subjects were given the following instructions (in parentheses the instructions refer to the "ticket" condition whereas in square brackets they refer to the "goal-directed note" condition):

Own fault

"You have decided to go to a show. The ticket costs 50,000 Lire. In the afternoon, (returning from the box office where you have bought the ticket) you meet a friend who asks you to play a game of dice with him. You bet 50,00 Lire (the ticket) [which you had put in your pocket on purpose for the show. Your friend bets 50,000 Lire, too] and your friend the same amount (50,000 Lire). You are unlucky and lose 50,000 Lire (the ticket).

Would you still spend (50,000 Lire for another ticket) 50,000 Lire to buy the ticket to the show?"

As in Experiment 1, subjects had to answer "yes" or "no" to the question and justify their answer.

Results and discussion

Tables 2a and 2b show that the effect reported by Singer and colleagues is replicated in the "control" situation and cancelled in the "own fault" situation.

Tab.2a: Percentages of affirmative/negative answers in the control situation across the two types of losses (in square brackets are reported Singer et al.'s findings)

Control

	Note	Ticket directed Note
Yes	76 (84%)[81%]	18 (62%)[64%]
No	15 (16%)[19%]	11 (38%)[36%]
	91	29

$\chi^2(1) = 5.97, p < .025$

Tab.2b: Percentages of affirmative/negative answers in the "own fault" situation across the two types of losses.

Own fault

	Note	Ticket directed Note
Yes	14 (50%)	11 (42%)
No	14 (50%)	15 (58%)
	28	26

$\chi^2(1) = 32$, n.s.

The disappearance of the target effect is not accounted neither by the economic transaction nor by the script hypotheses. According to the former hypothesis, if the presence (or the absence) of an imagined transaction such as "I'll give you some money, you will give me a ticket" induces subjects to take into account (or not to take into account) the loss of the note, then the different account of the loss across the two "type of loss" conditions should be maintained when subjects are presented, in both conditions, with causal information specifying "personal responsibility" for the loss occurrence. As for the script hypothesis, the different status of the two losses related to the "going to the theater" script should not change when subjects are presented, in both conditions, with the cause of the loss.

The disappearance of the target effect is due to a different effect of the presence/absence of the causal information on the persistence decision across the two type of loss conditions. Said differently, whereas the presence/absence of the cause of the loss did not affect choices in the "goal directed note" condition, the presence/absence of such an information affected choices in the "note" condition. Affirmative answers do not differ across the two situations related to the loss of the "goal-directed note" [χ^2 (1) = 2.15, n.s.], while they differ across the two situations related to the loss of the "note" [χ^2 (1) = 13.06, p < .001].

The target effect disappears when the two losses ("ticket" vs. "note") are caused either by a "carelessness act" of the subject such as forgetting the note/ticket in an unwatched book left in the studying room (X^2 (1) = 1.42, n.s.), as reported in the previous experiment, or by an "imprudence act" such as putting them at stake in a dice game (X^2 (1) = 1.40, n.s.). These findings show that the presence of causal information suggesting "personal responsibility" for the loss eliminates the target effect. Finally, it should be noted that, contrary to Singer and colleagues' results, the tendency to persist associated with the "ticket" loss does not differ from that related to the "goal-directed" note [X^2 (1) = .61, n.s.].

In the two previous experiments, the difference between the two loss conditions related to the presence or the absence of an economic transaction, be it real or imaginary, carried out by the subject. This transaction is represented by the real or imaginary buying of a theater ticket through a cash outlay *totalling the amount required* to see the show.

Would the target effect still stand if the subjects paid, whether really or fictitiously, *only a part of the amount* necessary to see the show? For instance, subjects could book the theater ticket (or imagine to do that) by paying a part of the 50,000 Lire needed to purchase the ticket.

Both the economic transaction and the cognitive script hypotheses envisage a different tendency to persist across the two "type of loss" conditions. In particular, they would predict less tendency to persist when subjects lose a "ticket reservation" than when they lose a "generic note". Furthemore, subjects should exhibit less tendency to persist when they lose a "booking-directed note" than when they lose a "generic note". The difference in the persistence decision across the loss conditions should be due to a different account of the suffered loss.

The aim of the third experiment is to check the predictive validity of the economic transaction and the cognitive script hypothesis when another type of loss is considered by subjects. It should be noted that in the next experiment the factor "cause" of loss is not manipulated. That is, in both loss conditions subjects are not presented with information specifying how the loss occurred.

EXPERIMENT 3

Method

Subjects. The subjects taking part in the experiment were 179 students attending a psychology degree course at the University of Padova.

Experimental design. The design is made up of one three-level factor, "type of loss". One condition focuses on the loss of the "booking", another on the loss of the "booking-directed note", and the third on the loss of the "generic note". The instructions for the three loss conditions are the following (the instructions in parentheses relate to the "booking" loss and those in square brackets refer to the "booking-directed note" loss):

"You have decided to go to a show. The ticket costs 50,000 Lire. It is not possible to buy the ticket in advance. You can either buy it the day of the show or book it beforehand. In the latter case you must pay a deposit of 20,000 Lire at the time of booking and the remaining 30,000 when you pick up the ticket on the day of the show.

You have chosen to book the ticket (booked the ticket and, the same evening, on returning home you realize you have lost the booking receipt. The booking is not numbered and you cannot prove you have already paid 20,000 Lire). At the time of booking you realize you have lost 20,000 Lire [the two 10,000 Lire notes you had put aside for the booking]. You have some more money in your wallet, but you need it for your shopping. You are forced to put off buying the ticket till the next day, the day of the show.

Would you still spend 50,000 lire to buy the ticket to the show?"

Subjects must answer "yes" or "no" to the question and justify their answer.

Results and discussion

Tables 3a and 3b show that the target effect is not replicated when the economic transaction involves a cash outlay which is only a part of the total price of the ticket. This result is not accounted neither by the economic transaction hypothesis nor by the cognitive script one.

Tab.3a: Percentages of affirmative/negative answers in the control situation across the two types of losses.

Control

	Reservation	Note
Yes	41 (62%)	45 (68%)
No	25 (38%)	21 (32%)
	66	66

$\chi^2(1) = .52$, n.s.

Tab.3b: Percentages of affirmative/negative answers in the control situation across the two types of losses.

Control

	Reservation Directed Note	Note
Yes	34 (72%)	45 (68%)
No	13 (28%)	21 (32%)
	47	66

$\chi^2(1) = .23$, n.s.

In the three previous experiments, the two "type of loss" conditions differed in terms of the presence (e.g. the "ticket" or the "goal-directed note") or the absence (e.g. the "generic note") of an economic transaction undertaken by the subject. Such a transaction could be either real or fictitious and could refer to either a partial or a total payment.

In Experiment 4, the predictions envisaged by the economic transaction and by the cognitive script hypotheses are checked in a condition where, for both types of loss, the subject is not engaged in any economic transaction. In fact, the subject receives the ticket (or the note) as a birthday gift. This is an interesting situation because allows to discriminate between the economic transaction and the script hypothesis in terms of their predictions.

As for the economic transaction hypothesis, no difference should be found in the tendency to persist between the loss of a "given ticket" and the loss of a "given note". In fact, in both conditions the subjects have engaged in no economic transaction.

As for the script hypothesis, if the loss of a ticket is more relevant than the loss of a note related to the theater script , then the loss of a"given ticket" should be taken more into account than the loss of a "given note". This in turn, should affect the persistence decision across the two "type of loss" conditions.

EXPERIMENT 4

Method

Subjects. Subjects taking part in the experiment were 78 students attending a psychology degree course at the University of Padova.

Experimental design. The design includes only one two levels factor, "type of loss": loss of the"given ticket" vs. loss of the "given note".

The instructions are the following (in parentheses are the instructions used in the "given note" condition):

"You have decided to go to a show. The ticket costs 50,000 Lire. In the afternoon, at your birthday party, your friends give you an envelope. Inside there is a ticket to the show (a 50,000 Lire note. You take the note out of the envelope and put it in your wallet). The evening of the show, before leaving home, you realize you have lost (the 50,000 Lire note you were given) the envelope with the ticket inside. The seats are not numbered and you cannot prove you actually had a ticket.

Would you still spend 50,000 Lire to buy the ticket to the show?"

The subjects had to answer "yes" or "no" to the question and justify their answer.

Results and discussion

The results reported on Table 4 show an asymmetry in the persistence decision across the two "type of loss" conditions. Subjects are more reluctant to persist with their previous decision when they lose a "given ticket" than when they lose a "given note". This finding is similar to that reported by Tversky and Kahneman (1981).

Tab.4: Percentages of affirmative/negative answers in the "gift" situation across the two types of losses.

Gift

	Given Ticket	Given Note
Yes	27 (71%)	39 (98%)
No	11 (29%)	1 (2%)
	38	40

$\chi^2(1) = 10.44, p < .001$

This finding can not be predicted by the economic transaction hypothesis. However, it can be predicted by the cognitive script hypothesis. Thus, results related to the "gift" experiment allows to discriminate between the two hypotheses in terms of their predictive validity.

GENERAL DISCUSSION

The manipulation of the cause of losing (or gaining) a note or a theater ticket, allowed us to assess the predictive validity of two main explanations of findings that relate to the theater problem. Furthemore, it allowed us to investigate to what extent the way a loss is presented affects the persistence decision.

Assessing the predictive validity. The economic transaction (cf. Tversky and Kahneman, 1981; Singer, Singer, and Ritchie, 1986) and the cognitive script hypotheses (cf. Henderson and Peterson, 1992) can not adequately account for the results reported in this study.

Results of Experiment 1 and 2 show that the effect reported by Tversky and Kahneman (1981) and Singer, Singer, and Ritchie (1986, hereafter, the "target effect"), disappears when subjects are presented with causal information suggesting "personal responsibility" for the suffered loss. This result suggests the relevance of the factor "subject's personal control" for the suffered loss on the persistence decision. The influence of this variable has been established on counterfactual reasoning (cf. Girotto, Legrenzi and Rizzo, 1991). Experiment 3 demonstrates that the target effect disappears when subjects engage in a partial rather than a full economic transaction. Experiment 4 demonstrates that the target effect is found when subjects lose a "ticket" vs. a "note" that were received as a gift for their own's birthday. All in all, results of the four Experiments suggest that the presence vs. the absence of an economic transaction (be it a real or a fictitious one) is neither a necessary nor a sufficient condition for making appear the target effect.

As for the cognitive script hypothesis, it can not adequately explain results of the first three experiments. In fact, same predictions can be advanced from the script and the economic transaction hypotheses across the first three experiments. However, Experiment 4 shows that only the script hypothesis accounts for gathered results. This suggests that the two hypotheses may be regarded as alternative explanations of the target effect.

The cause of the loss and the persistence decision. Experiments 1 and 2 show that the presence of information specifying the cause of the loss affects the persistence decision only in the "generic note" condition. Said differently, in the "ticket" and in the "goal-directed note" conditions the persistence decision does not change as a function of the presence/absence of such an information. This result can not be accounted by neither the economic transaction nor the cognitive script hypothesis

According to the latter hypothesis, if the loss of a "ticket" (of a "note") is taken (is not taken) into account while deciding whether to persist or not with the previous decision to go to the theater because of its relevancy (lack of relevancy) to the script "going to the theater", then this kind of relevancy should not change when a causal information specifying how the loss occurred is presented. Said differently, is far less probable that the category "going to the theater" includes the notion of "money loss" than the notion of "ticket loss", regardless of the cause of the loss. As for the economic transaction hypothesis, if the loss of a "ticket" (of a "note") is taken (is not taken) into account while deciding whether to persist or not with the previous decision because of the presence (absence) of an economic transaction, then the presentation of causal information specifying how the loss occurred should not change this difference in the loss account.

All in all, it seems that an interpretation of findings reported in this study by means of the economic transaction and script hypotheses is not sufficiently adequate. Although the authors do not have an alternative definitive hypothesis to advance, they suggest, as a contribution to the theoretical discussion, that the notions of "mental models" and "focussing" may give insights about the cognitive mechanisms implied in persistence decisions (cf. Legrenzi, Girotto and Johnson-Laird, 1993). For example, in the theater problem, perhaps some subjects will not buy another ticket to see the play because they have a mental model in which this would be to pay the theater twice for only one ticket. Saying to subjects that they have specifically set aside some money to go to the theater may give them a mental model in which the rest of their money is already committed to other activities. Thus, if the note for the theater is lost, there may not be unallocated money in their mental models for going to the theater. Finally, the presence (or the absence) of information specifying the cause of the loss of the "ticket" does not affect the persistence decision because in both situations a mental model is already set up in which going to the theater corresponds to pay twice for the play. On the contrary, the presence (or the absence) of causal information specifying the cause of the loss of a "note" may (may not) induce subjects to flesh out a mental model in which the note loss is coded as a "cost" rather than a "loss".

Whereas research on persistence decision has reported noteworthy effects, the cognitive mechanisms underlying the construction of the mental representation of this kind of decision dilemma are far from being understood. Further research should try to specify them, their conditions of application and their impact on choices.

REFERENCES

Arkes, H.R. & Blumer, C. (1985) The psychology of sunk cost. *Organizational Behavior and Human Decision Processes, 35*, 124-140.

Garland, H. & Newport, S. (1991) Effects of absolute and relative sunk costs on the decision to persist with a course of action. *Organizational Behavior and Human Decision Processes, 48*, 55-69.

Girotto V., Legrenzi P., & RIizzo A. (1991). Event controllability in counterfactual thinking. *Acta Psychologica, 78*, 111-133.

Henderson, P.W. & Peterson, R.A. (1992). Mental accounting and categorization. *Organizational Behavior and Human Decision Processes, 51*, 92-117.

Legrenzi P., Girotto V. & Johnson-Laird, P.N. (1993). Focussing in reasoning and decision making. *Cognition, 49*, 37-66.

Rumiati, R., Bonini, N. & Legrenzi, P. (1993) La persistenza nella decisione: quando una perdita diventa un costo e quando un costo rimane una perdita, *Giornale Italiano di Psicologia. Anno XX, Vol. 1*, 97-108.

Singer, A.E., Singer, M.S. & Ritchie, G. (1986) Role of transactions in mental accounting, *Psychological Reports, 59*, 835-838.

Thaler (1993). "Mental Accounting matters". Presented at 14th SPUDM Conference, Aix-en-Provence, August 1993.

Tversky, A. & Kahneman, D. (1981) The framing of decisions and the psychology of choice, *Science*, 453-458.

Acknowledgements. Authors are grateful to Clara Giangasparo, Elena Parovel and Paolo Puntin for helping us in collecting data. Thanks also to Prof. Giulio Vidotto and Francesca Cristante for assisting us in statistical analysis. Finally, we want to thank David Over and Agnès Blaye for their review of the paper.

Contributions to Decision Making - I
J.-P. Caverni, M. Bar-Hillel, F.H. Barron and H. Jungermann (Editors)
© 1995 Elsevier Science B.V. All rights reserved.

DISTRIBUTED DECISION MAKING IN DYNAMIC ENVIRONMENTS:

TIME SCALES AND ARCHITECTURES OF DECISION MAKING[1]

Berndt Brehmer and Peter Svenmarck

Uppsala University P.O. Box 1854
Department of Psychology, S-751 48 Uppsala Sweden

Abstract. This paper addresses the problem of how people coordinate their activity in a dynamic environment using D^3FIRE, a new experimental paradigm for the study of distributed decision making. It simulates forest fire fighting at the level of the individual fire fighting unit and makes it possible to investigate how groups of four decision makers coordinate their activity on line. The results suggest that a hierarchical environment where all communication has to pass through one decision maker leads to better performance than a fully connected environment where every decision maker is free to communicate with any other decision maker, presumably because in the former environment, the chances are better that at least one decision maker has a picture of the task as a whole. This subject can then take on the responsibility for the coordination. However, subjects in the fully connected environment were quite successful in coordinating their activity locally without any one taking the responsibility for the overall coordination.

Many of the tasks that people undertake are simply too large to be carried out by single individuals; they require cooperation among many persons. This raises the question of how such cooperation can be ensured. There seem to be two alternatives. The first alternative is to rely on *feedforward control*, as implemented in some form of plan or organisation. The Tayloristic form of production represents an extreme form of such control. It involves dividing the task into small parts and assigning the parts to different persons who then work independently. This requires no coordination effort from the people involved; the coordination is produced automatically by the organisation. Such forms of

---

[1] This study was supported by a grant from the Swedish Council for Research in the Humanities and Social Sciences.

coordination are, however, successful only when the environment is stable. As noted in many recent papers (see, e.g., those in the volumes edited by Rasmussen, Brehmer & Leplat, 1991 and by Brehmer, 1992), we cannot always assume such stability in, for example, business, emergency management, or military environments. Therefore, we cannot rely on feedforward modes of control only. We also need more flexible forms that can function in a feedback mode, i.e., they must be able to adapt their work to changing circumstances. In such organisations, the coordination cannot be the result of fixed patterns of work. Instead, it must be the responsibility of those who work in the organisation. In short, we must move from centralised forms of decision making to more distributed forms.

Such distributed forms of decision making have always been a part of military organisations. Thus, in the military it has long been recognised that local conditions cannot be predicted in detail, and that commanders must be free to adapt their actions to whatever the local conditions require. Therefore, coordination in military planning is achieved by a mixture of centralised and distributed decision making. The centralised element consists of a coordinated set of goals that are fed down the command hierarchy. The commanders at the lower levels of the hierarchy are then free to achieve these goals in whatever way possible, given the resources that they have and the constraints introduced by local conditions (see Brehmer, 1988, for further discussion of military decision making).

Modern information technology and the pace of today's forms of battle are changing the preconditions for the traditional forms of coordination in military circumstances, however. It is therefore not surprising that the military were the first to realise the need to understand distributed decision making better. This led to a number of attempts at developing experimental paradigms for the study of distributed decision making in the 1980's (see Svenmarck & Brehmer, 1992a, for a brief review). However, apart from the vigorous research program pursued by Kleinman and his associates at the University of Connecticut (see, Miao, Luh & Kleinman, 1992, for a recent review of this research program), little came of this effort. Kleinman's program is concerned with the problem of how a team of decision makers share their resources in a dynamic context where each decision maker owns some part of the total resources, and where some of the decision tasks require cooperation in the form of sharing of resources while others must be solved by each decision maker alone.

Resource sharing is, however, only one aspect of distributed decision making. The other important aspect is coordination of effort. This is a problem because each decision maker will only have a limited window on the task. Therefore, coordination can only be achieved by communication. To understand the implications of this, we must consider the temporal aspects of the decision environment and that the decisions have to be made in real time.

That decisions must be made in real time is an important aspect of many dynamic decision tasks (Brehmer, 1992). One consequence of this is that the decision maker will be subjected to time pressure. This aspect of distributed decision making in dynamic environments has been studied by Kleinman and his associates in a number of experiments (see, e.g., Kleinman, 1991). Another consequence, stressed by Brehmer (e.g., 1988, 1991) is that the decision maker must consider the task in terms of the relevant time scales. An example will clarify this. Consider the case of a group of fire fighting units charged with the problem of fighting forest fires. They face two problems: the immediate problem of fighting whatever fires they face locally and the larger problem of coordinating their efforts so that the fire as a whole will be extinguished. Because coordination takes time, the commanders must consider the future development of the fire so that they have the time to move into the most effective positions for fighting the fire as a whole together with the other units. That is, they must increase their time horizon and consider not only the fast local development of the fire, but also the slower development of the fire as a whole. In short, they must consider the task in terms of two time scales. As we have noted elsewhere, time scales are often the basis for the organisation of work with different persons being in charge of different time scales (see Brehmer, 1991 for a general discussion, and A. Brehmer, 1988, for an application in the field of intensive care of patients with large burns). Such an organisation may be effective also in situations where the dynamic character of the decision problem makes it impossible to develop a Tayloristic organisation. However, organisations in such multi-time scale environments must be hierarchical. This is because the decisions in the slower time scales, which concern the problem as a whole, must always take precedence over those in the faster scales that only concern parts of the problem; however efficiently the fire fighting units extinguish fires locally, they will not master the fire as a whole if they do not fight the local fires in the right location. That is, the power relations in such a hierarchy cannot be arbitrary. They must be in harmony with the structure of the task facing the organisation.

The present study is concerned with this problem. We present an experiment in which we compare subjects' effectiveness in two different environments, or *architectures of distributed decision making* to borrow a term from Rasmussen (1991), in a dynamic decision environment: a *fully connected architecture* where every local decision maker can communicate with every other decision maker directly (this term comes from Kleinman's work, see, e.g., Miao, et al., 1992), and a *hierarchical architecture*, where all communication among decision makers must pass through a centrally located decision maker. These architectures correspond to what is usually called democratic, or decentralised, networks and hierarchical, or centralised, networks in studies of communication in social psychology (see, e.g., Shaw, 1964). As shown in Shaw's (1964) review of research with such networks, subjects in centralised networks send less messages, are slower, make more errors and are less satisfied when solving complex problems than subjects in decentralised networks. However, these results are not directly relevant to our purposes for they have not been obtained in dynamic environments where subjects must consider different time scales. Based on the analysis in terms of such time scales, we expect, in contrast to the findings for static tasks, that decision makers will be more effective in the hierarchical environment than in the fully connected environment. This is because in the hierarchical environment, the chances are better that all the information needed for the coordination of the different local units will be collected in one place. This increases the possibility of an adequate assessment of the situation as a whole in at least one place in the decision network. Therefore, the chances are better that at least one decision maker will have information that will allow him or her to also consider the slower time scale relevant to coordination.

METHOD

Subjects

Thirty-two undergraduate students were paid to participate in the experiment. The subjects were randomly assigned to the two experimental conditions. The subjects worked in subgroups of four subjects each. They came to the laboratory on four separate occasions and worked for about 2 hr each time. They were paid about USD 80 for their participation.

Experimental task

The experiment used D^3FIRE (Svenmarck & Brehmer, 1992a), a general experimental paradigm for the study of distributed decision making in dynamic systems.

Specifically, the paradigm simulates a situation where four decision makers have to cooperate to extinguish simulated forest fires. Each subject works in front of a PC and communicates with the other subjects through electronic mail. Consequently, all messages can be logged, and it is possible to vary the architecture of the distributed organisation by controlling who can communicate with whom. Thus, a fully connected architecture is created by allowing free communication among all subjects, while a hierarchical architecture is created by allowing three of the subjects to communicate with a fourth subject, but not with each other. In this case, therefore, all information communicated in the system has to pass one subject. This should maximise the possibility that relevant information is collected by at least one of the subjects in the system.

Since most persons are not used to communicating by means of electronic mail, one might, perhaps, expect that the requirement to communicate in this way could hinder the subjects from doing their best with the main task of these experiments. However, a recent experiment in our laboratory shows that subjects who are allowed to communicate orally under face-to-face conditions do not perform better than do subjects who have to communicate by means of electronic mail (Svenmarck & Brehmer, 1992b)

D^{3}FIRE (Svenmarck & Brehmer, 1992a) is based on the general definition of a distributed decision making environment as one where decision makers have to cooperate to reach a common goal but where each decision maker only has a limited window on the task as a whole (Brehmer, 1991). The subject's task in a D^{3}FIRE experiment is to assume the role of a fire chief and to extinguish simulated forest fires in cooperation with three other fire chiefs. Figure 1 gives a general overview of the characteristics of the experimental task. As can be seen from this figure, D^{3}FIRE is a close relative of DESSY (Brehmer & Allard, 1991) and NEWFIRE (Løvborg & Brehmer, 1991) our earlier experimental simulations for the study of individual dynamic decision making.

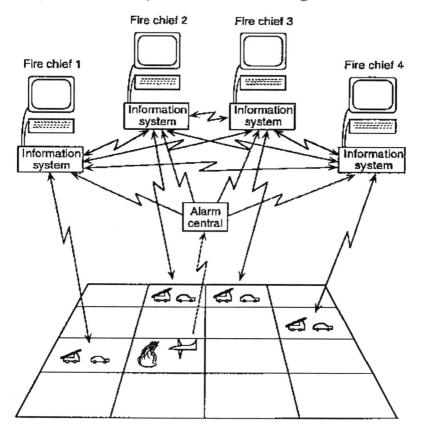

Figure 1. The general characteristics of the experimental task.

The definition of distributed decision making is reflected in the simulation in two ways. First each subject only controls *one* unit rather than all units as in DESSY and NEWFIRE. A unit consists only of one appliance, and it can only extinguish fire in one cell at a time. Second, each subject can "see" only the area just around his or her own unit. No one has the overview of the forest as a whole. Therefore, the subjects must communicate to build up the representation needed for coordination. The reduced view is explained to the subject in the following way. Each fire fighting unit has its own set of fire guards, with the following properties. First, the guards cannot extinguish any fires. They only observe the state of the forest area in which they are positioned, and report their observations to their unit. Second, their communication equipment has a very limited range, and therefore they can only report about the area right next to the unit. This means that a unit with 8 guards can only cover an area with the size of 3 x 3 cells. This local window offers no direct support for the monitoring of the time scale relevant to the problem as a whole. Instead, it probably invites a subject to think in a very short and local time scale.

As in NEWFIRE and DESSY, no special command is required to start fire fighting; a fire fighting unit will start fighting fire automatically if it is positioned in a cell where there is fire, or when the fire reaches the cell where it is positioned. The only command that the subjects can issue is that of ordering the unit to go to a new position and he or she does that by clicking on the new position with the mouse. The unit then starts moving immediately, although the subject can only see this when the screen has been updated after the command has been issued.

Figure 2 shows what the subjects actually see on the computer screen. Most of it is taken up by a map of the forest area, but the subject can, of course, only see what is within the set of nine cells that belongs to his or her fire fighting unit. To the right on the screen are two message areas, one for receiving messages and one for sending them. When a message arrives, there is a beep from the computer and a blinking text in the reception area. To read the message, the subject simply clicks in this area, and messages will appear in the order in which they have arrived as he or she continues to click. To send a message, the subject types in the message in the sending area. A message must fit in this area, so it has to be rather short. The subjects can send and receive messages also in between the updates of the screen.

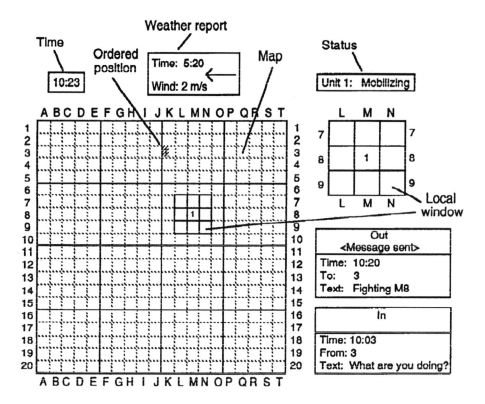

Figure 2. The experimental task as it appears to the subject on the computer screen. A subject can only see the fire and and fire fighting units that are in the nine cells comprising his or her window. The subject is located in the middle cell, and as he or she moves the unit, the whole window moves over the map of the forest.

To move his or her unit, the subject simply points with the mouse to the cell on the map to which he or she wants the centre of the 3 x 3 cell unit to move. The unit would then move towards that area at a pace of one cell per time unit, using the shortest possible route. A time unit is the interval between updates on the screen. In this experiment this was 30 seconds.

The quartet's goal is to fight the fires with a minimum loss of cells. A trial ends when the fire has been put out or when the maximum time of one hour is reached. The fire scenarios that the quartets faced in this experiment were selected to maximise the basic form of coordination in this context. Thus, there is always only one fire centre, and a constant light breeze. Still, the fires are so difficult that all four fire chiefs must cooperate to extinguish them. A fire always started in one of four areas E5, P5, E16, or P16, and spread towards one of the opposite sides. When a fire started, subjects were informed about this by an alarm central that also informed them about the location of the fire centre. This was necessary since it would take too long to find the fire by unplanned search.

Design

As already mentioned, the experiment was designed to compare two architectures of distributed decision making: a fully connected architecture where each subject could communicate directly with every other subject, and a hierarchical architecture where all communication was channelled through one subject in the quartet. In both conditions, the quartets received seven trials. Thus, the basic design of the experiment was a 2 (architectures) by 7 (trials) design with repeated measures of the second factor.

Procedure

All quartets were informed about the general nature of the task, about the restrictions in the communication network, and about the type of fire problem they would face (one fire and constant wind). They were further instructed to fight the fires with a minimum loss of cells. How they should coordinate to accomplish this task was left for the subjects to decide. They were then allowed to familiarise themselves with the display and the electronic message system for 30 minutes. Each quartet performed a total of seven trials. They came to the experiment on four days. They performed one trial on the first day, and two trials on every day after that.

The time interval between updates on the screen (one of the factors that can be varied in D^3FIRE), was set to 30 seconds. As already mentioned, a fire fighting unit moved at a pace of one cell per time unit, and it took 6 time units for a fire to spread from one cell to the next in the direction of the wind.

RESULTS

D^{3}FIRE registers everything that happens on a trial. From this information it is possible to construct a number of dependent variables. Three of these will be analysed here. They are (1) the number of cells lost to fire, which shows the extent to which the subjects were able to meet the main goal that they had been given, (2) the number of messages that are sent, and (3) the different types of messages that were sent and received by the subjects.

Number of cells lost to fire

Figure 3 shows the average number of cells lost to fire for the two architectures. As can be seen from the figure, there is a dramatic improvement over time for both architectures (F 6/36 = 18.75, p<0.001). As predicted, the quartets in the hierarchical condition performed better than those in the fully connected condition (F 1/6 = 7.77, p < 0.05).

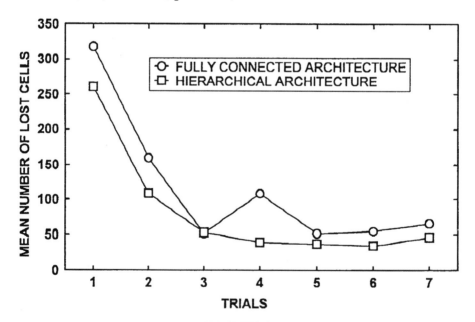

Figure 3. Mean number of cells lost to fire at the end of a trial as a function of architecture and trial.

Time per trial

The average time per trial decreased from 60 minutes to 25 minutes. The main effect of trials is significant (F 6/36 = 13.29, p < .001) but there was no difference between the two experimental conditions and no trials by conditions interaction.

Number of messages

Because of the decrease in time per trial, it is not meaningful to compare the number of messages over trials directly; the subjects simply did not have the time to send as many messages in the last trials as in the first. The messages were therefore normalised by computing the number of messages per minute in each trial. Figure 4 shows the average number of messages sent per minute in the two architectures. As would be expected from the fact that they have many more communication channels, the subjects in the fully connected architecture send more messages than those in the hierarchical architecture. The difference is not quite significant (F 1/6 = 5.28, p = 0.06), however, and there is neither a main effect of trials nor a trials by conditions interaction.

Message types

The messages from each subject were classified into 17 mutually exclusive categories. The categories were selected because they were theoretically relevant and because they actually cover most of the messages. Since the electronic messages are short and, in most cases, to the point, there was no problem in categorising them into the 17 categories listed below.

Communication concerning strategy (S)

4 kinds of questions

  . questions about some other subject's intentions (QI)

  . questions about the location of the fire (QE)

  . questions about some other subject's activity (QA)

  . questions about some other subject's location (QL)

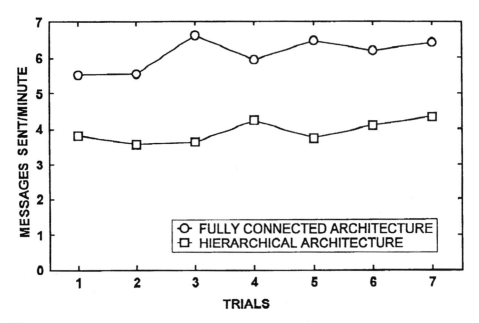

Figure 4. Mean number of messages per minute as a function of archictecture and trial.

4 kinds of messages providing information (often in response to questions)

- . information about intentions (II)

- . information about fire (IE)

- . information about own location (IL)

- . information about own activity (IA)

Commands (C)

Request for clear command (RC)

Requests for help (RH)

Offers of help (OH)

Acknowledgements (A)

Miscellaneous (M)

The "Miscellaneous" category contains mainly social chitchat. In this experiment it comprised about 6% of all messages. Communications concerning strategy are concerned with the implementation of some strategy or suggestions concerning some possible strategy. There were very few messages of this type in the present experiment, so this category is not analysed here. The "Commands" category comprises all cases when one subject has told another subject to go to a certain location and/or suggested that the other subject should do so. Questions about intentions concern what the addressee is planning to do, mainly where he was planning to go. Questions about fire concern the location of fire, and questions about location are concerned with the current location of the addressee. Questions about activity, finally, concern the current activity of the addressee. The information items were either responses to these questions, or spontaneous offers of information, usually concerning intentions.

For the current purposes, QI, QE, QL, QA, II, IE, IL, IA and C are the most interesting categories in that they are directly related to the fire fighting activity, and they also make up the majority of the messages. The analysis was therefore limited to these. Two sets of analyses were performed. The first concerned differences between architectures, the second differences among kinds of subjects.

Differences between architectures. For each category, an analysis of variance was conducted on mean frequency of messages sent per minute. The results showed significant effects of conditions for QI (F $1/6$ = 9.05, $p < .05$), QL (F $1/6$ = 6.01, $p < .05$), II (F $1/6$ = 6.23, $p < .05$), and IL (F $1/6$ = 6.82, $p < .05$). In all these cases, the mean frequency of messages was higher in the fully connected architecture than in the hierarchical architecture. Significant changes over trials in the number of messages per minute was obtained for QI (F $6/36$ = 2.42, $p < .05$, due to an increase over trials), QL (F $6/36$ = 6.11, $p < .01$, indicating a slight decrease in QL messages over trials), QE (F $6/36$ = 2.61, $p < .05$, caused by a slight increase, but this increase was greater for subjects in the fully connected architecture than for those in the hierarchical architecture as shown by a significant trials by conditions interaction, F $6/36$ = 4.16, $p < .01$), IL (F $6/36$ = 7.31, $p < 01$, due to a general decrease which was greater for the subjects in the fully connected architecture than for those in the hierarchical architecture as shown by a trials by conditions interaction, F 6/36 = 2.96, p < .05). These results show, then, that subjects in the fully connected architecture asked for more information about the location and intentions of the other subjects in their quartets and that they also sent out more information about these aspects. Interestingly, subjects became more concerned with intentions and the fire as the experiment progressed and less concerned with the location of other units. That subjects in the fully connected architecture ask more questions and send more information is not surprising: since information is not collected centrally, each subject must find out from the other subjects what he or she needs to know in this kind of architecture and this, of course, increases the message frequency. An analysis only in terms of architectures is, however, not sufficient since the subjects in the hierarchical architecture have very different roles. We must also examine possible differences among the three kinds of subjects in the experiment: subjects in the fully connected architecture and central and non central subjects in the hierarchical architecture. We now turn to this problem.

Differences between messages sent and received among subjects in the fully connected architecture and central and non central subjects in the hierarchical condition. Despite the changes in some of the message categories over trials, the relative frequencies of the different message categories were highly similar across trials. We therefore concentrate on the overall frequencies in this analysis.

Figure 5 shows the distribution of different kinds of messages sent for the central subjects and the non central subjects in the hierarchical architecture as well as for the subjects in the fully connected architecture. As can be seen from this figure, there are considerable differences among these three kinds of subjects with respect to the frequency of messages. Thus, for the Command category (C) we find the highest frequency for the central subjects in the hierarchical architecture. According to a Tukey HSD test, the differences between the number of messages sent per minute by these central subjects and the non central subjects and the subjects in the fully connected architecture are significant (p < .01 in both cases) but there is no difference between the latter two kinds of subjects. Subjects in the fully connected architecture, on the other hand, sent many more messages with information about intentions than the subjects in the hierarchical architecture (p < .01) but there was no difference between the central and the non central subjects in the hierarchical architecture.

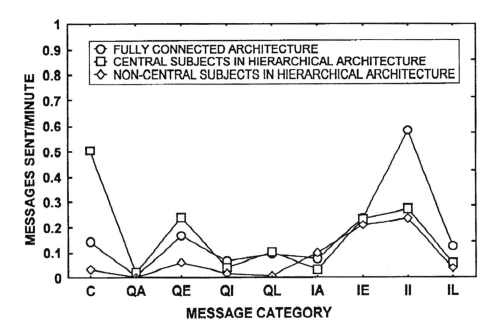

Figure 5. Mean number of messages sent per minute by the subjects in the fully connected condition, and by the central and non central subjects in the hierarchical condition.

Figure 6 shows the mean number of messages received per minute. The figure shows that there are no differences with respect to questions or commands, all differences are found with respect to information categories. Here, the results of the Tukey HSD tests show that the central subjects in the hierarchical architecture received more information about activity (IA) and intentions (II) than the non central subjects (p < .05), more information about fire (IE) than both the non central subjects in that condition and the subjects in the fully connected architecture (p < .01). The subjects in the latter condition received more information about intentions than the non central subjects in the hierarchical architecture. It may seem surprising that there is no difference in commands received given the great difference in commands sent shown in Figure 5. However, it must be remembered that the commands sent in the hierarchical architecture have to be distributed over three subjects, so there will not be as many commands per subject.

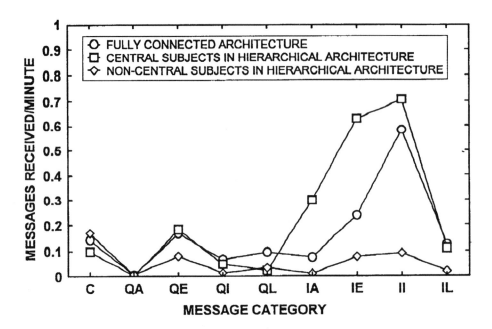

Figure 6. Mean number of messages received per minute by the subjects in the fully connected condition, and by the central and non central subjects in the hierarchical condition.

The messages sent and received by each individual subject in the quartets in the fully connected architecture were also analysed to search for possible informal leaders, i.e., for subjects who asked for and/or received more information about fire and sent out more commands than the other subjects in the quartet, i.e., subjects who were similar to the central subjects in the hierarchical quartets. No such subjects could be found, however.

DISCUSSION

The main results from this experiment are:

1) Subjects in both conditions improve with practice.

2) Subjects in the hierarchical architecture perform better than those in the fully connected architecture.

3) The content of the messages sent and received by the subjects in the hierarchical architecture differed from that of the messages sent and received by the subjects in the fully connected architecture suggesting that their methods for coordination were different.

That subjects in both conditions improve, and reach respectable levels of performance, shows that subjects in both conditions were able to cope with the fire fighting task. However, they obviously did so in different ways. In the hierarchical condition the central subjects received more information about fire, activity and intentions than the non central subjects and more information about fire than the subjects in the fully connected architecture. The central subjects in the hierarchical architecture were therefore better informed than the other kinds of subjects, and they took on the task of coordination and issued commands to the other three subjects. These commands were presumably based on the better picture of the fire as a whole, or better "situational awareness", to use a term that is popular in the studies of command and control, that this subject was able to develop on the basis of the information he/she received. In the fully connected architecture, on the other hand, most of the messages concerned intentions and there were relatively few messages concerning the fire and its location. This suggests that in this condition, no subject in the quartets was able to form a very good picture of the fire as a whole. Therefore, no one felt confident enough to try to coordinate the efforts of their fellow subjects by means of commands. This is not to say that they did not send out commands, however. Indeed, the subjects in the fully connected condition sent and received about as many commands as the subjects in hierarchical condition. But these commands were sent between pairs of subjects, rather than from one subject to all other subjects. That is, no informal leaders emerged. Thus, the coordination in the fully connected condition was local, rather than centralised. It is not surprising that this form of coordination was less effective than that in the hierarchical condition. It must be less effective because it is not based on a picture of the fire as a whole. However, that the subjects in this condition were able to solve the task at all shows that coordination is possible also when no one assumes responsibility for the coordination as such, and without specific commands issued to achieve coordination.

It is interesting to note the high frequency of II messages in the fully connected architecture. These messages are likely to be an important part of the coordination effort. If subjects are to coordinate their activity, they cannot do so on the basis of information about what the other subjects are doing. Coordination takes time, and if one subject moves his or her unit to a new location in an attempt to coordinate with another subject on the basis of information about what that subject is doing when the coordination attempt is initiated, he or she is likely to be too late; when in the intended position, the subject with whom he or she is trying to coordinate may then have moved on to a new location. To coordinate, the subjects need to know what the other subjects are planning to do so that they have time to coordinate, not what they are doing, which will give them no time for coordination. Therefore, successful coordination requires that the subjects send information about their intentions, rather than their actions. That is, the frequency of II messages should be greater than the frequency of IA or IL messages. This is exactly what we find in the fully connected architecture, and this may well explain at least part of the subjects' success at coordinating in this condition. The role of various forms of information for coordination is now being investigated in more detail in new experiments with D^{3}FIRE.

The difference in performance between the two conditions was not as great as one might have expected. This suggests that local coordination may be more effective than anticipated. Alternatively, the rather small difference in performance, despite considerable differences in communication content, may indicate that the commands issued by the central subjects were not as effective as they should have been. One reason for this may be that the subjects in this experiment had very little time to consider the situation and to communicate; in the experiment, the picture on the computer screen was updated every 30 seconds. Thus, the subjects may have been under too much time pressure to communicate effectively and to use the information that they received as well as they should have. Kleinman (e.g., 1991) has pointed to the central importance of time pressure in distributed decision making, and hypothesised that coordination on the basis of communication becomes difficult or impossible as the time pressure increases. The role of this factor in D^{3}FIRE is currently being investigated in our laboratory.

It is interesting that the hierarchical architecture in this experiment works as hypothesised, despite that no formal power relations have been specified in the experiment. That is, the central subject in the hierarchical quartets was not given any formal power over the other subjects in the quartet, nor was he or she told to take on the task to coordinate the activities of the four subjects in the quartet. His or her authority instead derived only from the communication structure. A consequence of this structure was that the central subject had more and better information about the task than the other subjects in these quartets, and this seems to have been sufficient for him or her to take on the task of coordination, thus illustrating the old saying that "knowledge is power". Whether the effectiveness of this centrally placed subject can be further improved by also giving him or her formal power is an interesting question now subject to experimental investigation in our laboratory.

REFERENCES

Brehmer, A. (1989). *Brännskadeintensivvård som hierarkiskt organiserat system.* Uppsala: Center for Human Computer Studies, Uppsala University CMD Report No. 4.

Brehmer, B. (1988). Organization of decision making in complex systems. In L. P. Goodstein, H. B. Andersen & S. E. Olesen (Eds), *Tasks, errors and mental models.* London: Taylor & Francis.

Brehmer, B. (1991). Modern information technology, time scales and distributed decision making. In J. Rasmussen, B. Brehmer & J. Leplat (Eds.), *Distributed decision making: Cognitive models of cooperative work.* Chichester: Wiley.

Brehmer, B. (1992). (Ed.). *Distributed decision making. Vol 1-2.* Proceedings of the Third MOHAWC Workshop. Belgirate, May 15-17, 1991. Roskilde: Risø National Laboratory.

Brehmer, B., & Allard, R. (1991). Dynamic decision making: The effects of task complexity and feedback delay. In J. Rasmussen, B. Brehmer & J. Leplat (Eds.), *Distributed decision making: Cognitive models of cooperative work.* Chichester: Wiley.

Kleinman, D. (1991). *Coordination in human teams: Theories, data and models.* Paper presented at IFAC, Tallin, June, 1991.

Løvborg, L., & Brehmer, B. (1991). *NEWFIRE. A flexible system for running simulated fire fighting experiments.* Roskilde: Risö National Laboratory Report M-2953.

Miao, X., Luh, P. B., & Kleinman, D. L. (1992). A normative-descriptive approach to hierarchical team resource allocation. *IEEE Transactions on Systems, Man, and Cybernetics, 22,* 482-497.

Rasmussen, J. (1990). Modeling distributed decision making. In J. Rasmussen, B. Brehmer & J. Leplat (Eds.), *Distributed decision making: Cognitive models of cooperative work.* Chichester: Wiley.

Rasmussen, J., Brehmer, B., & Leplat, J. (Eds.) (1990). *Distributed decision making: Cognitive models of cooperative work.* Chichester: Wiley.

Shaw, M. E. (1964). Communication networks, In L. Berkowitz (Ed,), *Advances in experimental social psychology Vol. 1* (Pp. 111-147). New York: Academic Press.

Svenmarck, P., & Brehmer, B. (1992a). D^3FIRE: An experimental paradigm for the study of distributed decision making. In B. Brehmer (Ed.), *Distributed decision making*. Proceedings of the Third MOHAWC Workshop, Belgirate, Italy, May 15-17, 1991. Roskilde: Risö National Laboratory.

Svenmarck, P., & Brehmer, B. (1992b). Face-to-face communication versus communication by means of electronic mail in distributed decision making. In B. Brehmer (Ed.), *MOHAWC: Separate papers*. Roskilde: Risø National Laboratory.

Contributions to Decision Making - I
J.-P. Caverni, M. Bar-Hillel, F.H. Barron and H. Jungermann (Editors)
© 1995 Elsevier Science B.V. All rights reserved.

A DYNAMIC MODEL FOR MULTI-ATTRIBUTE DECISION PROBLEMS

Adele Diederich

C.v.Ossietzky Universität Oldenburg
Institut für Kognitionsforschung
Fachbereich 5 – 26111 Oldenburg – Germany
email: Diederich@psychologie.uni-oldenburg.de

Abstract : This paper presents a decision model that takes into account both the dynamic and the stochastic nature of decision making. Its goal is to describe the cognitive and motivational mechanisms that guide the deliberation process involved in decision making with multi-attribute decision problems. It provides an explanation for why preferences waver over time and presents a mechanism for determining how long deliberation lasts. In principle, the approach proposed here provides a unified theoretical treatment of a wide range of measures of preference. It constitutes an extension to multi-attribute decision problems of the Decision Field Theory (DFT) approach recently developed by Busemeyer & Townsend (1993). This Multi-Attribute Decision Field Theory (MDFT) is shown here to predict choice probabilities and choice response times. In particular, the well-known preference reversal phenomena are accounted for by the model. Finally, experimental procedures for developing empirical tests are discussed.

INTRODUCTION

Imagine that you are confronted with the following decision problem. Your car's engine has broken down and you must decide whether to keep your current car and fix the engine, or purchase a new car. There are a large number of things to consider. Can you afford a new car now? If the old car is fixed, how long will it last? How much would you enjoy driving a new car? How safe is your old car? How much would you save on gas? The list of considerations seems to grow without end as you deliberate.

Decision theorists call this type of decision a multi-attribute decision. Each course of action needs to be evaluated with respect to a set of attributes. Over the past twenty years, considerable progress has been made in the development of formal theories of multi-attribute decision making. One class of theories employs algebraic measurement theory to represent multi-attribute preferences (cf. Keeney & Raiffa, 1976). Another class of theories employs heuristic information processing notions to describe multi-attribute choice (cf. v.Winterfeldt & Edwards, 1986). The purpose of this article is to present an approach to multi-attribute decision making based on a recently developed model called "Decision Field Theory" by Busemeyer and Townsend (Busemeyer & Townsend, 1992, 1993) and an information processing model developed by Diederich (1992, 1993). The multi-attribute decision field theory (MDFT) incorporates both stochastic and dynamic aspects of the multi-attribute decision making process providing a new prospective on an old and important problem.

The outline of the article is as follows. First, I present an intuitive description of the theory. Then I develop MDFT piece by piece starting with Multi-Attribute Utility Theory (MAUT) and showing that MAUT is a special case of MDFT. Due to space limitations, a thorough discussion of how this approach relates to other attempts to account for the dynamics of the multi-attribute situation must be postponed to another paper. Moreover, only one prediction of the new theory, the prediction of preference reversals as a function of time will be discussed in detail. At this stage, the model has not yet been subjected to empirical tests. However, in the latter part of this paper several experimental procedures for a rigorous empirical test of various aspects of the model will be proposed.

MULTI-ATTRIBUTE DECISION FIELD THEORY

Assume that starting from a large set of alternatives the decision maker finally ends up to make a decision between two alternatives, say alternative A and alternative B. She thinks about some attributes and compares the alternatives according to these attributes. To make it more concrete let us go back to the car example. In this case, those attributes could be "safety", "price", "design", etc. Attribute in this context is interpreted as a memory retrieval cue, i.e., a relative abstract or complex attribute retrieves many concrete ideas (aspects) connected with it. Consider e.g. the attribute "safety" of the car example, the decision maker might really think of air bags, how the safety belts are fastened to the passenger, steel reinforced sides, ABS brakes etc. and how important it would be in case of an accident. Or thinking of "price" might not only include the actual amount of money the decision maker has to pay but also the annual taxes for that car, insurance, repair costs, gas consumption etc. The decision maker tries to anticipate and evaluate all possible consequences produced by choosing either of the alternatives. These consequences are retrieved from a complex associate memory process and it takes time to retrieve, compare, and integrate the comparisons. An alternative is chosen once the preference for one alternative is strong enough to exceed a certain criterion.

To be more specific, when confronted with a decision problem, a *preference state* process is activated representing the tendency to choose alternative *A* or alternative *B*. The preference state changes as the decision maker deliberates over different aspects and various possible consequences involved in choosing each alternative, producing a new preference state at each point in time, denoted *D(t)*. The decision maker may start thinking about one attribute that both alternatives may or may not have in common. Presumably, the most important attribute for her is considered first. The preference for alternative *A* or *B* is assumed to change by very small amounts during small time intervals, producing a gradual drift in preferences over time towards *A* or *B*. After spending some time thinking about an attribute and its attached consequences the decision maker might consider another attribute. Again she contemplates the aspects of the attribute for alternative *A* and *B* and now her preference state might tend to that alternative that was less preferred after considering a previous attribute. The decision maker might consider further attributes or reconsider attributes. This process goes on until the decision maker has strong enough preference to make a decision in favor of either of these alternatives. To illustrate the process consider the figure below.

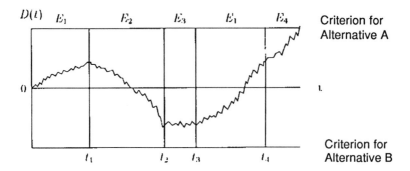

Figure 1. A stochastic trajectory representing a hypothetical decision process.

In this example, at the very beginning of the decision problem the decision maker has neither a preference for alternative *A* nor a preference for alternative *B*, i.e., she is indifferent to *A* or *B*, so $D(0) = 0$. When she starts thinking about the first attribute clearly her preference is directed towards alternative *A*. After a period of time, the decision maker starts considering the second attribute. Now her preferences strongly reverses towards alternative *B*. Again, after some time, she contemplates a third attribute. But reflecting on this attribute does not change her preference for either alternative, i.e., the aspects regarding this attribute and the anticipated consequences might be considered to have the same effect for both alternatives. Then the attribute the decision maker started with comes back into consideration. This time the deliberation for this attribute lasts longer than the first time. This might be due to spending more time thinking about certain aspects and their consequences or about new aspects of the same attribute. In any case, this attribute seems to be so important to the decision maker that she reconsiders it and alternative *A* clearly is favored with respect to this attribute. Finally, one last attribute is considered, and the decision maker has a strong enough preference to decide for alternative *A*, i.e. the preference state reaches a preset criterion, established by the decision maker.

Since the preference state at any point in time is not observable and not necessarily open to introspection, the hypothetical process described above is not directly observable. Nevertheless, some properties of the model are obvious:

- The preference for alternative *A* or *B* changes during the deliberation process.

- The strength of preference changes depending on the attribute considered momentarily.

- Changing the criteria may have an impact on the final decision.

- The decision maker may be biased towards an alternative and therefore have a higher *a priori* preference for this alternative.

- Setting the decision maker under time pressure may reverse a decision, e.g., forcing the decision maker to make her decision by time t_2 she would probably decide for alternative *B*.

- The order of the attributes the decision maker is considering may be crucial for the decision outcome.

In the next section we develop a formal model for capturing important features of this situation.

DEVELOPING MDFT

Rather than presenting the entire model at once, MDFT is developed piece by piece from multi-attribute utility theory (MAUT), similar to the way DFT is developed from subjective expected utility (SEU) theory by Busemeyer & Townsend (1993). Note, however, that this way of introducing the model is chosen for a clear understanding of the basic assumptions of the model by an audience most familiar with MAUT. The model originally stands in the tradition of the information-processing approach based on stochastic process mechanisms.

The most widely applied model in multi-attribute utility theory is based on the additive multi-attribute utility function, written as

$$u(\mathbf{x}) = \sum_{i=1}^{n} w_i u_i(x_i) \tag{1}$$

where $\mathbf{x} = (x_1, x_2, ..., x_k)$ and x_i is a specific amount of attribute X_i. The aggregate utility of an alternative is a weighted average of its single-attribute utilities $u_i(x_i)$. The weights w_i serve as scaling parameters that express the tradeoffs among the attributes with $\Sigma_i w_i = 1$. From a cognitive point of view, the weights can be interpreted to reflect the amount of attention paid to the attributes (Busemeyer & Townsend, 1993). The preference for alternative A or alternative B is determined by the sign of the difference in utility for each alternative,

$$d = u_A(\mathbf{x}) - u_B(\mathbf{x}) = \sum_{i=1}^{n} w_i [u_A(x_i) - u_B(x_i)]. \tag{2}$$

Alternative A is chosen if $d > 0$, and alternative B is chosen if $d < 0$. Since the weights and the utilities are assumed the same on every repetition of the choice task, this model cannot account for the observed variability of human preference. One way to overcome this problem is to allow the decision maker to change the weight for the importance of an attribute when confronted with the same decision at a different point in time. This is intuitively reasonable: what seems to be very important today may be less important tomorrow. We can express this formally by letting the weights w_i be random variables. This means, the aggregate utility of an alternative becomes a random variable

$$U(\mathbf{x}) = \sum_{i=1}^{n} W_i u(x_i) \tag{3}$$

and, therefore, the difference between two aggregated utilities determining the preference state on each trial,

$$D = U_A(\mathbf{x}) - U_B(\mathbf{x}) \tag{4}$$

is a random variable. Thus, preference for alternative A, say, is a probabilistic event with probability $p = Pr(D>0)$.

But it is plausible that the decision for alternative A or B, in terms of the difference between the "random" utilities is not based on just a single sample. For example, considering the attribute "safety" of our car example, the decision maker might think about the consequences of having this particular air bag, in case of an accident and the very next moment she might worry about the air bag opening too easily and causing an accident. She might also reconsider how important it really is to have double safety belts or whether it is also annoying.

Thus, the importance of single aspects of an attribute may change over time within a single decision task while considering different consequences. Moreover, new aspects of an attribute could come to the decision maker's mind as she is actively seeking more information about an attribute. For the following development let us consider aspects within only one attribute.

An initial comparison of an aspect determines the preference state for the first sample,

$$D(1) = U_A(1) - U_B(1).$$

A moment later the importance of that aspect may have changed or a new aspect is considered. The preference state for alternative A or B is now determined by adding this new utility difference to the previous preference and so on, i.e.,

$$
\begin{aligned}
D(2) &= D(1) + [U_A(2) - U_B(2)] \\
D(n) &= D(n-1) + [U_A(n) - U_B(n)] \\
&= \sum_i [U_A(i) - U_B(i)], \qquad i = 1, \ldots, n
\end{aligned} \tag{5}
$$

The process stops when the preset criterion c is reached by $D(n)$. Positive preference states represent a momentary preference towards alternative A and it is taken as soon as $D(n)$ exceeds the criterion c, negative preference states represent a momentary preference towards alternative B and it is taken as soon as $-D(n)$ exceeds the criterion c. The number of samples N needed to reach the criterion is a random variable, and the decision time is an increasing function of N.[1]

The next step is that we allow the decision maker to be biased towards an alternative, i.e. she has a higher preference for one alternative *a priori*, based on knowledge or past experience. We can express the bias towards an alternative by letting the initial preference state be larger than the neutral point, $D(0) > 0$, favoring alternative A in this case, or by letting the initial preference state be smaller than the neutral point, $D(0) < 0$, favoring alternative B. One may also want to account for the fact that aspects that have been considered early on may be weighed differently from aspects considered later in determining a current preference state. For example, early aspects may have a strong impact ("primacy effect") or late aspects may be more important than early ones ("recency effect"). An easy way to incorporate these position effects is to weigh the previous preference by a parameter s, say, called growth-decay rate. Given the value for $D(0) \equiv z$, the preference state is

$$
\begin{aligned}
D(0) &= z \\
D(1) &= (1-s)z + [U_A(1) - U_B(1)] \\
D(n) &= (1-s)D(n-1) + [U_A(n) - U_B(n)] \qquad\qquad (6) \\
&= (1-s)^n z + \sum_i (1-s)^{n-i}[U_A(i) - U_B(i)], \qquad i = 1, \ldots, n
\end{aligned}
$$

If the growth-decay parameter is strictly between zero and one $(0 < s < 1)$ Eq. 6 produces recency effects so that the more recent

---

[1]Note that although there is a formal similarity between Eq. 2 and Eq. 5 the interpretation is quite different. In Eq. 2, we sum across attributes, in Eq. 5 we sum over aspects within attributes.

samples have greater impact. If the growth-decay parameter is less than zero, Eq. 6 produces primacy effects so that earlier samples have greater impact. Setting $s = 0$, no position effect is incorporated[2].

To make quantitative predictions for decision time let the deliberation time become continuous. Then the process of considering one attribute can be presented by a diffusion process called "Ornstein-Uhlenbeck Process with drift and two absorbing boundaries" (For details see Busemeyer & Townsend 1992, 1993; Diederich 1992, 1993a, 1993b). This process is characterized by a drift coefficient μ driving the approach to the boundaries (cf. Cox & Miller, 1965). In DFT, this parameter takes the following form:

$$\mu(D(t)) = d - s \cdot D(t)$$

where d is the difference in utility for each alternative and s represents the position effect defined earlier.

Now consider a choice problem with two alternatives and with each alternative having three attributes E_1, E_2, and E_3, say. For each attribute considered by the decision maker a drift coefficient is defined:

$$\mu_j(D(t)) = d_j - s \cdot D(t) \tag{7}$$

respectively, where d_j is the mean utility difference for alternative A and B for the jth attribute.

In Figure 2, it can be seen how the drift coefficient $\mu(D(t))$ relates to the preference for alternative A and B.

---

[2]Busemeyer & Townsend (1993) build in another dynamic variable in DFT, called *goal gradient*, that accounts for the fact that the time to make a decision depends on the approach-avoidance nature of the conflict of deciding between alternative A and B. This possible extension of MDFT is not followed up here for lack of space, however.

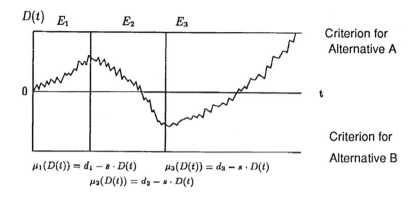

Figure 2. A decision process described by a stochastic diffusion process called Ornstein-Uhlenbeck process with drift and two absorbing boundaries.

d_j determines the asymptotic direction and magnitude of the mean preference state, i.e. d_j reflects the force directed towards the criterion (in this example, $d_1 > 0$, the force is directed to the criterion for alternative A). The parameter s reflects a restoring force directed towards the origin and of a magnitude proportional to the distance. Next, the decision maker considers the second attribute. Clearly, in our example, d_2 is smaller than 0, favoring alternative B. For the third attribute, d_3 is larger than 0, favoring alternative A. Finally the process reaches the criterion for alternative A, i.e. the decision maker has a strong enough preference to settle for this alternative.

Note that there is no claim that the decision maker consciously carries out the computations for the preference state at any moment in time. Rather, MDFT should be conceived as a possible description of the dynamics of the deliberation process.

MODES OF ATTRIBUTE SELECTION

There are different ways how the decision maker may draw upon the attributes. One possibility is to consider the attributes in a fixed order at fixed points in time. The order of attributes contemplated might be fixed because the decision maker thinks first about the attribute most important to her, then about the second most important attribute, etc. In our car buying example, the decision maker might first consider the attribute "safety" because she has to drive a lot in heavy traffic, has children to take with her and so on. For a decision maker with a very limited budget the most important attribute may be the price for the car and all expenses for it. Or, in a sales situation the decision maker may first attend to the attribute most emphasized by a salesperson. The point in time when the next attribute is considered may be fixed, for example, when a person instructs the decision maker to think about the next attribute. Another possibility is that the order of the attributes is still ordered by importance, but the time the decision maker spends with each attribute varies randomly. Furthermore, neither the order of attributes considered nor the time the decision maker deliberates about its attached consequences may be fixed. The decision maker starts thinking about any of the attributes and spends some time thinking about it. There may be no plausible hierarchy of importance of the attributes nor another point of view inducing a reasonable order. This appears to be a more realistic approach for many real life situations.

Finally, I discuss here in more detail the case where the decision maker has no predetermined order to consider the attributes and also switches back and forth between a set of attributes. The decision maker may spend more time with an attribute that is more important for her or that is of particular complexity, i.e., an attribute having many aspects. She may also switch back more often to this attribute. Formally, this can be described by assigning probabilities for staying in one attribute and probabilities for switching to another attribute. For our three-attribute-problem, the following state transition diagram is obtained:

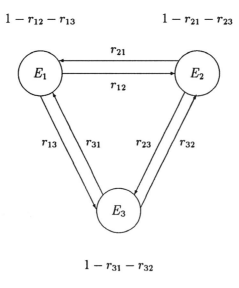

$$1 - r_{12} - r_{13} \qquad\qquad\qquad 1 - r_{21} - r_{23}$$

$$1 - r_{31} - r_{32}$$

Figure 3. A transition state diagram for three attributes.

The smaller r_{ij} is, the less likely it is to switch from attribute i to attribute j. This means increasing r_{ij} increases the weight or importance of attribute j.

Some interesting phenomena can be predicted by this model. Perhaps the most important phenomenon is the reversal behavior of the decision maker over time, i.e. the decision maker has a high probability for choosing, say, alternative B early on and, as time goes by, she tends to decide for alternative A. We can get this result in at least two different ways.

1. Let the mean differences in utility for the three attributes be $d_1 = .45$, $d_2 = .45$, and $d_3 = -.3$, and let the r_{ij} be all the same for all attributes, i.e. the importance is the same for all three attributes. Let the decision maker start with the third attribute first. The results for different r_{ij} are shown in Figure 4.

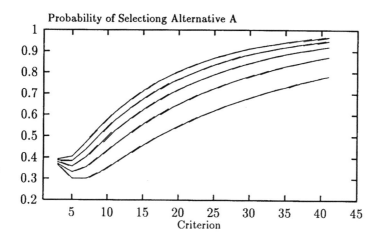

Figure 4. Change of preference over time when the decision maker focusses her attention at the beginning of the decision problem on the attribute that favors altertanive B, $(d_3 < 0)$. For the uppermost curve $r_{ij} = .06$, for the second upper curve $r_{ij} = .05$ and so on up to the lowest curve where $r_{ij} = .02$.

At the beginning of the decision problem the decision maker focusses her attention on the attribute that favors alternative B, $(d_3 < 0)$. Therefore, her preference is directed to that alternative. Then she considers those attributes that are in favor of alternative A, $(d_1, d_2 > 0)$ and her preference gradually drifts towards this alternative. Spending more time on the decision problem the decision maker reverses her initial preference for alternative B into a preference for alternative A since overall there is more evidence to decide for alternative A.

Increasing r_{ij} increases the frequency the decision maker switches from one attribute to the next reducing the amount of time the decision maker reflects on an attribute each time. Comparing, e.g., the lowest curve, where $r_{ij} = .02$ and the uppermost curve, where $r_{ij} = .06$ in Figure 4 shows that the decision maker reverses her preference sooner when r_{ij} is larger because she spends less time considering the attribute that favors alternative B before she switches to those attributes that favor alternative A.

2. A similar result, though in a different direction, can be obtained by letting the decision maker consider any of the attributes first, i.e. she starts with probability 1/3 reflecting on any attribute. But the attribute in favor for alternative B gets a higher importance by increasing the probability to switch to that attribute, i.e. r_{13}, $r_{23} > r_{12}$, r_{21}, r_{31}, r_{32}. With the same parameters d_1, d_2, and d_3 as above, with $r_{12} = r_{21} = r_{31} = r_{32} = .02$ and with $r_{13} = r_{23}$ reaching from .06 to .09, Figure 5 shows the result for this situation.

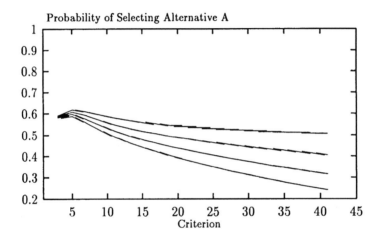

Figure 5. Change in preference over time when the attribute in favor for alternative B gets a higher importance. The uppermost curve indicates $r_{13} = r_{23} = .06$, the second upper curve indicates $r_{13} = r_{23} = .07$, the lowest curve indicates $r_{13} = r_{23} = .09$. r_{12}, r_{21}, r_{31}, r_{32} equal in all cases .02.

Note that there is an important difference between DFT and the multi-attribute extension. In DFT the timebased preference reversals can only be received if the decision maker has a strong bias towards an alternative, i.e. $D(0) \neq 0$ whereas in MDFT no bias towards an alternative has to be assumed because there are drift coefficients that allow the process to take different directions in the course of time.

EMPIRICAL TESTING

MDFT is meant to model complex decisions in real life. However, these real-life decisions do not permit the experimental control necessary to distinguish between competing models. Therefore, it is necessary to develop simple experimental procedures designed to investigate important features of the theoretical build-up. For the following experimental procedures, it is assumed that the relevant attributes are known *a priori* or given by the experimenter.

MDFT models the dynamics of preference strength and its stochastic process assumptions lead to quantitative predictions of choice reaction time and choice probabilities. To estimate these entities empirically, many replications of the choices are required. However, presenting the same choice alternatives again and again does not make much sense for alternatives that are easily discriminable, since the subject will remember the choices made and people would probably not be willing to participate in that kind of experiment. To overcome this problem, a paradigm for decision *under uncertainty* will be employed to test the model. Assume two alternatives are defined by a number of attributes. Each attribute is characterized by a single aspect, i.e., in this context attribute and aspect can be treated as the same. However, the quantitative value of each aspect is not fixed but is determined by a probability distribution. At each presentation of the alternatives a random value is taken on for each attribute. In analogy to natural situations where the decision maker at first does not have a good idea about the possible range of values of an attribute, the decision maker will learn and infer the probability distribution attached to the attributes after repeated presentations of the alternatives.

One possible experimental procedure is to vary systematically the amount of time the decision maker may spend for coming up with her decision. Under extreme time pressure the decision maker should tend to consider fewer attributes than without a deadline and this should show in the observed choice probabilities. Moreover, manipulating the distributional variance of the attributes should have specific effects on the time spent with an attribute. Another variation is based on the fact that attributes may covary over the alternatives to different degrees. For example, the attributes price and quality may have a high correlation and it is conceivable that the decision maker treats them as a single attribute. This calls for a cross-validation analysis where it is important to construct the most parsimonious model possible.

Another type of interaction of attributes may occur that seems to question the validity of the assumption that attributes are considered sequentially. As noticed by one of the reviewers, there may be a tradeoff between attributes. For example, in buying a car one may ask oneself the question "Am I paying too much for this car's reliability?" One way to test this is to consider tradeoffs as separate attributes. Thus, the decision maker may think of reliability, then price, and then reliability per price.

SUMMARY

The theory presented here strives to model the deliberation process of a decision maker trying to make a decision between two alternatives possessing a multi-attribute structure. In agreement with decision field theory (Busemeyer & Townsend, 1993), it is assumed that the decision maker undergoes a time-consuming process of retrieving, comparing, and integrating the information over time. It goes beyond DFT in specifying how the relevant attributes determine the decision time and the final choice. This multi-attribute decision field theory (MDFT) is formalized as a stochastic diffusion process and permits precise quantitative predictions of choice response times and choice probabilities. Since MDFT formally reduces to DFT in the case where only one attribute is considered, all assumptions and predictions of DFT are valid for this multi-attribute extension of the theory.

REFERENCES

Busemeyer, J.R. ,& Townsend, J.T. (1992). Fundamental derivations from decision field theory. *Mathematical Social Sciences, 23(3)*, 255-282.

Busemeyer, J.R., & Townsend, J.T. (1993). Decision Field Theory: A dynamic-cognitive approach to decision-making in an uncertain environment. *Psychological Review, 100(3)*, 432-459.

Cox, D.R., & Miller, H.D. (1965). *The theory of stochastic processes.* London: Chapman and Hall.

Diederich, A. (1992). *Intersensory facilitation: Race, superposition, and diffusion models for reaction time to multiple stimuli.* Frankfurt: Verlag Peter Lang.

Diederich, A. (1993). A diffusion model for intersensory facilitation of reaction time. G.H. Fischer, & D. Laming (Eds). *Mathematical Psychology, Psychometric, and Methodology.* New York, Springer Verlag.

Keeney, R.L., & Raiffa, H. (1976). *Decisions with multiple objectives: preferences and value tradeoffs.* New York: Wiley.

von Winterfeldt, D., & Edwards, W. (1986). *Decision analysis and behavioral research.* Cambridge: Cambridge University Press.

Contributions to Decision Making - I
J.-P. Caverni, M. Bar-Hillel, F.H. Barron and H. Jungermann (Editors)
193

DESIRABILITY AND HINDSIGHT BIASES IN

PREDICTING RESULTS OF A MULTI-PARTY ELECTION

Ilan Fischer [1] and David V. Budescu[2]

1 Department of Psychology, University of Haifa, Haifa, 31905, Israël

2 Department of Psychology, University of Illinois, Champaign,
Il 61820, USA

Abstract. Three weeks before the 1992 elections to the Knesset, the Israeli parliament, 250 students were asked to predict the election outcomes and to rate their identification with the six major political parties. The predictions were positively correlated with the respondents' political preferences, revealing a significant Desirability Bias.

Three weeks after the elections these subjects were contacted and 110 of them attempted to reconstruct their predictions. Comparison of the pre- and post-election predictions revealed a systematic Hindsight Bias, i.e. a tendency to shift the reconstructed ratings in the direction of the actual results.

Secondary data analysis efforts, taking advantage of the special features of multi-party elections, revealed that: (i) the Desirability Bias is inconsistent with traditional Wishful Thinking and Bandwagon accounts, and is best explained by the selective Social Interaction hypothesis (e.g. Ross, 1977), and (ii) as suggested by Hawkins and Hastie's (1990) hybrid model, the Hindsight Bias reflects a combination of memory and self-relevance factors.

In the last two decades research on human judgment and decision making has been dominated by the "heuristics and biases paradigm" (e.g. Kahneman, Slovic & Tversky, 1982). Following the seminal work of Kahneman and Tversky numerous researchers have demonstrated repeatedly that judgments under uncertainty are often accomplished by simple heuristic rules which are not necessarily consistent with standard probability theory. Because the results of these heuristics occasionally deviate from the normative rules they were labeled biases. Comprehensive reviews of these judgmental biases can be found in books by Hogarth (1987) and by Kahneman, Slovic and Tversky (1982).

Most empirical evidence for the existence of these heuristics was obtained in laboratory studies, but they have also been replicated in "real life" settings such as medical diagnosis, and political, sport and economic forecasting.

The current study focuses on two biases - Desirability and Hindsight - in the forecasting of political events. A distinctive feature of the present study is that the target events are embedded in the context of prediction of the outcomes of multi-party parliamentary elections by a large sample of motivated and highly involved voters. This context provides a natural, and ecologically valid, opportunity to test conflicting explanations regarding the sources of the two biases.

DESIRABILITY BIAS (DB)

The terms "desirability bias", "wishful thinking" and "optimism" (e.g. Bar-Hillel & Budescu, 1992) have been used interchangeably to describe the existence of normatively unjustified relationships between people's preferences, or desires, and their expectations and predictions regarding outcomes of future events. The existence of DB in the context of elections was documented more than half a century ago: 93% of those who preferred Roosevelt in the 1932 US Presidential elections expected him to win, whereas only 27% of those who preferred Hoover thought Roosevelt would win (Hayes, 1936). Granberg and Brent (1983) estimated the correlation between preferences and expectancies to be .65.

Several other studies have reported similar preference-expectations relationships (Brown,1982; Carroll, 1978; Frenkel and Doobs, 1976; Granberg, 1983; Lazarsfeld, Berelson, and Gaudet, 1944; Lemert,1986). The overall preference ratio (i.e. the ratio of the number of people expecting their favorite candidate to win / to lose) is 4: 1, and the correlations between preferences and expectations range between 0.42 and 0.68 (Granberg and Brent, 1983). The effect is especially strong in close, and hard to predict, elections but it is also significant in elections with relatively certain outcomes. The bias has been replicated in other countries such as Canada, New Zealand, Great Britain, Sweden and Israel, with different political (parliamentary vs. presidential) and electoral (national vs. regional elections) systems, (Badad and Yacobos, 1993; Badad, Hills and O`Driscoll, 1992; Frenkel and Doobs, 1976; Granberg, 1983).

Two intuitive explanations for this result are Wishful Thinking (WT) and Bandwagon (BW) (Granberg & Holmberg, 1988). The WT model assumes that voters' preferences determine their expectations. This causal relationship is best explained by Heider's theory of cognitive balance, according to which people modify their expectations, to achieve congruence with their desires (Heider, 1958). The BW model assumes an opposite causal relationship, namely that one's expectations affect political preferences (e.g. Lazarsfeld et al., 1944). However, because most relevant studies are correlational in nature, it is difficult to distinguish between these theories. A third account is offered by the Social Interaction hypothesis (SI) (Ross, 1977), which stipulates that many voters (including fully rational ones) fail to appreciate the degree to which their perceptions of the electorate mood and opinions are biased (Ross, 1977). Voters are likely to observe a degree of agreement between their preferences and those of others in their social environment, and may conclude that a majority of the public will vote as they, and others in their social surrounding, plan to. Consequently, they overestimate the chances of their favorite candidate to win the elections. Such a process reflects proper inference based on a highly biased sample of evidence.

HINDSIGHT BIAS (HB)

People's tendency to claim that they had predicted (in foresight) uncertain outcomes after the events have already occurred, is commonly known as the "Hindsight Bias" (e.g. Fischhoff, 1975; Fischhoff and Beyth, 1975) or the "I knew it all along" feeling (Wood, 1978). A typical within-subject study of HB consists of two stages: The first session takes place before the target event, and the second takes place after the results of this event have become known. During the first session subjects are required to assess the chances of the possible outcomes of the event, and in the second session they are instructed to reconstruct their original judgments. The term HB applies to the following pattern of empirical regularities: (i) People exaggerate what could have been anticipated in foresight; (ii) They believe that others could, and should, have been able to anticipate and forecast events with higher accuracy; (iii) They "misremember" their own forecasts: In hindsight they recall being wiser before the event than was actually the case (e.g. Fischhoff, 1975; Fischhoff and Beyth, 1975).

It is not clear whether HB is caused by cognitive or other (motivational) factors. Empirical findings are inconclusive and provide partial support for both explanations. According to Fischhoff (1975), the bias is purely cognitive: When outcome information becomes available, it is assimilated and incorporated within the existing memory data base. Hence, the foresight state can't be fully recovered in hindsight. Empirical support for the cognitive explanation of the bias has been provided, among others, by Connolly and Bukszar (1990). Their subjects analyzed different business cases. Half the subjects were provided with "real" outcomes, while the other half saw how the results were generated by flipping a coin. Yet, both groups showed significant, and equally large, hindsight shifts. Christensen-Szalansky and Willham (1991) meta-analyzed results of 122 studies and, as predicted by the cognitive explanation, found that the bias was stronger for events that actually occurred than for events that did not. Alternative cognitive explanations such as anchoring on the known outcome and insufficient adjustment to infer the original judgment have been reviewed by Hawkins and Hastie (1990).

Other studies have demonstrated lawful relationships between the HB and motivational factors, where motivation is interpreted in a broad, and sometime quite vague, fashion. For example, Schkade and Kilbourne (1991) concluded that the bias was significantly larger for undesirable than for desirable outcomes. They also uncovered a significant "disappointment effect": The greatest bias occurred when strong expectations were disconfirmed by a negative outcome. Campbell and Tesser (1983) found that several individual constructs such as need for control and for predicting one's environment were positively associated with the amount of HB exhibited by the subjects.

Hawkins and Hastie (1990) claim that all explanations of HB are "hybrids" of motivational and cognitive factors, and that it is impossible to distinguish unequivocally between the two classes. This claim is supported by results reported by Hell, Gigerenzer, Gauggel, Mall and Mueller (1988). They found poor memorability to be a necessary condition for the appearance of HB. Yet, this effect interacted with, and was moderated by, the intensity of the subjects' motivation to recall their original judgments.

Fischhoff and Beyth (1975) were the first to find HB in a political context: They asked subjects to predict the outcomes of Nixon's trips to China and the Soviet Union in 1972. The probabilities of the various outcomes, when recalled after the trip, were systematically enhanced by the actual outcomes. Leary (1981, 1982) studied predictions of the 1980 US presidential elections, and Synodinos (1986) examined the predictions regarding the 1982 gubernatorial elections in Hawaii, using between-subjects designs. They found HB, but only limited support for any motivational explanation. Other researchers have used (more appropriate in our opinion) within-subjects designs: Pennington (1981) found only weak support for HB in predictions made by members of the Conservative and Labor parties regarding the results of the British General Elections of May 1979. He speculated that the bias may be less pronounced when people make judgments about matters of concern to them, to which they have devoted a considerable amount of thought. Powell (1988) compared pre- and post-election predictions regarding the 1984 US national and three state races. Although HB was not found in all cases subjects recalled having assigned higher probabilities to the actual winners, remembered having more confidence in the accuracy of these predictions, and claimed to have had more knowledge of the candidates than they actually had reported before the elections. Finally, in a recent poll (results published in *USA Today*, Dec 30, 1993) 70% of the respondents (n=1,002) reported voting in the 1992 US presidential elections (the actual turnout was only 61%), and 50% of the respondents reported voting for Clinton (who actually obtained only 43% of the votes).

THE PRESENT STUDY

Most studies of judgmental biases in the context of elections have been conducted in political systems with two parties. In such systems one can vote for, and identify with, only one party. Furthermore, one party's success coincides (and is confounded) with the other's failure. The primary goal of the present investigation was to study DB and HB in the context of a multi-party election. Such an electoral system offers the voters a wider variety of parties to choose from, and one can identify (possibly at different levels of intensity) with more than one party. It also provides researchers an opportunity to elicit judgments regarding several interrelated events simultaneously. Consequently, studies conducted in multi-party elections are better suited for distinguishing between the competing explanations of the various biases.

Our second goal is to take advantage of this feature in order to shed some light on the sources of DB and HB. Some of the special features of the multi-party system allow us to (i)contrast the standard WT/BW and SI explanations for the DB, and (ii)compare the cognitive and motivational explanations of HB.

According to the standard WT/BW hypothesis, one would expect to find DB for all political parties in an election, i.e. consistent overestimation of the chances of all one's favored parties and underestimation of all the disliked ones. A modified (and weaker) version of the WT explanation predicts a significant DB only for the one party the respondent would like to see win, but not necessarily for all others. Such a pattern cannot be explained as a BW effect, but it is consistent with the SI hypothesis, which predicts bias only in judgments regarding the party that defines the voter's immediate social environment. Thus, removing the voter's favorite party from the set of predictions should eliminate the relationship between identification and predictions.

To test various explanations for HB we examine accuracy measures calculated only for some of the outcomes and / or subjects. For example, to validate the cognitive explanation we compare accuracy measures for events which actually occurred and those events which did not. To test a "self flattery" explanation, i.e. subjects' tendency to present themselves in a favorable light, half of the respondents were told that their original predictions were lost. Their reconstructed predictions are compared with the judgments of the other group (respondents who know that the original data are available). If HB is caused by self flattery, we expect to find a larger bias for the first group. To test an alternative "self relevance" explanation, i.e. subjects' tendency to predict differentially the outcome of their favorite party, we compared the predictions of subjects with different political identifications regarding the two major political blocks. If HB is driven by this factor (which follows quite naturally from the notion of DB), we would expect to find higher levels of bias in people's predictions of the block they identify with.

The present study was conducted during the general national elections to the Israeli parliament, the "Knesset", in June, 1992. A total of 25 parties participated in the elections. For the purpose of the study, they were grouped into seven major political "clusters": (1) The Likud party (identified as right - center, which has been in power since

1977); (2) Three small right wing parties (running separately). We will refer to 1 and 2 combined as the Right Block. (3) The Labor party (identified as left-center, which had been in power between 1948 and 1977); (4) Three small left wing parties (that had merged prior to the elections). We will refer to 3 and 4 combined as the Left Block. (5) Four independent religious parties; (6) Three Arab parties; (7) A few "others".

Historically, no political party has ever achieved an absolute majority of the votes in the Israeli national elections, and Israel has always been governed by coalition governments (with either the Labor or Likud parties as leaders). Thus, although a large number of parties was involved in the elections, we also analyzed the results according to the inferred winning coalition (the Left or Right Block).

METHOD

Subjects: 250 undergraduate students at the University of Haifa volunteered to participate in the first stage. They were first, or second, year students in several large Social Sciences departments (Psychology, Economics, Political Science, and Statistics). All subjects were Israeli citizens above the legal voting age (18). The participation rate in the national elections is over 80%, so the respondents can be considered potential voters.

Instruments: Subjects responded to a questionnaire with two sections. First they were asked to predict the number of parliament seats for each of the seven parties. Subjects were reminded that the predictions should add up to 120 (The total number of seats in the Knesset). For each prediction, subjects also provided a confidence rating on a 10 point scale. Next, they were asked to rate their identification with every party except "Others" on seven point scales from 1:"Absolutely no identification" to 7: "High identification".

Procedure: The questionnaire was administered twice. The first administration took place three weeks before the elections and was based upon voluntary participation in class settings. The questionnaire was filled either at the beginning or end of large classes. Upon completion of the questionnaire all respondents received small gifts (pens valued at $2) in appreciation of their cooperation. Over 90% of the students approached agreed to participate in the study.

Subjects also provided personal information including name and address, and were told that it might be used to contact them for further studies. Each questionnaire was identified by a numerical code, but the sheet with the personal information was separated from the questionnaire in the presence of the subjects, to assure the confidentiality and anonymity of the responses.

The second administration took place three weeks after the elections. Identical questionnaires were mailed to the 250 subjects, who were asked to reconstruct, as accurately as possible, their responses on the first administration. The subjects were asked to use their original numerical code. This allowed us to match the two sets of responses. No names, or other identifying information, appeared on the forms or the return envelope. Half the subjects (randomly selected) were sent letters explaining that their previous responses were lost, and asking them to reconstruct their original predictions. The other half were not given any specific explanation, but simply asked to attempt to reproduce their responses. Subjects were informed that all responses mailed back within two weeks would participate in a lottery with several monetary prizes (amounts of $3, $7, and $17). One hundred and ten of the original respondents (44%) mailed back the forms within the designated period

RESULTS

Desirability Bias

The total number of seats allocated was different from 120 in 44 questionnaires, which were excluded from the analysis[1].

Table 1 presents the mean predictions and sample sizes in each cell, and the last column presents the actual results of the elections. The predictions for each of the parties were analyzed as a function of the respondents' level of identification with that party. One way ANOVAs uncovered significant effects for four parties (see Table 1). Post hoc Student-Newman-Keuls tests showed that in three cases the effects were due only to the difference between the small and extreme groups with the highest (7) identification level and all other respondents (identification levels 1 - 6). The former group consistently overestimated the party's success. The predictions for the Labor party

---

[1] One of the reviewers suggested rescaling all the responses to add up to 120, and re-analyzing the data without excluding anyone from the sample. All the major results reported in this section were replicated under this approach, and all the conclusions hold.

followed a different pattern, with the party's fiercest opponents (identification levels 1 and 2) underestimating its success, by comparison to the others (levels 3-7).

Table 1

Mean Predictions for Each of the Political Parties as a Function of the Respondent's Level of Identification with the Party

Political Party	Level of Identification								Election Results
	1	2	3	4	5	6	7	Mean	
LIKUD $(F_{6,192}=3.1*)$									
Mean	37	37	37	37	38	39	44	38	32
n	35	53	32	22	28	23	7	202	
LABOR $(F_{6,192}=5.5*)$									
Mean	38	39	41	42	42	43	44	42	44
n	11	21	23	18	42	58	26	202	
LEFT $(F_{6,191}=0.7)$									
Mean	10	11	11	11	10	11	11	11	12
n	32	17	24	17	24	47	37	202	
RIGHT $(F_{6,192}=5.8*)$									
Mean	9	8	9	10	9	10	12	9	11
n	72	42	10	15	18	23	19	202	
RELIGIOUS $(F_{5,193}=2.2)$									
Mean	10	10	13	9	12	13	--	11	16
n	123	34	14	15	7	6	0	202	
ARAB $(F_{6,190}=3.2*)$									
Mean	5	6	4	4	5	4	9	5	5
n	107	30	18	28	8	2	4	202	

Note: Means rounded to the nearest integer
*: $p < (0.05/6 = 0.008)$.

The number of seats predicted for each party was also correlated with the respondent's level of identification with that party. For three parties the correlations between the two variables are significantly larger than 0 (Likud: r=.16; Labor: r=.35; and Right: r=.33; p<.05 in all cases).

The respondents rated their level of identification with each party, and the previous analysis treated each set of predictions separately. Another way to illustrate the effect is to compare the Knesset compositions predicted by people with opposing political views. For all individuals we identified the party with which they reported the highest level of identification (which was not necessarily 7). Then, we compared the predictions of the 53 respondents who reported the highest levels of identification with the Right block, and of the 126 respondents who most identified with the Left. Table 2 displays the average prediction of these two groups.

Table 2

Mean Predictions for the Knesset Composition by two Groups of Respondents with Opposing Political Identifications

Political Party	Identification with	
	Left Block (n=126)	Right Block (n=53)
Likud	37.2	38.5
Labor *	43.1	38.9
Left	10.8	11.2
Right *	8.8	10.8
Religious	10.7	10.5
Arab	4.7	4.5
Others	5.7	7.1

Note: *: p < .05

The two "projected parliaments" are significantly different by a MANOVA ($F_{6,170}=10.8$, p < .05). The difference is due to the fact that the left oriented voters predicted more seats for Labor ($F_{1,175}=36.9$, p < .05), and those leaning to the right predicted more seats for the small Right parties ($F_{1,175}=16.5$, p < .05).

To distinguish the WT/BW and the SI explanations of the effect, we repeated the analysis after eliminating the subjects' predictions regarding their favorite parties[2]. Consistent with the SI hypothesis, the desirability bias vanished. The only significant ANOVA was obtained for the Labor party: $(F_{4,96}=5 °\sim P <.05; r = 0.41, p < .05)$

Hindsight Bias

Twenty of the individuals who responded on both occasions were excluded from this analysis because the total number of seats they allocated differed from 120 on one at least one of the questionnaires[3] .

The accuracy of the predictions was quantified by the Mean (across all political blocks) Absolute Deviation of the Predictions (MADP) from the actual results. Measures of accuracy were also calculated for the judgments regarding the Left (MADPL), and the Right (MADPR) blocks[4] . Accuracy measures were calculated for the pre- and post-election judgments. Most conclusions were based on the analysis of the *signed* difference: HB = (MADP$_{pre}$ - MADP$_{post}$). The expected HB effect (post-election judgments closer to the actual results than their pre-election counterparts) yields positive differences.

We conducted a preliminary analysis to determine whether the respondents differed from the nonrespondents in any important way. The comparison revealed that the two groups were identical in terms of their age and gender composition, and reported similar political preferences. Furthermore, both groups predicted, correctly and with equal confidence, that the Left block would win the elections. On the average, the pre-election predictions of the respondents were slightly more accurate than those of the nonrespondents.

Table 3 presents the MADPs of the pre- and post-election judgments and HB, the signed difference between the two, for the three target events. As expected, all differences are positive, indicating that the post election judgments were closer to the actual outcomes.

---

[2] A few subjects reporting equally high identification with more than one party were excluded from this analysis.

[3] One of the reviewers suggested rescaling all the responses to add up to 120, and re-analyzing the data without excluding anyone from the sample. All the major results reported in this section were replicated under this approach, and all the conclusions hold.

[4] Generally, (MADPL + MADPR) < MADP, because they are based on only 4 of the 7 parties participating in the elections.

A one sided within-subject t test revealed a significant HB effect across all parties (MADP) ($t_{89}=2.6$, p < .05). The effect was also verified by a sign test comparing the number of subjects for which post-election MADP was larger than pre-election MADP, with the number of respondents displaying the opposite pattern. As predicted, the former pattern was more prevalent ($X^2_1=10.0$, p < .05).

The memory-update hypothesis predicts a larger HB effect for the event which eventually occured (victory for the Left block), than for events which failed to materialize (victory for the Right). In agreement with this prediction we found a significant HB effect for MADPL, i.e. the Left block ($t_{89}=2.6$, p < .05), but not for MADPR, the Right block ($t_{89}=1.4$, p > .05).

Table 3

Mean Absolute Deviation of the Predictions from the Election Results and the Hindsight Effect for the Total Sample (n=90)

	MADP Before elections	MADP after elections	HB Effect
MADP	22.47	20.14	2.33 *
MADPL	6.32	5.21	1.11 *
MADPR	8.90	8.14	0.76

Note: *: p < .05

To test the self-flattery explanation we compared the post-election MADP of the two groups of subjects who were provided different justifications prior to the second administration. Contrary to this explanation, we found no significant differences between the two groups ($F_{1,89}$ <1). An Analysis of Covariance (ANCOVA) of the post-election judgments using the pre-election predictions as a covariate (Cronbach & Furby, 1970) yielded identical results.

Table 4

Mean Absolute Deviation of the Predictions Regarding the Left Block from the Election Results, and Hindsight Effect, as a Function of Respondents' Political Preference and Original Prediction Pattern

Political Preference	Predicted Winner	n	MADPL Before elections	MADPL after elections	HB Effect
Left	Left	59	5.3	4.3	1.0
Left	Right	5	8.4	6.8	1.6
Right	Left	17	6.7	5.6	1.1
Right	Right	9	11.1	9.8	1.3
Left	Mean	64	5.5	4.5	1.0
Right	Mean	26	8.2	7.0	1.2
Mean	Left	76	5.6	4.6	1.0
Mean	Right	14	10.1	8.7	1.4
Mean	Mean	90	6.3	5.2	1.1

The test of the self-relevance hypothesis relies on a partition of the subjects according to their political preferences and their original predictions of the elections outcome. Respondents were classified into four groups defined by their identification with the two major blocks, and by their predicted winner in the election. The groups are not equal in size (most respondents identified with, and predicted victory for, the Left) and the two variables are not independent (75% of the subjects predicted victory for their favorite block)[5] . ANOVAs of the HB effects revealed different patterns for the two events: The bias in the prediction of the Left block is uniform across the groups ($F_{1,86} < 1$, for respondents' identification, predicted winner and their interaction);

---

[5] The high correlation between the two classifications is, of course, a reflection of the previously discussed DB.

However, the accuracy of predictions regarding the Right block is related to the respondents' political identification ($F_{1,86}$=5.6, p < .05). Tables 4 and 5 display accuracy measures for the pre- and post-election judgments, and the HB effects, regarding the Left and Right blocks, respectively.

<u>Table 5</u>

Mean Absolute Deviation of the Predictions Regarding the
Right Block from the Election Results, and Hindsight Effect,
as a Function of Respondents' Political Preference and
Original Prediction Pattern

Political Preference	Predicted Winner	n	MADPR Before elections	MADPR after elections	HB Effect
Left	Left	59	8.5	7.0	1.5
Left	Right	5	8.0	5.8	2.2
Right	Left	17	9.2	9.4	-0.2
Right	Right	9	11.2	14.9	-3.7
Left	Mean	64	8.5	6.9	1.6
Right	Mean	26	9.9	11.3	-1.4
Mean	Left	76	8.7	7.5	1.2
Mean	Right	14	10.1	11.6	-1.5
Mean	Mean	90	8.9	8.1	0.8

Interestingly, subjects who identified with the losing Right block, and especially the small group who went as far as to predict its victory, showed the opposite of an HB effect (see also Mazursky & Ofir, 1990): They "remembered" having predicted a larger share of the vote to their favorite party.

DISCUSSION

The present study found a Desirability Bias in preelection predictions, and a Hindsight Bias in the postelection reconstruction of these judgments in multi-party national parliamentary elections. Note that both biases were relatively small (1 - 4 seats out of a total of 120). This is consistent with Pennigton's (1981) observation regarding the accuracy of judgments of important political events by motivated and involved subjects.

The predictions regarding four of the six major parties were biased in the direction of the respondents' political identifications. The correlations between predictions and identification, ranging between 0.12 and 0.35, were somewhat lower than those reported by Granberg and Brent (1983). This may be due to the different nature of the political and electoral system in Israel, and/or the nature of our sample (younger, more homogeneous and more left oriented than the national electorate).

One of the goals of this study was to distinguish between the WT/BW and the SI explanations of the DB. Both BW and WT assume the existence of a general tendency to achieve high congruence between one's predictions and preferences. Hence, the removal of one party (in this case the preferred one) should not affect significantly the overall pattern. On the other hand, the SI hypothesis predicts that people make correct inferences on the basis of biased evidence. It is assumed that people know and interact primarily with others with similar values, beliefs, attitudes, and political preferences, and tend to generalize from these interactions to the entire electorate and to overestimate the performancé of their favorite party. However, one's predictions about other parties should not be biased by this selective pattern of social interactions, and should not exhibit any systematic relationship between political identification and actual predictions.

The empirical results tend to favor the SI hypothesis. After removal of the voters' predictions for their favorite parties, the effect diminished considerably. In fact it persisted (although diminished in magnitude) only for the Labor party. This can be attributed to the unusual pattern of predictions observed for this party: While in most other cases the DB was due to a minority of fervent backers of the party, the differences in predictions about the Labor success were due primarily to its most vehement opponents.

We conclude that the relation between identification and outcome prediction cannot be explained by WT or BW, and it is driven primarily by a selective pattern of social interactions. This latter conclusion is only tentative and requires further rigorous tests. Specifically, one could argue that removal of predictions regarding one's favorite party eliminates effects which do not reflect exclusively the influence of one's social environment. It is also possible that the process operating is different from the one postulated by SI. Although no specific suggestions for such effects and processes have been offered, future studies should attempt to go beyond establishing the pattern of relationships between predictions and political preferences. One promising possibility calls for an attempt to map the voters' social environment and their pattern of interactions and sample voters with various political preferences who live in different social environments.

Joint analysis of the two waves of responses revealed a significant HB: People were unable to ignore, or suppress, the information regarding the election results. Consequently, their reconstructed predictions were systematically biased in the direction of the actual results.

We used special features of the multi-party elections to test cognitive and other hypotheses (loosely described as motivational) regarding the source of HB. As predicted by the cognitive memory update hypothesis (e.g. Christensen-Szalansky & Willham, 1991), we uncovered a strong significant bias concerning the event that occurred (victory of the Left block), but only a weak (statistically nonsignificant) bias for the event which did not occur (victory for the Right block). One of the reviewers pointed out that the postelection judgments regarding the Left (Right) are affected not only by the actual outcome for the Left (Right), but also by the results of the Right (Left). If such mutual influences indeed exist, one would expect them to be symmetric, and affect predictions of the Left and Right in identical fashion. Our results show a clear asymmetry in the predicted direction which is best interpreted through the memory update hypothesis.

We found no evidence to support a general tendency for "self flattery" (Connolly & Bukszar, 1990). Subjects who were led to believe that they could get away with a retroactive "adjustment" of their (supposedly lost) predictions, did not adjust more than those who knew that their reconstructed judgments could be compared with their original predictions. This seems to indicate that the problem is one of faulty memory rather than motivation. We cannot, however, rule out the possibility that subjects simply did not believe our cover story regarding the loss of the data.

The self relevance hypothesis was tested by comparing the accuracy of pre- and post- election judgments regarding the left and right blocks (MADPL and MADPR) by subjects who predicted victory for, and favored, one of the two blocks. We speculated that those who identify with a given block (Left or Right) will display greater HB in their predictions regarding the performance of that block, but this expectation was not confirmed. Whereas all groups of subjects displayed approximately equal levels of HB with respect to the results of the Left block, an intriguing and unexpected pattern emerged in the analysis of the predictions for the Right ` block: The judgments of the subjects identifying with the left were biased in the expected direction. The subjects who favored, and predicted victory for, the right exhibited a larger (in absolute terms) but "reversed" HB (e.g. Mazursky & Ofir, 1990): They falsely recalled predicting better outcomes for their favorite, but losing, candidates. It is impossible to determine whether this pattern should be attributed to extremely cautious (or pessimistic) pre-election predictions, or to attempts to demonstrate, in retrospect, high loyalty to one's favorite party, or a combination of both factors.

The most important aspect of this finding is that the lack of an overall HB in the prediction of the results of the Right block appears to be artifactual. The sample consists of two groups with opposite political orientations and, consequently, different interests and aspirations. The two sets of judgments are biased in opposite directions and cancel out in the aggregate. Furthermore, the pattern of predictions can not be fully predicted by cognitive factors alone. As suggested by Hawkins and Hastie (1990) and Hell et al.(1988), it appears that HB is best explained by a hybrid model involving both cognitive (memory update) and additional, yet to be fully understood, motivational factors.

REFERENCES

Babad,E., & Yacobos,E. (1993) Wish and reality in voters predictions of election outcomes. *Political Psychology, 14*, 37-54.

Babad,E., Hills,M., & O'Driscoll, (1992) Factors influencing wishful thinking and predictions of election outcomes. *Basic and Applied Social Psychology, 13,* 461-476.

Bar-Hillel,M., & Budescu,D.V. (1992) The elusive wishful thinking effect. Paper Presented at the 33rd Annual Meeting *of the Psychonomic Society.* St.Louis, MO.

Brown, C. (1982) A false consensus bias in 1980 presidential preferences. *Journal of Social Psycholoay, 118,* 137-138.

Campbell,J.D., & Tesser,A. (1983) Motivational interpretations of hindsight bias: An individual differences analysis. *Journal of Personality, 51,* 605-620.

Carroll,J. (1978) The effect of imagining an event on expectations for the event: An interpretation in terms of the availability heuristics. *Journal of Experimental Social Psychology, 14,* 88-96.

Christensen-Szalanski,J.J., & Willham,C.F. (1991) The hindsight bias: A meta-analysis. *Organizational Behavior and Human Decision Processes, 48,* 147-168.

Connolly,T., & Bukszar,E.W. (1990) Hindsight bias: Self flattery or cognitive error? *Journal of Behavioral Decision Making, 3,*205-211.

Cronbach, L., & Furby, L. (1970) How we should measure change --- or should we ? *Psychological Bulletin, 74,* 68-80.

Fischhoff,B. (1975) Hindsight # foresight: The effect of outcome knowledge on judgment under uncertainty. *Journal of Experimental Psycholoqy: Human Perception and Performance, 1,* 288-299.

Fischhoff,B., & Beyth, R. (1975) "I knew it would happen" -Remembered probabilities of once-future things. *Organizational Behavior and Human Performance, 13,* 1-16.

Frenkel,O., & Doobs,A. (1976) Post-decision dissonance at the polling booth. *Canadian Journal of Behavioral Science,,8,* 348 -350.

Granberg,D.(1983) Preference, expectations, and placement judgment: Some evidence from Sweden. *Social Psychology Quarterly, 46,* 363-368.

Granberg,D., & Brent,E. (1983) When prophecy bends: The preference - expectation link in U.S. presidential elections, 1952-1980. *Journal of Personality and Social Psychology, 45,* 477-491.

Granberg,D., & Holmberg,S., (1988) *The political system matters.* New York: Cambridge University Press.

Hawkins,S.A., & Hastie,R. (1990) Hindsight: Biased judgments of past events after the outcomes are known. *Psychological Bulletin, 107,* 311-327.

Hayes,S. (1936) The predictive ability of voters. *Journal of Social Psychology, 7,* 183-191.

Heider,F. (1958) *The psychology of interpersonal relations.* New York: Wiley,

Hell,W., Gigerenzer,G., Gauggel,S., Mall,M. & Mueller, M. (1988) Hindsight bias: An interaction of automatic and motivational factors? *Memory and Cognition, 16,* 533-538.

Hogarth,R.M. (1987) *Judgment and choice.* New York:Wiley.

Kahneman,D., Slovic,P., & Tversky,A. (1982) *Judgment under uncertainty: Heuristics and biases.* Cambridge, England: Cambridge University Press.

Lazarsfeld,P.F., Berelson,B., & Gaudet H. (1944) *The people's choice.* New York: Duell, Sloan and Pearce.

Leary,M.R. (1981) The distorted nature of hindsight. *The Journal of Social Psychology, 115,* 25-29.

Leary,M.R. (1982) Hindsight distortion and the 1980 presidential election. *Personality and Social Psychology Bulletin, 8,* 257-263.

Lemert,J.B. (1986) Picking the winners: Politician vs. voter predictions of two controversial ballot measures. *Public Opinion Quarterly, 50,* 208-221

Mazursky,D., & Ofir,C. (1990) "I could never have expected it to happen": The reversal of the hindsight bias. *Organizational Behavior and Human Decision Processes, 46,* 20-33.

Pennington,D.C. (1981) Being wise after the event: An investigation of hindsight bias. *Current Psychological Research, 1,* 271-282.

Powell,J.L. (1988) A test of the knew-it-all-along effect in the 1984 presidential and statewide elections. *Journal of Applied Social Psychology, 18,* 760-773.

Ross,L. (1977) The intuitive psychologist and his shortcomings: Distortions in the attribution process. In L. Berkovitz (Ed.), *Advances in experimental social psychology (Vol. 5).* New York: Academic Press.

Schkade,D.A., & Kilbourne,L.M. (1991) Expectation-outcome consistency and hindsight bias. *Organizational Behavior and Human Decision Processes, 49,* 105-123.

Synodinos,N.E. (1986) Hindsight distortion: "I knew-it-all-along and I was sure about it". *Journal of Applied Social Psychology, 168,* 107-117.

Wood,G. (1978) The knew-it-all-along effect. *Journal of Experimental Psychology: Human Perception and Performance, 4,* 345-353.

AUTHORS' NOTES

Portions of this work were supported by a grant from the Israel Foundations Trustees (1990 - 92) to the second author.

We wish to thank Maya Bar-Hillel and two anonymous reviewers for their useful comments on the original version of the manuscript, and to acknowledge the assistance provided by Osnat Avraham and Ayelet ben Ziv in data collection and entry.

STRATEGIES IN DYNAMIC DECISION MAKING: DOES TEACHING HEURISTIC STRATEGIES BY INSTRUCTIONS AFFECT PERFORMANCE ?[1]

Anders Jansson

Department of Psychology, Uppsala University,
S-75148 Uppsala, Sweden

Abstract. Several studies have reported that some subjects when working with systems characterized as complex, opaque and dynamic exhibit a special ability, referred to as heuristic competence, i.e. a general competence for coping with complex, dynamic systems. The concept of heuristic competence has two important implications for research on dynamic decision making. First, those subjects who possess such an ability seem to be able to organize their behaviour in a better way. Second, it suggests a strategy for approaching the task which will improve one's chances to understand and control the particular system. The aim of the present study was to investigate whether it was possible to convey to naive subjects through heuristic instructions, the behaviours associated with heuristic competence and, whether as a consequence one could improve the subjects' performance. Subjects in three experimental groups were subjected to the Moro-system, i.e. a microworld frequently used in the research paradigm. Two groups of subjects received instructions with two different heuristic strategies, emphasizing either a systematic-elaborate approach (SEI), or a goal-planning approach (GPI). A control group (GI), received general instructions of the kind used in earlier experiments with Moro. The results showed that both the groups with heuristic instructions improved their control over the system, the SEI-group having the overall best performance followed by the GPI-group. Moreover, the subjects' behaviours were altered according to the a priori hypothesis. It thus seems possible to influence people's behaviour with heuristic instructions and, as a consequence, improve their ability to control a system such as Moro. Further, the result of a post-experimental task knowledge questionnaire suggests that the reason for the improvements could be explained in terms of better models of the system within subjects with overall better performance.

[1] This research was supported by the Swedish Council for Research in the Humanities and the Social Sciences. The author is indebted to Berndt Brehmer for comments on earlier drafts of this paper and also to Thea Stäudel for providing our research group with the moro-program and the instructions belonging to the program.

Recent studies of dynamic decision making (for a review, see Brehmer, 1992), suggest that there may be stable individual differences among people with respect to performance. For example, Schaub and Strohschneider (1989), compared university students with industrial managers in Moro, a microworld which requires the subject to assume the role of advisor to a tribe living in the Sahel zone in South Sahara. They found that the manager-group performed significantly better than the student-group. Further, they demonstrated that the difference in performance was due to differences in strategies. Specifically, Schaub and Strohschneider found that the industrial managers spent more time representing the problem in the beginning of the task, made fewer decisions, collected more information and, finally, checked on the results of their decisions to a higher degree than the students. Since the groups did not differ in epistemic knowledge, i.e. domain knowledge relevant to the task, Schaub and Strohschneider concluded that the managers had knowledge, helping them to cope with complex, opaque and dynamic systems of the kind that Moro represents. The students on the other hand, seemed to lack this kind of knowledge. The managers judged that the demands made by Moro were similar to those made by their ordinary work of running a company, whereas the students did not judge the demands made by Moro as similar to anything they had experienced. Following earlier research by Dörner, Kreuzig, Reither and Stäudel (1983), and by Stäudel (1987), the ability of the manager-group to cope with this task was referred to as heuristic competence, i.e. a general competence for coping with complex, dynamic systems.

The strategies used by the industrial managers in the study by Schaub and Strohschneider (1989), seem to be highly adaptive in a dynamic task, and it can therefore be argued, that these strategies make it possible for the managers to develop more appropriate models of system. Appropriate models of the task are a prerequisite for good performance (Conant & Ashby, 1970). This hypothesis is supported by the results of a recent study by Jansson (in press).

Using the Moro-system, the relation between performance in a complex and opaque task and certain pathologies, i.e. maladaptive strategies, was assessed. Jansson showed that six out of seven pathologies were found significantly more often in subjects who later showed bad performance than among subjects who showed better performance. Furthermore, all seven pathologies were found before the subjects had received feedback about any catastrophes in Moro, suggesting that the pathologies should be understood as precursors of failure, not the consequence, as had earlier been suggested by Dörner (see e.g. Dörner 1980; 1983; 1990). However, the exact relation between the pathologies on the one hand and the subjects' models of the system on the other hand, was not ascertained in any detail in this study. It is reasonable to assume, however, that some of the pathologies, e.g. "insufficient systematization", "insufficient control of hypotheses and strategies" and "no self-reflexion", are responsible for the insufficient models developed by the subjects, i.e. they are maladaptive strategies. Others should, instead, be seen as consequences of these imperfect models, e.g. "acting directly on feedback", "selective decision making" and "thematic vagabonding". All pathologies reviewed in the study by Jansson (in press), can be seen as indications of lack of heuristic competence. That is, the pathologies are examples of what one should *not* do in a dynamic task.

A reasonable explanation for the more successful performance of the better subjects in Jansson's (in press) study, is that these subjects have better heuristic competence. In this study, two salient features of this ability seemed to be the ability to adopt a systematic and elaborate strategy, and the ability to keep in mind goals and plans for coping with the system. Thus, the behaviours manifested in the pathologies are very much opposite to that of the managers in Schaub and Strohschneider's (1989) study. It could be argued that the successful subjects in these previous experiments with the Moro-system adopted two qualitatively different aspects of heuristic strategies. The first of these emphasizes a systematic-elaborate approach, and the second a goal-planning approach. These approaches are explained in the next section.

An important problem is whether heuristic competence can be taught to naive subjects and in what form it can be taught. As part of the now classic Lohhausen study, Dörner, et. al. (1983) investigated this problem in an experiment where two kinds of instructions were compared. The first one consisted of a general strategic training (Globaltraining). This instruction emphasized the importance of general rules for solving complex problems. The second instruction consisted of both this general strategic training and additional training in tactical aspects, stressing the importance of relatively concrete action alternatives (kombiniertes Training). The results showed no significant effect of either of these instructions compared to a control group which did not receive any form of special instruction. One possible interpretation of this negative result is that it is impossible, or at least very difficult, to acquire heuristic competence through instructions. This would amount to attempts to explain heuristic competence as an ability, purely acquired by experience. An alternative interpretation is that the methods of training used in the experiment did not fully capture the real nature of heuristic competence. As reported by Dörner and Schölkopf (1991), and Jansson (in press), an important feature of heuristic competence seems to be the ability of working with a systematic-elaborate strategy i.e., to collect information systematically, to take measures on a regular basis, to check on the measures taken continuously etc. However, for such a strategy to be effective for other subjects than those who already have heuristic competence, they must know what to base this strategy upon, i.e. a certain minimum level of domain knowledge of the environment they are supposed to perform in. Results in general support of this interpretation were reported by Voss and his colleagues (e.g. Voss, Tyler & Yengo, 1983; Voss, Greene, Post & Penner, 1983), who studied expert problem solving in the area of political science. They found that a prerequisite for non-experts on former Soviet Union to represent the problem in an appropriate way and to provide solution processes at the same level of abstraction as experts on this area, is to have both heuristic knowledge and a minimum of domain knowledge.

Following Dörner and Schölkopf (1991) and Jansson (in press), another aspect of heuristic competence is the ability to work with a goal-planning strategy, i.e. to control hypothesis and strategies about the nature of the system, to evaluate one's own actions in the long term, to detect and control developmental trends etc. This interpretation stresses the importance of different time scales in a dynamic task, something which has attracted research in the paradigm for distributed dynamic decision making (see e.g. Brehmer & Svenmarck, 1994), and whether a subject is able to use these scales. A related issue is that of self-reflexion which is an important aspect of action regulation. Tisdale (1992) concluded that self-reflexion had a positive effect on the quality of problem solving and that this effect was stable and transferable to other problem settings.

The purpose of the present study is to provide subjects in two different experimental groups with either a Systematic-Elaborate Instruction (SEI) or a Goal-Planning Instruction (GPI), and compare the performance and strategies of subjects in these experimental groups with those of a control group. Both instructions are similar to the general strategic training (Globaltraining) in the study by Dörner, *et al.* (1983). However, the GPI-instruction involves an extra emphasis on the long term perspective, while the SEI-instruction involves an extension of the original concept of heuristic competence. In the present paper, the effects of these instructions are investigated in a study using the Moro-system. Moro (Dörner, Stäudel & Strohschneider, 1986) requires the subject to assume the role of a development worker in charge of the welfare of a tribe of semi-nomads in the southern part of the Sahel-area, in the long term (see below for a description of the system), and is one of the most frequently used microworlds within the experimental paradigm of dynamic decision making (for a review, see Brehmer & Dörner, 1993). The first hypothesis of this study is thus as follows:

Hypothesis 1: Subjects in the two groups with the heuristic instructions should perform better than those in the control group. The reason is that the heuristic instructions should help the subjects to form a better model of the system. For subjects receiving the SEI-instruction this will be possible because they will not suffer from the opaqueness characteristic to the same degree as the other groups in the experiment. For subjects receiving the GPI-instruction this should, instead, be possible because the long term planning should make it easier to detect the more important variables in the system.

The changes in the subjects' performance, as an effect of learning the strategies, should be attributable to altered behaviours.

Hypothesis 2: The SEI-group should collect more information, use more categories of information, spend more time on the task and check on decided measures to a higher degree than the GI-group. The GPI-group should collect more information about central variables, take more measures concerning central variables and check on decided measures to a higher degree than the GI-group.

In addition to the predictions concerning performance and behaviour of the subjects, another interest of the present paper is to find out more specifically how well the subjects understand the structure of the system. This problem has also attracted some interest from Funke (1985). To investigate this problem, all subjects were given a post-experimental questionnaire designed to measure how well they could describe the relation between different variables in the system and decisions that have direct or indirect impact on these variables. This should enable us to understand the nature of the models of the system that the subjects develop during their interaction with the system better.

METHOD

Subjects

Thirty six subjects, 18 males and 18 females, all undergraduate university students, participated in this study. Their age ranged from 23 to 30 years. Half of the subjects were paid at a rate of 50 SEK (about 6 US dollars) per hour and the other half of the subjects participated as part of the course requirement. The subjects were randomly divided into three experimental groups, with the restriction that gender and form of compensation should be evenly distributed over the different experimental conditions.

The task

The program used to conduct the experiment was Moro (Dörner, *et al.*, 1986). Moro is an interactive computer program, simulating the living conditions of a small Sahel tribe, the moros. According to the taxonomy for dynamic systems (Brehmer, 1990), Moro is a complex dynamic system, meeting the criterion for a microworld. In the Moro task, the subject is required to assume the role of a development worker, employed to care for the welfare of the moros. The subject's task is to improve the living conditions for the tribe in the long term. The subjects can affect a large number of elements by deciding to implement one or more of about 25 different measures. They can also ask for detailed information about 45 specific issues which describe aspects of the state of the system. It is also possible to ask about the general nature of the task. This gives the subjects information about what is possible to do and what is not possible. The subjects receive feedback about some obviously changed conditions at the beginning of every decision time (once a year in the simulation). They also get feedback in the form of complaints from the moros. This information is mainly based on the background information that the subjects can ask for to inform themselves about the habits and traditions of the moros. This information is generally not sufficient to make a good decision so the subject should interrogate the system by asking the experimenter for more specific information. Figure 1 shows the structure of the

Moro-system and whether the connections between various aspects are positive or negative.

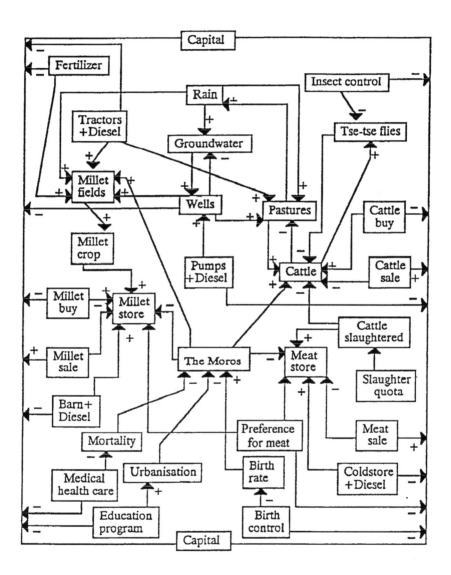

Figure 1. The structure of the Moro-system

Apparatus

The experimenter conveyed information from the program and implemented the decisions made by the subjects on a Commodore PC 20. The subjects were not allowed to use calculators, but only paper and pen.

Procedure and design

The general instruction and the task procedure as well as the specific moro-version that was used were the same as that in earlier studies with Moro (e.g. Brehmer & Jansson, 1993; Jansson, in press; Schaub & Strohschneider, 1989; Stäudel, 1987). The subjects were randomly divided into three experimental groups. All groups received the same general instruction. The first experimental group (SEI) then received a systematic-elaborate instruction. The second experimental group (GPI) received an additional goal-planning instruction. Finally, one group of subjects (GI) got only the general instruction and acted as a control group in the experiment. The two additional instructions for the two experimental groups are described in detail below.

The Systematic-Elaborate Instruction (SEI)

Subjects receiving the SEI instruction were told that they got this extra instruction because it was important to know more about the moros and their society. In these instructions, they got information about the moros, that they would otherwise have had to ask for. They received information about more central variables, i.e. the cattle, the millet crop and the millet fields, but also about variables of less central concern i.e. education, religion etc. All information provided to the subjects was taken from the background information that all subjects (including the control group) could ask for to inform themselves about the habits and traditions of the moros. The relations between these variables were stated in qualitative terms. This information is not available to subjects only receiving the GI-instruction; they have to find it on the basis of their own experience. Subjects were also instructed to ask for detailed information in all situations and for all aspects of the system. The instructions stressed that they should base their decisions on this kind of information over the simulated years. By instructing the subjects in this way, the relations between several variables in different parts of the system were made salient.

The Goal-Planning Instruction (GPI)

Subjects in this condition were told that they received this extra instruction because the importance of long-term planning and goal-relevant acting had to be stressed. In this instruction they were told to combine an overall perspective, i.e. decisions about what to achieve in the long term, with detailed measures, i.e that they should implement their decisions and check their effects carefully. By doing this, they were told that they would enhance their chances of finding a state of balance in the system so that they could feel that they had the situation under control. They were also told that by examining changes from one situation to another, they should be able to understand what things are more important than others and what is important to check continuously. The great importance of adapting one's thinking and behaviour to the demands and circumstances of the situations was stressed. The subjects were told that this sometimes meant demands for careful examinations and new decisions, while at other times it may be better to wait and see.

After having read the instructions, subjects were told that they could keep them for the whole experiment. The experimenter explained the general procedure of the experimental session and the subjects were told that they had to manage the system and complete the period of thirty simulated years within two and a half hours. If they were unable to do so, the program would continue where the subject ran out of time. After 15 simulated years, the subjects had to take a short break from working with the system. The subjects could dispose the two and a half hours as they wished. During a simulated year, they could ask for information and take measures and when they had completed a year, the experimenter was told to jump to the next year. After having finished their work with the simulation, the subjects had to fill in a post-experimental questionnaire. This form ascertained the subjects' understanding of the relation between variables in the system and decisions affecting these variables.

Measures

Task performance

Six of the most important of the variables affected in the simulation were chosen as the dependent measures. These were used to classify the subjects into six criterion groups for assessing the overall performance of the subjects. The same groups have been used in earlier research with the moro-system (see, e.g. Brehmer & Jansson, 1993). In each of these criterion groups, criteria for each of the six variables were set up (see Table 1). To be included in a criterion group, a subject had to meet all of these criteria. Following Brehmer and Jansson (1993), performance in criterion-groups 1-4 is regarded as good performance, while performance in criterion-groups 5-6 is regarded as bad performance.

Table 1. The criteria for each dependent variable for each of the six criterion groups.

	Criterion groups					
	1	2	3	4	5	6
Groundwater in %	99 %	95 %	90 %	80 %	-	-
Capital in Rika	750.000	0	- 100.000	-	-	-
Dead moros	0	0	0	0	0	-
Pastures in km²	300	300	300	100	10	-
Number of cattle	5.000	5.000	5.000 or	5.000 or	-	-
Millet crop in kilos	15.000	15.000	15.000	15.000	-	-

Behaviour assessments

For each subject, all the specific information he or she asked for and all of the decisions made by him or her while working with the system were stored automatically in a data-protocol during the experiment. From these protocols, the number of pieces of information collected, the number of information categories used, the number of pieces of information collected about five central variables, the number of decisions made for two central variables, the total amount of time spent on the task and, finally, the number of decisions checked relatively to the total number of decisions made was computed. All computations extended over the first 15 years in the simulation, except for the measure of central decisions, which was computed over all 30 years in the simulation.

The task knowledge questionnaire

This form was divided into three different parts. The first part consisted of seven single feedback questions such as: *If you introduce a medical health-program with the aim to improve hygiene and elementary medical care which of these factors do you think will be affected a) as a direct consequence and b) more as an indirect consequence ?* For each such question, the subjects could choose between five different variables. They were told that only one of the alternatives was affected directly and that two of the remaining alternatives were affected indirectly. The second part consisted in seven single feedforward questions such as: *Which measure is the most effective if you want to increase the amount of cattle ?* For each such question, the subjects could choose between three different variables. They were told that only one of them was the right answer. In the third part, the subjects were presented with seven different complex decision sequences. Each such sequence consisted of five different decisions and the task for the subjects was to decide how the whole decision sequence affected either one of seven different variables in the system. For each one of these variables, the subjects had to decide whether it increased, decreased or stayed the same after the decisions had been made.

RESULTS

Performance data

The performance of the subjects was assessed for each of the six most important outcome variables in the system. The variables are listed in Table 2. The state of the variables was measured at year 30, that is, the last year during which the subjects interacted with the system. The state of the system was also assessed at year 40. This was possible by bringing the simulation ten years further after the subjects had quit. In this way, it was possible to ascertain the state of the system not only once, but twice, for each subject.

Table 2 shows the means for each of the six dependent variables at year 30 and 40 for the three experimental conditions, respectively. A one-way ANOVA for each of the dependent variables showed significant differences for three of the variables at year 30 and for five of the variables at year 40, respectively. For the capital-variable, the GI-group

A. Jansson

had significantly less money left at year 30 than the SEI- and the GPI-group. The difference maintained and was significant also at year 40. For the population-variable and for the millet crop-variable, the GPI-group had significantly more population and larger millet crop at year 30 than the other two groups. These differences were even more pronounced at year 40 with the GPI-group having the most population and the largest millet crop, the GI-group having the smallest population and the smallest millet crop and the SEI-group performing in between them. No significant differences were found at year 30 for the groundwater- pasture- or cattle-variable, but the GI-group differed in all three variables from the other two groups. At year 40, these differences were significant for the pasture-variable and for the cattle-variable, respectively.

Table 2. The means for the six dependent variables for each of the experimental conditions for years 30 and 40, respectively.

		SEI-Group	GPI-Group	GI-Group	
Groundwater in %	Year 30	93 %	94 %	87 %	$F_{2,33} = 2.141, p > .05$
	Year 40	88 %	92 %	78 %	$F_{2,33} = 3.107, p > .05$
Capital in Rika	Year 30	4.585.081	5.231.883	396.125	$F_{2,33} = 5.849, p < .01$
	Year 40	6.587.971	6.548.208	- 383.296	$F_{2,33} = 4.646, p < .05$
Population	Year 30	825	1.330	642	$F_{2,33} = 5.996, p < .01$
	Year 40	884	1.397	269	$F_{2,33} = 7.665, p < .01$
Pastures in km²	Year 30	437	435	269	$F_{2,33} = 1.351, p > .05$
	Year 40	425	433	182	$F_{2,33} = 3.814, p < .05$
Number of cattle	Year 30	6.384	6.083	3.703	$F_{2,33} = .704, p > .05$
	Year 40	9.288	3.455	1.039	$F_{2,33} = 6.040, p < .01$
Millet crop in kilos	Year 30	53.598	112.806	41.731	$F_{2,33} = 7.398, p < .01$
	Year 40	47.761	116.622	18.568	$F_{2,33} = 10.388, p < .001$

According to the results with respect to the six dependent variables, each subject was assigned a rank corresponding to a criterion group for years 30 and 40 respectively. This way of classifying the overall performance of the subjects is the same as was used in

Brehmer and Jansson (1993), and in earlier research with Moro (Schaub & Strohschneider, 1989). Table 3 shows the frequency of subjects in each of these criterion groups for each of the experimental conditions. By using the same procedure as that used by Brehmer and Jansson (1993), subjects that were assigned a rank between 1 and 4 were classified into the Good Performance Group (GPG) and subjects that were assigned a rank of 5 or 6 were classified into the Bad Performance Group (BPG). Two Fisher's Exact Tests were performed at year 30, showing significant differences in frequencies with respect to performance between the SEI- and GI-groups on the one hand and between the GPI- and GI-groups on the other hand ($p < .05$ for both comparisons). The same two tests were performed at year 40, showing even larger differences ($p < .01$ for both comparisons) between the SEI- and the GI-groups and between the GPI- and the GI-groups, respectively.

Table 3. Number of subjects in each criterion group for each of the experimental conditions year 30 and year 40. Subjects classified in criterion group 1-4 belong to the Good Performance Group (GPG) and subjects classified in criterion group 5-6 belong to the Bad Performance Group (BPG).

Criterion	SEI-Group		GPI-Group		GI-Group	
group	Year 30	Year 40	Year 30	Year 40	Year 30	Year 40
1	6	5	4	2	1	0
2	0	1	0	0	0	0
3	2	1	1	3	0	0
4	1	1	4	3	2	1
GPG Total	9	8	9	8	3	1
5	2	2	2	1	4	1
6	1	2	1	3	5	10
BPG Total	3	4	3	4	9	11
Grand Total	12	12	12	12	12	12

Behavioural data

According to the second hypothesis, it should be possible to explain differences in performance among the three experimental conditions in terms of altered behaviours for the groups with the experimental instructions. Relevant behavioural data were analysed to see whether there were differences in behaviour in accordance with the hypothesis. As can be seen from Table 4, the SEI-group collected more information, used more categories of information, checked on the results of their decisions to a higher degree, and spent more time on the task than the GI-group did. Further, the GPI-group collected more information about five central variables, made more decisions for two central variables, and checked on the results of their decisions to a higher degree than the GI-group did. Moreover, the two experimental groups did not differ substantially from each other with respect to any of these particular behavioural measures.

Table 4. Behavioural data for the three experimental conditions for the six behavioural measures that were analysed.

	SEI-Group	GPI-Group	GI-Group	Contrasts of interest
Number of pieces of information collected	132.33	138.33	86.08	$\Psi_{1,3}, t = 2.27, p < .05$
Number of information categories used	13.42	13.5	11.58	$\Psi_{1,3}, t = 1.94, p < .05$
Total amount of time spent in minutes and seconds	85.48	73.54	61.55	$\Psi_{1,3}, t = 2.22, p < .05$
Number of decisions checked relative to total number of decisions made	0.733	0.812	0.507	$\Psi_{1,3}, t = 2.28, p < .05$ $\Psi_{2,3}, t = 4.15, p < .001$
Number of pieces of information collected for five central variables	46.83	51.17	29.5	$\Psi_{2,3}, t = 5.21, p < .0001$
Number of measures taken for two central variables	10.92	15.25	4.58	$\Psi_{2,3}, t = 3.65, p < .001$

Results of the task knowledge form

There were no significant differences in the direct or in the indirect part, for the single feedback questions. For the part of the form which consisted in complex decision sequences, there were no significant differences among the experimental conditions even though both the groups with heuristic instructions performed better ($\overline{x}$ for SEI = 29.83, $\overline{x}$ for GPI = 29.0) than the control group ($\overline{x}$ for GI = 26.92).

Correlations between the overall performance of the subjects in the two experimental groups at year 30 in the simulation and the scores on the complex decision sequence part of the form reached an association of r = .53 which was signiflcant at p <. 01. At year 40 in the simulation, the correlation was r = .46, which was significant at p < .05. The subjects from these two groups were then divided into two performance groups in the same way as described above, that is, they were classified into either the GPG- or the BPG-group. This resulted in 18 subjects being classified as Good and 6 subjects as Bad at year 30. The same procedure was used for classifying the subject's performance at year 40. This resulted in 16 subjects classified as Good and 8 subjects as Bad. After this, all subjects were again divided into two groups according to how well they had been scoring on the complex decision sequence part of the form. This partitioning was made by dividing all subjects by the median. This resulted in 12 subjects performing above median and 12 subjects performing below median. By using Fisher's Exact Test, it was then possible to test whether subjects with better performance in the moro-system also were scoring higher on this part of the form. The difference between the two performance groups in this part of the form did not quite reach significance at year 30, but for year 40, this difference is significant (p < .05).

A one-way ANOVA showed significant differences between the experimental groups on the result of the scores on the single feedforward part of the form ($F_{2,33}$ = 4.395, p< .05). The SEI-group had the highest scores ($\overline{x}$ = 4.92), the GI-group had the lowest scores ($\overline{x}$ = 3.67) and the GPI-group were scoring in between them ($\overline{x}$ = 4.08).

DISCUSSION

In this study, it was shown that the two different heuristic instructions clearly affected the performance of the subjects in these groups. Since the SEI-Group and the GPI-Group performed better than the GI-Group, respectively, it can be concluded that it is possible to teach subjects strategies for coping with an opaque and complex dynamic system such as Moro. This result is contrary to the conclusions drawn by Dörner, et al. (1983). However, besides the fact that their study was conducted on a different system, the instructions used in this study are partly different from the instructions they used. The group with the best performance in this study was the group with the systematic-elaborate instruction. This group did not only receive a heuristic instruction, but also information about the task content, i.e. they started with more domain knowledge than the other groups. Appearantly, this combination of a heuristic strategy and an early knowledge structure of the task content helped the subjects in this group to control the system rather well. The main difference between the instruction (Globaltraining) used by Dörner, et al. (1983) and the SEI-instruction in this study is this particular early domain knowledge structure which functions as a remainder for the subjects' information gathering and decision making activities. As a consequence, subjects receiving this instruction knew what information to ask for and what decisions to make, i.e the microworld will appear a little less opaque and uncertain.

The performance of the GPI-group indicates that they too improve their control over the system. However, a closer look at Table 3 shows that most subjects in this group are allocated to performance groups three and four. This means that this group is performing in between the SEI-group and the control group. Moreover, the GPI-group also looses more subjects to higher ranks (that is, worse performance) between year 30 and 40 in the simulation. Accordingly, the subjects' performances in this group are much more unstable and not so resistent to changes in the system as the performance of the subjects in the SEI-group, but still, subjects in this condition are improving. The main difference between this instruction and the instruction (Globaltraining) used in Dörner, et al. (1983), is that the former one puts an extra emphasis on the system development in the long term. To realize such a strategy, subjects must find out what the more important variables are and try to control the system through the use of these variables. As a consequence, subjects receiving this particular instruction will ask for and make decisions about very central aspects of the moro-system such as the cattle and the groundwater, i.e. the microworld will appear somewhat less complex. At a first glance, the effect of this goal-planning instruction contradicts the result of the study by Brehmer and Jansson (1993). They failed to show any dramatic effect of a goal-specific instruction. However, since the subjects in that study had to accomplish seven different specific goals while the subjects in the present study focused on the two or three most central variables only, the difference in performance could be in terms of a decrement complexity.

Examination of behavioural data showed that the differences in performance were accompanied by differences in behaviour between each one of the experimental groups on the one hand and the control group on the other hand. On the one hand, the SEI-group did collect information and make decisions much more systematically than the control group and this was also manifested by the longer time this group had to use to accomplish this systematic strategy. The GPI-group on the other hand, realized their strategies through the use of information and decisions that were central to the system in a much more systematic way than did the control group. However, the differences in performance between the two experimental groups could not be fully accounted for in terms of differences in the behaviours that were examined. In fact, the behaviour of the two experimental groups was quite similar, with respect to the behavioural data that were assumed to be relevant for assessing the difference in performance. Although there were some indications in line with the hypotheses, this suggests that the subjects' behaviour must be analysed at a more detailed level than was done here. We may have to consider the timing and quantitative aspects of the subjects' decisions and not only whether a certain decision was made. Despite this, it seems possible to explain the improvements made by the subjects in the two experimental conditions with the fact that they seem to control their behaviour in a better way than the subjects in the control group. As noted by Brehmer and Jansson (1993), such a control of one's own behaviour is a first step toward control of a system.

What is the common denominator for the improvements made by the groups with the heuristic instructions? The results of the post-experimental questionnaire suggest an explanation for the superior performance of these groups. They show that the better overall performance of the SEI-group is accompanied by higher scores on the feedforward part of the form, i.e. on the questions that concern what measure is the most appropriate if one is to achieve a certain subgoal. This suggests that subjects in this group have a better model of the system, an interpretation that seems quite probable, considering the instruction this group of subjects received. Further, the overall performance of the subjects in the groups with heuristic instructions was highly correlated with their ability to predict how central variables in the moro-system are affected by certain complex combinations of decisions. Again, this is likely to be an effect of the better models developed by the subjects with better performance.

One may argue, however, that the overall better performance of the experimental groups compared to the control group is due to motivational factors, i.e. that subjects in the control group in general exhibited a lower level of aspiration. However, with respect to achievement, there is no difference between any of the three experimental groups. All subjects received the same general instruction whithin which all the general goals were stated. The difference is instead in the emphasis on *how* one can achieve these very general goals. The appropriate explanation for the performance of the control group should instead be sought for in terms of subjects' experiences of interacting with the system. Motivational factors are one part of these experiences, a part that cannot be disconnected from any other, and may be more important parts as, for example, deficient goal formulations and insufficient mental models of the system within the subjects. In addition to this, the control group in this experiment performed similar to groups subjected to the moro-system with identical general instructions in previous studies (Brehmer & Jansson, 1993), or, very similar instructions (Schaub & Strohschneider, 1989; Stäudel, 1987). To explain the overall better performance of the experimental groups in terms of motivation thus not make sense.

In conclusion, then, the results of this study suggest that it is possible to teach subjects strategies for coping with systems such as Moro. This leads to the question of whether the fact that it was possible to teach subjects heuristic strategies means that these subjects now possess general heuristic competence ? Probably not. It may instead be that the results of this study only demonstrate the effects of using heuristic strategies. That is, the subjects behaved in accordance with the instructions and as a consequence they appeared to act as if they controlled their behaviour better and by this, in turn increased their ability to control the system. To ascertain what the subjects have learned, we need to examine the extent to which the subjects' strategies will generalise. Moro is high in opaqueness and complexity but rather low in the dynamic aspects (Brehmer, 1990). A first attempt at such a generalisation is that a systematic-elaborate strategy is possible and needed when people are subjected to systems with severe opaqueness, while a goal-planning strategy is helpful when the systems one is about to control is fairly complex. In view of this, the results of this study may seem rather trivial at a first glance. The performance of the subjects in the SEI-group depends on the instruction these subjects received. As was noted earlier in this paper, this instruction decreases the opaqueness of the system in that it gives information about the nature of the system that the subjects would otherwise have had to find for themselves. If the performance of the subjects in this group can be attributed to this fact, it may seem rather trivial. However, when trying to reveal the nature of heuristic competence, we need to know what the effects are of any particular strategy that is associated with the concept of heuristic competence. The results of the post-experimental questionnaire show that lowering the demands made by the opaqueness characteristic is followed by a better model within these subjects. The results of the GPI-group show that a strategic goal-planning instruction help the subjects to keep in mind more important things in favour of other things. A reasonable explanation for this is that they too develop a good model of the system, but at a later stage in the experiment. This explains the rather good, but unstable performance of this group. Both strategies, then, seem to be sufficiently good at developing the models the subjects need to control a complex and opaque system.

REFERENCES

Brehmer, B. (1990). Towards a taxonomy for microworlds. In J. Rasmussen, B. Brehmer, M. de Montmollin & J. Leplat (Eds.), *Taxonomy for Analysis of Work Domains*. Proceedings of the first MOHAWC-workshop. Roskilde. Riso National Laboratory.

Brehmer, B. (1992). Dynamic decision making: Human control of complex systems. *Acta Psychologica, 81*, 211-214.

Brehmer, B., & Dörner, D. (1993). Research with computer simulated microworlds: Escaping the narrow straits of the laboratory as well as the deep blue sea of the field study. *Computers in Human Behavior, 9*, 171-184.

Brehmer, B., & Jansson, A. (1993). Swedes in Moro: I. Effects of goal specificity. Department of Psychology, Uppsala University. *Manuscript.*

Brehmer, B. & Svenmarck, P. (1994). Distributed decision making in dynamic environments: time scales and architectures of decision making. In J.P. Caverni, M. Bar-Hillel, F.M. Barron & H. Jungermann (Eds.), *Contributions to Decision Making I*, Amsterdam: Elsevier Science Publishers (North-Holland).

Conant, R.C., & Ashby, W.R. (1970). Every good regulator of a system must be a model of that system. *International Journal of System Science, 1*, 89-97.

Dörner, D. (1980). On the difficulties people have in dealing with complexity. *Simulation and Games, 11*, 87-106.

Dörner, D. (1983). Heuristics and cognition in complex systems. In R. Groner, M. Groner & W.F. Bischof (Eds.), *Methods of Heuristics*. Hillsdale: Lawrence Erlbaum.

Dörner, D. (1990). The logic of failure. In D.E. Broadbent, J. Reason & A. Baddeley (Eds.), *Human Factors in Hazardous Situations:* Proceedings of a Royal Society Discussion Meeting. Oxford: Clarendon Press.

Dörner, D., Kreuzig, H.W., Reither, F., & Stäudel, T. (1983). *Lohhausen: Vom Umgang mit Unbestimmtheit und Komplexität.* Bern: Huber.

Dörner, D., & Schölkopf, J. (1991). Controlling complex systems or: Expertise as "Grandmother's Wisdom". In K.A. Ericsson & J. Smith (Eds.), *Toward a General Theory of Expertise: Prospects and Limits.* New York: Cambridge University Press.

Dörner, D., Stäudel, T., & Strohschneider, S. (1986). Moro-Programmdokumentation. *Memorandum 23,* Lehrstuhl Psychologie II, Bamberg University.

Funke, J. (1985). Steuerung dynamischer Systeme durch Aufbau und Anwendung subjektiver Kausalmodelle (Control of dynamic systems through development and application of subjective causal models). *Zeitschrift fur Psychologie, 193,* 443-465.

Jansson, A. (in press). Pathologies in dynamic decision making: Consequences or precursors of failure ? *Sprache & Kognition.*

Schaub, H., & Strohschneider, S. (1989). Die Rolle heuristischen Wissens beim Umgang mit einem komplexen Problem oder: Können Manager wirklich besser managen ? *Memorandum 71,* Lehrstuhl Psychologie II, University of Bamberg.

Stäudel, T. (1987). *Problemlösen, Emotionen und Kompetenz. Die Überprüfung eines integrative Konstrukts.* Regensburg: Roderer.

Tisdale, T. (1992). Self-reflection and its part in action regulation. In B. Brehmer & J. Leplat (Eds.), *Simulations, Evaluations and Models.* Proceedings of the fourth MOHAWC workshop. Roskilde. Riso National Laboratory.

Voss, J.F., Greene, T.R., Post, T.A., & Penner, B.C. (1983). Problem-solving skill in the social sciences. In G. Bower (Ed.), *The Psychology of Learning and Motivation. (Vol. 17).* San Diego: Academic Press.

Voss, J.F., Tyler, S.W., & Yengo, L.A. (1983). Individual differences in the solving of social science problems. In R.F. Dillon & R.R. Schmeck (Eds.), *Individual Differences in Cognitive Processes (Vol. 1).* New York Accademic Press.

Contributions to Decision Making - I
J.-P. Caverni, M. Bar-Hillel, F.H. Barron and H. Jungermann (Editors)
233

WELL CALIBRATED CONFIDENCE JUDGMENTS FOR GENERAL KNOWLEDGE ITEMS, INFERENTIAL RECOGNITION DECISIONS AND SOCIAL PREDICTIONS[1]

Peter Juslin

Department of Psychology, University of Uppsala,
Box 1854, S-751 48 Uppsala, Sweden

Abstract. This paper argues that ecological models (Gigerenzer, Hoffrage & Kleinbölting, 1991; Juslin, 1993 a) are the only models that attempt to provide a detailed account of how beliefs in single, unique (true or false) facts become related to long-run frequencies. The ecological models also predict the circumstances that allow this relationship to approach identity (good calibration) viz. random selection of items from naturally constrained reference classes. The paper presents data from three areas: General knowledge items, inferential recognition decisions, and social predictions. The data suggest that: (a) When items are selected in a way that minimazes the role of informal selection procedures, subjects are often well calibrated; (b) Provided that difficulty is operationalized in ecologically relevant ways, subjects can be well calibrated both for harder and for easier tasks (in contrast to the hard-easy effect). This suggests that biases that cannot be explained by biased selection of tasks need to be explained by specific circumstances that create poor cognitive adjustment, rather than by a general, cognitive bias. It is argued that a detailed account of the relationship between belief and frequency, and consideration of the associated problems with different and possibly biased reference classes is an important preliminary step in any investigation of calibration. The paper discusses a number of objections to the ecological models.

There is a current debate on the status of the *overconfidence phenomenon* in the area of general knowledge. The overconfidence phenomenon is manifested by hit-rates which are too low as compared to expressed levels of confidence, e.g., correct only 70% of the time when 100% certain, correct only 65% of the time when 90% certain, and so on. This leads to a mean confidence $\bar{x}$ considerably higher than

[1] This research was supported by the Swedish Council for Research in the Humanities and Social Sciences. The author is indebted to Mats Bjorkman, Anders Winman, and two anonymous reviewers for useful comments on an earlier version of this paper.

the overall proportion $\bar{c}$ of correct answers. This result ($\bar{x} - \bar{c} > 0$) has been a frequent finding in studies with informally selected, two-alternative general knowledge items (e.g., Allwood & Montgomery, 1987; Arkes, Christensen, Lai & Blumer, 1987; Keren, 1985; Lichtenstein & Fischhoff, 1977; Ronis & Yates, 1987). The norm relevant to studies on overconfidence is defined by the *calibration score* C (Murphy, 1973),

$$C = 1/N \sum_{1}^{T} n_t (x_t - c_t)^2 \tag{1}$$

where x_t is probability (confidence) category t (t = 1...T), n_t is the number of responses in probability category t, and c_t is the proportion of correct responses in category t. If the subjective probabilities match the corresponding relative frequencies, the assessor is said to be well calibrated with a calibration score of zero (i.e., $x_t = c_t$ and thus $\bar{x} - \bar{c} = 0$).

According to the *heuristics and biases* tradition (Kahneman, Slovic, & Tversky, 1982; Nisbett & Ross, 1980), the overconfidence phenomenon reflects a *cognitive bias.* Another line of argument, largely originating with the work of Regine May (1986 a, b), focuses on the relationship between subjects' knowledge structures and the specific tasks provided in typical studies on overconfidence. According to recent *ecological models* (Gigerenzer, Hoffrage & Kleinbölting, 1991; Juslin, 1993 a, b, 1994), people are well calibrated in their natural environments, and overconfidence is mainly seen as a *pseudo-phenomenon* which has been boosted by biased selection of items, rather than a general, cognitive bias.

The purpose of this paper is twofold: First, to argue that the ecological models attempt to make sense of the whole notion of realism (or calibration) of confidence in general knowledge, i.e., they attempt to provide a detailed account of how beliefs in *single* and *unique* facts become related to relative frequencies. Second, to review data which suggest that people have cognitive abilities that allow them to become well calibrated to their environments, and provided that tasks are selected in an unbiased manner people are often well calibrated, both for harder and for easier items.

THE ECOLOGICAL MODELS

In view of the definition of calibration a natural first concern seems to be: How can belief in a single and unique (true or false) fact become related to a relative frequency in the first place? How does my belief that Pakistan has a larger population than Sri Lanka relate to any relative frequency? Most models (e.g., Ferrell & McGoey, 1980; Griffin & Tversky, 1992; Koriat, Lichtenstein & Fischhoff, 1980) merely take this relationship for granted, without explicit discussion or treatment. Further, calibration is defined in terms of relative frequency and, consequently, we need to confront a second and neglected issue: In terms of what reference class (i.e., possible sequence of outcome indices) can we expect subjects to be well calibrated?

The ecological models (Björkman, 1994; Gigerenzer *et al.*, 1991; Juslin, 1993 a) attempt to answer these questions, as well as to account for the overconfidence phenomenon and the *hard-easy effect* (i.e., the observation that overconfidence is inversely related to the solution probability of almanac items; see Lichtenstein & Fischhoff, (1977), and Juslin (1993 a)). According to these models, whenever subjects are unable to retrieve or deduce the correct answer (i.e., to use a *Local Mental Model*, in the words of Gigerenzer *et al*, 1991), they will rely on probabilistic cues (*Probabilistic Mental Models*; Gigerenzer *et al.*, 1991). Consider the almanac item: "Which country has the larger population? (a) Spain, (b) Greece". When faced with this item, a subject may be able to retrieve only one relevant fact: Spain has a fairly large area, while Greece has a smaller area. The subject may believe that a large area tends to go with a large population and use area as a cue to which country has the larger population. Most cues define an *extension*, which is a naturally constrained reference class of situations in the environment where the cue can be applied, e.g., pairs of countries. For most situations within the extension, the cue will lead to selection of the correct answer (e.g., for Spain and Greece), but for some items it will not (e.g., Saudi-Arabia has a larger area but a smaller population than Iraq). The cue attains its probabilistic validity within the extension and the relative frequency of successful decisions within the extension defines the *ecological cue validity* of the cue.

The ecological models assume that confidence equals the ecological validity of the cue, i.e., a cue with ecological cue validity .XX leads to confidence .XX. A decision based on a cue that leads to

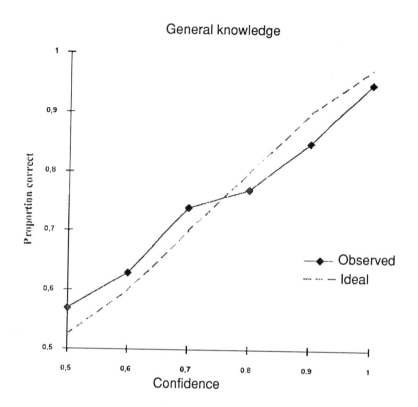

Figure 1. The calibration curve for the entire representative sample of general knowledge items from Juslin (1993 a).

In Juslin (1993 b), subjects were provided with representative samples of two-alternative, almanac items. The items involved six target variables that describe the world countries: Overall population, population of capitals, latitude of capitals, area, population density, and mean life expectancy. The countries (capitals) compared in each item were randomly selected from the world countries. Figure 1 presents the calibration curve, where c_t are plotted against x_t, for the entire response sample. As is evident from Figure 1, the subjects revealed a quite remarkable calibration (see also the first row of

Table 1) [2] . Familiarity ratings by 20 (other) subjects served to define a measure of content familiarity for each almanac item. The items received by each subject in the calibration study were divided into four levels of difficulty, where difficulty was operationalized in terms of content familiarity (i.e., as a way to create item samples with different average solution probability). Note that the criterion of familiarity does not capitalize on knowing the outcomes of the subjects' cue-based inferences in the same systematic manner as the criterion of solution probability (see Juslin, 1993 b). We have no reasons to expect a hard-easy effect due to the creation of biased reference classes. Indeed, subjects were well calibrated both for hard and easy items[3] . Table 1 presents data for two extreme categories of difficulty (very unfamiliar and very familiar contents). $\bar{x}$

Table 1. Calibration of general knowledge. Data for the entire sample of items, and for two levels of content familiarity (from Juslin, 1993 b). Numbers within parentheses refer to the variance of confidence.

Condition	Mean confidence $\bar{x}$		Proportion correct $\bar{c}$	$\bar{x}-\bar{c}$	Calibration score C
The entire sample	.73	(.0339)	.74	-0.01	.0024
Very unfamiliar (hard)	.64	(.0253)	.67	-0.03	.0026
Very familiar (easy)	.82	(.0304)	.80	+0.01	.0036

---

[2] Confidence is assessed on a scale with six alternatives (50%, 60%, 70%, 80%, 90, and 100%). If we assume that subjects are well calibrated and round their subjective probabilities to the six values on the confidence scale the expected proportion correct for confidence .5 is above .5 and the expected proportion correct for confidence 1.0 is below 1.0. More specifically, if the underlying subjective probabilities are continuously and uniformly distributed in these extreme intervals the expected proportions are .525 and .975, respectively. The elbows in the curve for perfect calibration in Figures 1 to 3 are based on this assumption.

[3] Throughout this paper, whenever calibration for different categories of difficulty are compared, the difference in difficulty $\bar{c}$ is statistically significant (p < .01).

These two categories are not very extreme in their proportions correct $\bar{c}$ ranging between .67 to .80. In an attempt to arrive at more extreme levels, over/underconfidence and proportion correct were computed for the 10 % least familiar items (480 items: $\bar{c}$ = .62; $\bar{x}$ - $\bar{c}$ = - 0.019), and the 10 % most familiar items (480 items: $\bar{c}$ = .80; $\bar{x}$ - $\bar{c}$ = + 0.021). There was still no hard-easy effect. At the same time, dividing items into hard and easy on the basis of post hoc solution probability (i.e., the proportion of subjects who selected the correct answer) leads to extreme hard-easy effects (e.g., $\bar{x}$ - $\bar{c}$ = .25 for hard items and $\bar{x}$ - $\bar{c}$ = - 0.11 for easy items, see Juslin, 1993 a). These results demonstrate that the difference between informal, experimenter guided item selection and representative item selection cannot be accounted for as a mere capitalization on the hard-easy effect (as argued by Griffin & Tversky, 1992). The sample with the 10% least familiar items is associated with close to zero over/underconfidence, despite a proportion correct below the proportion correct for the selected sample in Juslin (1994) which is characterized by overconfidence ($\bar{c}$ = .63 and $\bar{x}$ - $\bar{c}$ = + 0.08)[4].

The observation of good calibration for representative item samples was replicated with a set of eight other target variables sampled to cover a wider variety of everyday knowledge (e.g., prices of train tickets, sales of car makes, spatial distances between locations at the centre of Uppsala). For each of the target variables, a naturally delineated pool of objects in the environment was defined (e.g., the major railway junctions in Sweden) and pairs of objects were randomly selected from these pools. Once again, there was good calibration for a representative item sample ($\bar{x}$ = .71 (.0371), $\bar{c}$ = .71, $\bar{x}$ - $\bar{c}$ = 0, C = .0049), suggesting that this conclusion is not restricted to the geographic and demographic contents used by Juslin (1993 a; 1994) and Gigerenzer et al. (1991).

The ecological models have been formulated with reference to general knowledge items, but the ideas, of course, apply also to other inferential responses, such as recognition decisions based on reconstructions and social predictions. A common conception of inferential memory is that reconstructions supplement retrieval with probable knowledge, where "probable" refers to what is generally the case within the reference class of situations that may be encountered

---

[4] Both Juslin (1994) and Juslin (1993 a) relied on the same tasks and the same subject-population.

in the environment. As with general knowledge items, confidence is based on life-long experience with the environment and may thus be expected to reflect the validity of these reconstructions within the environmental reference class. Also in analogy with general knowledge items, overconfidence may be created by "over-representation" of misleading distractor items in a recognition test (e.g., the test item "philosophy" after reading a text about Ludwig Wittgenstein which actually did not contain the word "philosophy"). However, if people are adapted to their environments and if test items are selected in an unbiased manner, namely with no eye to difficulty or misleadingness, subjects should be reasonably calibrated.

Similarly, when confronted with the task of predicting the preferences of a peer (social prediction) the subjects may rely on their knowledge of social stereotypes (e.g., a professor) and assess probability according to the relative frequency of a behavior (e.g., preferring Mozart to Guns & Roses) in the reference class defined by this stereotype (i.e., the class of encountered professors). Once again, if tasks and target persons are representative samples from a natural environment, we expect reasonable calibration. If we accept that the argument presented by the ecological models can be generalized to inferential memory processes and social predictions a natural question is: Will unbiased item selection be associated with good calibration in these areas too?

CALIBRATION OF ASSOCIATIVE AND RECONSTRUCTIVE RECOGNITION RESPONSES

The heuristics and biases tradition (e.g., Kahneman *et al.*, 1982) embodies a rather negative view of probabilistic inferences, wherein overconfidence is largely regarded as the consequence of unwarranted trust in reconstructions of limited validity. Thus, Wagenaar (1988) suggested that overconfidence and poor calibration could be regarded as indicators of reconstructive and inferential processes, in contrast to immediate retrieval which should be associated with good (or at least considerably better) calibration. In Wagenaar's (1988) Experiment 1, subjects were exposed to unintentional learning of three-letter (nonsense) syllables, three-digit numbers, or words. Half an hour later, subjects made recognition decisions, i.e., they had to decide whether each of 32 presented items where "old" (part of the training list) or "new" (not part of the training list), and to assess confidence on a scale from .5 to 1.0. They were informed that 16 out of 32 test items were old.

In all three conditions Wagenaar (1988) reported good calibration for old items, with hit-rates that increased steadily with confidence levels. For new items, on the other hand, there was extremely poor calibration with almost no relationship between stated confidence and hit-rates, i.e., with an almost entirely flat calibration curve. Wagenaar interpreted these results in terms of the distinction between retrieval and inference. He suggested that, while subjects could base their confidence on the strength of a retrieved memory trace in the case of old items, for new items they necessarily had to rely on some form of inference, since they had never been presented with these items. Hence, one should expect good calibration for old items (retrieval processes), but poorer calibration for new items (inferential processes).

These two views of the calibration of reconstructive and inferential responses were compared in a study designed to compare highly abstract and artificial material which requires retrieval and material allowing considerable reconstruction and inference (Juslin, Winman, & Persson, in press). The first of three conditions (N = 20 in each) was designed to resemble Wagenaar's Experiment 1. This condition involved the incidental learning of a list of nonsense syllables (during 15 minutes of sorting them). After half an hour the subjects were required to make new/old judgments for 50 nonsense syllables, 25 of which were part of the original list.

In the second condition, the word list consisted of 50 words selected randomly from the words of 20 texts taken from Swedish morning and evening papers (covering a variety of topics, e.g., sports, entertainment, accidents, economics). In the test phase, there were 25 words from the training list and 25 distractors randomly sampled from the same pool of words from 20 everyday texts (no word appeared both in the training list and as a distractor). In the third condition, each subject was presented with one of the 20 stories as a whole for 30 seconds. Each story contained 50 to 60 words. In the test phase, subjects were confronted with 25 words randomly selected from the text (old items) and 25 distractors (new items) randomly selected from the words of the remaining 19 stories. In all conditions, subjects made confidence judgments after each choice (old/new) in the test phase. The conditions were similar, aside from the fact that as we go from condition 1 (nonsense syllables) to 3 (coherent texts) there is more and more room for reconstructive and inferential processes, i.e., based on the semantic representations of stimuli. In all three conditions test items were selected randomly from pools of similar content (i.e., by the computer), with no eye to difficulty or misleadingness.

Recognition Decisions

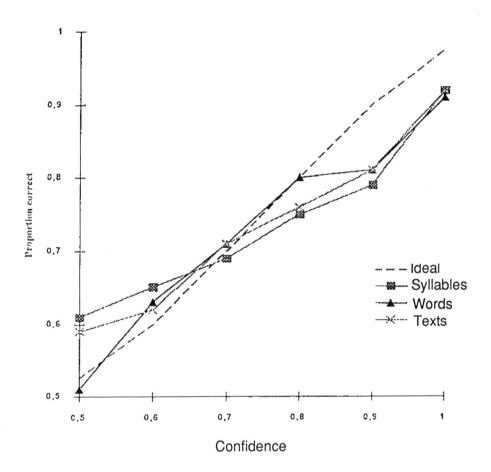

Figure 2. Calibration curves for recognition decisions. (From Juslin, Winman, & Persson, in press).

The results are reported in Table 2 and Figure 2. The subjects were well calibrated in all three conditions (proportions correct $\bar{c}$ were almost identical to those in Wagenaar's study). If we look at the text-

and syllable conditions in more detail there are differences, however. The condition with nonsense syllables replicates Wagenaar's results with a good slope of the calibration curve for old items (C = .0053) and an almost entirely flat calibration curve for new items (C = .0147). For the more "real-life-like" text condition which allowed a richer cue structure for both old and new items, subjects were quite well calibrated for both old and new items (C = .0056 for old, and C = .0093 new items).

Table 2. Calibration of recognition decisions for three kinds of material that differ in the degree to which the correct decision can be arrived at by inference and reconstruction. The text and syllables conditions were investigated at two retention intervals (30 minutes and 2 months). Data from Juslin, Winman, and Persson (in press).

Condition	Mean confidence $\bar{x}$		Proportion correct c	$\bar{x} - \bar{c}$	Calibration score C
Texts (30 minutes)	.77	(.0348)	.75	+0.02	.0048
(2 months)	.72	(.0331)	.69	−0.03	.0083
Words (30 minutes)	.78	(.0338)	.76	−0.02	.0036
Syllables (30 minutes)	.80	(.0270)	.77	+0.03	.0054
(2 months)	.72	(.0226)	.52	+0.20	.0613

For the text- and syllables conditions, subjects were contacted two months later for a similar recognition test, but with 25 new test items from the text or list of nonsense syllables respectively, and 25 new distractors (see Table 2). For the nonsense syllables there was profound overconfidence after two months (C = .0163; $\bar{x} - \bar{c}$ = +.20). In the text condition, subjects were still fairly well calibrated after two months, despite a lower proportion correct. These results were replicated in a second experiment which confirmed the prediction of different distributions of solution probabilities in the text- and the syllable conditions (see Juslin et al., 1993, for more details). In general, then, these data provide no support for the idea that inferences should be associated with poorer calibration. The artificial and abstract content in the condition with nonsense syllables, which allowed little opportunity for inference and reconstruction, was associated with poor calibration for new items, and severe overconfidence after two months. The more real-life-like text condition, with the richest opportunities for reconstructive processes, was associated with good calibration for both old and new items, after both 30 minutes and two months (Juslin et al, in press).

CALIBRATION OF SOCIAL PREDICTIONS

A number of studies have reported overconfidence for social predictions (e.g., "What magazine subscription would your peer prefer? (a) Playboy, (b) The New York Review of Books"), a result explained as due to the subjects relying too much on their implicit personality theories (e.g., social stereotypes) at the expense of information about base-rates (Dunning *et al.*, 1990; Vallone *et al.*, 1990). If we extend the general argument presented by the ecological models to social predictions, this would suggest that once the social stereotypes are allowed to have their everyday validity, subjects should reveal reasonable calibration also for social predictions.

We provided subjects with samples of social predictions that concerned the preferences of a peer in seven areas (e.g., future professions, university courses, TV-programs)[5.] In the selection of tasks we tried to minimaze the role of those informal selection procedures known to affect calibration in the area of general knowledge. For each kind of preference, a natural pool of options was defined (e.g., a list of professions provided at the employment exchange bureau, the university courses available at Uppsala University, the programs broadcasted by Swedish television in one specific week). Two-alternative, half-range tasks were generated by selecting pairs of options randomly from these pools. Thirty subjects (undergraduate students, 13 male and 17 female, with an average age of 23 years), in 15 pairs, performed both self-ratings where they indicated their own preferences (e.g., "Which profession would you prefer? (a) Social Worker, (b) Engineer"), and social predictions ("Which university course would your peer prefer? (a) Mathematics, (b) Anthropology"). The acquaintance of the pairs ranged from those who met for the first time at the experimental occasion, to those who had been living in the same dormitory for more than a year. Within each subject-pair, subject

---

[5] This study is an unpublished undergradute thesis (Morley, 1993) available from the author. Aspects of method not discussed here conform to standard practise in calibration research as described in, e.g., Juslin (1993 a).

A indicated his or her preferences for a set of items and subject B predicted these preferences. Thereafter the roles were reversed for another set of items. The subjects rated confidence in the social predictions and the self-rated preferences allowed us to score the social predictions as correct or wrong.

Table 3. Calibration of social predictions for the entire subject-sample (N = 30) and two levels of acquaintance between the subject making the predictions and the target-person (N = 10, in each) (from Morley, 1993).

Condition	Mean confidence $\bar{x}$		Proportion correct $\bar{c}$	$\bar{x}-\bar{c}$	Calibration score C
All subjects	.70	(.0287)	.72	-0.02	.0050
Low acquaintance (hard)	.62	(.0177)	.62	0	.0051
High acquaintance (easy)	.77	(.0321)	.76	+0.01	.0043

Table 3 presents data on calibration for the social predictions and Figure 3 shows the corresponding calibration curve (in addition, the subjects responded to geography items and this calibration curve is also presented in Figure 3). Subjects were well calibrated for both contents. A natural way in which the difficulty of a social prediction can vary is in terms of the degree of acquaintance between the person making the prediction and the target person. Table 3 also presents data for the ten subjects with the lowest level of acquaintance and the ten subjects with the highest level of acquaintance based on self-rated acquaintance on a scale from 0 to 100. The subjects who knew each other well provided more accurate predictions, of course, but both groups were well calibrated. In particular, the social predictions by the subjects with low-acquaintance are difficult ($\bar{c}$ = .62), but there is still no sign of overconfidence ($\bar{x}$ - $\bar{c}$ = 0) (the same difficulty as in Dunning et al., 1990).

Calibration curves

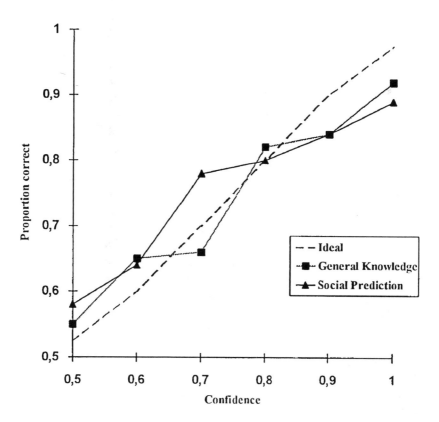

Figure 3. Calibration curves for social predictions and general knowledge items (From Morley, 1993).

CONCLUSIONS

The ecological models suggest that subjects reason in terms of the reference classes defined by their natural environments. In agreement with this conjecture, subjects often seem well calibrated for representative item samples, i.e., where tasks have been randomly selected from naturally constrained reference classes. For general knowledge items, representative selection is most often associated with reasonable calibration (Gigerenzer *et al.*, 1991; Juslin, 1993 a; b; 1994). We can create or eliminate overconfidence depending on the selection procedure (Gigerenzer *et al.*, 1991; Juslin, 1994), an effect that is not reducible to a mere capitalization on the hard-easy effect

(Juslin, 1993 a; b). Similarly, recognition based on reconstruction and inference was well calibrated when test material was selected in an unbiased manner, both after 30 minutes and 2 months. The social predictions were well calibrated once selection effects were kept to a minimum, both for subjects with high and low acquaintance. These results are also consistent with the observation that overconfidence has been less pronounced when experts have been studied in their everyday work environments (see Keren, 1991; Lichtenstein & Fischhoff, 1982; Wallsten & Budescu, 1983). When difficulty was varied in ecologically more relevant ways (i.e., content-familiarity, forgetting, level of acquaintance) and the tasks involve realistic and meaningful material, subjects were well calibrated for both hard and for easy items (at least for the moderate variations of difficulty observed in the studies reviewed above).

Only the ecological models have tried to provide a detailed account of how beliefs in single facts become related to long-run relative frequencies, or indeed for why subjects have the confidence they have. Therefore, they are the only models that can account for the remarkable achievement evidenced by the calibration curve in Figure 1. The remaining slight "regression" of the calibration curve, with underconfidence for the lowest confidence levels and overconfidence for the highest confidence levels, can be accounted for as end-effects that arise due to errors in the process from ecological cue validities to confidence, e.g., in the translation of beliefs into subjective probabilities (Björkman, 1994). Errors in the translation of beliefs into numbers will introduce a regression of the hit rates on the overt confidence variable. Models that take errors in the process from ecological cue validities to confidence into account seem a promising way to extend the basic ideas of the ecological models (see Erev, Wallsten, & Budescu, in press, on different models that incorporate errors in the process of subjective probability assessment).

It should be stressed, however, that a serious limitation to the ecological models is that thus far they have only been applied to the case of two-alternative, half-range items. Although it has been shown that selection procedures that create different laboratory reference classes have a powerful effect on calibration for the two-alternative format, it remains an open question whether the ecological models can account for overconfidence with other formats too, e.g., subjective probability distributions for continuous quantities. In addition, there are biases that cannot be accounted for in terms of the selection of tasks, e.g., overconfidence for extremely difficult item samples (Griffin & Tversky, 1992), and for samples of comparisons of frequencies of death causes (Winman & Juslin, 1993), and underconfidence for sensory discriminations (Björkman, Juslin, & Winman, 1993). But the results presented here suggest that these biases need to be explained by *specific circumstances,* rather than by a general, cognitive overconfidence bias (Juslin, 1993 b).

A common objection to the demonstrations that subjects often are well calibrated to randomly generated item sets is that people do not encounter randomly selected tasks in their natural environments. So, the argument goes, even if people are calibrated to randomly generated item sets, they are still poorly calibrated to the (non-random) tasks that they meet in their natural environments. This argument, that may seem to have some face validity, is based on a superficial interpretation of the rationale for the randomization procedure. The biased selection of items in most previous studies with general knowledge items is due to the experimenter, or item-selector, *knowing the correct answers to the items.* Since the item-selector is in position of roughly the same knowledge structures as the subjects and knows the correct answers, he or she can predict the answers selected by most subjects (see Juslin, 1994, for an illustration). The item-selector may even be in position of the "solution probabilities". In the subjects natural environment (i.e., outside the context of Trivial Pursuit and elementary school exams) as well as in most professional decision environments (e.g., meteorologists, economists) the outcome is unknown at the time of the decision and there is nobody that "over-selects" those situations where the cues fail at the expense of the situations where they are successfully applied. The cues are allowed to have their ecological cue validity. Hence, the randomization is not an end in itself, but an attempt to generate item sets that are unbiased in this sense.

As noted in the introduction, somewhat similar ideas were expressed by May (1986 a; b). May discussed the relationship between subjects' knowledge structures and the specific tasks selected in calibration studies. She also stressed the issue of representative selection of items. But in view of the ecological models it seems that she was too concerned with the notion of "*misleading items*" (i.e., items with solution probability below .5 in a two-alternative task) and with the criterion of "*itemwise calibration*". Misleading items were regarded as reflecting distorted and wrong knowledge, and it was presumed that subjects were unable to account for this source of error in their confidence assessments, thus leading to overconfidence. It has been shown, however, that misleading items are perfectly compatible with good calibration in regard to the entire task environment (Juslin, 1993a; Juslin et al., in press)

The criterion of itemwise calibration requires that the confidence assessment for each item should coincide with the solution probability of the item. Itemwise calibration presumes that each subject that selects an answer to a specific item can be regarded as an *independent* random event (Juslin et al., in press). Since the inferences made by the subjects reflect experience with the same environment (where, e.g., population of countries is correlated with area) the decisions made by the subjects will often be highly correlated (e.g., when all subjects use exactly the same cue in a perfectly consistent manner). When all subjects select the same answer we either get a solution probability of 1.0 or 0, depending on whether this is an item where the inference leads to the correct answer or not. Even if all subjects use the same cue, it may still be a cue with low validity which is associated with low confidence. Hence, for most cognitive tasks, we have no reasons (normative or other) to expect itemwise calibration (see Juslin, 1993 a; Juslin et al., in press for further details) and calibration can only be assessed for representative samples of items from the environmental reference class.

The signal detection model presented by Ferrell and McGoey (1980) still remains little more than a reformulation of empirical phenomena into the lingua of signal detection theory. Further, many of the results of fitting the signal detection model to data are consistent with the predictions made by the ecological models, e.g., that there should be the same cut offs for selected and representative item sets (Ferrell, in press). As with the other theoretical approaches (e.g., Koriat, Lichtenstein, & Fischhoff, 1980; May, 1986 a; 1986 b), the signal detection model cannot *predict* or *explain* the major results that support the ecological models, viz. good calibration for representative item samples and the overconfidence phenomenon for selected item sets. The same could be said about the creation and the elimination of the hard-easy effect reported by Juslin (1993 a). The ecological models account for the relationship between belief and frequency, and predict the circumstances that lead to good calibration and to observation of overconfidence without fitting parameters from data (see Juslin &

Winman, in press, for a more extensive comparison of the ecological model and the signal detection model).

Throughout this paper I have discussed "representative" item samples as if this notion was a trivial one. The point, of course, is not to argue that it is easy to ascertain in terms of what reference class the subjects are (or should be) reasoning, or that the notion of representative item samples is easy to operationalize. It most certainly isn't. The argument is that we *have* to consider these issues when we investigate calibration. A proper understanding of the relationship between belief in single facts and relative frequencies, and the associated problems with different and possibly biased reference classes, is an important preliminary step in any investigation of calibration. Future research should concentrate on identifying the conditions that promote or prevent realization of the good calibration observed for the representative item samples presented in this paper.

REFERENCES

Allwood, C. M., & Montgomery, H. (1987). Response selection strategies and realism of confidence judgments. *Organizational Behavior and Human Decision Processes, 39*, 365383.

Arkes, H. R., Christensen, C., Lai, C., & Blumer, C. (1987). Two methods of reducing overconfidence. *Organizational Behavior and Human Decision Processes, 39*, 133-144.

Björkman, M. (1994). Internal cue theory: Calibration and resolution of confidence in general knowledge. *Organizational Behavior and Human Decision Processes, 58*, 386-405.

Björkman, M., Juslin, P., & Winman A. (1993). Realism of confidence in sensory discrimination: The underconfidence phenomenon. *Perception and Psychophysics. 54*, 75-81.

Dunning, D., Griffin, D. W., Milojkovic, J. D., & Ross, L. (1990). The overconfidence effect in social prediction. *Journal of Personality and Social Psychologvy 58 (4)*, 568-581.

Erev, I., Wallsten, T. S., & Budescu, D. V. (in press). Simultaneous Overconfidence and Conservatism in Judgment: The Role of Error in judgment Processes. *Psychological Review*.

Ferrell, W. R. (in press). Calibration of sensory and cognitive judgments: A single model for both. *Scandinavian Journal of Psvchologvy*

Ferrell, W. R., & McGoey, P. J. (1980). A model of calibration for subjective probabilities. *Organizational Behavior and Human Performance, 26*, 32-53.

Gigerenzer, G., Hoffrage, U., & KleinbÖlting, H. (1991). Probabilistic mental models; A Brunswikian theory of confidence. *Psychological Review, 98*, 506-528.

Griffin, D., & Tversky, A. (1992). The weighing of evidence and the determinants of confidence. *Cognitive Psychology, 24,* 411-435.

Juslin, P. (1993 b). An explanation of the hard-easy effect in studies of realism of confidence in one's general knowledge. *European Journal of Cognitive Psychology, 5 (1),* 55-71.

Juslin, P. (1993 a). An ecological model of realism of confidence in one's general knowledge. Ph. D. Dissert. *Acta Universitatis Uppsaliensis: Studia Psychologica Upsaliensia* serial nᵒ. 14. Almquist & Wiksell: Stockholm.

Juslin, P. (1994). The overconfidence phenomenon as a consequence of informal experimenter-guided selection of almanac items. *Organizational Behavior and Human Decision Processes, 57,* 226-246.

Juslin, P., & Winman, A. (in press) Reply to William R. Ferrell's paper "Calibration of sensory and cognitive judgments: A single model for both". *Scandinavian Journal of Psychologvy*

Juslin, P., Winman, A., & Persson, T. (in press). Can overconfidence be used as an indicator of reconstructive rather than retrieval processes? *Cognition.*

Kahneman, D., Slovic, P., & Tversky, A. (1982). *Judgments under Uncertaintvy Heuristics and Biases.* New York: Cambridge University Press.

Keren, G. (1985). On the calibration of experts and lay people. Paper presented at the 10th SPUDM-conference in Helsinki, 1985.

Keren, G. (1991). Calibration and probability judgments: Conceptual and methodological issues. *Acta Psychologica, 77,* 217-273.

Koriat, A., Lichtenstein, S., & Fischhoff, B. (1980). Reasons for confidence. *Journal of Experimental Psychologvy Human Learning and Memory. 6,* 107-118.

Lichtenstein, S., & Fischhoff, B. (1977). Do those who know more also know more about how much they know? *Organizational Behavior and Human Performance, 20,* 159-183.

Lichtenstein, S., Fischhoff, B., & Phillips, L. D. (1982). Calibration of subjective probabilities: The state of the art up to 1980. In D. Kahneman, P. Slovic, & A. Tversky (Eds.), *Judgments under Uncertainty: Heuristics and Biases* (pp. 306-334). New York: Cambridge University Press.

May, R. S. (1986 a). Inferences, subjective probability and frequency of correct answers: A cognitive approach to the overconfidence phenomenon. In B. Brehmer, H. Jungermann, P. Lourens, & G. Sevon (Eds.), *New Directions in Research on Decision Making.* New York: North-Holland.

May, R. S. (1986 b). Overconfidence as a result of incomplete and wrong knowledge. In R. Scholz (Ed.), *Current Issues in West German Decision Research,* Frankfurt, Bern, New York: Peter Lang Publisher.

Morley, R. (1993). Good calibration of social predictions. Unpublished undergraduate thesis. Department of Psychology, Uppsala University.

Murphy, A. H. (1973). A new vector partition of the probability score. *Journal of Applied Meteorology, 12*, 595-600.

Nisbett, R. E., & Ross, L. (1980). *Human Inference: Strategies and Shortcomings of Social Judgment.* Englewood Cliffs, N. J.: Prentice-Hall.

Ronis, D. L., & Yates, J. F. (1987). Components of probability judgment accuracy: Individual consistency and effects of subject matter and assessment method. *Organizational Behavior and Human Decision Processes, 40*, 193-218.

Wagenaar, W. A. (1988). Calibration and the effects of knowledge and reconstruction in retrieval from memory. *Cognition, 28*, 277-296.

Vallone, R. P., Griffin, D. W., Lin, S., & Ross, L. (1990). Overconfident prediction of future actions and outcomes by self and others. *Journal of Personality and Social Psychology 58 (4)*, 582-592.

Wallsten, T. S., & Budescu, D. V. (1983). Encoding subjective probabilities: A psychological and psychometric review. *Management Science, 29 (2)*, 152-173.

Winman, A., & Juslin, P. (1993). Calibration of sensory and cognitive judgments: Two different accounts. *Scandinavian Journal of Psychology 34*, 135-148.

Contributions to Decision Making - I
J.-P. Caverni, M. Bar-Hillel, F.H. Barron and H. Jungermann (Editors)
© 1995 Elsevier Science B.V. All rights reserved.

CATEGORICAL DECISION ANALYSIS FOR ENVIRONMENTAL MANAGEMENT: A SIBERIAN GAS DISTRIBUTION CASE[1]

Oleg Larichev[1], Rex Brown[2], Elena Andreyeva[3] and Nicholas Flanders[4]

1 Institute of Systems Analysis, Russian Academy of Science,
Oktiabrja 9, 117312 Moscow, Russia
2 George Mason University, 2018 Lakebreeze Way-Reston,
VA 22091 Virginia, USA
3 Arctic Systems Laboratory, Institute of Systems Analysis,
Russian Academy of Science, Oktiabrja 9, 117312 Moscow, Russia
4 Institute of Arctic Studies, Dartmouth College, Hanover,
New Hampshire, USA

Abstract. This paper illustrates a Russian approach to decision aiding, which characterizes judgments by categories (as opposed to numbers). The case deals with a choice between sea and land gas pipeline routes on the Yamal peninsula. Several Russian agencies participated, with conflicting perspectives on the appropriate balance between economic, social and environmental considerations. Based on a qualitative but formal analysis of variants under consideration, a promising new option was developed, more appealing to all parties. A contrast is made with how Western decision analysts might have approached the same consulting task, and a start has been made at developing a balancing Alaskan case.

---

[1] Paper presented at 14th International SPUDM Conference, Aix-en-Provence, August 22-27, 1993. Supported primarily by the Arctic Social Sciences Program of the National Science Foundation, through grant DPP9213392 to George Mason University, with some additional support from the National Institutes of Health. Authors thank Hutton Barron and one anonymous reviewer in particular for most helpful comments on an earlier draft.

I. INTRODUCTION

Society's need to preserve the physical integrity of the Arctic and to manage its natural resources soundly and defensibly calls for systematic integration of conflicting economic, social and environmental considerations. This paper presents early results of an effort by Russian and American decision analysts to develop logical frameworks, based on certain approaches to decision aiding. In particular it presents one complete approach to a current problem in the exploitation of gas in Western Siberia and a discussion of its implications. It is intended as a contribution to prescriptive (rather than descriptive) decision research, along the line proposed by Brown and Vari (1992), which distinguishes it from other papers in this book.

A. Larger project.

This effort is part of a larger project to advance the state of the art of decision aiding, in the context of Arctic natural resource development, drawing on Russian and American approaches. As practiced by the authors, these differ mainly in the degree to which they quantify judgment. For convenience we will characterize the Russian as categorical and the American as numerical decision analysis (CDA and NDA respectively).

Our research strategy is primarily "build-test-build-test," a type of "divergent" research which often characterizes the early stages of developing decision aiding art (Brown, 1989; Brown and Vari, 1992). It will be time to converge on something approaching controlled experimentation when the "treatments" have settled down, and "hypotheses" involving them are mature enough to be worth testing; in this case, when the appropriate form of CDA and NDA for this class of problems (governmental natural resource risk management) is clearer and critical innovations have been developed.

The test bed is the Arctic. Society's need to preserve the physical integrity of the Arctic and to manage its natural resources soundly and defensibly calls for systematic integration of conflicting economic, social and environmental considerations. It is an area of concern to both Russia and America, and presents some distinctive technical issues.

Case studies are drawn from current difficult or controversial decisions for each country. In each case both approaches are considered, using the same data and judgments, and attempting to contribute to the same decision processes (not necessarily formulating the task in the same way). The acid test is whether we can add something useful to how choices are made (or justified). Do we help the client make effective use of available knowledge? How burdensome is the exercise? How well do the approaches fit psychological realities? What is the best way to take account of institutional differences in how decisions are made in the two countries?

B. Focus of present effort.

We are starting by having the exponents of each approach address one problem situation in their own country, much as they would normally conduct a decision aiding consulting assignment, and on having both sides review its implications as such. The research strategy is essentially inductive, proceeding from specific practice to generalization later. Part of the motivation for this sequencing is to leave enough time within the four years of the project for the upshot of the cases to unfold and to stimulate more directed technical development. The results of literature review will be integrated later.

The first complete round of a Russian case study is now complete and is the primary focus of this paper. (A balancing American case, aimed at the process of permitting oil and gas development in Alaska, is in the early stages of development).

II. A RUSSIAN GAS DISTRIBUTION PROBLEM

Senior Russian officials are choosing between a sea and a land route for a gas pipeline on the Yamal Peninsula. The Russian side of our team has been working intensively with them in a consulting capacity.

A. Background.

The Northern regions of West Siberia are famous for great deposits of natural gas discovered during the last 10-15 years. The most outstanding gas fields, with reserves of more than 20 trillion cubic meters, are situated on Yamal Peninsula. The peninsula is characterized by severe climatic conditions and a vast expanse of permafrost soils.

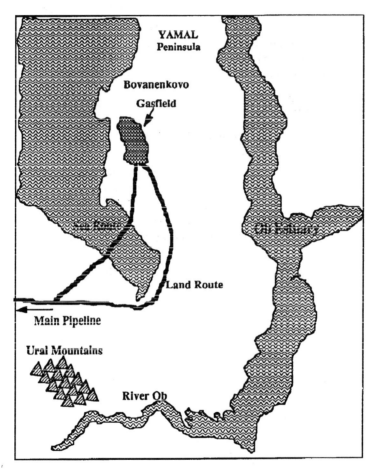

Figure 1. Pipeline options

For the Central Government of Russia and institutions responsible for energy, the issue of gas development on the Yamal peninsula is clear: the resources must be developed. The logic of such decision is easy: gas reserves elsewhere are exhausted and gas exports can noticeably increase Russia's national income.

Gas development on the peninsula requires the selection of a pipeline route from the gas fields on Yamal Peninsula to the existing gas pipeline system. The sea route was initially suggested as a shortening of the proposed land route. The land route crosses the Yamal Peninsula to the East of Baidaratskaya Bay, an inlet of the Kara sea. The sea route entails a straightening of the pipeline, achieved by crossing Baidaratskaya Bay (see Figure 1). The choice is constrained by the President's decree that pipeline construction would begin in 1993[2]. Reports prepared by institutes researching the decision were a major input to this analysis.

Thus, this decision-making task consists of choosing between two specific options. The multiple groups with influence on the decision have different interests, differ in their appraisals of the options on several criteria and are forced to rely on incomplete characterizations of the environmental conditions for each option. Detailed descriptions of the options follows.

B. The two options.

The two options are shown in Figure 1: a sea route crossing the bay and a land route. The following distinguishing characteristics have been included in the analysis:

1. *Length of the route.* The sea route is 160km shorter than the land route.

2. *Terms of construction.* Construction conditions are demanding for both options: a large expanse of permafrost and enormous rivers and lakes. But there is an essential difference: the need to cross the bay (about 68km).

---

[2] As of submission, a start had not been made.

3. *Construction cost.* Construction for both options depends on how the work is organized. Uncertainty is greater for the sea route, since there is no appropriate technology in Russia for pipeline construction at the bottom of the sea (though foreign forms have offered their help in constructing the sea segment of the pipeline). In principle, the cost of the land route can be estimated from the quantity and prices of tubes needed for the pipeline, technological and building equipment, fuel and labor cost. However, estimating ruble expenditures is complicated by harsh hyperinflation.

4. *Construction time.* A preliminary estimate is that the required time is 5-7 years for both options. An unstable economic situation can impact the starting time. This factor is of great importance, but very difficult to estimate.

5. *Impact on the environment.* The land route would cross many ecologically valuable areas, including reindeer pastures, wildlife refuge, hunting lands as well as rivers and lakes famous for their high productivity and fishing resources. The sea route also has a negative environmental impact but much less, because it does not cross valuable and vulnerable land on Yamal.

6. *Risk of pipeline rupture.* The probability of a land route accident may be assessed from data on other pipeline operations in the North. Statistical information on gas pipeline accidents in mountain regions can help to make this assessment more precise and adapted to the Polar Ural region. On the other hand, risk assessment for the sea route is rather difficult. The operation of an underwater pipeline under such severe Arctic conditions is unprecedented, so no accident statistics are available. Several features of the suggested route across Baidaratskaya Bay increase the likelihood of accidents, specifically:

a) instability of the shore sites with permafrost processes and impact of sea ices;

b) rupture of or damage to the pipeline by underwater ices;

c) probable appearance of iceberg sections in the Kara Sea capable of reaching Baidaratskaya Bay.

7. *Consequences of pipeline rupture or damage.* In the land route case an accident on the pipeline is associated with explosion and fire. As a result, the impact on the natural environment would be very high: complete destruction of the vegetation cover and thermal regime of permafrost soils, and the death of numerous wild animals. An underwater accident has less environmental impact: gas is not dissolved in water and is not toxic. The ice cover is not solid and gas can escape through cracks into the atmosphere.

8. *Time to recover from accident.* In the underwater part of the sea route, repair of a destroyed segment would be limited to the two to two and a half months a year when the Bay is free of ice. Such repairs would require special techniques and equipment (e.g., barges, caisson apparatus).

Most of these factors are unknown and would require long-term observation and prolonged investment in scientific research to characterize satisfactorily. Thus, the choice between the land and sea routes for gas development on the Yamal Peninsula must be made under great uncertainty, given the planned 1993 construction start date.

C. Groups actively involved in choice.

No comparison of options would be sufficient without an analysis of who is likely to make the choice and how. It is unlikely that the choice will be made by a single decision maker, because of the high cost of the project. Several institutions and organizations, which we call active groups, are involved either directly or indirectly.

1. A holding company, Gaskontsern, which is essentially a Russian Ministry of Gas, is responsible for selecting one option.

2. Two research institutes had been charged by Gaskontsern with making a feasibility study for the project. Yusniiprogas is the official leader and supports the sea option, while Giprospezgas favors the land option. There has been bitter discussion between the two, over the last two years, with arguments on either side.

3. Nadymasprom is the *operational arm* of Gaskontsern in the Tyumen region, responsible for the construction and exploitation of the gas pipeline system.

4. The *Ministry of Economy* evaluates economic considerations and especially the economic efficiency of the proposed project, and approves it.

5. The *Ministry of Ecology* evaluates the ecological and economic aspects of the project, impact on the environment, and confirms it.

6. *Local authorities* in the Yamal region also must agree to the pipeline choice.

7. *Local population* (or representatives of native peoples) whose territory and resources will be impacted by the construction of a very large pipeline system.

The resulting preferences of these active groups to the choice was not made known explicitly (but is surmised based on the analysis below). The procedure for approving the project includes a preliminary selection by the institutes of one option, which is submitted to Gaskontsern and then to all other groups. With necessary concurrences, the project may be approved.

III. THE RUSSIAN CATEGORICAL DECISION ANALYSIS

In order to be able to communicate with the representatives of active groups and to play a constructive role, the firm position of the Russian analysts is that a language of problem description accepted by all active groups is needed. This must be a verbal, understandable language, in which all analysis is done from the beginning to the end (Larichev, 1987, 1992). (By contrast, multi-criteria utility theory and other variants of NDA, require deterministic or probabilistic evaluations of options, which may be difficult to make.)

A. Evaluation of options.

Many reports have been prepared by the two project organizations - reports containing calculations based on different models and assumptions. Accordingly, their evaluations differ and sometimes contradict each other.

The options are seen through a "fog of uncertainty" deriving partly from the difficulty of measuring them in terms of appropriate criteria. How should cost be evaluated in a time of rapid inflation? How can the probability of accidents be estimated and compared in the absence of reliable models, historical information, and adequate characterization of those features of each option which might lead to accidents?

We take into account only those criteria where we can see something really different between options through the fog. For example, one cannot measure the difference in the time for construction, because so many uncertainty factors influence both options and one cannot find a significant difference, based on the existing data. The sea route is designated option A and the land route is designated option B.

1. *Cost.* The cost of crossing Baidaratskaya Bay (Ca) is determined by a foreign firm in dollars. To estimate the cost of the land route (Cb), we convert all expenses into dollars: to find equivalent prices for equipment (some of it is selling abroad), materials (the same), labor cost (some Russian workers have had foreign contracts), tubes (will be bought abroad). Unfortunately, it is difficult to estimate the distribution of the expenses over time. That is why only general expenses for two options are compared. Initial approximate estimates made by one project institute suggest Ca to be a little larger.

2. *Ecological impact.* Both options have a negative impact on the environment. It is much larger for option B, since it occupies a lot of land and crosses many rivers, though there is some uncertainty about the influence of option A on marine life. But according to expert opinion, (including one author of this paper) option A is much better.

3. *Probability of accident.* The probability of an accident is larger for option A, due to unstable shores and heavy blocks of undersea ice. This is the opinion of two project institutes and the experts.

4. *Consequences of the accident.* An accident is usually connected with an explosion and destruction of the environment for option B. In the case of option A there would not be an explosion. The gas would rise through the water and cracks in the ice. Option B according to experts' estimation is clearly worse.

5. *Reliability of gas supply.* The repair of the pipeline after an accident requires much more time for option A, particularly since the bay is free from ice only 60-70 days per year. Option A is clearly worse.

6. *Uncertain and unknown factors.* There are many uncertain and unknown factors connected with the unique project of crossing the Baidaratskaya Bay. According to experts, option A is clearly worse. The comparative evaluations of two options are given in Table 1.

TABLE 1. The evaluation of the options by the criteria:

The underline indicates which option is to be preferred on that criterion

Criteria	Option A (Sea)	Option B (Land)
Cost	Ca	C̲b̲
Ecological Impact	E̲a̲	Eb
Probability of Accident	Pa	P̲b̲
Consequences of Accident	I̲a̲	Ib
Reliability of Gas Supply	Ra	R̲b̲
Uncertain and Unknown Factors	Ua	U̲b̲

B. Developing a new variant.

Table 1 shows the results of a preliminary comparison of options noting the better evaluations. Comparative measurements are practically all we can make. How can we draw conclusions from such weak measurements?

In this case, as in many others, the practical value of decision analysis consists not only in comparing existing options, but in creatively inventing new ones. A method for aiding strategic choice, ASTRIDA (Berkeley et al., 1991), has been developed which permits, not only comparing several options, but also defining the requirements of a new, desirable and potentially best option. Simon (1960) defined three stages in decision making: intelligence, design, and choice. So far most research methods have been devoted to the third stage, which is easier to formalize. But in real life we have all three stages, for which it is necessary to develop new tools to help decision makers to solve real-life problems effectively. ASTRIDA uses verbal evaluations of the options on each criterion, and calls for the decider to make pair-wise comparisons. Such comparisons can be made from the point of view of different active groups. We shall give below an analysis reflecting the interests of Gaskontsern.

In Figure 2 the two options are presented in the framework of ASTRIDA as it appears on a computer screen. For the elicitation of preferences, psychologically valid operations (Larichev, 1992) are used. First the decision maker ranks the disadvantages of two options separately. Then special reference options are created. In Figure 3 an example is given of pair-wise comparison for "reference" options, which are constructed from real ones in the following way: each has the best evaluations for the real options on all criteria, except for one or two on which real disadvantages are given (option A is on the left). When comparing the two reference options, the decision maker again performs a psychologically valid operation--the comparison of two objects which differ only on two or three criteria.

By giving the decision maker different pairs of reference options we are trying to create a pair of options where the disadvantages of one option are dominated by the disadvantages of the other. But CDA does not guarantee that this is always possible. By doing only qualitative comparisons one can determine incomparability, when some evaluations are better for the first option and some better for the second, which was the case here. The greater uncertainty and lesser reliability of gas supply for option A are worse than ecological impact for option B. But the negative consequences of an accident for option B is worse than the larger probability of an accident for option A.

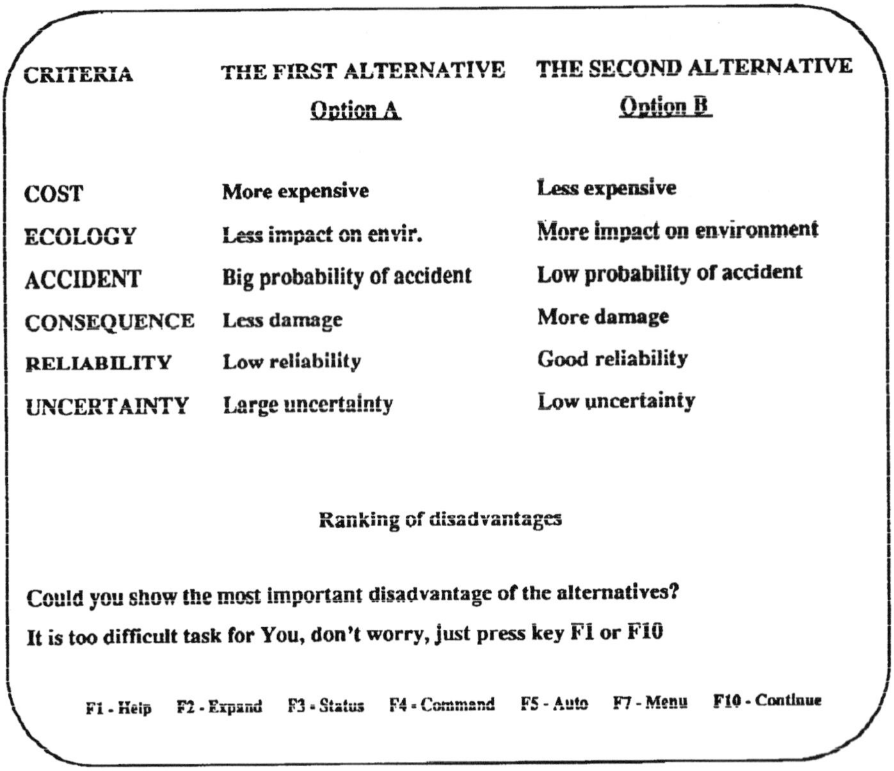

CRITERIA	THE FIRST ALTERNATIVE Option A	THE SECOND ALTERNATIVE Option B
COST	More expensive	Less expensive
ECOLOGY	Less impact on envir.	More impact on environment
ACCIDENT	Big probability of accident	Low probability of accident
CONSEQUENCE	Less damage	More damage
RELIABILITY	Low reliability	Good reliability
UNCERTAINTY	Large uncertainty	Low uncertainty

Ranking of disadvantages

Could you show the most important disadvantage of the alternatives?
It is too difficult task for You, don't worry, just press key F1 or F10

F1 - Help   F2 - Expand   F3 - Status   F4 - Command   F5 - Auto   F7 - Menu   F10 - Continue

Figure 2. Ranking the disadvantages of the two options to be made by the decision maker (screen display)

In the case of incomparability, the ASTRIDA method proposes to the user a direction for developing a new promising option, by adjusting the evaluations for one existing option. The analysis shows that one cannot change much of option B (the traditional way of construction). But it may be possible to change option A. The main interconnected disadvantages of option A are large uncertainty and larger probability of accident. The possible direction of development of new variants consists in finding a way to change these characteristics. Discussion with experts led to ideas on how to do it.

Let us consider a new variant A1 in which we decrease uncertainty by adding certain new technically feasible features to option A.

1. To eliminate the influence of seashore instability it is possible to construct special *shafts* located at a safe distance from the sea and put the pipeline through the shafts. This will incur additional cost Cs.

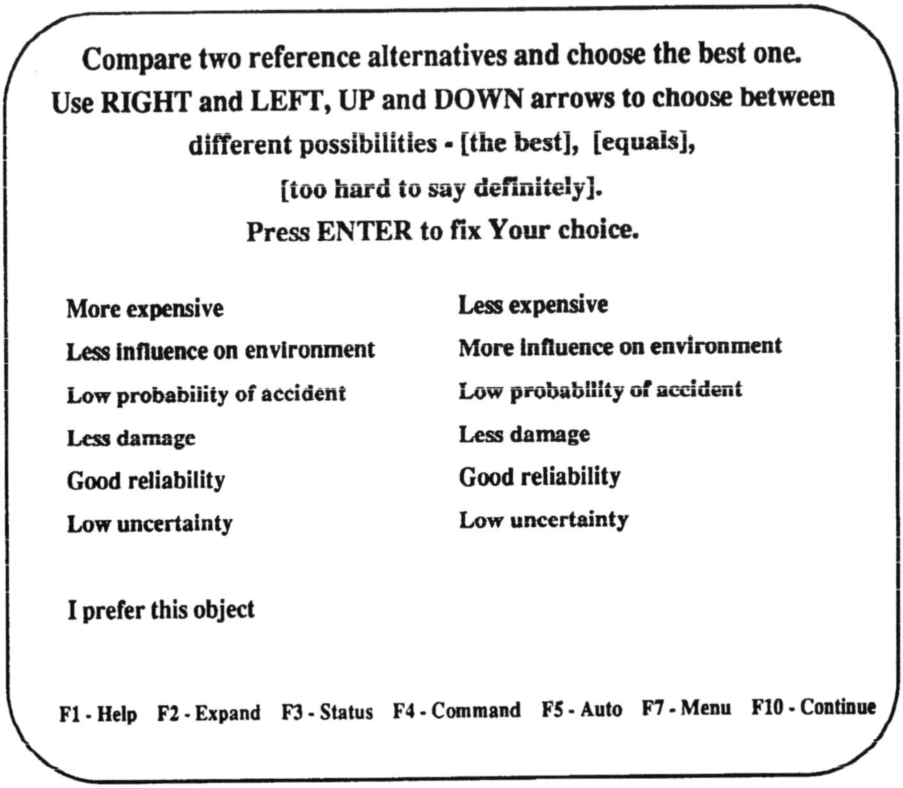

Compare two reference alternatives and choose the best one.
Use RIGHT and LEFT, UP and DOWN arrows to choose between
different possibilities - [the best], [equals],
[too hard to say definitely].
Press ENTER to fix Your choice.

More expensive	Less expensive
Less influence on environment	More influence on environment
Low probability of accident	Low probability of accident
Less damage	Less damage
Good reliability	Good reliability
Low uncertainty	Low uncertainty

I prefer this object

F1 - Help   F2 - Expand   F3 - Status   F4 - Command   F5 - Auto   F7 - Menu   F10 - Continue

---

Figure 3. An example (screen display) of pair-wise comparison of reference options

2. To avoid the damage of the pipeline from underwater ice, the pipeline can be laid in special trenches at a depth of 1.5-2 meters

(deeper than the floor of the bay). It is deeper than provided by the project and creates additional cost, Ct.

3. A very rare but a dangerous event in the bay is an iceberg. An iceberg moving in shallow waters may destroy the pipeline even lying in a trench. To avoid this danger it is necessary to have a special observation service and a special ship to drag the piece of iceberg from the bay. Let us denote the cost of service by Ci.

These new features of variant A1 allow us to say that the degree of uncertainty for options A1 and B is approximately equal. The probability of accident for variant A1 is not very different from that for option B. Given the possibility of additional service for repairing the tubes underwater, the reliability of gas supply is estimated to be not very different for A1 and B. Thus, there is no significant difference between options A1 and B except cost (Ca=Ca+Cs+Ct+Ci) and ecological impact. The cost of variant A1 will clearly be greater than that of option B. But the environmental destruction will be greater for option B.

From Gaskontsern's perspective, we must now make a detailed calculation of cost (in the way proposed above) and then again compare the two options, which now differ on only two criteria. Analogous analyses for other active groups would allow one to guess at their positions on the option. Two project organizations would support contrary options of the Ministry of Ecology and representatives of local population would support variant A1. It is difficult to define the position of Gaskontsern. Other groups will probably support the option B.

IV. IMPLICATIONS FOR COMPARISON OF CDA WITH NDA

A. Comparative research strategy.

The first stage of our effort to make a comparative evaluation of CDA and NDA has been to let each of the two lead exponents loose on a "client" problem of their own, solve it as they see fit, and then together draw any lessons for the comparison. This is a report on the Russian case, but all lessons will not be drawn until the practical impact of the CDA becomes clearer over the next three years, during which time the decision will be made and there will be some indication of its success. The initial American case is in progress and will be reported later[3].

At one stage we had considered making a stab at controlled experimentation, by rerunning the whole exercise with NDA, including working with the same clients and seeing how they respond. In order to compare the two approaches reasonable in the Yamal case, the NDA would need to replicate the knowledge and client interaction available to the CDA. This would require major participation of the Russian team, using the American team as a technical resource on NDA. Apart from the logistical, institutional and cost problems of having the American team implement their approach in Russia and secure another complete round of collaboration with senior government officials, the scientific pay-off is likely to be quite limited. The relative effectiveness the two approaches will be confounded by the "home ground" phenomena, interaction between the two approaches and the difficulty of attributing the client aftermath to one of them. (There is still scope for controlled comparison, but in more tractable circumstances like the traditional student subject experiments.)

B. A numerical approach to the Yamal problem.

Without attempting a "bitter-end" analysis and implementation, it may be instructive to give some thought to how the same problem situation might have been addressed with NDA and reflect on how the two approaches might have compared.

1. *Basic model.* Figure 4 shows a basic model format could be used to model the preferences of any of the several "active groups". The model proposed here takes essentially the same attributes addressed in the above CDA -- cost, ecological impact, etc. -- and treats them as attributes in a linear additive multi-attribute utility analysis (MUA). The sequence of modeling steps the American team would be inclined to follow (by no means conventional) is in the direction of progressively more complex quantification.

---

[3] It is to help State and Federal regulators devise a general test to determine which oil and gas development ventures in Alaska (such as drilling in the wildlife refuge) should be permitted.

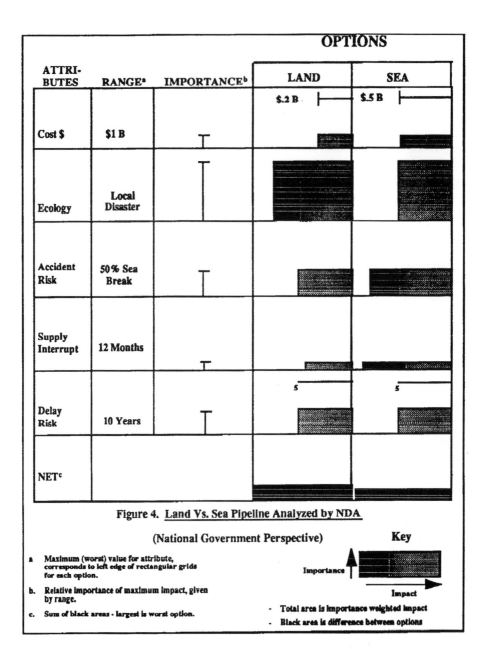

Figure 4. Land Vs. Sea Pipeline Analyzed by NDA

(National Government Perspective)

a   Maximum (worst) value for attribute,
     corresponds to left edge of rectangular grids
     for each option.

b.   Relative importance of maximum impact, given
     by range.

c.   Sum of black areas - largest is worst option.

2. *Regular MUA.* In figure 4 the boxes in the two right columns give the contribution of each option to utility (negative, since all attributes are undesirable). It is the product of importance and impact score. The black part is the excess of one box over the other, leaving identical gray parts. The preferred option is the one for which the rectangle areas thus defined sum to the smallest[4].

Each attribute is scaled as follows: 0 is worst plausible and 100 best plausible value (a clear illustration must be given for each anchor point). This includes attributes with a natural numeraire like money or delay. The second column in figure 4 illustrates plausible scales.

Each attribute is then scored on that scale in the analog box format proposed. Uncertainty is taken into account, by reducing the score for risk aversion (certain equivalent where there is numeraire - dollar cost and years delay here). Attribute importance is weighted in the same analog format, by comparing the "swing" of their scales.

The assessments shown in figure 4 are notional, purely to illustrate an approach, but as shown the "sea" option is slightly preferred, since it has the smallest net contribution to negative utility (black area).

3. *Further quantification.* In theory, uncertainty is automatically accommodated by making each score a certain equivalent, which, for example, incorporates a penalty for risk aversion. The uncertainty is, however, hidden from view, and a possible next step would be to display it explicitly (e.g., with bands).

Another natural extension in the direction of more complex quantification would be to decompose the assessed impact of "accident risk" as consequence times probability. Modeling can proceed in ever finer decomposition in this way, to the extent that interaction with deciders and other players in the decision process indicate. One stops when further decision aiding effort appears unproductive.

---

[4] The additive formulation makes simplifying assumptions, which may not be entirely realistic, but are unlikely to be less so than a corresponding CDA.

4. *Role of analysis.* Different decision-aiding tasks can be assessed by the numerical analysis suggested, not necessarily the same tasks as the Russian team addressed, though it could be. Indeed, the appropriate approach may depend on the task as formulated.

For example, it could be that CDA is best suited to modeling individual deciders or agencies, but NDA to a more integrative analysis. The "client" for NDA could be taken to be the Russian government acting in a legitimate capacity (regardless of how the decision is actually to be made, or of the parochial motives of the players). The analyst is thus acting on behalf of "Russia," using whatever knowledge and informed judgment are available.

C. Comments by American team.

1. *Comparative pros and cons.* In principle, the two approaches to decision aiding have significant shared elements. They are both personalized, in the sense that they attempt to represent systematically and unambiguously judgments of fact and value experienced by those humans who, in some sense, are responsible for the decision to be made.

The primary argument for the CDA qualitative approach is that, if the prescriptive models are to be appropriate for a given person (decider), or capture his knowledge (expertise), their inputs should reflect the cognition or values of the person to whom they refer. The questions asked should be readily understood, calling for judgments the subject is familiar with and skilled in providing. It is often argued that human subjects have great difficulty in providing quantitative probabilities, utilities, and such, no matter how skillfully the questions are formulated. Furthermore, the burden and discomfort they experience disinclines them to participate in the exercise or to have confidence in the results.

A dominant argument for a quantitative NDA approach is that it can be finely and precisely adapted to the decision problem at hand and that any relevant judgmental or factual input can be unambiguously characterized without loss of information. However, it may require extracting *more* information than is strictly needed to resolve the dilemma at hand, with an added cost. For example, if no more than ordinal input is needed to select an option, it is wasteful and inconvenient to require that complete probability distributions or utility functions be specified. However, conversely, an ordinal approach may throw away relevant information (for example, if the subject is able to say more that is relevant than ranking and give *some* indication of the size of differences).

It may be feasible to rely primarily on qualitative, natural language approaches to elicit knowledge and judgment and to communicate the findings of analysis to the decider(s); but to employ quantitative models in-between.

2. *Familiarity of concepts.* The closer fit between subject's usual way of thinking and CDA trades off against NDA's potential for enhancing that thinking by virtue of the very fact that it is different. In the extreme, which no-one is urging, CDA would simply be playing back what the subject was thinking anyway, and little has been added.

Since any coherent qualitative argument can, in principle, be elaborated in quantitative NDA terms (but not necessarily the reverse), a plausible combined strategy would be to start with CDA and "graduate" to NDA if it seems worth the trouble. In the Yamal case, these was a first, tentative effort to build on CDA with NDA, but in a purely hypothetical way, with no client contact. However, the main reason for having the NDA track the CDA as close as possible was to aid comparison of essential differences.

3. *Reviewable rationale.* In a highly controversial public policy issue, like this one, it helps to have an argument whose pieces can be examined and resolved (or at least argued over) separately. Again there seems to be a trade-off between analytic approaches: CDA is easier to communicate; but NDA may permit action implications to be more readily -- or at least more unambiguously -- derived, according to maximum expected utility parts of the analysis can also be delegated to more disaggregated approaches (like engineering and economic modeling in this case), without losing any relevant information contained in the quantitative probabilistic output. (This argument

would not apply in other cases where, for example, an individual's informal thinking is being aided.)

In the above CDA, the client judged that the greater probability of an accident for the land option was "worse" than the larger consequence of the sea option. If the client is logically consistent, he would presumably assign the land option a minus for the composite criterion: accident risk. However, quantifying the two components, in an NDA formulation, as the product of accident probability and consequence (utility), would provide an explicit logical check. In the event that the qualitative and quantitative evaluation disagree, neither has any necessary logical precedence. It reduces to which approach one believes taps more accurately into the client's cognitive field.

4. *Confounding effect of task formulation.* It immediately became clear that the difference was as much to do with formulating the problem as analyzing it. For example, CDA may lend itself particularly well to managing the interaction between key players; while NDA may lend itself to evaluating clear-cut options from the perspective of one party. At least, that is how these consultants were disposed to address the issue.

However, there is a real question of whether the central feature of the Russians' analysis -- developing a new variant A1 which improves on option A and simplified comparison with B -- is really distinctive of their approach; or is just a good idea, which could also be used just as effectively with a numerical approach. Comparison of basic approaches should not be confounded by orthogonal technical issues. An example is whether the translation of cost rubles into dollar equivalents should be what will actually be spent (with rubles converted at some realistic exchange rate); or what the international market would pay for the items.

5. *Cognitive enhancements to NDA.* Presenting a quantitative argument in a graphic analog form may gain some of the advantages of cognitive accessibility, without giving any of its appeal of logical completeness.

6. *Natural language interface.* This is a strong plus for CDA, but it need not be, since in principle we can use natural language to elicit our inputs and communicate our outputs, even though there is a quantitative model in-between. However, it is not easy, not commonly done by NDA practitioners, and techniques for doing it need to be developed. This might be the way to get the best of both worlds.

D. Comments from Russian team.

1. *Decision Theory perspective.* The problem discussed here is of a strategic nature, oriented 7-9 years ahead. There is much uncertainty in the execution of any of the options. That is why we must take into account only the factors on which it is possible to find a big, essential difference between the options.

In strategic decisions the analysis is to be oriented, not only to the comparison of existing options (Berkeley et al., 1991), but to the invention of new, promising variants of problem solution. The invention of new options may not be part of any formalized approach, NDA or CDA. The member of the family of CDA methods presented above only defines the direction of possible improvement of existing options, to work with the experts. But the direction of search is also important.

2. *Psychological validity.* In the process of analysis, the analyst has to try to reduce the problem to one with psychologically valid information processing operations. In our case, the comparison is of options having different evaluations only on two criteria. In the execution of such operations, people demonstrate much more reliable answers (Larichev, 1992).

3. *Natural language interface.* According to the experience of the Russian authors, using a language natural to the participants is a very productive way to go quickly to the essence of the problem. The thinking of the participants is stimulated, not by numbers but by good questions posed in an understandable way. CDA can be used as initial stage of NDA, but the quantification is not always needed for problem solution.

4. *Horses for courses.* Different problems in real life may call for different approaches. For unstructured problems (where the problem is poorly formalized, the main factors are of a qualitative nature, relations between factors is unknown) CDA is better than NDA. But NDA is more suitable for well-structured and some ill-structured problems.

5. *Analog devices.* The interesting idea of analog devices in the context of NDA needs further elaboration and psychological validation.

V. NEXT STEPS IN LARGER PROJECT

The next round of research to gain insight into a comparison of decision analytic approaches is to reverse roles and have the American team apply NDA to an Alaskan case, and have the Russian team consider how they might have approached it with CDA.

A major concern of American industry, government and the general public is to assure that the regulation of oil and gas projects in Alaska is responsible and predictable. It is typified by controversy and legislative "flip-flops" over whether exploratory drilling for oil should be permitted in the Alaskan National Wildlife Refuge. The American team has begun developing a scientific basis for permitting oil and gas projects in Alaska. The resulting regulatory procedure is designed to be predictable, reviewable, and defensible, and to responsibly balance conflicting economic, social and environmental considerations and the interests of competing constituencies.

It would have two components:
a standard format that industry and government would use to characterize a development project; and
a decision rule that regulators would use to determine if it is acceptable.

Several technical approaches are being considered which build on existing processes under the National Environmental Protection Act (NEPA) and conform to established decision science (Brown, 1993). Impacts can be described in general or problem-specific terms, either quantitatively or qualitatively. Acceptable limits can be set on each impact or on a combination of impacts permitting compensation among them or on an explicit cost-benefit comparison. The limits reflect, implicitly or explicitly, trade-off between public and private impacts, which may change with national priorities.

IMPACT TYPE COSTS	SCALE (UPPER END)	WT	SCORE	NRML	LIMIT
ACCIDENTAL OIL SPILLS	50% PROB SPILL OVER 3 YRS	-6	0.1	0.2	0.5
ROUTINE OIL SPILLS	> 500 BBL/YR	4	200	0.4	.4
OTHER WATER QUALITY	EQUIVALENT RETURN SPILL	--	100	0.2	No
ENDANGERED SPECIES	BOWHEAD 10 YEARS	1	--	0.6	0.5
SOCIO-CULTURAL: LOCAL	SEA HARVEST	-2	--	0.3	0.5
SOCIO-CULTURAL: REGIONAL	ARCHEOL LOSS	-1	--	0.2	0.7
OTHER COSTS	EQUIVALENT SOCIO REG.	--	--	0.1	No
TOTAL COSTS	[WTD. SUM]	--	--	25	30
BENEFITS					
ECONOMY: LOCAL	20% EMPLOYMENT	4	10	0.5	--
ECONOMY: REGIONAL	5% GDP	1	0.02	0.4	--
ECONOMY: OTHER	EQUIVALENT GDP	1	0.01	0.2	--
INDUSTRY EARNINGS	25% ALASKAN OPERATIONS	2	0.15	0.6	--
STRATEGIC INTEREST	OIL IMPORTS DOWN 8%	5	0.02	0.25	--
OTHER BENEFITS	EQUIVALENT LOCAL ECONOMY		0.05	0.25	--
TOTAL BENEFITS	[WTD. SUM]	--	--	18	--
NET BENEFIT	[POSITIVE - NEGATIVE]	--	--	-7.1	0

FIGURE 5. Hypothetical Evaluation of OCS Lease Sale

A candidate procedure is illustrated in the context of a hypothetical Outer Continental Shelf (OCS) lease sale decision by the Secretary of Interior. The form and content of how a project might be characterized and evaluated is shown in figure 5.

Costs and benefits of a proposed project are scored on criteria, specific to this type of case. Where a natural scale (such as dollars) does not exist, as in the case of ecological intangibles, artificial scales are constructed, anchored to good and bad scenarios, which is consistent with common EIS practice. Unspecified "anything else" impacts are handled by adding an adjustment to a related specified impact, on the same scale.

Numbers used in this demonstration are imaginary and incomplete. If realistic, they would imply that the lease sale meets all environmental impact limits except one. If the limits are non-binding targets (illustrating one possible set of impacts which meet a combined limit), variances from individual limits could compensate for each other and be acceptable overall. However, when benefits are valued and compared explicitly with environmental costs, the net benefit is negative. Thus, the acceptability of a project with a given total impact assessment depends critically on which decision rule is adopted.

Whether any procedure, within the same philosophical paradigm, is politically feasible depends primarily on how the legitimacy of uncertain measurements and controversial value tradeoffs is established. Our measurement procedure has a precedent in common EIS (Environmental Impact Statements) practice, which characterizes impacts as being "very high/low" etc, and provides an illustrative scenario for each such rating.

The valuation issue is more problematic. Tradeoffs can be elicited directly from individuals (e.g., sample members of the public, experts, officials), using well-established techniques, but their subjectivity may make them suspect. They can, however, be reinforced by, or coalesced with, more indirect (and therefore, some hold, less arbitrary) valuations. These include:

inferring issue-specific tradeoffs from more universal tradeoffs, of the type issued by several regulatory agencies ($3M for the value of a life; $1000 for one person-rem of radio-active dose); and

calculating the actual economic consequences of a lost environmental resource. (This is distinct from a personal judgment of what monetary sacrifice would equate to a non-monetary impact, which is a variant of the direct valuation, discussed above).

We now plan to work with "active groups" involved in this issue, including the Alaskan Oil and Gas Association and the Minerals Management Service of the Department of Interior, and to review progress with the Russian team in the Summer of 1994.

REFERENCES

Berkeley D., Humphreys P., Larichev, O., & Moshkovich, H. (1990) "Aiding strategic decision making: derivation and development of ASTRIDA," In Y. Vecsenyi and H. Sol, (Eds.) *Environment for support decision processes*, Proc. IFIP TC-8.3 Conference, Budapest.

Brown, R.V. (1993) "Permitting Arctic Oil and Gas Activities: a Scientific Basis for Regulatory Decisions." Unpublished Report to NSF Arctic Social Science Program and U.S. Arctic Research Commission. George Mason University, 7 December.

Brown, R.V. (1989) Toward a prescriptive science and technology of decision aiding. *Annals of Operations Research, Volume on Choice Under Uncertainty,,* 19, 467-483.

Brown, R.V. (1992) "The state of the art of decision analysis: a personal perspective," *Interfaces,* 22, N6.

Brown, R.V. & Vari, A. (1992) "Toward an agenda for prescriptive decision research." *Acta Psychologica,.*

Larichev, O. (1987) "Objective models and subjective decisions" (in Russian), Moscow, Nauka.

Larichev, O. (1992) "Cognitive validity in design of decision-aiding techniques," Journal of multi-criteria decision analysis, v. 1, N3, 127-138,

Simon, H.A. (1960)*The new science of management decision,* Harper and Row, New York: New York.

Contributions to Decision Making - I
J.-P. Caverni, M. Bar-Hillel, F.H. Barron and H. Jungermann (Editors)
1995 Elsevier Science B.V.

FRAMING ELABORATIONS AND THEIR EFFECTS ON CHOICE BEHAVIOUR: A COMPARISON ACROSS PROBLEM ISOMORPHS AND SUBJECTS WITH DIFFERENT LEVELS OF EXPERTISE.

A. John Maule

School of Business & Economic Studies, University of Leeds
Leeds LS2 9JT, UK

Abstract. Two experiments are reported in which groups of social work and general students were presented with classic decision framing problems and a set of isomorphs of these problems based in social work settings. Two current framing theories, Security-Potential/Aspiration Theory (Lopes, 1987) and Elaboration Theory (Maule, 1989) were investigated. From elaboration theory it was predicted that, given their knowledge and expertise in the area, social work students would develop more elaborate frames when solving social work problems and that this would lead to a reduced framing effect. In study one there was support for this view in one of the three decision problems, as well as an overall tendency in all subjects to be generally more risk averse in the social work problems. In study two the problem demonstrating the effect in experiment one was further investigated using concurrent verbal protocols. Hypotheses from both theories were tested with very limited success. The discussion considers the implications of these findings for the two theories, highlights the need for a clearer theoretical and methodological definition of decision framing and considers some important limitations in the way previous studies have investigated framing in experts.

INTRODUCTION

In a series of papers Kahneman & Tversky have demonstrated that seemingly trivial changes in the way decision alternatives are described can crucially affect choice behaviour, even though these changes do not affect the objective outcomes associated with the alternatives (e.g. Kahneman & Tversky, 1984). This framing effect is best exemplified by the Asian disease problem in which respondents are asked to choose between two programmes to combat a disease threatening the lives of 600 people. In one version of the problem subjects choose between two programmes described in terms of the lives saved by each, in the other version the same programmes were described in terms of the lives lost by each. The two versions are formally identical. Tversky & Kahneman (1984) reported that a majority of subjects presented with the version of the problem emphasising lives saved preferred the certain alternative to a risky alternative of equal expected value, whereas a majority preferred the risky alternative when the programmes were described in terms of lives lost. It was argued that this represents inconsistent behaviour and has subsequently been referred to as the framing bias (e.g. Bazerman, 1990).

To explain this and other similar findings Kahneman & Tversky developed Prospect Theory. The theory assumes two phases in the decision-making process. First, an editing phase in which the decision maker frames or develops an internal representation of the decision problem. Editing depends upon a number of mental operations, the most important of which is coding, responsible for representing the values associated with alternatives. It is assumed that values are represented relative to a neutral reference point such that values above the reference point are conceptualised as gains, and those below the reference point as losses. Second, an evaluation phase in which the framed alternatives are evaluated as a basis for choice. Critical in evaluation is the value function, assumed to be S shaped such that people prefer a sure thing to a gamble of equal expected value (risk aversion) in gains, but a gamble to a sure thing of equal expected value (risk seeking) in losses. Returning to the Asian disease problem, the version of the problem emphasising lives saved is framed as a choice between an uncertain and certain gain leading to a preference for the certain alternative. In contrast, the version emphasising lives lost is framed as a choice between a certain and an uncertain loss, leading to a preference for the risky alternative.

Research on framing has expanded considerably with many replications of gain/loss effects like the one illustrated above and a wide range of other effects demonstrated in both individuals and organisations (e.g. Fiegenbaum & Thomas, 1988; Tversky & Kahneman, 1986). This has led some authors to highlight framing effects as one of the key biases inhibiting effective decision making (e.g. Bazerman, 1994) and others to develop procedures to help professional decision makers overcome this bias (Russo & Schoemaker, 1994).

In recent years there has been increasing dissatisfaction with the Prospect Theory account of framing (see Schneider, 1992 for a review). For instance, Hershey & Schoemaker (1980) used a wide range of two outcome gambles and their certainty equivalents and found that the tendency for risk aversion in gains and risk seeking in losses was the exception rather than the rule. Fagley & Miller (1987) found variable evidence for framing effects suggesting that effects may be sensitive to such issues as choice of subjects and problems. On the basis of a review of previous research and findings from two studies of her own, Schneider (1992) argued that preferences in gains are, as predicted, strongly risk averse, whereas preferences in losses are much less consistent and not strongly risk seeking.

Though failures to support the Prospect Theory account of framing have been frequent, there have been very few attempts to develop alternative theories. Two of these alternative accounts are the focus for the present paper. One of these, Security-Potential/Aspiration (SP/A) theory (Lopes, 1987; Schneider 1992), assumes that choice is determined by two key factors. One, Security-potential, is a dispositional bipolar factor reflecting the relative attention that people place on security (avoidance of the worse case outcomes) and potential (approach of best-case outcomes). The other, aspiration, is a situational factor reflecting an individual's hopes and needs to achieve an outcome at or above a particular aspiration level. The majority of people are assumed to be security seekers and generally risk averse. Schneider (1992) argued that this theory may account for the strong tendency for risk aversion in gains and the lack of consistency in choice behaviour in losses. She argued that in gains both security needs and aspiration levels generally favour the certain alternative thereby leading to strong and consistent preferences for it. In contrast, in losses the two factors often favour different alternatives, with the certain alternative attractive from the stand-point of security needs, but often below the aspiration level. This leads to conflict and a lack of a strong preference for either alternative. Though an explanation in terms of SP/A Theory is consistent with previous research data Schneider (1992) provides no direct test of the theory.

Maule (1989) presented, in very general terms, a rather different explanation for the reported inconsistencies in framing. He analysed verbal protocols generated whilst subject were engaged on the Asian disease problem and used these as a basis for categorising the different frames used by subjects. Some protocols only included saving words; these were classified as *gain frames* and were always associated with choice of the certain alternative. Other protocols only included losing words, and were classified as *loss frames;* these were always associated with choice of the risky alternative. Finally, some protocols involved both saving and losing words and/or made reference to moral principles associated with the choice. These were called *elaborated frames* since subjects had developed their representation of the problem beyond its formal description. Elaborated frames occurred in both versions of the task and were associated with no strong preference for one alternative rather than another. Maule argued that Prospect Theory only held when subjects did not elaborate their frames i.e. had only simple gain or loss conceptions of the task. It was argued that elaboration was more likely to occur in important situations where the increased effort associated with this more complex cognitive activity was justified. This suggests that the account offered by Prospect Theory is partial and limited to situations where the decision itself is relatively unimportant.

The present paper reports two studies exploring these alternative accounts of decision framing. In the first, elaboration theory is evaluated by exploring the effects of expertise on decision framing. Previous research has indicated that a key distinction between experts and novices is the knowledge that the former bring to situations, allowing them to build more elaborate representations of problems (e.g. Lesgold, 1984). If Maule's theory is correct then the greater tendency for experts to elaborate their frames should induce a reduced framing effect in this group. To test this prediction, three framing problems were used each in two forms - the original and an isomorph involving the same choice alternatives developed in the context of a cover story based on social work. Groups of social work students and general social science students were given either the social work or the original problems. Elaboration theory predicts that there will be a reduced framing effect when social work subjects are given social work problems as compared with social work subjects presented with the original problems and all the general students regardless of problem type.

METHOD

Subjects

All subjects were students at Huddersfield University. One group of 141 were in the second year of a social work course and had a minimum of two years work experience in social work. The other group were 205 students drawn from social science and management courses. None had any previous experience of social work.

Problems

Three classic framing problems were used: the Asian disease problem, the Cancer problem, and the Business transaction problem. From each of these an isomorph was constructed based on the same alternatives but a social work cover story: the Child abuse problem, the Truancy problem, and the Electricity board problem (see appendix 1).

Procedure

Eight different problem sheets were constructed. Four of these contained different combinations of either the positive or negative version of each the three control problems; the other four contained different combinations of either the positive or negative version of each the three social work problems. Each student completed one problem sheet. Problem sheets were handed out and completed at the beginning of students' lectures making it impossible to ensure equal numbers within each condition.

RESULTS

Figure 1 illustrates the choice behaviour of social work and control subjects across the three pairs of problem isomorphs. The first pair, based on the Asian disease problem, supported previous research in showing a strong preference for the certain alternatives in the gain versions of both problems. In addition, there was the predicted increase in the attractiveness of the risky alternatives in the loss versions of the tasks, though there was still an overall preference for the certain alternatives in the social work problem for both groups. Further analysis was undertaken to see whether the choice behaviour of each group was different across the two problems. A Chi-square analysis of the frequency of choosing the riskless alternative across the positive and negative versions of each problem revealed no difference in the pattern of choice behaviour of control subjects (Chi-square=0.31, df =1) but a significant difference for social work subjects (Chi-square =4.635, df =1, p<0.05). This difference supports the research hypotheses in showing that social work subjects showed a significantly reduced framing effect across the two versions of the social work problem as compared with the Asian disease problem.

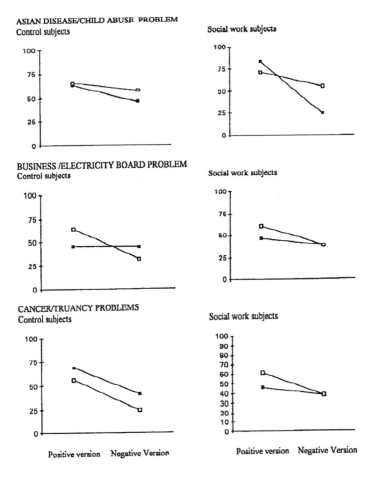

Figure 1. Percentage of control and social work subjects choosing the certain alternative in the positive and negative versions of the control problems (filled squares) and the social work problems (unfilled squares), for each of the three pairs of problem isomorphs.

The second pair of problem isomorphs, the business transaction and electricity board problems, also revealed a general tendency for risk aversion in gains and an increased preference for risk seeking in losses, though Figure 1 suggests that this was less pronounced than the previous pair of problems. A similar analysis of group and problem differences across the positive and negative versions of each task revealed that the choice behaviour of control subjects was different across the two problems (Chi-square=4.09, df=1, p<0.05), with a greater reversal of preference in the social work as compared with the control problem. There was no such difference for social work students (Chi-square=0.82, df=1). Figure 1 also strongly suggests that choice behaviour for the third pair of problems, based on the Cancer Therapy and Truancy, also showed the predicted reversal in preference. The analysis of group and problem differences revealed no differences in the pattern of choice behaviour for control or social work subjects across the problems (Chi square=0.13 and 0.47 respectively, df =1).

DISCUSSION

The findings from experiment one, in general, supported previous research demonstrating changes in preference for alternatives across the positive and negative versions of each problem. In all but one case (control subjects in the business problem), there was a higher percentage of subjects choosing the certain alternative with the positive version than with the negative version of each problem. However, in two of the three social work problems (Child abuse and Electricity board) this trend was not sufficient to eliminate an overall preference for the certain alternative in the negative as well as the positive version. The findings provided contradictory evidence concerning the prediction that expertise would increase the incidence of frame elaboration and thereby reduce the framing bias. The Asian disease problem and its isomorph showed the predicted reduction in the framing bias, but this was not evident in the other two. Indeed, control subjects showed a significantly reduced framing effect in the control version of the business transaction problem. Together, these findings show a rather inconsistent set of effects, supporting Fagley & Miller (1987) in their suggestion that effects are sensitive to choice of subjects and problems.

To further explore these findings a second study was undertaken focusing just on the expert group, giving two separate groups of social work students either the social work or the control version of the three problems used in experiment one. Each subject generated a concurrent verbal protocol and completed both versions of each problem in two sessions separated by a three-week interval. This provided the basis for using Maule's procedure for identifying the frame used by subjects and how this relates to choice behaviour. The present paper focuses on just one of the pairs of problems based on the Asian disease, since this was the pair revealing the expert differences in study one. The second study tested the following hypotheses: (i) following the results of experiment one it was predicted that there would be a greater framing effect in the control as compared with the social work version of the problem; (ii) given the knowledge and experience that social workers bring to the social work situation, it was predicted that the incidence of elaborated frames will be greater for subjects completing the social work versions of the task; (iii) following Maule (1989) it was predicted that risk aversion in the gain version of the task and risk seeking in the loss version of the task will only occur when subjects adopt simple gain or loss frames, not when they use elaborated frames; (iv) as indicated above, Schneider (1992) argued that, in the context of SP/A theory, the greater inconsistency in choice behaviour found in the loss version of framing tasks was due to conflict between the two factors Security-potential and Aspiration. If such conflict and diffficulty is a distinctive feature of the loss versions, then it would be predicted that protocols for this condition, as compared with the gain conditions, should be longer and/or should contain a greater number of words reflecting conflict and difficulty.

EXPERIMENT TWO

METHOD

Subjects

31 subjects were recruited from the same second year social work course as described in experiment one. One subject failed to turn up for the second session.

Problems

Positive and negative versions of the same three pairs of framing problems as experiment one were used and these were embedded in three further filler problems designed to make it more diffficult for subjects to recall the details of problems and their choice behaviour from the first to the second experimental session.

Procedure

Subjects attended two experimental sessions a minimum of three weeks apart. At each session they were presented with one version of each of the three experimental and filler problems. At the second session the other versions of the problems were presented. Versions of problems and the order in which they were presented were randomly determined for each subject. At the outset of each session subjects were given instructions concerning the procedure to be followed for completing the choice problems and the need to think aloud. Subjects were told to read the instructions aloud as a way of priming protocol generation and, prior to the first session, also had a brief practice at generating protocols based on two simple problem solving tasks. Following the suggestions set out by Svenson (1989) the experimenter sat back to back with the subject and prompted them by saying "what are you thinking now?" whenever the subject paused for more than a few seconds. 18 subjects completed both versions of the social work problems and 12 both versions of the control problems.

RESULTS

(i) Choice behaviour

To allow comparison with experiment one based on a between subjects design, choice behaviour was considered in terms of the percentage of subjects choosing the riskless alternative in each of the three pairs of problems considering each version of the problem separately. These data are illustrated in Figure 2. Choice behaviour was similar in all three, revealing, as predicted by Prospect Theory, a consistent reduction in preference for the riskless alternative in the loss versions of all problems. In addition, there was a generally higher overall preference for the riskless alternative in the social work versions of all problems. The major focus of the present experiment is the Asian disease problem and its social work isomorph. A comparison of the frequency of risk averse responding across the positive and negative versions of the two problems failed to show a significant difference (Chi-square= 0.07, df =1). Thus, the first hypothesis predicting a difference in choice behaviour between the two problems was not supported, though Figure 2 does indicate a trend in the same direction as experiment one.

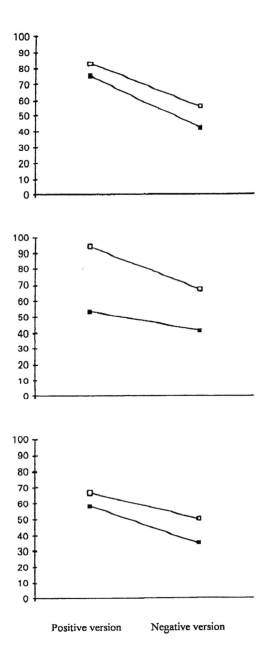

Positive version   Negative version

Figure 2. Percentage of subjects choosing the certain alternative in the positive and negative versions of the Asian disease (filled squares) and Child abuse (unfilled squares) problems.

(ii) Protocol Analysis

Each taped protocol was transcribed and, following suggestions by Svenson (1989), unitised by the experimenter by segmenting the protocol into separate units each involving one 'idea', then typing each segment on a separate line. Protocols were analysed in this form.

Protocol length

Inspection of the protocols indicated that, having read the problem once, some subject reread parts or all of the protocols on one or more occasions whilst others generated protocols involving no further reading of the problem. It is unclear whether these differences are important, so two calculations of protocol length were derived - one based on a count of all the words uttered following the first reading of the problem, called *total length,* and the other excluding any sequence of 3 or more words that were identical to the problem description as presented on the problem sheets, called *non reading length.* Table 1 illustrates the mean and range of protocol length expressed in these ways for positive and negative versions of the two problems. The first point to note is the extreme range of protocol lengths - lengths based on both measures varied from as little as 7 words to 443 words. This implies a considerable degree of variation between subjects as to the nature of the cognitive processing underlying their decision making. A comparison of protocol lengths based on both measures was undertaken for positive and negative versions of each problem, using a two-way analysis of variance. None of the main effects nor interactions were significant (F=2.07 or less, df =1.28, p>0.05). The failure to find longer protocols for the negative versions of the problems represents a lack of support for one part of hypothesis four based on SP/A theory, suggesting that the negative version of the problem is subject to greater difficulty and conflict.

Classification of Frames

Following the procedure described by Maule (1989) the protocols were analysed to determine the frame type. Each protocol was analysed by two judges, instructed to underline every instance of the words 'saving' and 'losing' or synonyms of these words, and then write the letter 's' or 'l' in the margin. The two judges then compared their analyses and resolved any discrepancies. In all but two cases, discrepancies were due to one judge agreeing that he/she had missed a word or its synonym. The other two cases were resolved by discussion of the meaning implied within the protocol. Having completed this the two judges analysed the protocols a second time identifying all examples when reference was made to moral principles (e.g. "it's like playing God" - Sub 13, positive version, Asian disease problem), any elaborations defined in terms of subjects referring to information that was not contained within the formal problem definition (e.g. "that is certainly what good social work practice is about" - Sub 7, positive version, Child abuse problem), and any examples of cognitive strain or perceived difficulty making a decision (e.g. "that sounds very complicated" Sub 5, negative version, Child abuse problem). There was a higher degree of disagreement in these judgements (15 in all) but these were readily resolved by discussion.

Table 1. Two measures of protocol length for subjects engaged in the positive and negative versions of the Asian disease and Child abuse problems.

	Total Length		Non-reading Length	
	Pos Version	Neg Version	Pos Version	Neg Version
Asian Disease Problem	80.1	89	63.8	60.8
	(17 - 137)	(38 - 146)	(17 - 106)	(18 - 123)
Child Abuse Problem	112	121	89.6	87.8
	(7 - 443)	(7 - 443)	(25 - 285)	(25 - 285)

Following these analyses, protocols only containing saving words were classified as gain frames, those containing only loss words were classified as loss frames, and those containing both gain and loss words were classified as both frames. In addition, if the protocol contained reference to moral principles or other elaborations it was classified as an elaborated frame. Table 2 summarises the frame classification for the positive and negative versions of the two problems and the choice behaviour associated with each frame.

This table shows that for both problems, a majority of subjects adopted a gain frame in the positive version of the task and a loss frame in the negative versions of the task. The number of elaborations was, however, very similar for both problems with 4 examples over both versions of each problem. This finding leads to a rejection of the second hypothesis predicting greater degrees of elaboration when experts are solving problems in their area of expertise.

Table 2. The frequency with which subjects adopted simple frames (gain or loss) and elaborated frames and associated choice behaviour for the positive and negative versions of the Asian disease and Child abuse problems.

ASIAN DISEASE PROBLEM

Frame	Positive Version			Negative Version		
	Total	RA Choice	Rs Choice	Total	RA Choice	RS Choice
G	7	6	1	1	1	0
L				8	3	5
B	1	0	1	1	0	1
G/E	3	2	1			
L/E	1	1	0			
B/E				2	1	1

CHILD ABUSE PROBLEM

Frame	Positive Version			Negative Version		
	Total	RA Choice	Rs Choice	Total	RA Choice	RS Choice
G	17	14	3			
L				13	7	6
B				2	1	1
G/E	1	1	0			
L/E				2	1	1
B/E				1	1	0

A further analysis was undertaken to assess the relationship between frame type and choice. This was considered by classifying frames as simple (gain or loss) or elaborated (both frames or those involving elaborations). Maule (1989) showed that the choice behaviour associated with simple frames could be predicted by Prospect Theory i.e. risk aversion in gains and risk seeking in losses. Collapsing across both versions of both problems revealed 46 instances of simple frames, with 70% of these leading to choice as predicted by Prospect Theory. There were 14 examples of elaborated frames and in just over half of these, 57%, was choice behaviour consistent with Prospect theory. Though this analysis suggests, as predicted, that choice behaviour based on simple frames was more consistent with the predictions of Prospect Theory than choice behaviour based on elaborated frames, the effect was much smaller than that reported by Maule (1989) and failed to reach significance (Chi-square=.81, df =1).

The final analysis of protocols focused on the frequency with which subjects reported difficulty and conflict when solving the problems. For the Asian disease problem 3 of the 12 subjects indicated strain/diffficulty in the positive version and 5 in the negative version. For the Child abuse problem the figures were 4 out of 18 and 3 out of 18 respectively. Together, these data provides little support for the prediction from SP/A theory for greater conflict and difficulty in the negative versions of framing problems.

DISCUSSION

The choice behaviour of subjects in experiment two was broadly similar to that exhibited by comparable groups in experiment one. There was support for the framing effect in terms of a reduction in preference for the certain alternative in the loss version of all the problems, though an overall preference for the certain alternative remained in both versions of all three social work problems. The results of experiment two generally failed to support the research hypotheses. First, there was a failure to replicate the findings of experiment one showing a significantly reduced framing effect in the social work version of the Asian disease problem. This may be due, in part, to the small number of subjects tested, leading to a lack of power in the statistical analyses (protocol studies are intensive, making it very difficult to test large numbers of subjects). In addition, it further demonstrates the variability and lack of consistency in framing effects often reported by other researchers (e.g. Fagley & Miller, 1987).

A failure to support hypothesis two, predicting a higher incidence of elaborated frames in social workers solving social work problems, was much more surprising. There appear to be two possible explanations for this lack of effect. One is to assume that the group were not expert. Though it is not usual to claim expertise in a student group, all of these students had at least two years social work experience prior to starting their course, and had further work experience during it. This would be expected to take the group well beyond the simple novice stage making an explanation based on lack of expertise unlikely. A second and apparently more plausible explanation reflects the fact that the social work problems used in these experiments are not typical of those found in everyday social work settings. Social workers rarely make decisions about whole programmes in the way demanded by the problem, making the acquired body of social work knowledge and expertise less relevant.

This suggests that simply developing decision problems based in a particular area and giving it to experts in that area may not provide an adequate test of the effects of expertise. Rather, the content and form of the problems must closely mirror those typically confronting experts. This principle does not appear to have been recognised by previous research investigating framing effects in expert decision makers (e.g. Mowen & Mowen, 1986; Neale & Northcraft, 1986), limiting the conclusions that can be drawn about the framing bias in experts. There is a strong need for future research to investigate framing in experts using more ecologically valid tasks.

The third hypothesis was based on elaboration theory and suggested that choice behaviour was consistent with the predictions of Prospect Theory when subjects adopted simple gain and loss frames but was inconsistent with the theory when subjects adopted elaborated frames. There was weak support for this in experiment two, suggesting that this may not be as important a factor as originally suggested. However, the protocols in the present study were generally longer than those reported by Maule (1989). Longer protocols include greater amounts of problem restructuring, involving changes to the internal representation of the problem over time. It is unclear whether all problem representations are of equal importance when defining the decision frame, or whether the representation current at the point of choice is the critical one. If the latter is the case then an analysis of the complete protocol will include irrelevant information leading to a misclassification of the frame type. This raises important methodological and theoretical issues. Developing a methodology to determine the frame at the point of choice is complicated by the fact that, in many protocols, the point of choice is difficult to determine and varies from very early to very late in the process. Theoretically, there is a need to better understand the role of restructuring across the decision process and the extent to which the different problem representations determine final choice. The analysis of the protocols in the present experiment shows a wide range of different frames, including one case of a gain frame in the loss version of the task. Such findings caution against developing theories that assume a simple relation between problem versions and frames. Indeed, previous researchers have often referred to the two versions of framing problems as being positively and negatively framed (e.g. Schneider, 1992). The present findings suggest both a need to distinguish between problem versions and frames and a need to define decision frames in the context of the changes in problem representation which occur across the decision making process.

The fourth hypothesis was based on SP/A theory predicting that the assumed conflict between the two factors Security-potential and Aspiration in losses should increase protocol length and/or reveal greater incidence of conflict or difficulty in the protocols generated in negative versions of the problems. There was no evidence for either of these elements, thereby failing to provide any support for this part of the theory.

A final issue emerging from the results of experiment two was the great variability in protocol lengths across subjects. The protocols of a few subjects involved less than ten words in about five seconds, whereas other protocols involved several hundred words over many minutes. This finding has two implications. First, it questions the adequacy of contemporary theories of decision making like Prospect Theory since they are unable to explain such disparate behaviour. Second, previous framing research has asked subjects to solve framing problems in groups, assuming that they take approximately equal time to complete problems. The fact that some individuals take considerably longer than others suggest that a proportion will be under time constraints, a condition that is known to influence framing effects (Svenson & Benson, 1993).

In conclusion the two experiments have, together, provided further support for the framing effect. The effect was, however, less strong with social work problems, with a continuing preference for certainty exhibited even in the negative versions of these problems. Neither SP/A Theory nor Elaboration Theory was supported by the analyses undertaken in experiment two, though a discussion of these findings have identified a number of important issues and priorities for future research.

REFERENCES

Bazerman, M. (1994). *Judgement in managerial decision making*. 3rd Edition; Chichester: Wiley.

Fagley, N.S., & Miller, P.M. (1987). The effects of decision framing on choice of risky v certain options. *Organizational Behavior & Human Decision Processes, 39*, 264-277.

Fiegenbaum, & Thomas, (1988). Attitudes towards risk and the risk-return paradox: Prospect theory explanations. *Academy of Management Journal, 31*, 85-106.

Hershey, & Schoemaker, (1980). Prospect theory's reflection hypothesis: a critical examination. *Organizational Behavior & Human Performance, 25,* 395 - 418.

Kahneman, D., & Tversky, A. (1984). Choices, values & frames. *American Psychologist, 39,* 341- 350.

Lesgold, A. (1984) .Acquiring expertise. In J.R. Anderson (Ed.), *Tutorials in learning & memory.* San Francisco: Freeman.

Lopes, L.L. (1987). Between hope and fear: The psychology of risk. In L. Berkowitz (Ed.), *Advances in experimental social psychology,Vol 20.* New York: Academic Press.

Maule, A.J. (1989). Positive and negative decision frames: a verbal protocol analysis of the Asian disease problem of Kahneman & Tversky (1981). In O. Svenson & H. Montgomery (Eds) *Process tracing approaches to decision making.* Chichester: Wiley.

Mowen, M.M., & Mowen, J.C. (1986). An empirical examination of the biasing effects of framing on business decisions. *Decision Sciences, 17,* 596 602.

Neale, M.A., & Northcraft, G.B. (1986). Experts, amateurs, and refrigerators. *Organizational Behavior & Human Decision Processes, 38,* 305 - 317.

Russo, J., & Schoemaker, P. (1990). *Decision traps: the ten barriers to brilliant decision making and how to overcome them.* Simon & Schuster.

Schneider, S.L. (1992). Framing and conflict: aspiration level contingency, the status quo, and current theories of risky choice. *Journal of experimental Psychology: Learning, memory and cognition, 18,*1040-1057.

Svenson, O. (1989). Eliciting and analysing verbal protocols in process studies of judgement and decision making. In O. Svenson & H. Montgomery (Eds.), *Process tracing approaches to decision making.* Chichester: Wiley.

Svenson, O., & Benson, (1993). Framing and time pressure in decision making. In O. Svenson & A.J. Maule (Eds.) *Time pressure and stress in human judgement and decision making.* New York: Plenum.

Tversky, A., & Kahneman, D. (1986). Rational choice and the framing of decisions. *Journal of Business, 59,* Part 2, 251- 278.

APPENDIX 1

The three control problems and their social work isomorphs:

1. Control Problem: Asian disease problem

Imagine that the US is preparing for the outbreak of an unusual Asian disease, which is expected to kill 600 people. Two alternative programmes to combat the disease have been proposed. Assume that the exact scientific estimates of the consequences of the programmes are as follows:

Positive version

If Program A is adopted, 200 people will be saved.

If Program B is adopted, there is one-third probability that 600 people will be saved and two-thirds probability that no people will be saved.

Negative version

If Program A is adopted, 400 people will die.

If Program B is adopted, there is a one-third probability that nobody will die and a two-thirds probability that 600 people will die.

1. Social Work Problem: Child abuse problem

Imagine that in a certain region it is known that 600 children suffer from non-accidental injury. Two alternative programmes to combat this have been proposed by the Social Services Department. Assume that the exact scientific estimates of the consequences of the programmes are as follows:

Positive version:

If programme A is adopted 200 children will be saved from non-accidental injury .

If programme B is adopted there is a one-third chance that 600 children will be saved and a two thirds chance that no children will be saved from non-accidental injury.

Negative version

If programme A is adopted 400 children will suffer non-accidental injury.

If programme B is adopted there is a one-third chance that no children will suffer and a two-thirds chance that 600 children will suffer from non-accidental injury.

2. Control problem: Business transaction

Imagine that you are currently £200 down on a business transaction. You have identified two different ways of proceeding with this transaction.

Positive version

Method A You will get £50 for certain

Method B You have a 25% chance of getting £200 and a 75% chance of getting nothing.

Negative version

Method A You will still be £150 down

Method B You have a 25% chance of having nothing to pay and a 75% chance of having all £200 to pay.

2: Social Work Problem: Electricity board problem

Imagine that one of your cases is a family that owes £200 to the Electricity Board. You have identified two different ways of helping the family get financial support for this problem:

Positive version

Method A The family will get £50 for certain .

Method B The family has a 25% chance of getting £200 and a 75% chance of getting nothing.

Negative version

Method A The family will still have £150 to pay .

Method B The family has a 25% chance of having nothing to pay and a 75% chance of having all £200 to pay.

3. Control problem: Cancer treatment

Imagine that you are advising someone as to the most appropriate course of action to take to treat cancer. There are two therapies available, based on surgery and radiation therapy, and you must choose between them. The two schemes differ in terms of the number of people who survive at various points in time. Records of previous cases show:

Positive version

Surgery: Of 100 people having surgery, 90 survive treatment, 68 survive by the end of one year and 34 survive by the end of five years.

Radiation Therapy: Of 100 people having radiation therapy, all survive treatment, 77 survive by the end of one year and 22 survive by the end of five years.

Negative version

Surgery: Of 100 people having surgery, 10 die during treatment, 32 die by the end of one year and 66 die by the end of five years.

Radiation Therapy: Of 100 people having radiation therapy, none will die during treatment, 23 will die by the end of one year and 78 will die by the end of five years.

3. Social work problem: Truancy problem

Imagine that one of your clients is a ten year old boy who has not attended school for sometime. There are two schemes for truants in your area, and you must choose which one to send him on. The two schemes differ in terms of the number of children who remain on the scheme at various points in time. Research shows that all children who absent themselves from the scheme remain truants and do not return to school. Records of previous cases show:

Positive version

Scheme A Of 100, 10 yr olds sent there, 90 continued going after the induction, 68 still attended at the end of the first year and 34 still attended at the end of 5 years.

Scheme B Of 100, 10 yr olds sent there, all completed the induction, 77 still attended at the end of the first year and 22 still attended at the end of 5 years.

Negative version

Scheme A Of 100, 10 yr olds sent there, 10 absented themselves at the induction, 32 had absented themselves by the end of the first year and 66 had absented themselves by the end of 5 years.

Scheme B Of 100, 10 yr olds sent there, none absented themselves at the induction, 23 had absented themselves by the end of the first year and 78 had absented themselves by the end of 5 years.

Contributions to Decision Making - I
J.-P. Caverni, M. Bar-Hillel, F.H. Barron and H. Jungermann (Editors)
© 1995 Elsevier Science B.V. All rights reserved.

RISK ORIENTATION IN DYNAMIC DECISION MAKING

Eva Pascoe and Nick Pidgeon

Birkbeck College (University of London) Department of Psychology,
Malet Street, London WC1 7HX, United Kingdom

Abstract. This paper reports an investigation exploring Lopes' (1987) Two-Factor model of risk in the context of dynamic decision making. The study is focused on the influence of the Dispositional Factor (ie risk orientation) on the behaviour of individuals during a dynamic decision task. The experimental task was a computer-based simulation of an alcohol distillation process. Subjects were classified into Risk Seeking and Risk Averse groups on the basis of choices made in static gambles, and subsequently trained to operate the dynamic production system. The basic task required subjects to maximise the goal of alcohol production, while maintaining an overall safety for the process. The results indicated a relationship between individual risk orientation and strategies used to control the dynamic production process. Specifically, subjects who were classified as Risk Seeking in the gamble task consistently selected more risky strategies in the dynamic context. The Risk Seeking subjects achieved higher performance levels, but their preferred strategies during normal operation caused significantly more safety problems. However, there was some evidence that Risk Seeking subjects would cope better with abnormal high complexity conditions.

INTRODUCTION

Traditional research on decision making under risk has been carried out primarily in static contexts, often using gamble paradigms. However, the characteristics of real-world decision making tasks are often very different from those of static gambles. Many real-world problems are distinguished by their dynamic properties. In a dynamic context the decision maker has the opportunity to correct problems caused by earlier decisions in later decisions. Such an adaptive decision making process is typically time-dependent with the environment changing both autonomously *and* as a function of the decision maker's action. Recent empirical studies have begun to investigate decision making in such contexts (reviewed in Brehmer, 1991; Funke, 1991). However, there is as yet no comprehensive theory of individual risk taking in dynamic tasks. One important aspect of such a theory would be to describe how individual characteristics affect risk taking, and their interaction with the characteristics of the dynamic task. Although most theories of decision making in static contexts have not concerned themselves with individual differences *per se,* some evidence does exist that there is a general risk taking propensity which influences behaviour across, and interacts with a range of decision making tasks (MacCrimmon & Wehrung, 1986). Furthermore, in dynamic contexts the role of the individual decision maker deserves special attention, since his or her actions have more influence over the progress and the outcome of the task than is the case in most static contexts. The purpose of the present investigation was to begin to address this issue in a study of the relationship between task and individual characteristics in dynamic decision making under risk.

Previous studies of dynamic decision making have typically addressed either the properties of the individual or the characteristics of the task in isolation from each other. Regarding individual differences there is some evidence that a dynamic task may elicit different coping strategies from different subjects (Staudel, 1987). Also Wearing and Omodei (1991) report that in dynamic tasks personality traits such as extraversion are predictive of individual strategy although not overall performance. However, no clear explanations of these individual differences in dynamic decision making have as yet emerged.

With respect to task characteristics, important variables are opaqueness and complexity. Opaqueness has been investigated indirectly in terms of feedback delays and feedback quality (Brehmer & Allard, 1991). Complexity is a less precise concept (for a recent review see Bainbridge *et al.* 1993), but would typically be defined in systems terms as the number of elements within a task (Brehmer, 1991). However, it also needs to be recognised that complexity is to some extent relative to the capacity of the decision maker to cope with the task demands (Ashby, 1956). Aspects of complexity which may influence dynamic decision processes include: the number of goals; the number of processes to be controlled to reach the goals; control actions; and side effects of decisions (Brehmer & Allard, 1991).

We would argue that the separate treatment of both individual and task properties, while valuable, may fail to fully account for the interactive properties of behaviour in dynamic contexts. In terms of risk taking, there is recent evidence from research in static contexts that both individual and situational characteristics contribute to risk behaviour and, crucially, that the interaction of both elements should be addressed (Lopes 1987).

Lopes' (1987) framework conceptualizes risk behaviour as a function of two factors. The first of these, the Dispositional Factor, expresses an individual orientation towards risk. Congruent with earlier research on individual variations in risk taking (e.g., MacCrimmon & Wehrung, 1986), Lopes (1987) has demonstrated that some people tend to be interested in the *potential* or opportunity that uncertainty offers, seeking to maximise the possible gains available. These she labels *Risk Seekers*. Other subjects will be more concerned with their *security* in an uncertain environment, being motivated to avoid the risk of extreme losses by seeking safe choices. These she labels *Risk Averse*. Thus in a situation of uncertainty, different people may choose different goals (potential or security) depending on whether they are Risk Seeking or Risk Averse. Lopes' Dispositional Factor can be interpreted in terms of the assessment by subjects of the available choice alternatives on a continuum between security and potential. For example, a person who is Risk Averse is likely to pay more attention to the 'bad' results of any alternative due to his/her motivation to seek security. Alternatively a Risk Seeking subject may pay more attention to the 'good' results, due to his/her tendency to seek the maximum potential offered.

The second element of Lopes' model influencing risk behaviour is termed the Aspirational Factor. This describes how people's responses in a risky situation will also depend upon the constraints imposed by the environment, and in particular the immediate needs and opportunities present. For example, a generally Risk Averse individual might be induced to behave in a risk seeking manner if this offers the possibility to meet a pressing immediate need such as avoiding imminent bankruptcy (Bowman, 1982). The Aspirational Factor is assumed to play an adaptive role, organising actively the choice process around external demands and opportunities. The Aspirational Factor describes therefore the second element underlying the individual's choices of the outcome or goal to aim for.

The integrated influence of both Dispositional and Aspirational Factors on risk behaviour in static decision making has been investigated experimentally in several studies using gambling tasks, providing evidence for the model (Lopes, 1984; Lopes & Casey, 1987; Schneider & Lopes, 1986; Leon & Lopes, 1988).

We would argue that the theoretical approach to risk taking of Lopes (1987) provides a metaphor to model risk taking behaviour in dynamic decision making. The objective of the present experiment therefore was to examine the validity of the Two-Factor approach to risk behaviour in a dynamic decision making task. The study focuses primarily on the effects of the Dispositional Factor (ie Risk Orientation) on risk behaviour and it's relationship to the strategies chosen by subjects in a dynamic decision making task; specifically the control of a computer-based simulation of an alcohol production process. The experiment was also designed to provide information on the interaction of the Dispositional Factor with task complexity, operationalised as the number of goals to be achieved in real-time.

THE RESEARCH PARADIGM: PROCESS

A computer-based real-time simulation of a dynamic task was used for the experiment, representing closely a real-world task, specifically process control. Typically in such a task the subject (operator) supervises the state of a more or less automated production system. The simulation used in the present study is based on a water-alcohol distillation process. The task requires subjects to control the simulated distillation system shown in Fig.1.

The program runs on an IBM compatible PC (PROCESS, see Jelsma & Bijlstra, 1990, for a detailed description). It produces a high-fidelity simulation, with thermodynamic and heat transfer equations controlling the dynamics of the process, based upon a real-world process control environment. The simulation is fully dynamic, with all variables being updated, displayed on the screen and recorded every 6 seconds in real-time. The main elements of PROCESS displayed in Fig. 1 are as follows: Raw material enters through a pipe on the lefthand side regulated by a Feed Controller valve (1). The feed is then preheated by means of a closed steam pipe regulated by a Temperature Controller (2). The heated feed is then introduced continuously into the Distillation Column (3). A condenser then cools the vapours and the condensate is caught in the Reflux Tank (4). The final product flows through the pipe on the right side to the output vat (5).

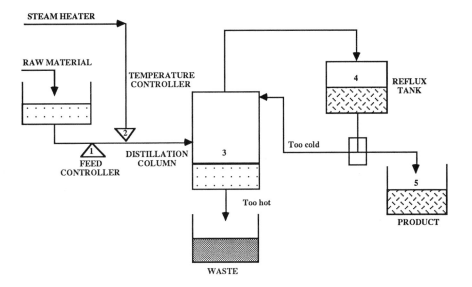

Figure 1. Simplified diagram of the simulated water-alcohol distillation system.

The operator's main goals are to maximise production within safety constraints. In order to achieve this he/she can vary the feedstock pump (1) and temperature settings (2) by either manual commands or using automatic controllers. Also, the operator can set the alarm safety bounds. A warning is subsequently triggered when the process flow parameters violate these preset limits. For the current experiment PROCESS was set up to output, under stable conditions, an average of 12.5 tonnes per hour of final product.

METHOD

Subjects

25 subjects completed the process control task. The data from 22 subjects (12 males, 10 females, all aged between 26 and 31 years old) was analyzed; 11 being Risk Seeking (6 females, 5 males) and 11 Risk Averse (4 females, 7 males), as classified on the basis of performance in the lottery tasks described by Leon and Lopes (1988). Subjects were paid an hourly rate plus a bonus contingent on results.

Independent Variables and Design

The main experiment was a 2x2 mixed design. The first independent variable was Risk Orientation resulting in two groups of subjects; Risk Seeking and Risk Averse. The second (repeated measures) independent variable was Complexity, operationalised as the number of goals the subjects had to attend to simultaneously. In the Low Complexity condition the simulation ran normally without disturbance. Here subjects had two goals, maintaining Safety and maximising Performance. In the High Complexity condition a third goal was introduced; that of coping with a pre-programmed fault. This appeared in the 33rd second of the run of a High Complexity trial. The fault was a leak in the material feed (1), causing emptying of the distillation column (3). The subjects had been trained in management of the fault and the diagnosis was made unambiguous. By operationalising complexity in this way, a qualitative change in the task and its cognitive demands was introduced, although clearly adding another goal also involves a quantitative difference in the demands that the task places upon subjects. A third independent variable, the number of trials (4 in each of the main conditions) was included in the overall design, but results from this will not be reported here.

Dependent Variables

PROCESS records several measures of performance and system states during each trial. Of these, four measures will be reported here. The first two represent the degree of achievement of the primary goals; *Performance* as measured by total production achieved at the end of each trial, and *Safety* measured by the total number of alarms per trial caused through exceeding the set alarm safety bounds. The second two are direct measures of the subjects' actions, which can be used to illustrate the strategies that they develop; degree of *Risk Taking* measured by increases of the alarm safety bounds, and the total number of *Control Actions* taken during a trial.

A measure of individual preference for the type of control strategy, A (Risky) and B (Safe), was taken before each trial. Strategy A (Risky) consisted of large increases in input volume, which could lead to significant performance gains. However, without corresponding changes in temperature and alarm safety bounds settings, this strategy might cause the alcohol to be either too cold and recycled, or too hot and burned. Strategy B (Safe) consisted of small increases in input volume, which could be made without adjusting the temperature or alarm settings, but would not lead to significant performance gains.

Procedure

Stage 1: Risk Seeking/Averse Classification:

Subjects were divided into Risk Seeking (RS) and Risk Averse (RA) on the basis of performance in the lottery task (described by Leon & Lopes, 1988; Leon & Gambara, 1991). The stimuli used are a set of six lotteries with multiple results, all of them with the same expected value of £100 (reproduced in Lopes,1987). All possible combinations of pairs of the six lotteries are formed, totalling 15. The *riskless* lottery (RL) is a positively skewed lottery with a minimum prize of £70 and maximum prize of £200. The *short shot* (SS) is a negatively skewed reflection of the riskless lottery with a £0 minimum and a £130 maximum. The *peaked* (PK), *rectangular* (RC) and *bimodal* (BM) lotteries are all symmetrical with a £0 minimum and £200 maximum. The *long shot* (LS) is a high-variance positively skewed lottery with a £0 minimum and £439 maximum. It has been observed that Risk Averse subjects typically chose RL, SS, PK, RC lotteries over BM or LS (Lopes, 1984; Schneider & Lopes, 1986). 42 subjects took part in this initial phase, and those subjects who chose the Long Shot and Bimodal lottery 4 times or less *and* the Long Shot lottery not more than 2 times were classified as Risk Averse (RA). Subjects who chose 5 or more Long Shot and Bimodal lotteries were classified as Risk Seeking (RS). The task was repeated after approximately 6 weeks for test-retest reliability purposes[1] and only these subjects who were consistently classified as Risk Averse and Risk Seeking on both occasions then took part in the dynamic decision making task.

Stage 2: Dynamic Decision Making Task

Training Phase

Subjects were trained to operate 'PROCESS' and instructed that they had two goals, to maximise the production and to maintain the security of the plant. They were also trained to manage the fault, which was the third goal in the High Complexity condition. Short instructions were read to subjects and a brief manual was provided and available during trials. Subjects were allowed to familiarize themselves with the display and the commands, and practice the commands on the keyboard in 4 training trials (2 in each Complexity condition) lasting 6 minutes each. They were instructed to use these runs to familiarize themselves with the physical task environment (computer display, keyboard). In order to check if subjects understood the system after the second training trial they were asked to draw a mental model of the system (cf. Bostrom, 1990). If misunderstandings were identified, relevant parts of the instructions were repeated. However, most subjects quickly understood PROCESS and were able to change the system states and recover from the fault scenario. Each training session lasted about 40 minutes. In keeping with the characteristic of dynamic contexts, uncertainty was induced by making salient to the subjects the interdependence of feed volume, temperature and output, but not providing them with the complete explanation of this relationship or its dynamics. The objective of the training was primarily to provide a basic understanding of the system and the ways of

---

[1] The classification procedure results in fact in three groups of subjects. Risk Seeking and Risk Averse as described above and an 'Undifferentiated' middle group, who chose Long Shot and Bimodal lotteries 4 times or less, with the Long Shot lottery being selected *more* than two times. Test-retest reliability of the procedure was checked in two ways. First each subject's score for the total number of Long Shots and Bimodal lotteries that was selected (a number that could vary between 0 and 10) was correlated across the two test sessions ($r=0.84$, $N=42$, $p<0.001$). Second, the percentage agreement of the final classification into RS, RA and Undifferentiated was 81% across the two test sessions.

controlling it, and not the achievement of any particular stable level of performance in advance of the main trials.

Experimental Phase

Subjects received 8 experimental trials lasting 6 minutes each, 4 of Low Complexity and 4 of High Complexity, in a pre-set sequence[2]. Before each trial, the subjects had available the descriptions of the Risky (A) and Safe (B) control strategies, and were asked to indicate a preference for either by circling one from the pair on a pre-prepared response sheet.

During each trial subjects could control the feed valve position, the temperature of the process, the mode of operation (manual or automatic) and the repair function. On automatic control, the system would yield about 12.5 tonnes per hour of product. The two objectives of maximising performance and maintaining safety were interrelated. If subjects wished to maximise production, they had to increase feed volume significantly. To do this without suffering excess alarms, they had to extend the alarm safety bounds. Increasing the alarm safety bounds might in turn have a negative effect on safety, as it would have decreased the sensitivity of the warning system, and alarms might have been triggered too late for recovery from the disturbance. The change of setting of the alarm limits was risky, as it exposed the subjects to a greater risk of negative consequences. Although the possibility of a total safety failure was explained to subjects, the simulation was set up to be relatively robust and in the event no subjects suffered such a failure of the process within the 6 minutes period of a trial.

Subjects had to learn how to meet each of the performance and safety objectives within the constraints of the other. Bonuses

---

[2] The sequence of Low complexity (L) and High complexity (H) trials was preset at LLHLHLHH. Separate ANOVAs were run using trials as a within-subjects factor, but the results from these are not reported here. Clearly the High Complexity trials tend to come later in the sequence, and hence complexity is partially confounded with trial position. However, this does not affect the broad conclusions drawn, since inspection of the trial means for all the dependent measures (with the single exception of Control Actions) indicates that differences between successive HL or LH trials were both systematic and far greater than those between successive HH or LL trials. Details of the trial results can be obtained from the first author.

were offered for achieving performance above the average of 12.5 tonnes per hour (£1 for each tonne of production extra). The safety goal required subjects to maintain the process within the set alarm safety bounds, minimising any out-of-bounds situations. Therefore penalties were deducted from subjects' final bonuses for safety related outcomes and actions (£1 deducted for each alarm caused, and 0.50 pence for each action to extend the alarm safety bounds by 5%). The gains and penalties were designed to approximately balance under the Low Complexity mode of system operation.

In the High Complexity trials a fault (a leak in the material feed which appeared in the 33rd second) was indicated by acoustic and visual alarm signals. To rectify the fault, subjects had to diagnose it and send a 'repair team' by issuing a keyboard command.

Hypotheses

It was predicted that RS subjects would tend to choose strategy A (Risky) in the expressed preference task and also exhibit more risky actions (eg large increases in alarm safety bounds) in the dynamic task. Conversely it was expected that RA subjects would prefer strategy B (Safe) and take less risky actions in the dynamic task. No specific predictions were made for performance (beyond the general expectation that higher complexity would degrade overall production), or for the interaction between Risk Orientation and Complexity.

RESULTS

Risk Orientation and Expressed Preference for Risky Versus Safe Control Strategies

Subjects indicated their preference for either the A (Risky) or B (Safe) control strategy before each of the 8 experimental trials. RS subjects selected A (Risky) on the average 7.41 times (out of a maximum 8), while RA subjects selected A only 3.2 times (t=6.31 df=20 p<0.01). Therefore risk orientation as measured in a static lottery task predicts expressed preference for riskiness of control strategy in the dynamic task.

Measures from the Dynamic Decision Task: Outcomes and Strategies

Results from four of the dependent measures obtained from on-line data collected by PROCESS are reported here. The first two relate to achievement of the primary task goals: (1) *Performance* measured in total production per trial, and (2) *Safety* measured by the number of alarms caused. The next two can be used to illustrate the strategies by which subjects went about achieving these goals: (3) *Risk Taking* measured by degree of increase in the alarm safety bounds, and (4) the total number of *Control Actions* taken. The data reported here is pooled over the 4 trials within each of the main experimental conditions in the 2 x 2 Risk Orientation by Complexity design.

Effects of Risk Orientation and Complexity on Achievement of the Primary Task Goals: Performance and Safety

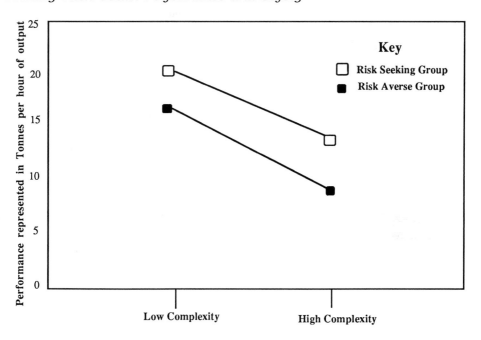

Figure 2. The Effects of Risk Orientation and Complexity on performance pooled over trials.

a) Performance: Volume of final product

Fig.2 represents the mean performance in each of the experimental conditions measured in tonnes per hour of production. RS subjects achieved consistently higher production than the RA group. The main effect of Risk Orientation was significant at p<0.001 F(1,20)=14.3. Increasing complexity led to a drop in production in both RS and RA groups indicated by a main effect of Complexity significant at p<0.001, F(1,20)=49.15. There was no interaction of Complexity and Risk Orientation.

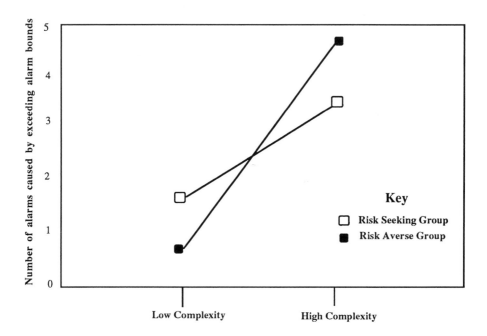

Figure 3. The Effects of Risk Orientation and Complexity on safety record represented as the number of alarms caused by exceeding the alarm safety bounds pooled over trials.

b) Safety: Number of Alarms Caused

Fig.3 shows the average number of alarms caused by subjects exceeding alarm safety bounds on the feed controller. The main effect of Risk Orientation was not significant. Both groups of subjects caused more alarms in the High Complexity condition compared to the Low Complexity condition: the main effect of complexity was significant at $p<0.001$, $F(1,20)=94.37$. The graph shows an interesting interaction in that in the High Complexity condition the relative increase in mean number of alarms was greater for RA subjects than for the RS group. This effect was reflected by a significant interaction of Complexity with Risk Orientation at $p<0.001$, $F(1,20)=19.13$.

Effects of Risk Orientation and Complexity on Risk Taking and Total Number of Control Actions

The final two dependent measures give some indication of the strategies used to achieve the primary goals.

a) Risk Taking: Increasing Alarm Safety Bounds to Maximise Production

Fig.4 shows the proportion of increase in the alarm safety bounds on the feed volume controller. Subjects could increase the alarm safety bounds in order to let the system accept more volume of raw material to maximise the production. However, this involved taking risk, as the alarm system became less sensitive to dangerous changes and alarms might have been triggered off too late to allow recovery from a disturbance. A score of 0 in Fig.4 represents maintaining the alarm safety bounds at a pre-set level. Both groups increased the alarm safety bounds above this level, despite the penalty points that resulted from such increases. However, the RS increases were higher, yielding a main effect of Risk Orientation significant at $p<0.001$, $F(1,20)=39.14$. There was no main effect of Complexity but there was an interaction of Risk Orientation with Complexity, significant at $p<0.001$, $F(1,20)=14.14$. From Fig.4 it may be seen that RA subjects selected less risky increases of the alarm safety bounds in the High Complexity condition. A few RA subjects stopped increasing the alarm bounds altogether, and only worked within the pre-set alarm bounds (5 out of 11 RA subjects). The RS subjects show the converse pattern with higher levels of alarm bound increases in the High Complexity condition. This significant interaction was an unexpected result and will be addressed further in the Discussion section.

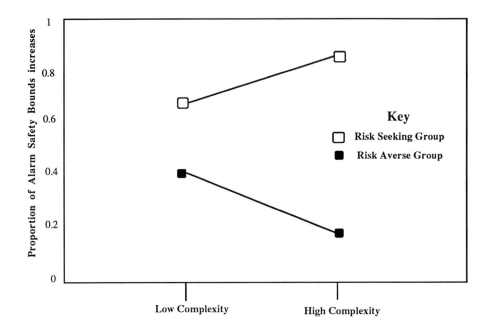

Figure 4. The Effects of Risk Orientation and Complexity on risk taking represented as a proportion of the total possible increase of the alarm safety bounds on the feed controller pooled over trials.

b) Total Number of Control Actions

Fig.5 illustrates the mean number of actions (all commands to request information or change the state of the system). RS subjects consistently took more actions than RA subjects yielding the main effect of Risk Orientation significant at $p<0.001$. $F(1,20)=30.75$. The main effect of Complexity was significant at $p<0.05$ with $F(1,20)=5.4$, indicating that the introduction of the High Complexity condition appears to lead to an increase of action for both groups[3]. There was no interaction between Risk Orientation and Complexity.

---

[3] The interpretation of this particular main effect has to be treated with some caution. On the one hand the introduction of the High Complexity condition would be expected to demand more 'recovery' actions from subjects irrespective of their Risk Orientation. On the other hand, and as mentioned earlier, the Control Actions dependent

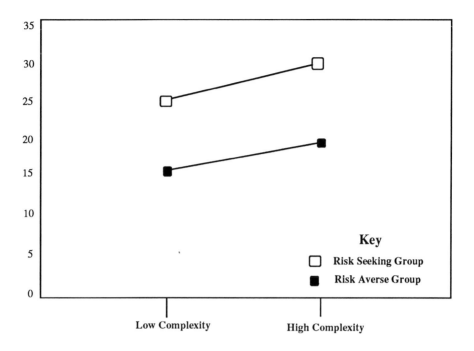

Figure 5. The Effects of Risk Orientation and Complexity on the number of control actions taken pooled over trials.

DISCUSSION

The results of the experiment confirm the prediction that there would be a systematic relationship between Risk Orientation as defined by the static lottery task and both expressed preferences for strategy, and actual risk taking in the dynamic water-alcohol distillation task. Specifically, the approach of the RA subjects could be described as less active than that of the RS group, and with less risk taking as measured by increases in the alarm safety bounds. The result was that the RA subjects achieved less production, but

---

measure was unlike the other three in that the by-trial data for the control actions gave some indication of a general trend of increasing control actions across trials (particularly for the RS subjects). Therefore, with this dependent measure one cannot rule out the possibility that the main effect for Complexity was in some way related to experience with the system.

obtained a better safety record under 'normal' Low Complexity conditions. In very general terms these findings indicate that the first factor of Lopes' (1987) model does indeed generalise to the dynamic case, accounting for some of the individual differences in risk behaviour in such contexts.

The results also show two interesting interactions between Risk Orientation and Complexity. First, compared to RS subjects the RA group caused less alarms under normal operation (Low Complexity). However, when the third goal of rectifying a fault (High Complexity) was introduced, the RA group caused more alarms than the RS subjects (Fig.3).

The second interaction (Fig.4) involved risk taking as measured by the increases in alarm safety bounds. In comparison to their behaviour in the Low Complexity condition, RS subjects appeared to compensate for the disruption caused by the introduction of the fault in the High Complexity condition (ie. the lost time and unfavourable drop of the raw material level in the distillation column) by taking more risk. RA subjects demonstrated the opposite pattern of results, since they reduced risk taking under High Complexity (or in some cases stopped taking risk altogether) as compared to the Low Complexity condition.

In interpreting the meaning of the interactions in Figs. 3 and 4 it should be recognised that the two dependent measures (alarms caused and risk taking measured by increase in alarm safety bounds) are not fully independent. One explanation for RA subjects causing more alarms in the High Complexity condition could be that RA subjects had set lower alarm safety bounds, making the system more sensitive. However, RA subjects set lower alarm safety bounds also in the Low Complexity condition as compared to the RS group. Therefore if the number of alarms caused was purely a function of the bounds set, we would expect the number of alarms caused by the RA group to be higher than RS in both Low and High Complexity trials. Fig.3 shows this not to be the case, as the RA safety record was better in the no-fault trials, despite having set more sensitive alarm safety bounds. Whether there is any partial dependence or not, this does not, however, alter the broad interpretation that we place on the interactions (particularly the most critical measure of risk taking).

Part of the reason for the interactions shown in Figs.3 and 4 might be found with reference to the Two Factor model of risk behaviour. This would predict that RA and RS subjects would prioritise the task goals (in this case Safety and Performance) differently. Lopes (1987) argues that RA subjects tend to pay more attention to 'bad results'. In the PROCESS simulation these would be the penalties for causing alarms and alarm bounds increases, and the avoidance of safety problems. Thus they could be expected to be less concerned than RS subjects with the goal of maximising production. The fact that in Fig.2 the RA subjects consistently show lower production levels provides some support for this. More importantly, however, in the High Complexity condition, the occurrence of the fault would have made the achievement of the Safety goal more difficult, as causing alarms was more likely due to the greater instability of the system. We can speculate that this might have affected the RA group more in terms of their confidence to control the task. As noted by Lee and Moray (1992), operators of complex dynamic systems may react to faults by losing confidence in their abilities to achieve control, because they may attribute the occurrence of the disturbances to their own mistakes. In the current case we did not measure subjective confidence directly, however, one could argue that since RA subjects' primary goal (Safety) was made more difficult by introduction of the fault, their confidence might have been more affected in the High Complexity condition compared to RS subjects, for whom safety would be less of a consideration. This is supported by the finding that there was a drop in risk taking by the RA subjects in the High Complexity condition (Fig.4). It may also partly explain why the RA safety record is relatively worse (Fig.3) in the High Complexity condition (loss of confidence leading to less effective control strategies), although further analysis of the Control Actions data from the trials would be needed to investigate this hypothesis.

Conversely the Two Factor model predicts that RS subjects would pay more attention to 'good' results (achieving above average production) and less to their safety record. Introduction of a fault (which has an immediate impact on production) might have the effect with this group of increasing risk in order to compensate for the loss (ie time spent on repairs and temporary drop in output), particularly after the fault has been successfully dealt with. Taken together, these rather complex set of results do suggest to us that the RA and RS subjects compensate for the introduction of the High

Complexity condition by developing qualitatively different control strategies.

The main effect between RS and RA subjects for Control Actions (Fig.5) has several interesting implications, since this difference was not predicted in advance. The finding in Fig.5, that the RA group took fewer control actions (spending more time monitoring), suggests that RA subjects may need more information before deciding on their next move. Corbin (1980) has pointed out that avoiding action until more information is available may be used by subjects as a way of coping with uncertainty. Since the information display was constantly being updated in real-time (every 6 seconds), it may be that RA subjects sought more information before reaching a decision and therefore would be at a disadvantage in some real-time dynamic decision tasks, particularly under high complexity. These tasks require not only the right decision, but more importantly timing, determined by the dynamic system rather than the decision maker.

Turning to the higher level of control action of the Risk Seeking group, in previous studies of dynamic decision making the strategy of a high level of activity has been interpreted as a 'pathology' (Dorner, 1991). In the present study it could be argued that the higher level of actions exhibited by the Risk Seeking subjects is associated with *good* performance (measured by better production and fewer alarms caused) under the High Complexity condition. This offers an alternative view on 'actionism': a high level of actions may be helping subjects to explore the complexities of the dynamic task.

Considering the uncertainty in the control task (induced by providing only partial information regarding the specific relationship between feed volume, temperature and output), the non-salient characteristics of the dynamic task were only identifiable by a trial-and-error strategy. Since control actions did not cost the subjects many penalty points, an *active* control strategy could have been perceived by subjects as optimal if the decision maker's objective was to increase production while maintaining safety. The precise understanding of the relationship of feed volume, temperature and output was less crucial if the subject's goal was merely to maintain safety. Therefore, the differences in activity of control actions may again be explained by possible differences in goal selection of Risk Averse (security orientated) and Risk Seeking (potential orientated) subjects, in line with the prediction based on Lopes' Two Factor model.

Although the evaluation of 'good' performance is obviously dependent upon the nature of the task, this does lead in the current context, to the somewhat counterintuitive conclusion that Risk Seeking subjects might cope better with abnormal, high complexity conditions.

In more theoretical terms, the control actions data are interesting since they point to a possible correlate of the Risk Orientation factor that would not readily be revealed by static tasks. Specifically, one could argue that the Risk Seeking subjects appear to work harder (in terms of direct actions) at achieving their goals. Of course, the question of whether such an 'achievement orientation'[4] is a result of Risk Orientation in combination with the specific demands of the PROCESS task as set up here, or a more fundamental individual characteristic that is correlated with Risk Orientation *per se*, is an interesting empirical issue and one that deserves further study. In any event, the results imply that Lopes' model should be investigated further in other dynamic contexts.

In conclusion, the study demonstrates that the PROCESS simulator is a useful research tool for investigating risk taking behaviour in dynamic real-time contexts. The results from the study support the suggestion that the Dispositional Factor from Lopes' (1987) model influences decision making in both static and dynamic contexts. In addition, the experimental findings indicate that explanations for performance in dynamic tasks can indeed by sought in terms of the interaction of characteristics of the individual and those of the task.

---

[4] We are indebted to an anonymous reviewer for raising this interesting suggestion.

REFERENCES

Ashby, W.R. (1956) *An Introduction to Cybernetics*. London:Chapman & Hall.

Bainbridge, L., Lenior, T.M.J., & Schaaf, T.W (1993). Cognitive processes in complex tasks. *Ergonomics, Vol 36*, (11), 1273-1279.

Bostrom, A. (1990) *A mental models approach to exploring perceptions of hazardous processess*. PhD thesis. School of Urban and Public Affairs, Carnegie Mellon University.

Bowman, E.H. (1982) Risk seeking by troubled firms. *Sloan Management Review. Vol.* 23, 3342.

Brehmer, B. (1991) Dynamic decision making: Human control of complex systems. *Proceedings from 13th Conf. on Subjective Probability, Utility and Decision Making* Fribourg, August 18-23.

Brehmer, B. ,& Allard, R. (1991) Real-time dynamic decision making. Effects of task complexity and feedback delays. In J. Rasmussen, B. Brehmer & J. Leplat (Eds), *Distributed Decision Making: Cognitive Models for Cooperative Work*. Chichester:Wiley.

Corbin, R. M. (1980) Decisions that might not get made. In T.S.Wallsten (Ed) *Cognitive Processes in Choice and Decision Behaviour*. Hillsdale (NJ): Erlbaum.

Dorner, D. (1991) The investigation of action regulation in uncertain and complex situations. In J. Rasmussen, B. Brehmer & J. Leplat (Eds), *Distributed Decision Making: Cognitive Models for Cooperative Work*. Chichester:Wiley.

Funke, J. (1991) Solving complex problems: Exploration and control of complex social systems. In R.J. Sternberg and P.A. Frensch (Eds) *Complex Problem Solving: Principles and Mechanisms*. Hillsdale: Lawrence Erlbaum Assoc.

Jelsma, O., & Bijlstra, J.P. (1990) Process: Program for research on operator control in an experimental simulated setting. *IEEE Transactions on Systems, Man and Cybernetics*, Vol 20,111-132.

Lee, J., & Moray, N. (1992) Trust, control strategies and allocation of function in humanmachine systems. *Ergonomics*, Vol 35 (10), 1243-1271.

Leon, O.G., & Gambara, H. (1991) Self-fulfilling prophecy and feedback in decision making under risk. *Psicothema*, Vol 3 (1), 219-230.

Leon, O.G., & Lopes, L. (1988) Risk preference and feedback. *Bulletin of the Psychonomic Society*, Vol 26 (4), 343-346.

Lopes, L. (1984) Risk and Distributional Inequality. *Journal of Experimental Psychology: Human Perception and Performance*, Vol 10, 465-485.

Lopes, L. (1987) Between hope and fear: the psychology of risk. *Advances in Experimental Social Psychology, Vol 20*, 255-295.

Lopes, L., & Casey, J.T. (1987) Tactical and strategic responsiveness in a competitive risk taking game. *Wisconsin Human Information Processing Program Technical Report, WHIPP*, 28.

MacCrimmon, K.R,, & Wehrung, D.A. (1986) *Taking risks. The Management of Uncertainty*. New York: The Free Press.

Schneider, S., & Lopes, L. (1986) Reflection in preferences under risk: Who and When may suggest Why. *Journal of Experimental Psychology: Human Perception and Performance*, Vol 12,535-548.

Staudel, T. (1987) Problemlosen, Emotionen and Kompetenz. Die Uberprufung eines integrative Konstrukts. Regansgurg: Roderer.

Wearing, A., & Omodei, M. (1991) Cognitive commitment and affect in a real-time dynamic decision-making task. *Proceedings from 13th Conf on Subjective Probability, Utility and Decision Making* Fribourg, August 18-23.

ACKNOWLEDGEMENT. This work was funded by the Cognitive Science/HCI Joint Council Initiative of the UK Research Councils by a graduate student scholarship to the first author. We are grateful for the comments of Mary Omodei, our colleague P.J. Barber and two anonymous reviewers.

Contributions to Decision Making - I
J.-P. Caverni, M. Bar-Hillel, F.H. Barron and H. Jungermann (Editors)
© 1995 Elsevier Science B.V. All rights reserved.

DISENCHANTING HINDSIGHT BIAS

Rudiger F. Pohl

FB-I Psychology, Universitat Trier Postbox 3825,
D-54286 Trier, Germany
e-mail: pohl@cogpsy.uni-trier.dbp.de

Abstract. One case of hindsight bias is the phenomenon that people who gave numerical estimates under uncertainty and who later received the correct numbers tend to „remember" having given better estimates than they actually did. While this effect appears remarkably robust, its proper interpretation is hindered by several methodological artifacts. In trying to avoid these problems, this paper claims that the observed distribution of imperfect recollections should be considered a compound of three distinct recollection types: unbiased new estimates, correct-value anchored judgments, and blended recollections.

INTRODUCTION

„Hindsight is easier than foresight" claims an English proverb. We all do know more *after* the event (because that's how we learn), but how do we judge our prior knowledge in retrospect? Often, we seem to overestimate the quality of our previous knowledge, thus concealing our true degree of ignorance. Fischhoff (1975) coined the term „Knew-it-all-along" effect. Suppose, for example, someone who estimates the length of the Danube river to be 1,800 km, is later told that it is 2,852 km, and is subsequently asked to recall the earlier estimate. A typical recollection will lie closer to the correct value than the original estimate did (e.g., 2,200 km). Shifts of this sort are commonplace in everyday situations.

Two recent papers reviewed the state of hindsight research in some detail (Christensen-Szalanski & Willham, 1991; Hawkins & Hastie, 1990). Both attested that hindsight bias is a very robust phenomenon: out of 122 studies (included in a meta-analysis by Christensen-Szalanski & Willham, 1991), only 6 failed to show the „normal" effect.

The bias index used in this paper is defined as follows (cf. Hell, Gigerenzer, Gauggel, Mall, & Müller, 1988):

$$\text{Bias-Index } (BI) = 100 \times \frac{\text{Estimate - Recollection}}{\text{Estimate - Correct Value}}$$

This index yields 0, if the original estimate was recalled correctly, and an absolute value between 0 and 100, if the recollection moved towards the correct value. In the above Danube river example, the recollected answer (i.e., 2,200 km) would have a bias index of 38. This finding is commonly interpreted as a hindsight bias. The effect is explained either through immediate assimilation of the correct value into one's knowledge representation (Fischhoff, 1975; Wood, 1978) or through reconstructive processes that are anchored at the correct value, and fail to adjust fully to the original estimate (Tversky & Kahneman, 1974). Motivational causes - like trying to appear more knowledgeable - seem to play only minor roles (Hawkins & Hastie, 1990; but see Campbell & Tesser, 1978, and Hell et al., 1988).

This paper claims that the overall shift of the distribution of recollections may reflect a number of methodological artifacts. The most severe critique of the common interpretation states that not a single one of the individual recollections is biased by means of interference between original estimate and correct value (cf. McCloskey & Zaragoza, 1985, for a similar argument regarding the eyewitness misinformation effect). Rather, the mean shift may be caused by (unjustifiedly) summing across two separate distributions corresponding to different recollection types (cf. the „summed distribution hypothesis" by Metcalfe & Bjork, 1991). Two further artifacts that may mimic a hindsight-biased recollection shift concern subjects who misunderstand the memory-test instructions and regression effects. The latter two problems will be tackled first, before I turn to the question of how to disentangle different recollection types.

TWO MINOR PROBLEMS

Failure to Follow Instructions

Although usually instructions clearly ask subjects to recall their earlier *estimates*, it occasionally happens that subjects try to recall the correct values. This can easily be understood, because asking what someone has learned is a natural task, while asking what someone had guessed some time ago (and before knowing the correct value) is an odd one. Subjects who erroneously attempt to recall the correct value will, of course, produce a large, systematic shift. But this shift has nothing to do with memory blends!

In this light, one should inspect collective hindsight data for signs of „suspect" subjects. For example, subjects who successfully recall most of the correct values, or subjects who gave only *round* numbers as original estimates, but *unrounded* values (as correct values usually are) for recollections, are suspect. My experience is that in about every third experiment one or two such subjects turn up. This might not seem a serious problem, but in order to interpret results adequately, these subjects should be excluded from further analyses. In some cases, it will be difficult to determine whether or not a subject really misunderstood the instructions. I suggest that even only slightly suspect subjects should not be considered further. While this rule may appear extreme, it leaves one on the safe side regarding what a recollection shift actually means.

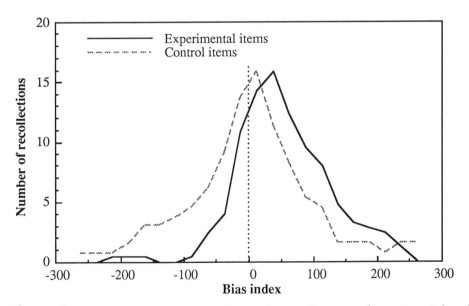

Figure 1. A typical bias-index distribution for recollections of experimental and control items (recollections with $BI = 0$ and $BI = 100$ excluded; data from the standard group of Experiment 2).

Regression Effects

The second minor artifact concerns regression effects. The chances of a positively biased recollection are always higher than those of a negatively biased one. (This is true except when the correct value lies outside the range of the estimates). Thus, regression alone may cause a shift of the bias-index distribution. That this is possible can be seen from Figure 1. The depicted data (taken from Experiment 2 described below) show a shift towards the correct value ($BI = 100$) not only for recalled *experimental* items, but for recalled *control* items as well. The control-items' shift cannot, of course, be interpreted as a hindsight bias, because they are, by definition, no-feedback items. The observed shift for experimental items may include similar regression effects. Thus, only the shift-„surplus" of experimental items should be subject to further investigation.

SEPARATION OF RECOLLECTION TYPES

A major problem is what types of recollection exist and how they can be separated. Following McCloskey and Zaragoza (1985), I assume three distinct recollection types. McCloskey and Zaragoza questioned the eyewitness misinformation effect (i.e., the erroneous recognition of misinformation as originally presented information) in the standard two-alternative forced-choice test. They argued that the observed effect may simply reflect different recall probabilities, rather than a memory interference phenomenon. For the original information, they assumed the same recall probability for control items as well as for experimental ones, that is, misinformation does not impair recall of the original information. But if the original information was not encoded or was forgotten, subjects in the experimental condition might remember (and report) the misinformation instead-leading to the typical misinformation effect. This line of reasoning can easily be transferred to hindsight research (cf. Pohl & Gawlik, in press; Stahlberg & Eller, 1993).

If subjects remember only their earlier estimates (and nothing else), then their recollections will center around those original estimates (with a mean of $BI \approx 0$). Because the correct value has no distorting effect in this case, the recollection type is labelled „unbiased". If, on the other hand, subjects remember only the correct value (and nothing else), then their recollections will be distributed around it (with a mean of $BI \approx 100$). This recollection type is therefore labelled „correct-value anchored".

Summing across unbiased and correct-value anchored recollections could yield the typical unimodal distribution, disguising its true constituents and erroneously suggesting a homogenous recollection shift (cf. Fig. 1 and Metcalfe & Bjork, 1991). If these were the only recollection types, then there would be no need to assume systematically distorted memories - as hindsight bias does.

„True" memory distortions constitute the third type of recollection, labelled „blended recollections" or simply „blends". Their distribution should have a mean of $0 < BI < 100$, because blends are considered to result from contamination of original estimates by correct values, leading to an amalgamation of both numbers (Fischhoff, 1975, 1977; Metcalfe, 1990; Metcalfe & Bjork, 1991; Schooler & Tanaka, 1991). The distortion might come about if encoding the correct value leads to a selective activation of one's knowledge base from which the earlier estimate was drawn.

This paper is not aimed at exploring *how* the three recollection types actually emerge, but rather focuses on whether blends *exist* or whether the first two recollection types are sufficient to account for the observed shift. I now turn to three possible approaches for separating the assumed recollection types: introspection, experimental manipulation, and statistical modeling.

Introspection

Although possibly valuable in other domains, introspective data in the hindsight paradigm seem to provide no clues towards the desired separation. At least that is what the results of the following experiment indicate.

Experiment 1

Method

Subjects were 50 students (of the University Trier) who underwent the typical hindsight procedure (memory design). They first estimated the solutions to 40 difficult almanac questions (e.g., „How long is the Danube river?"), received the true solutions to 20 of them one week later (like „The Danube river is 2,852 km long."), and were then immediately asked to recall all 40 of their earlier estimates. Additionally, for each item they had to indicate on a 6-point scale how confident they were in their recollection (C_R). In the case of experimental items, which were marked in the list, subjects were further asked to recall the correct value and to rate their confidence (C_V).

These confidence ratings were assumed to allow separation of the three recollection types: High C_R (irrespective of C_V) should accompany unbiased estimates (with $BI \approx 0$); low C_R and high C_V should accompany correct-value anchored judgments (with $BI \approx 100$); and low C_R and low C_V should denote blended recollections (with $0 < BI < 100$). A necessary precondition, though, is the validity of the confidence ratings, that is, both C_R and C_V should positively correlate with the recollections' precision.

To further elucidate the influence of recall strategies, the recall mode was varied between subjects: One group first recalled all original estimates and then - for experimental items - all correct values, while a second group recalled all available information for each item at a time.

Results and discussion

All estimates, correct values and recollections were transformed to standardized scores, thus allowing to compute the mean shift (Δz) across all recollections. Experimental items exhibited the usual trend: Recollected estimates revealed a mean shift of $\Delta z = .14$ towards the correct value, while control items remained unshifted ($\Delta z = -.03$; $F(1,48) = 45$, a $< .0001$, for the difference between experimental and control items). The recall mode showed neither a main effect nor an interaction with the item type (both Fs < 1).

Analyzing the confidence ratings for recalled estimates (C_R) found only one valid clue: C_R was higher for perfect than for imperfect recollections (4.7 vs. 3.8; $F(1,48) = 308$, a $< .0001$). For imperfectly recalled values, however, C_R showed no relation to the precision of recollections - independent from item type and recall mode (all $|r| < .06$). The same was true for imperfectly recalled correct values and the appropriate confidence ratings (C_V; $|r| < .03$ for both recall modes). Consequently, the confidence ratings were useless for separating the assumed recollection types.

    This result resembles an outcome reported by Gigerenzer, Hell, and Hoffrage (1990): They found the same shift irrespective of whether or not subjects remembered having received the (actually given) correct value. Findings like this show that the ability to consciously monitor what happens during reconstructive memory processes is rather limited. Most probably, hindsight bias is caused by automatic processes that either assimilate the correct value (Fischhoff, 1975) or just can't by-pass it while attempting to recall one's earlier estimate (Tversky & Kahneman, 1974). If the underlying processes are indeed automatic, then it is no wonder (in hindsight...) that the collective confidence ratings proved to be unreliable.

Experimental Manipulations

    A second approach to separation of recollection types consists of comparing different experimental conditions devised to promote or inhibit one or the other of the assumed recollection types. Generally it cannot be concluded unequivocally whether only *one* type of recollection was affected or more. If, for example, an experimental manipulation leads to a reduced shift, all three recollection types might be involved: There could be fewer blended and/or fewer correct-value anchored and/or more unbiased recollections. It is therefore important to consider carefully how experimental manipulations and recollection types might be related. Experiment 2 tried to pursue this path.

Experiment 2

Method

    Subjects were 48 students (of the University Trier) who were randomly assigned to one of three groups. All groups followed the same hindsight procedure as in Experiment 1. They differed only with respect to the final test phase. Group 1 (*standard*) tried to recall their earlier estimates without any further information present. Group 2 (*correct value*) had the correct values still at hand. Subjects of Group 3 (*cue*) additionally were cued whether originally they had over- or underestimated the correct value.

    The resulting set of recollections should be composed differently for each group. Group 1 could exhibit all possible recollection types, as in any other standard experiment. Assuming that the correct value automatically influences memory, Group 2 recollections should be either blended or correct-value anchored, excluding unbiased ones. Group 3, finally, was restricted to blended or correct-value anchored recollections with a bias index of $BI < 100$, because the correct value and the direction of deviation of one's earlier estimate were given.

The material consisted of a fictitious auction catalogue with 20 to-be-sold objects (cf. Pohl & Gawlik, in press). Each item was depicted and described on a separate page with one (numerical) detail missing (e.g., the year of origin). This detail had to be estimated by the subjects.

Results and discussion

While recollections of control items revealed no bias ($\Delta z = -.03$), experimental items exhibited the typical shift towards the correct value ($\Delta z = .23$; $F(1,45) = 40$, a $< .0001$). The group variable showed no main effect ($F < 1$), but a significant interaction with the item type ($F(2,45) = 4.9$, a $= .012$): The separate shifts for experimental items were $\Delta z = .39$ for the standard group, $\Delta z = .15$ for the correct-value group, and $\Delta z = .22$ for the cue group. Close inspection of the data suggested that the unexpectedly large effect in the standard group was mainly caused by source confusion ($BI = 100$). The frequency of such confusion was 18.5 % in the standard group, but only 1.6 and 0 % in the correct-value and cue groups, respectively. Therefore, a second analysis was performed excluding cases of source confusion. While control items showed no shift ($\Delta z = -.04$), experimental items revealed the typical bias ($\Delta z = .18$; $F(1,45) = 27$, a $< .0001$). Differing from the first analysis, the group variable showed neither a main effect nor an interaction with the item type (both $Fs < 1$). The separate shifts for experimental items were $\Delta z = .20$, .13, and .22 for the standard, the correct-value, and the cue groups, respectively.

This finding (once more) underscores the importance of detailed analysis. Rather than concluding that hindsight bias was unaffected by the experimental manipulations, I suggest that the overall shift disguises more subtle differences in the data. Therefore, a more fine-grained analysis was undertaken and proved to be valuable. Comparing the frequencies of recollections with $BI \neq 0$ and $BI \neq 100$ across the three groups for several bias-index categories provided some important clues concerning the distribution of the assumed recollection types (see Table 1). For example, 16 % of the recollections of Group 2 showed a shift beyond the correct value ($BI > 100$).

Following the assumptions given above, these were considered „correct-value anchored" recollections. Approximately the same proportion should be found with $BI < 100$, leaving 36 % „biased" recollections in that category. If the distribution of correct-value anchored recollections is assumed to be symmetrical around $BI = 100$, then one third of the biased recollections is found in the category $BI < 0$, while two thirds are found in the category $0 < BI < 100$. Note that the same ratio (1:2) holds for the corresponding data frequencies of Group 3. To assume blends with $BI < 0$ might seem strange at first sight, but consider the following theoretical argument: The biasing process (assimilation or anchoring) that leads to blends could be viewed as a selective activation of one's earlier knowledge base. The resulting estimation interval is thus shifted towards the correct value, but drawing a *single* value (as recollection of the original estimate) need not necessarily reflect this shift. Only the *mean* of all recollections will exhibit the typical bias. It would therefore not be surprising to find blended recollections with $BI < 0$.

Table 1. Frequencies (%) of recollections of experimental items for different bias-index categories (Experiment 2).

	Group		
Data category	Standard	Correct value	Cue
$BI<0$	12.6	18.7	23.1
$BI=0$	11.0	29.9	24.6
$0<BI<100$	40.3	33.7	52.2
$BI=100$	18.5	1.6	0.0
$100<BI<200$	12.6	8.6	0.0
$BI≥200$	5.0	7.5	0.0

In sum, the major use of experimental manipulations seems to lie in the provision of cues that may clarify the types and distribution characteristics of different recollection types. This approach is still limited, because it appears difficult to isolate a single type. Besides, certain processes underlying hindsight bias could well be resistant to *any* kind of manipulation, if the effect is produced at an entirely automatic level. Therefore, it is essential to examine how far the third approach - statistical disentangling - may lead.

Multinomial Model

The model class that seems best to suit the goal of disentangling unobservable states are *multinomial models*. Because these models are simple to construct and rather easy to evaluate, they provide valuable tools for experimental research. Applying multinomial modeling to hindsight data was originally proposed by Erdfelder (1991). The basic procedure entails three steps (cf. Riefer & Batchelder, 1988, for a basic instruction): Sorting all recollections into mutually exclusive categories, laying out a theoretical model that specifies the relations between data categories and assumed recollection types, and fitting the model to empirical data. In principle, this approach can say whether the whole model was successful in describing the data (goodness of fit), and how many recollections out of the total set may belong to each type (parameter estimates). These probability estimates help determine whether or not a particular data set includes true blends.

A complete and detailed version of such a model has been outlined elsewhere (Pohl & Gawlik, in press). That model was fitted to a total of 30 data sets that were collected in 14 experiments (including the ones described above) all of which reported a similar and significant overall shift in recollections.

In almost all cases the model led to an acceptable fit. Most noteworthy, the estimated proportion for each recollection type varied considerably across data sets. The probability of blended recollections, for example, ranged from 0 % up to 76 %. As a further result, the correlation between amount of shift (Δz) and probability of blends was found to yield a non-significant value ($r = .08$, a > .10). Thus, the estimated parameters generally suggested an entirely different interpretation of the data than the conventional analysis did.

SUMMARY AND CONCLUSIONS

This paper establishes that an observed distribution of recollections (using numerical items in a typical hindsight study) should be considered a compound of different recollection types, only one of which comprises the sought-after „blends". After pointing out two minor artifacts - „suspect" subjects and regression effects - the major part of this paper was devoted to the problem of how to separate the assumed recollection types. In addition to introspective data and experimental manipulations, a third approach - multinomial modeling - was sketched and discussed.

These considerations have important consequences for conventional ways of data analysis. A shift towards the correct value need not mean that blended recollections were responsible, nor that they even occurred. Unless more detailed results are available, like those provided by the multinomial modeling described above, it remains questionable whether reported hindsight findings really contain what they claim. The proposed approach supplies the necessary separation of different recollection types, thus allowing a proper interpretation of the data. Moreover, the same disentangling can (and should) be applied to eyewitness misinformation data - given they used numerical information as material (Loftus, 1977; Pohl & Gawlik, in press; Pohl, Schumacher, & Friedrich, 1993) (Five such data sets were included in the above analysis).

Two problems were not thoroughly discussed. These concern the specific validity of the proposed model and the explanation of how and when blended recollections actually emerge. The present paper rather focused on the avoidance of some methodological problems that may be confounded in traditional hindsight-bias research. Whatever is obtained through the attempt to identify true blends should be subject to further psychological inquiry.

REFERENCES

Campbell, J. D., & Tesser, A. (1983). Motivational interpretations of hindsight bias: An individual difference analysis. *Journal of Personality, 51,* 605-620.

Christensen-Szalanski, J. J. J., & Willham, C. F. (1991). The hindsight bias: A meta-analysis. *Organizational Behavior and Human Decision Processes, 48,* 147-168.

Erdfelder, E. (1991). *Kognitive Täuschungen.* [Cognitive illusions.] Discussant at the 33. Tagung experimentell arbeitender Psychologen, Gießen/Germany.

Fischhoff, B. (1975). Hindsight ≠ foresight: The effect of outcome knowledge on judgment under uncertainty. *Journal of Experimental Psychology: Human Perception and Performance, 1,* 288-299.

Fischhoff, B. (1977). Perceived informativeness of facts. *Journal of Experimental Psychology: Human Perception and Performance, 3,* 349-358.

Gigerenzer, G., Hell, W., & Hoffrage, U. (1990). *Hindsight bias and biased recall of the correct information.* Unpublished manuscript, Universität Konstanz, Konstanz/Germany.

Hawkins, S. A., & Hastie, R. (1990). Hindsight: Biased judgments of past events after the outcomes are known. *Psychological Bulletin, 107,* 311-327.

Hell, W., Gigerenzer, G., Gauggel, S., Mall, M., & Müller, M. (1988). Hindsight bias: An interaction of automatic and motivational factors? *Memory and Cognition, 16,* 533-538.

Loftus, E. F. (1977). Shifting human color memory. *Memory and Cognition, 5,* 696-699.

McCloskey, M., & Zaragoza, M. (1985). Misleading postevent information and memory for events: Arguments and evidence against memory impairment hypotheses. *Journal of Experimental Psychology: General, 114,* 1-16.

Metcalfe, J. (1990). Composite holographic associative recall model (CHARM) and blended memories in eyewitness testimony. *Journal of Experimental Psychology: General, 119,* 145-160.

Metcalfe, J., & Bjork, R. A. (1991). Composite models never (well, hardly ever) compromise: Reply to Schooler and Tanaka (1991). *Journal of Experimental Psychology: General, 120,* 203-210.

Pohl, R. (1992a). Der Rückschau-Fehler: systematische Verfälschung der Erinnerung bei Experten und Novizen. [Hindsight bias: Systematic alteration of recollections of experts and novices.] *Kognitionswissenschaft, 3,* 38-44.

Pohl, R. (1992b). Misinformed and biased: Genuine memory distortions or artifactual phenomena? *Proceedings of the Fourteenth Annual Conference of the Cognitive Science Society* (pp. 153-158). Bloomington, Indiana. Hillsdale, NJ: Erlbaum.

Pohl, R., & Gawlik, B. (in press). Hindsight bias and misinformation effect: Separating blended recollections from other recollection types. *Memory.*

Pohl, R., Schumacher, S., & Friedrich, M. (1993). The eyewitness-misinformation effect: Distorted recollections based on contradictory information. In G. Strube & K. F. Wender (Eds.), *The Cognitive Psychology of Knowledge* (pp. 33-52). Amsterdam: Elsevier.

Riefer, D. M., & Batchelder, W. H. (1988). Multinomial modeling and the measurement of cognitive processes. *Psychological Review, 95,* 318-339.

Schooler, J. W., & Tanaka, J. W. (1991). Composites, compromises, and CHARM: What is the evidence for blend memory representations? *Journal of Experimental Psychology: General, 120,* 96-100.

Stahlberg, D., & Eller, F. (1993). Hindsight-Effekte: Eine urteilstheoretische Erklärung. [Hindsight effects: A decision theoretic explanation] In L. Montada (Eds.), *Bericht über den 38. Kongreß der Deutschen Gesellschaft für Psychologie in Trier 1992* (Vol. 2; pp. 735-741). Göttingen: Hogrefe.

Tversky, A., & Kahneman, D. (1974). Judgment under uncertainty: Heuristics and biases. *Science, 185,* 1124-1131.

Wood, G. (1978). The "knew-it-all-along" effect. *Journal of Experimental Psychology: Human Perception and Performance, 4,* 345-353.

AUTHOR'S NOTE. I am indebted to Edgar Erdfelder for his ingenious idea of applying multinomial models to hindsight-bias data. I also thank all the students and a number of co-workers who helped in collecting the empirical data. Very appreciated comments on an earlier draft were provided by Maya Bar-Hillel, Martin Friedrich, Ralph Hertwig, and Christof Körner. The research was supported by grant We 498/14 from the Deutsche Forschungsgemeinschaft.

Contributions to Decision Making - I
J.-P. Caverni, M. Bar-Hillel, F.H. Barron and H. Jungermann (Editors)
© 1995 Elsevier Science B.V. All rights reserved.   335

TESTING IN A RULE DISCOVERY TASK:

STRATEGIES OF TEST CHOICE AND

TEST RESULT INTERPRETATION

Fenna H. Poletiek

Leiden University, PO BOX 9555,
2300 RB Leiden, The Netherlands

Abstract. In this paper, hypothesis testing behavior is addressed from a Bayesian point of view. The Bayesian normative relation between test choice and test result interpretation is demonstrated both formally and intuitively. If two predictions are equivalent as to their likelihood given the hypothesis, the less probable of these two can subsequently provide the best support for the hypothesis. A similar Bayesian testing model has recently been experimentally investigated by Skov and Sherman (1987) and Slowiaczek, Klayman, Sherman and Skov (1992). However, in these studies the stimuli consist of statistical descriptions of tests. In a variation of Wason's (1960) rule discovery task, designed to reduce the shortcomings of probabilistic stimuli and to investigate the test choice and interpretation of subjects more directly, it was found that testers prefer those tests believed likely to produce a confirming result. But subjects do not discriminate, in the interpretation phase, between confirmations resulting from tests involving high or low probability. This finding is similar to what Skov and Sherman (1986) and Slowiaczek et al. (1992) found in their studies.

This paper deals with the strategies people use in choosing tests for hypotheses and the subsequent interpretation of the test results. Hypothesis testing is a daily activity for experts and lay persons; e.g., medical diagnoses can be seen as hypotheses being tested by means of making observations of the patient. Lay persons make social judgements about other people by means of checking hypotheses about them.

Previous research on hypothesis testing relies on the concepts of confirmation and falsification (see for recent reviews Klayman and Ha,

1987; Gorman, 1992; McDonald, 1992; Friedrich, 1993). Conducting a testing strategy directed at falsification of the hypothesis is generally considered superior to trying to confirm the hypothesis. However, the concepts of a confirming and a falsifying strategy of testing have been analyzed and criticized from different points of view, demonstrating the serious problems regarding these concepts for describing testing behavior. The crucial problem is that testing behavior labeled by authors as 'falsifying' or 'confirming', turns out to have little to do with subjects' prior intentions or even expectations of having their hypothesis falsified or confirmed (Klayman and Ha, 1987; McDonald, 1992; Poletiek, 1994).

Recently, a new approach to hypothesis testing has been proposed, which meets this criticism (Fischhoff & Beyth-Marom, 1983; Skov & Sherman, 1986; Slowiaczek, Klayman, Sherman & Skov, 1992). This new approach takes into account the interpretation of the test result a posteriori, in addition to the test choice beforehand. Moreover, this approach makes use of a Bayesian analysis of testing (cf., Fischhoff & Beyth-Marom, 1983). It provides normative statements about how test results should be interpreted a posteriori, depending on the properties of the test conducted. In this manner, the formal relation between test *choice* and test result *interpretation*, poorly justified in previous models of testing, can be clearly accounted for. Moreover, in an experimental setting, it can be observed to what extent and under which conditions hypothesis testers 'correctly' relate a test choice to the interpretation of the test result.

In the hypothesis testing experiments based on this Bayesian approach, probabilistic stimulus materials, mostly likelihoods, are used. However, a disadvantage of defining and presenting tests with likelihoods is that some statistical reasoning is required from the subjects as well as testing behavior. Indeed, the subject must detect the important properties of the tests by mental calculation. The properties of the tests are hidden in the likelihoods. It thus remains unclear whether subjects make test choices on the basis of the properties derived from the likelihoods, or whether their test choice is based on the likelihoods only.

This paper has two purposes. First, to show how Bayes' theorem can be used for modeling testing behavior and moreover to show that this model is intuitively understandable as well. Secondly, I shall show that this principle can be investigated experimentally without the need of probabilistic stimuli. A variation of Wason's (1960) rule discovery task is presented in which the Bayesian model is used for studying subjects' test choices and their result interpretations.

THE BAYESIAN MODEL OF TEST CHOICE AND TEST INTERPRETATION

Basically, Bayes' theorem implies the following for an observation with respect to a hypothesis: The less probable an observation, as compared to its likelihood given the hypothesis, the more support it can provide for the hypothesis when it is observed.

Given that observation A and observation B are predicted by H, under which conditions does A give stronger support to the hypothesis H than B? A supports H better than B does if and only if the revision of belief after observing A is greater than after observing B.

$$\frac{p(H \mid A)}{p(H)} > \frac{p(H \mid B)}{p(H)}$$

Thus, $p(H \mid A) > p(H \mid B)$.

It follows from Bayes' theorem that:

$$\frac{p(A \mid H) * p(H)}{p(A)} > \frac{p(B \mid H) * p(H)}{p(B)}$$

Thus,

$$\frac{p(A \mid H)}{p(A)} > \frac{p(B \mid H)}{p(B)}$$

which can also be expressed as:

$$\frac{p(A)}{p(B)} < \frac{p(A \mid H)}{p(B \mid H)}$$

This conclusion represents the condition under which observing A gives more support to hypothesis H than does observing B. This is true in the case mathematically expressed above: when observing A is less probable compared to its likelihood under H, than B is as compared to its likelihood under H. When p(A|H) and p(B|H) are both equal to one, A gives more support to H to the extent that it is less probable to occur than B. Under this condition, the Bayesian principle of testing is intuitive. Consider the following simple example. We have the hypothesis that a particular melon at the greengrocer's will taste good (the hypothesis being tested is 'tasty'). We know that a tasty melon is necessarily yellow and smells sweet (p(yellow|tasty) = 1 and p(sweet|tasty) = 1). Suppose we can test our hypothesis by examining either the particular melon's color or its smell. Now, if almost all the other melons are as yellow as the particular one (p(yellow) = .90), then testing the color and finding it yellow cannot give a very strong confirmation of the tasty melon hypothesis, since the probability of occurrence is very high. Suppose that about half of all melons only smell sweet in general (p(sweet) = .50). Observing a sweet smell will confirm relatively well our tasty-melon hypothesis. Thus, we have a hypothesis (this melon is tasty) which generates two predictions (the melon is yellow and the melon smells sweet). Now, from these two predictions the less probable one can better confirm our hypothesis afterwards. Testing the aroma can provide us with greater confidence in the truth of our hypothesis than checking its color, since the probability of observing a good smell is lower than the probability of observing yellow, a priori.

PREVIOUS HYPOTHESIS TESTING STUDIES WITHIN A BAYESIAN FRAMEWORK.

In Skov and Sherman (1986) and Slowiaczek et al.(1992), different tests are presented to the subjects as different likelihoods. The subject is required to choose a test on the basis of the properties of those likelihoods which seem preferable to him or her for testing the hypothesis. Presenting subjects with likelihoods entails that they have to derive test properties, such as the probability of a hypothesis confirming result, by making mental calculations. Characteristically, in Skov and Sherman (1986) and Slowiazcek et al. (1992), the likelihoods (p(A|H) and p(A|~H)) are given for each test and the p(H) and p(~H) (both are generally set to .50). Now, the probability of result A from a particular test must be derived from these data. The subject can do that by mental calculation of p(A):

$$p(A) = p(A|H) * p(H) + p(A|~H) * p(~H).$$

Skov and Sherman (1986) and Slowiaczek et al. (1992) found that subjects tend to prefer tests with a high probability of a hypothesis-confirming result. Subjects also interpret a confirming result, from such a test, too strongly as supporting evidence for the hypothesis, compared to the prescription of the Bayesian model. But the test characteristics, like the probability of a confirming answer A, must be derived by a calculation from the likelihoods given in the stimuli before they can be considered as a ground for test choice. The question thus remains exactly what kind of reasoning exactly precedes the test choice.

OBSERVING BAYESIAN STRATEGIES OF TESTING IN WASON'S RULE DISCOVERY TASK

In order to avoid statistical reasoning, while still observing Bayesian testing strategies, an experiment was designed based on Wason's (1960) rule discovery task to observe subjects' preferences for tests with a low or high probability of a hypothesis confirming result (p(A)), and in addition the subjects' interpretation of the test result, in terms of their revision of belief. It was assumed that the likelihoods of the tests (p(A_i|H) for several possible $A_{i,1...n}$ are equivalent. In other words, it was assumed that all possible test items predicted by a subject's hypothesis, had an equal likelihood one (p($A_{i,1...n}$|H) = 1) under this hypothesis. This is a reasonable assumption in the rule discovery task situation. Suppose a tester has the following hypothesis about the rule governing strings of three numbers: "three increasing numbers". All strings satisfying this hypothesis have a likelihood equal to one. Indeed, *if* the hypothesis is true, all possible hypothesis compatible strings (e.g., 3-4-5, 80-81-82) *must* be observed (p(A_i|H) = 1).

Now, it can first be observed which kind of tests subjects prefer beforehand. Do they prefer tests with a high probability of observing a confirming result (p(A) is high), as was found by Skov and Sherman (1986) and Slowiazcek et al. (1992)? Secondly, it can be observed how they interpret the result. Do subjects, choosing tests with a high probability of a confirmation, make a smaller revision of belief afterwards as compared to subjects choosing tests with a low probability of a confirming result? In the present experiment, the p(A) were not given. Subjects rated the p(A) themselves for five possible tests (p($A_{i,1...5}$)), and subsequently chose one from among these five tests.

Two predictions were tested based on the findings of Skov and Sherman (1986) and Slowiaczek et al. (1992) .

1 Subjects prefer tests with a high probability of a hypothesis confirming result.

2 Once the confirming result is obtained, all subjects interpret it in the same way, regardless of the test choice beforehand; i.e., the revision of belief is the same for all kinds of tests chosen.

METHOD

Wason's rule discovery task served as a basis, but was varied in several respects. In Wason's original task, subjects are asked to discover a rule about sequences of three numbers. They are given one example of this rule. Subsequently, they are asked to generate hypotheses about that rule, which they are asked to test by proposing new sequences to the experimenter. The experimenter answers "yes" if the particular sequence fits the rule and "no" if it doesn't.

We introduced some major variations on this methodology. First another rule was chosen than the one used by Wason (1960). This was done to avoid misleading subjects into believing a false hypothesis to be true (see also Klayman and Ha, 1987).

Second, we didn't mention anything about a 'rule' governing the sequences of numbers until the latest phase of the experiment. Focussing subjects on any hypothesis about the rule at the beginning of the task was avoided because we wanted them to assess the *un*conditionalised probability (p(A)) of the sequences. In the case they had a hypothesis in mind at the moment they had to assess the p(A), they may be tempted to give instead the conditionalised probability (p(A|H)). We will come back to this problem in the discussion. Moreover, the experimenter's feedback was not expressed in "yes" and "no" but as two neutral different feedbacks. This also was done to avoid subjects thinking of a rule underlying the feedback. Indeed subjects might interpret the yes-no feedback as: "Yes, the sequence fits the rule" or "no it is not in accordance with the rule".

Thus, in order to obtain the ratings we wanted to get, the task was built up as follows:

phase 1: Subjects are told that some sequences provoke Feedback 1 and other sequences provoke Feedback 2 (c.f. the Dax-Med methodology in Tweney et al. (1980)).

phase 2: Subjects are asked to generate some sequences and assess the probability to obtain Feedback 1 for each of these sequences.

phase 3: Subjects are told about a rule governing the feedbacks. Make them generate a hypothesis (H) about the rule, and ask their subjective probability about the hypothesis.

phase 4: Subjects are asked to choose one among the proposed sequences to test H.

phase 5: Subjects are asked how confident they are now that H is true if the sequence has indeed provoked Feedback 1.

These adaptations of Wason's rule discovery task allowed to observe the subjects' ratings about $p(A)$ (in phase 2), $p(H)$ (in phase 3), and $p(H|A)$ (in phase 5).

Subjects Thirty six students of the department of Language and Literature from the University of Tilburg participated in this experiment as voluntary subjects.

Procedure The experiment was administered with paper and pencil. Subjects were given a booklet with the instructions. The task was presented as a problem solving task. The true rule was 'even-uneven-even'. Subjects were given one example of the rule: 2-15-6. Subjects were allowed to perform only one test. They were asked to imagine the following problem:

"Suppose you have a machine with a keyboard with 10 digits and a board with two lights in front of you: A yellow light and a blue light".

This was drawn on the instruction as follows:

YELLOW   BLUE

O   O

1	2	3	4	5
6	7	8	9	0

"When you give an input of three numbers to the machine, one of the lights goes on; either the yellow or the blue one. It is known that the input 2-15-6 causes the yellow light to go on".

At this point subjects were asked to generate five strings of three numbers and to rate each string on a 10 point scale (the extremities being 'very uncertain' and 'very certain') as to the probability that it will make the yellow light go on. Subsequently, on a new page of the booklet, subjects were asked to state the rule according to which the machine works, to write down their hypothesis about the rule, and to indicate their confidence in this hypothesis on a 10 point scale. Next, they were told that they could have one opportunity to test their hypothesis by giving an input string to the machine. They were asked:

"Which one of the five strings you wrote down, provides the best test of your hypothesis?".

After having answered, the subjects were asked to give their reason for choice. The instruction followed on the next page:

"Now, suppose that you have given the chosen string as input, and the yellow light indeed goes on. How much confidence do you *now* have in your hypothesis?".

Subjects were given the same 10 point scale as previously to express their confidence in the hypothesis. The subjects were debriefed after all booklets had been handed to the experimenter.

Variables *Test Preference:* The preference for tests with a high or a low probability of a hypothesis confirming result was measured by comparing the probability of the *chosen* test string with the mean probability of all five generated test strings. The ratio of these two probabilities ($p(A_{chosen})$ / ($A_{i,1...n}$)) is the test preference score. A high ratio (greater than one) of the probability of the chosen test to the mean of all strings[1] indicates a preference for strings believed likely to produce a confirming answer. A low ratio indicates a preference for test strings believed unlikely to do so.

Revision of Belief: The revision of belief is measured by the ratio of the confidence in the hypothesis after the test has been performed in relation to the prior confidence in the hypothesis. This is the same ratio as used in the demonstration above ($p(H|A)$ / $p(H)$). Thus, the more the hypothesis tester interprets the observation as a stronger confirmation for the hypothesis, the more this ratio exceeds one.

Reasons for Choice: Subjects reasons for test choice were categorized with prior defined categories. The primary goal of asking for reasons was to find out whether and how subjects referred to the relation between test choice and evidential value of the result, in justifying their choice. In accordance with this goal, categories were defined as in Table 2. Reasons were categorized in the first or second categories when the subject justified his or her choice by referring to the high or low probability of the string he or she chose. When the subject expected to obtain high evidential value with the chosen test (such as "I will be very sure I'm right if this test string makes the light go on"), the answer fell in the third category. The fourth and fifth categories were used when the subject said that "the string is (in)compatible with my hypothesis, that is why I use this one".

RESULTS

In Figure 1 the distribution of the test preference scores is shown. To test their hypothesis, most subjects preferred test strings which have an equal or higher probability of making the yellow light go on (thus, to confirm their hypothesis) than the mean probability of all

---

[1] It was verified for all generated strings whether they were compatible with -- i.e., predicted by -- the hypothesis the subjects proposed later. Those strings which were not were omitted from the calculation of the Test Preference. Indeed, for those strings it cannot be assumed that $p(A|H)$ is equal to one. Actually, strings which are not compatible with the hypothesis have a likelihood equal to zero. These strings are not predicted by the hypothesis, thus $p(A|H) = 0$.

generated test strings. Actually, 15 of the 36 subjects preferred a hypothesis confirming test string, i.e., strings satisfying $p(A_{chosen})$ / $(A_{i,1...n}) > 1$.

Eighteen subjects preferred strings with a probability equal to the mean probability of all generated test strings $(p(A_{chosen})$ / $(A_{i,1...n}) = 1)$. These subjects rated all the strings they proposed equally (all p(A)'s were equal).

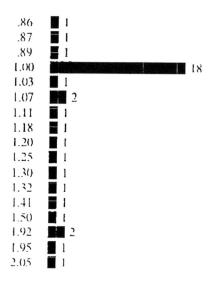

Figure 1. Frequency distribution of test preference scores (N=36).

With respect to the interpretation of the test result after the confirmation had been obtained, there was no correlation between test preference and revision of belief ($r = .01$; $p > .10$). Table 1 shows the mean revision of belief of subjects having chosen hypothesis falsifying, hypothesis confirming and neutral tests.

Table 1. Test Preference in Terms of the Probability of a Confirming Result of the Chosen Test, and Interpretation of the Confirming Test Result in Terms of Revision of Belief (N=36)

		Revision of Belief	
		M	SD
Probability of Confirming Result of Preferred Test	n		
High	14	1.2	1.3
Medium	18	1.7	3.0
Low	3	1.5	1.6

Note   Due to a missing datum of Revision of Belief, one subject was omitted from this analysis.

Neutral tests are tests with a score of one on the variable test preference. The revision of belief did not differ significantly between groups. None of the differences in the means in Table 1 were significant. Thus, as can be deduced from the correlation and the means in Table 1, test preference did not influence the interpretation of the test result.

Table 2. Reasons for Test Choice (N=36).

Reasons for Test Choice	f
Test string has a low probability to provide a confirming result	0
Test string has a high probability to provide a confirming result	4
Test string can give high support in the hypothesis afterwards	3*
Test string is compatible with my hypothesis	16**
Test string is incompatible with my hypothesis	0
Uncategorizable or no reason given	15

Note: When a subject gave more than one differently categorizable reason, each individual reason was counted.

The reasons for test choice are presented in Table 2. It can be seen that most subjects justified their choice by saying that the chosen test string was compatible with the hypothesis they proposed. Only three subjects referred to the value of the potential confirming result in justifying their choice. Moreover, only one subject from among those three had chosen a test string which was believed to falsify the hypothesis (marked with an asterisk).

DISCUSSION

The Relation Between Test Choice and Test Interpretation

The present experiment provides similar results to those found by Skov and Sherman (1986) and Slowiaczek et al. (1992). First, subjects prefer tests with a high probability of providing them with a hypothesis confirming result. Second, they do not interpret the confirming observation resulting from this test as relatively weak support of their hypothesis. Hypothesis testers seem not to be aware of the *inverse* relation between the *probability* of a confirming outcome before the test and the evidential *value* of the confirming outcome after the test. Thus, subjects do not interpret test results as a function of their test choice. They are not normative with respect to the Bayesian view on testing proposed in this paper. Note that this Bayesian approach does not put any normative constraint on the test choice. Indeed, it is the interpretation of a test result, *given* a particular test choice, which is prescribed by the Bayesian algorithm. The bias subjects display, with respect to the interpretation of their test result, has two consequences: First, when subjects test a hypothesis by means of a test with a high probability of a confirming result, they tend to overestimate the evidential value of the result, if it is obtained. Second, if they use a test with a low probability of a confirming result they underestimate the value of the confirming result, if it is obtained. Actually, hypothesis testers do not take into account the prior probability of the test to provide a confirming result, when they interpret the test posterior test result. Since testers seem to prefer the first type of test (hypothesis confirming tests), the mistake of overestimating the evidential value of a test result will be more frequent in real life testing (cf. Slowiaczek et al., 1992).

Do subjects rate p(A|H) or p(A)?

However, the last word on testing behavior within the Bayesian framework has not yet been uttered. An important question, for example, is whether subjects really did assess $p(A)$ rather than $p(A|H)$

when rating the strings in the first stage of the task. Slowiaczek et al. also mention the problem of separating the p(A) from p(A|H) in experimental materials. Although this is a major problem in this field of research, we feel that the present methodology allows the interpretation of subject's ratings of their sequences as subjective ratings of p(A) rather than p(A|H). First, subjects were not instructed about any rule at the moment that they did the ratings. Second, suppose they had one or several hypotheses about a rule in mind in the first stage of the experiment, and suppose further that they had proposed sequences generated by these hypotheses. Would they interpret the probability that the test sequence makes the yellow light go on, as "the probability that the light goes on *under the condition* that the putative hypothesis is true"? It is very implausible that the subject reasons like this. If he or she has a hypothesis, and deduces a sequence from this hypothesis ("if this is the system, this particular sequence should work") he or she will think of it as being fully determined by the hypothesis. There is no ground to make another assessment, and it would be a very complex cognitive task. It would require reasoning like "what is the extent to which my hypothesis generates this particular sequence".

However, subject's ratings of the sequences may be biased in another way. The subjects may have given their confidence in the hypothesis which lies behind the proposed sequence, thus the ratings would reflect the belief in the putative hypotheses. This is a more plausible alternative explanation of the ratings. The reasoning may have been "if this hypothesis is true, then this sequence should work, but I'm not so sure that this hypothesis is right, so I'm equally unsure that this sequence will work". However, in this last case, then the subject's given ratings of the p(A)'s are still useful in modelling testing choice in the way we did. Indeed, the inverse relation between $p(A_{chosen})$ and $p(H|A)$ still holds, and the conclusions about subjects' test choice and interpretation are still valid.

Improving The Ecological Validity of Experimental Tasks on Testing Behavior

Although the present study has removed some problems with regard to the descriptions of the tests, in the sense that less statistical reasoning is needed to estimate the properties of the tests, this is only a first step towards improving the ecological validity of the stimulus materials. Indeed, the principle that among all equivalent test predictions of our hypothesis, the one which is least probable (or 'most surprising') gives us the best proof of our hypothesis, is quite intuitive, as has been illustrated in the greengrocer's example. Experiments on hypothesis testing with stimulus materials which account for this intuition can provide interesting new findings on testing behavior. E.g., it is probable that testers will no longer make the interpretation error when they are made aware of the relation between the test property and the evidential value of a test result, by means of the realistic presentation of the tests (cf., the tasty melon test example). Moreover, if this relation is intuitively clear to subjects in an experimental setting, interesting hypotheses concerning hypothesis testing can be studied. Under which conditions do subjects prefer high probability confirming tests, taking the low value of the confirming result for granted? And when do they examine less probable or more surprising predictions, in the hope of finding a conclusive proof of their theory? These are some questions generated by the present Bayesian approach to hypothesis testing; an approach suggesting promising future experimentation on hypothesis testing behavior.

REFERENCES

Fischhoff, B., & Beyth-Marom, R. (1983). Hypothesis evaluation from a bayesian perspective. *Psychological Review, 3*, 239-260.

Friedrich, J. (1993). Primary error detection and minimization (PEDMIN) strategies in social cognition: A reinterpretation of confirmation bias phenomena. *Psychological Review, 100*, 298-319.

Gorman, M. E. (1992). Experimental simulations of falsification. In Keane, M. T., & Gilhooly, K. J. (Eds.), *Advances in the psychology of thinking, Volume I.* London: Harvester Wheatsheaf.

Klayman, J., & Ha, Y.-W. (1987). Confirmation, disconfirmation and information in hypothesis testing. *Psychological Review, 94*, 211-228.

McDonald, J. (1992). Is strong inference really superior to simple inference? *Synthese, 92*, 261-282.

Poletiek, F. H. (1994). Paradoxes of Falsification. Submitted.

Skov, R. B., & Sherman, S. J. (1986). Information gathering processes: Diagnosticity, hypotheses confirmatory strategies and perceived hypothesis confirmation. *Journal of Experimental Social Psychology, 22*, 93-121.

Slowiaczek, L. M., Klayman, J., Sherman, S. J., & Skov, R. B. (1992). Information selection and use in hypothesis testing: What is a good question and what a good answer? *Memory and Cognition, 20*, 392-405.

Tweney, R. D., Doherty, M. E., Worner, W. J., Pliske, D. B., Mynatt, C. R., Gross, K. A., & Arkkelin, D. L. (1980). Strategies of rule discovery in an inference task. *Quarterly Journal of Experimental Psychology, 32*, 109-123.

Wason, P. C. (1960). On the failure to eliminate hypotheses in a conceptual task. *Quarterly Journal of Experimental Psychology, 12*, 129-140.

Author Notes. I thank Joshua Klayman for his constructive comments on an earlier version of this paper. Correspondence concerning this article should be addressed to Fenna H. Poletiek, Leiden University, PO BOX 9555, 2300 RB Leiden, The Netherlands. E-mail: poletiek@rulfsw.leidenuniv.nl.

Contributions to Decision Making - I
J.-P. Caverni, M. Bar-Hillel, F.H. Barron and H. Jungermann (Editors)
© 1995 Elsevier Science B.V. All rights reserved.   351

FRAMING AND TIME-INCONSISTENT PREFERENCES

Peter H.M.P. Roelofsma & Gideon Keren

Cognitive Psychology Unit, Department of Psychology,
Free University of Amsterdam, De Boelelaan 1111,
1081 HV Amsterdam, The Netherlands

Abstract. Recent research on intertemporal choice (e.g., Ainslie, 1991; Herrnstein, 1990; Loewenstein & Elster, 1992) exhibits several pervasive effects that are incompatible with the basic tenets of the "rational" or "normative" economic theory. In particular, people show time-inconsistent preferences when asked to choose between payoffs occurring at different moments in time. Following an example from Herrnstein (1990), our first experiment demonstrates such time-inconsistent preferences. Using a *present* time perspective the majority of subjects portrayed a positive time preference by choosing the smaller but more immediate payoff; in contrast, when a *future* time perspective was employed (delaying all possible outcomes by a constant duration) most subjects portrayed a negative time preference for identical payoffs. Two additional experiments tested the robustness of this effect by (1) using an isolation procedure (Kahneman and Tversky, 1979), and (2) manipulating the certainty associated with the payoffs. Our results suggest that time-inconsistent preferences, as described by Herrnstein, can be interpreted as an analog of the certainty-effect (Kahneman & Tversky, 1979) in the time domain.

The value people place on time and on differential timing of outcomes has evoked considerable interest in recent research on human decision making. It is often the case that people have to make a choice between outcomes that will be realized at different points in the future. Such decisions are usually referred to as *intertemporal choices* (e.g., Loewenstein & Elster, 1992). Many important decisions in daily life possess an intertemporal component since most choices have future consequences, like the money people set aside for their pension funds or for preventing future ecological and environmental disasters.

An interesting aspect of intertemporal choice concerns a systematic preference for receiving a commodity immediately rather than at some later time, or the preference for immediate over delayed consumption. This phenomenon, described as *positive time preference* reflects the tendency to downgrade delayed consumption and is an empirically well documented finding (e.g., Björkman, 1984; Jungermann & Fleisher, 1988; Loewenstein, 1988; Mischel, Grusec & Masters 1969).

The phenomenon of positive time preference is related to the concept of *time discounting,* which underlies most conventional economic and decision-theoretical analyses of intertemporal choice (Loewenstein, 1988; Fishburn & Rubinstein, 1982). Following time discounting, time is evaluated according to a time-outcome value function, which represents the subjective value of a given outcome at different moments at which it may occur. Subjective time discounting implies that every option is converted (according to the discount function) separately into its present value, and that subjects subsequently choose the option with the largest value. Moreover, according to conventional economic theory, the time-outcome value function is subject to *exponential* decay, that is, with a fixed discount rate.

The validity of this normative or "rational" economic model for *describing* intertemporal decisions has recently been examined by several researchers (Ainslie, 1991; Herrnstein, 1990; Loewenstein & Elsler, 1992; Loewenstein & Thaler, 1989; Prelec & Loewenstein, 1991). They question the rational model by stating that an exponential declining discount function cannot explain the empirical finding of time-inconsistent preferences as a function of elapsed time. As a prototypical illustration of time-inconsistent preferences, Herrnstein (1990) suggested the following example: "Suppose you are asked to imagine winning a lottery and are given a choice between $100 tomorrow and $115 a week from tomorrow. Which would you prefer?" Although Herrnstein did not perform a formal experiment, he observed that people tended to choose the earlier but smaller payoff. However, when asked to choose between $100 52 weeks from now, or $115 53 weeks from now, he observed that many persons who chose $100 in the first lottery reversed their preference to the $115 alternative in the second lottery. Such a reversal of preferences is incompatible with the standard discounting model and cannot be accounted for by any exponential discount function (for a detailed discussion, see Ainslie & Haslam, 1992). According to the exponential model one may well prefer a smaller payoff now over a larger payoff at some later time. However, such preferences should not change with the introduction of a constant additive time delay to the relevant choice alternatives.

The purpose of the studies reported in the present article was to test Hermstein's observations in a more rigorous experimental setting (Experiment 1), and investigate its robustness (Experiments 2 and 3). By delineating the conditions under which inconsistent choices are being observed, additional insight into the underlying mechanisms may be obtained. In the final discussion we briefly discuss potential explanations to Herrnstein's observations in light of our reported results.

GENERAL METHOD

The studies were based on the responses of university students to hypothetical choice problems. Respondents were presented with problems like:

Which of the following would you prefer?

Receive: A: Hfl 100, now   or   B: Hfl 110, 4 weeks from now.

The outcomes refer to Dutch currency ($ 1.00 is approximately equal to 2 Dutch Hfl). The respondents were students from the Free University of Amsterdam who received Hfl 12.50 for their participation in this and several other decision making tasks. They were asked to imagine that they were actually faced with the choice described in the problem, and to indicate the decision they would made in such a case. Each of the five problems described below were presented to subjects as part of a 45 minutes paper and pencil session with several other unrelated judgement and choice problems. Subjects were tested in groups of four to five persons, and each subject received one and only one of the following five choice problems. To counterbalance possible order effects several orders of the problems in the paper and pencil session were constructed.

Experiment 1: Testing the Herrnstein Observation.

The first pair of choice problems consisted of a variation on Herrnstein's above mentioned example. The number of respondents to each problem is denoted by N, and the percentage of subjects who chose each option is given in brackets.

PROBLEM 1

Which would you prefer?

Receive:

    A) Hfl 100, now.   or   B) Hfl 110, 4 weeks from now.

N=60   [82%]   [18%]

PROBLEM 2

Which would you prefer?

Receive:

    C) Hfl 100, 26 weeks from now.   or   D) Hfl 110, 30 weeks
                                             from now.

N=60   [37%]   [63%]

Note that Problem 2 is obtained from Problem 1 by adding a constant 26 week delay to both outcome prospects. The standard discounting model predicts that utilities (u) should change in such a manner so that if u(100, now) > u(110, 4 weeks), then u(100, 26 weeks) > u(110, 30 weeks). As more time elapses the value functions of both payoffs become closer. However, regardless of the length of the additive delay, the preference in both problems should be the same.

Evidently, the pattern of results is incompatible with the above prediction. The data show that 82 percent of the subjects choose A in Problem 1, and 63 percent of the subjects chose D in Problem 2. Thus, when asked for their preference most subjects said that they would rather have Fl 100 immediately. Yet, a large majority preferred receiving Fl 110 in 30 weeks to Fl 100 in 26 weeks. The shift of preference is highly significant. (X_1^2=52.375, p < .001). The pattern of results confirm Herrnstein's observations and violates a simple time-discounting model, in which the rate of decline of the value function is constant per unit of time.

Experiment 2: Imposing Different Time Frames.

How robust are the time inconsistent preferences obtained in Experiment 1? Ainslie and Haendel (1983) report results congruent with ours though their experimental setting and subject population was different. A question that can be raised concerns the extent to which time-inconsistent preferences are susceptible to different time frames. Specifically, Experiment 1 suggests that despite the common difference (of 4 weeks) in outcome delay in both Problems 1 and 2, subjects preferences were different. Evidently, the difference in outcome delay is assessed relative to the overall magnitude of delay[1]. This implies that manipulating the overall time frame should affect subjects choice as was indeed the case in Experiment 1.

An alternative way to manipulate the overall time frame is by isolating the common time delay component from the overall magnitude component. Such a manipulation can be achieved by using a procedure similar to that used by Kahneman and Tversky (1979) in their demonstration of the "isolation" effect. For example, the time delay for each of the two alternatives in Problem 2 can be represented as the sum of two components: The common delay which is the same for both alternatives (26 weeks), and a unique component that distinguishes between the two alternatives.

Our prediction was that under such conditions, subjects would base their preferences solely on the distinctive time delay (and disregard the overall magnitude) and would thus exhibit positive time preferences also in Problem 2. Consequently, the preference reversals observed in Experiment 1 should be eliminated. Problem 3 is thus identical to Problem 2 except that the common and distinctive components of the time delay are separated.

PROBLEM 3

Imagine the following two-stage game. In the first stage you may receive a letter either 6 weeks or 26 weeks from now. If the letter has been received 6 weeks from now the game has ended without winning anything. If the letter arrives after 26 weeks the second stage of the game has been reached which provides a choice between:

Receive:

A) 100, immediately.	B) 110, 4 weeks later.
N=57 [70%]	[30%]

---

[1] The overall magnitude of delay can be assessed for instance by taking the average of the two delays. In problem 1 this is 2 weeks compared with 28 in problem 2.

Your choice must be made before the game starts, i.e. before the outcome of the first stage is known.

Note that one has a choice between receiving 100, after 26 weeks or 110, after 30 weeks. Thus, in terms of final outcomes and timing one faces an identical choice as in Problem 2 above. Yet, the pattern of results is radically different. The majority of the subjects chose the latter prospect (contrary to the preference in Problem 2), thus exhibiting positive time preference as was the case for Problem 1. This difference in choices between Problems 2 and 3 is highly significant ($X_1^2=50,1$, p <.001). Evidently, people ignore the first stage of the game (the common component) and consider Problem 3 as if it were Problem 1.

Experiment 3: Uncertainty and Time-inconsistent Preferences.

An essential element inherent in any decision regarding delayed outcomes is uncertainty. The more remote the outcome from the present, the higher the uncertainty (or ambiguity) associated with it. In the previous 2 experiments the subject may implicitly assume that the outcomes, regardless of the length of delay, are certain. In reality, however, any future outcome carries some uncertainty.

Consider the case in which the payoffs in Experiment 1 are introduced with some uncertainty. Would the preference reversals observed in Experiment 1 be maintained? A plausible account for the phenomenon of positive time preferences (like in Problem 1) is the existence of uncertainty.

The preference for the immediate but smaller reward in Problem 1 may thus be explained in terms of the "certainty" effect (Kahneman and Tversky, 1979). If uncertainty is attached to the outcomes of both alternatives in Problem 1, the immediate outcome may loose its appeal relative to the higher but more delayed outcome. Experiment 3 was designed to test this hypothesis. Accordingly, Problems 4 and 5 were identical to Problems 1 and 2 respectively, except that the payoffs were changed to be probabilistic.

PROBLEM 4

Which would you prefer?

Receive:

    A) 100, now   B) 110, 4 weeks from now

    with probability .50   with probability .50

N=100   [39%]   [61%]

PROBLEM 5

Which would you prefer?

Receive:

    C) 100, 26 weeks from now   D) 110, 30 weeks from now

    with probability .50   with probability .50

N=100   [33%]   [67%]

In contrast to Problem 2 and 3, the last pair of problems show similar choice patterns ($X_1^2 = .781$, $p > .75$). Apparently under conditions of uncertainty the time-inconsistent preferences observed in Experiment 1 have disappeared.

GENERAL DISCUSSION

Several conclusions can be drawn from the present experiments. Experiment 1 confirms that Hernstein's observations represent indeed a reliable phenomenon. It provides formal evidence that in a *present* time perspective the majority of subjects portray a positive time preference by choosing the smaller but more immediate payoff. In contrast, employing a *future* time perspective most subjects portray a negative time preference for identical payoffs. The results of Experiment 2 have shown that this phenomenon is related to the time frame in which the choice alternatives are presented. Isolating common and different components of the choice alternatives, leads to a present time perspective and consequently yields a shift from negative to positive time preferences. Experiment 3 presents evidence that the time-inconsistent preferences observed in Experiment 1 disappear by introducing uncertainty. Reducing the certainty of the payoffs in a time perspective of the present resulted in a shift from positive to negative time preferences.

How can these lindings be explained? Two alternatives will be briefly outlined, one stemming from perceptual theory and one from reinforcement theory.

One possible explanation could be based on the application of Weber's Law to time perception. Accordingly, the choice problems used in our experiments are determined by a joint function of two independent features, namely time perception and monetary value. Following Weber's Law, the perceived difference between two stimuli, on a particular sensory dimension, depends on the absolute magnitude of the relevant stimuli. That is, a constant difference in time does not produce a constant difference in perceived time. Referring to Problem 1 and 2 in Experiment 1, a difference in delay between 26 and 30 weeks is perceived to be considerably less than a delay from now to four weeks. As a result the time factor becomes less prominent relative to the monetary component of the choice alternatives. Consequently, subjects choose the largest payoff and show a negative time preference.

It should be noticed, however, that Weber's law remains controversial and is not always applicable to the time domain (e.g., Allan, 1977; Thomas & Brown, 1974; Getty, 1976). Moreover, Weber's law can obviously not account for the results of Experiment 3 since it does not deal with uncertainties.

An alternative explanation for our findings is based on Herrnstein's Matching law (Herrnstein, 1961, 1990). The Matching law has been applied as an alternative to the normative exponential time discounting theory. It describes the valuation of reinforcers as a function of the rate of reward, amount of reward, the expected moment of received reward and the moment that behavior is carried out. The time-value function underlying the matching law is hyperbolic rather than exponential (Ainslie & Haslam, 1992). The point is that, in contrast to the exponential function of the time discounting theory, hyperbolic value functions cross as a function of time. The hyperbolic function can account for the observation that a lower payoff that is originally preferred due to its immediacy[2] may, as time elapses be valued less than the higher more delayed payoff. Indeed, Herrnstein has applied the matching law to account for his observations of time

---

[2] According to Ainslie (1975), this is a reflection of the tendency to be overly influenced by immediate reinforcers.

inconsistent preferences as portrayed in his example that we tested in Experiment 1. Unfortunately, the matching law does not address in any direct way the component of uncertainty inherited in the time dimension and consequently cannot account for the results of Experiment 3.

A final way of explaining our findings is by relating them to the *certainty* effect as described by Kahneman & Tversky (1979). The certainty effect refers to the phenomenon that people overweigh outcomes that are considered certain, relative to outcomes which are probable. It can be illustrated by the following example adapted from Kahneman & Tversky (1979). When asked for their preference between receiving $4000 with a probability of .80 or $3000 with certainty, most subjects (80%) said that they would rather have $3000 with certainty. Yet, a large majority (65%) preferred receiving $4000 with a probability of .20 to $3000 with a probability of .25. Note that the second choice is obtained from the first by dividing the outcome probabilities by four. Evidently, reducing the probability of winning from 1.0 to .25 has a larger effect than the reduction from .8 to .2. This is mainly so because in the former case there is not just a quantitative but also a qualitative change, namely the transition from certainty to uncertainty. Applying this line of thought to intertemporal choice, a change from immediate to delayed payoff transforms the option from a certain to a probabilistic gain. From this perspective, we propose that the time-inconsistent preference in Problem 1 and 2 of Experiment 1 can be viewed as a specific example of the certainty effect. Accordingly, our results give empirical evidence for Prelec & Loewenstein's (1991) assertion that the patterns of choice in the domain of time and uncertainty are closely related. They demonstrated the similarity between the behavioral violations of the normative theories for those domains, i.e. the expected utility and the time discounting framework. More specifically, they argue that both models share the independence axiom, which implies that preferences between outcomes should not be affected by multiplying the outcomes by a common factor (this principle is refered to as the common ratio effect in the domain of uncertainty). The certainty effect (Kahneman & Tversky, 1979) reflects a violation of this axiom in the domain of uncertainty. As corresponding anomalies in the domain of time, Prelec & Loewenstein suggest the *common difference effect* and the *immediacy effect.* The immediacy effect refers to the enhanced significance decision makers attach to outcomes that are experienced immediately. The common difference effect implies that the impact of a constant time difference between two payoffs becomes less significant as both outcomes are made more remote. Accordingly, subjects may shift preferences in favor of the larger and more delayed monetary outcome, as was observed in our findings in Experiment 1.

The isolation effect in Experiment 2 can also be explained in terms of a similarity between the domains of uncertainty and time. As a result of the isolation procedure, people may discard the common time delay component which contains the bulk of the uncertainty. Consequently, one alternative is perceived as being immediate and therefore as implying certainty. Consequently subjects portray a positive time preference, as observed in Experiment 2.

Introducing a probabilistic component in Problem 1 and 2, as was done in Experiment 3 is another way of substantiating the relation between the certainty effect and time-inconsistent preferences. Specifically, when a probabilistic element is added to Problems 1 and 2 as achieved in Problems 4 and 5 respectively, the certainty component is eliminated. As a result the monetary values of the two alternatives receive a higher weight in the decision process that may lead to negative time preferences in both problems, as found in Experiment 3.

We have demonstrated that time-inconsistent preferences as described by Herrnstein can indeed be interpreted in terms of an analogy between on the one hand the certainty effect in the domain of uncertainty and, on the other hand, the immediacy effect in the time domain. Immediate outcomes are always more certain in comparison to delayed outcomes and therefore reversals of time preference may result from overweighting the "certainty" aspect of the present, relative to the "uncertainty" of the future. Furthermore, we propose that the component of uncertainty in intertemporal decisions may override all other factors in the decision process, such as the desire for improvement and spreading preferences (see: Loewenstein & Prelec, 1993). Therefore, we affirm that any theoretical framework of intertemporal choices should explictely incorporate the component of uncertainty in the valuation of differential timing of outcomes.

REFERENCES

Ainslie, G. (1975). Specious reward: A behavioral theory of impulsiveness and impulse control. *Psychological Bulletin, 82*, 463-496.

Ainslie, G. (1991). Derivation of Rational Economic Behavior from Hyperbolic Discount Curves. *The American Economic Review, 81,(2)*, 334-353.

Ainslie, G., & Haslam, N. (1992). Hyperbolic Discounting. In Loewenstein G. & Elster J. (Eds) *Choice over Time*. Russel Sage Foundation New York.

Ainslie, G., & Haendel, V. (1983). The motives of the will. In E. Gottheil, K. Druley, T. Skodola, and H. Waxman (Eds.) *Etiology Aspects of Alcohol and Drug Abuse*. Springfield, Ill.: C. Thomas.

Allan, L.G. (1977). The perception of time. *Perception & Psychophysics, 26 (5),* 340-354.

Björkman, M. (1984). Decision Making, risk taking and psychological time: Review of empirical findings and psychological theory. *Scandinavian Journal of Psychology, 25,* 31-49.

Getty, D.J. (1976). Counting processes in human timing. *Perception & Psychophysics, 20,* 191-197.

Fishburn, P.C. & Rubinstein, A. (1982). Time Preference. *International Economics Review, 23,* 677-694.

Herrnstein, R.J. (1961). Relative and Absolute Strengths of Response as a Function of Frequency Reinforcement. *Journal of the Experimental Analysis of Behavior, 4,* 267-272.

Herrnstein, R.J. (1990). Rational Choice Theory. *American Psychologist, 45(3),* 356-367.

Jungermann, H., & Fleischer, F. (1988). As time goes by: Psychological determinants of time preference. In: G. Kirsch, P. Nijkamp & K. Zimmermann (Eds). The Formulation of Time Preferences in a Multidisciplinary Perspective. Aldershot, Gover.

Kahneman, D., & Tversky, A. (1979). Prospect Theory: an Analysis of Decision under Risk. *Econometrica, 47, (2),* 263-291.

Loewenstein, G.F. (1988). Frames of Mind in Intertemporal Choice. *Management Science, 34, (2),* 200 -214.

Loewenstein, G. F., & Elsler, (1992). *Choice over Time*. Russel Sage Foundation New York.

Loewenstein, G., & Thaler, R. (1989). Anomalies: Intertemporal choice. *Journal of Economic Perspectives, 3,* 181-193.

Loewenstein, G.F., & Prelec, D. (1993). Preferences for sequences of outcomes. *Psychological Review, 100,* 91-108.

Mischel, W., Grusec, J., & Masters, J.C. (1969). Effects of expected delay time on the subjective value of rewards and punishments. *Journal of Personality and Social Psychology, 8,* 253-257.

Prelec, D., & Loewenstein G. (1991). Decision making over time and under uncertainty: A common approach. *Management Science, 37, (7),* 770-786.

Thomas, E.A.C., & Brown, I., Jr. (1974). Time Perception and the filled duration illusion. *Perception & Psychophysics, 18,* 44-48.